# AMERICAN REICH

**ALSO BY ERIC LICHTBLAU**

*Return to the Reich*
*The Nazis Next Door*
*Bush's Law*

# AMERICAN REICH

A Murder in Orange County,
Neo-Nazis, and the New Age
of Hate

## ERIC LICHTBLAU

LITTLE, BROWN AND COMPANY

New York   Boston   London

Copyright © 2026 by Eric Lichtblau

Hachette Book Group supports the right to free expression and the value of copyright. The purpose of copyright is to encourage writers and artists to produce the creative works that enrich our culture.

The scanning, uploading, and distribution of this book without permission is a theft of the author's intellectual property. If you would like permission to use material from the book (other than for review purposes), please contact permissions@hbgusa.com. Thank you for your support of the author's rights.

Little, Brown and Company
Hachette Book Group
1290 Avenue of the Americas, New York, NY 10104
littlebrown.com

First Edition: January 2026

Little, Brown and Company is a division of Hachette Book Group, Inc. The Little, Brown name and logo are trademarks of Hachette Book Group, Inc.

The publisher is not responsible for websites (or their content) that are not owned by the publisher.

The Hachette Speakers Bureau provides a wide range of authors for speaking events. To find out more, go to hachettespeakersbureau.com or email hachettespeakers@hbgusa.com.

Little, Brown and Company books may be purchased in bulk for business, educational, or promotional use. For information, please contact your local bookseller or the Hachette Book Group Special Markets Department at special.markets@hbgusa.com.

ISBN 9780316564717
Library of Congress Control Number: 2025940231

10 9 8 7 6 5 4 3 2 1

MRQ-T

Printed in Canada

In memory of Blaze Bernstein and the
victims of hate everywhere

# CONTENTS

|  |  |  |
|---|---|---|
| Prologue: The Ashes of Western Civilization | | 3 |

### Part I: No One Can Ever Know

| Chapter 1: | I'm a Cancer | 15 |
|---|---|---|
| Chapter 2: | The Skinhead Capital of the World | 25 |
| Chapter 3: | Saboteur | 44 |
| Chapter 4: | The White Race Is Back in the Game | 56 |
| Chapter 5: | They Want to Build a Fourth Reich | 78 |
| Chapter 6: | Hate Camp | 95 |
| Chapter 7: | Right-Wing Death Squad | 116 |
| Chapter 8: | Text Is Boring but Murder Isn't | 136 |

### Part II: No Turning Back

| Chapter 9: | The Spigot Is on Full Blast | 143 |
|---|---|---|
| Chapter 10: | Who's Sam Woodward? | 155 |
| Chapter 11: | The Sword Has Been Drawn | 168 |
| Chapter 12: | Impunity to Violent Bigots | 181 |
| Chapter 13: | White Replacement | 199 |
| Chapter 14: | Go Back to Your Own Country | 212 |
| Chapter 15: | Is This America? | 228 |
| Chapter 16: | Pure Evil | 259 |
| Chapter 17: | Hate Will Never Be Tolerated | 262 |
| | Epilogue: Poisoning the Blood | 276 |
| | *Author's Note and Acknowledgements* | *291* |
| | *Notes* | *293* |
| | *Illustrations* | *325* |
| | *Index* | *327* |

# AMERICAN REICH

## PROLOGUE

# "THE ASHES OF WESTERN CIVILIZATION"

Sam Woodward parked his silver Nissan one moonlit night by the cul-de-sac in a leafy suburb of Orange County, California, lined with palm trees and stucco-sided, million-dollar homes, and he waited expectantly for his old classmate. Cool winds off the Pacific Ocean brushed the night air.

Sam, a tall, lanky twenty-year-old with a shock of dirty-blond hair and dark, sunken eyes, was meeting up with a high school classmate named Blaze Bernstein that night in 2018. Sam and Blaze hadn't really been friends in school; they were barely acquaintances, in fact, and Blaze knew him mainly by reputation: as a brooding loner known in school for his outbursts against minorities and for his love of the Confederate flag.

They hadn't seen each other for several years, and now their lives were on very different paths. Sam had dropped out of college and was floundering, living at home with his parents in his old bedroom in Newport Beach; Blaze, an artsy poet, was an Ivy League student at Penn who'd been thinking about medical school. They had reconnected via social media months earlier, and with Blaze back home in Orange County on winter break, Sam was anxious to see him again in person, he told him online, just to "catch up." His messages to Blaze had been friendly, even flirtatious. To Blaze, he seemed nothing like his bad-boy persona from their days in school together. He wondered: *Could this really be the same Sam Woodward?*

But it was. The friendly persona was a façade. Sam's dark side had only grown darker since their days together in school. Unknown to Blaze, his old classmate had now become a full-fledged neo-Nazi. He'd joined up with a menacing neo-Nazi cell, and he'd made a pilgrimage to visit with a notorious, resurfaced white supremacist leader of yesteryear. Another one of his heroes, Donald Trump, was in the White House, bashing minorities at every turn, and Sam had started writing what he called his "Diary of Hate" to catalogue all his angry racial grievances. Black people, Latinos, biracial couples, "mongrels," and all types of minorities—Sam Woodward loathed them all. But he held a special enmity for gays and Jews, and Blaze, his old schoolmate home on winter break, happened to be both.

Sam wrote in his journal of baiting gays online by posing as a gay man, then threatening them with violence as retribution; the terrified reactions from his online victims energized him. "They think they are going to get hate-crimed," Sam wrote. But he seemed to be growing bored with the online harassment, anxious for the real thing. "Text is boring but murder isn't," he had written just a few weeks earlier on a napkin, along with a chilling sketch he'd made of a bloody knife.

Now he was meeting up with Blaze. As Sam waited in his car by the cul-de-sac, Blaze slipped downstairs and out of his house around eleven o'clock at night. He was quiet about it; his parents and his two younger siblings never heard him leave. He got in the car with Sam, and they drove down the hill toward a serene, wooded park nearby, next to Blaze's old elementary school.

Blaze didn't make it home.

---

## "The Ashes of Western Civilization"

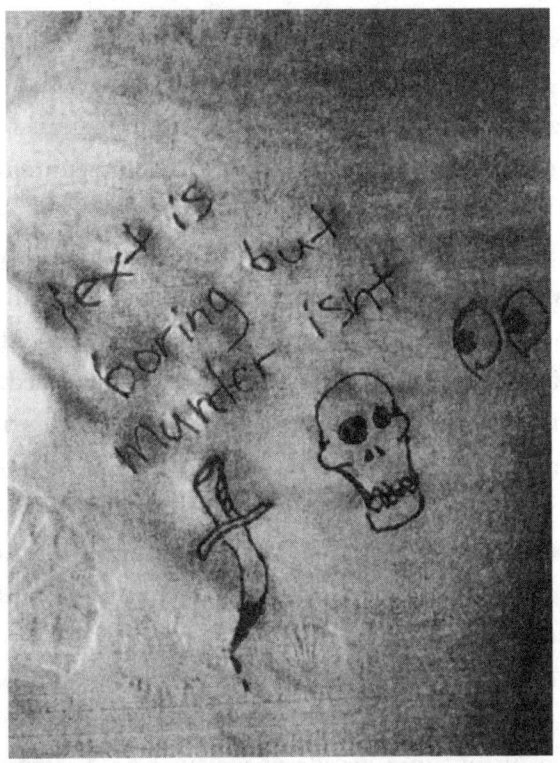

A note and drawing written on a napkin by Sam Woodward weeks before the killing of Blaze Bernstein.

Sam Woodward was part of something much bigger, something even more harrowing. America is seeing a huge, nationwide surge in violent bigotry and white supremacy unlike anything since the bloodiest days of the civil rights movement in the South in the 1960s. Often spurred on by the incendiary racial rhetoric of Donald Trump, young men like Sam Woodward have flocked to the "cause" of white supremacy by the thousands with violent results. It is a scourge endemic to America, ingrained deep in the nation's fabric, rearing its head time and again through American history in furtherance of a white-dominated society.

After a steady drop in reported hate crimes in the early 2000s, violent bigotry against the *others*—the non-whites, the non-Christians, the non-straight people—came roaring back with a vengeance behind a wave of nativist violence beginning in 2015, just as Trump, not coincidentally, was beginning his first run for president with a xenophobic, tone-setting attack on Mexican "rapists" and immigrants. So began a decade-long explosion of violent bigotry that was unrelenting in its hatred and bloodshed.

Hate crimes in America have now reached the highest levels recorded by the FBI since it began tracking them, more than doubling in a decade—even as crime overall was dropping. While the assailants could be found among practically every race and creed, one group dominates them all: whites, and typically white men, have made up the bulk of all hate-crime offenders—as many as three of every four, by one accounting. And the most violent and vicious of all the attacks have been carried out, almost always, by avowed white supremacists and proud neo-Nazis, some of them just teenagers, lashing out at the *others* in "defense" of the white race.

The scenes of mass carnage are wide and growing, with one minority group after another bearing the scars of some of the worst hate crimes in American history in a decade of violent hatred. Seven Asian and Hispanic shoppers, including three young children, murdered at a mall outside Dallas in 2023 in one of the worst massacres of people of color in modern history. Five gay club-goers at a Colorado Springs bar shot dead a year earlier in the worst massacre that authorities found had targeted LGBT people. Ten Black shoppers at a Buffalo grocery killed that same year in the worst massacre of Blacks in modern history, eclipsing the grim toll set at a historic Black church in South Carolina. The worst massacre of Hispanics in modern history, with twenty-three killed at a Walmart in El Paso in 2019, including many children and parents shopping for back-to-school supplies. The worst massacre of Jews ever on American soil, with eleven killed at a Pittsburgh synagogue a year before that. The worst massacre ever of Sikh Indian Americans before that, with seven killed at a temple in Milwaukee.

All carried out by avowed white supremacists armed with high-powered assault rifles, all flashes of fury in a blitzkrieg of hate crimes targeting the *others* for who they are and what they represent. And unlike the violence of the 1960s in the South against Black victims, the spree has been diffuse and wide-ranging—not limited to any one minority group or region, but targeting them all.

In between the mass-scale rampages came tens of thousands of other less headline-grabbing hate crimes. A few victims would be remembered by name, their stories so jarring: Ahmed Arberry, for one, a Black man out jogging in southern Georgia, who was chased down and shot to death in 2020 by three white men, all with racist pasts. But the bulk of the victims remain anonymous and faceless, except perhaps for the color of their skin; just statistics on a grim chart growing longer by the day.

Inevitably, this violent bigotry has fed off of racist propaganda and blatant misinformation targeting the *others*, oxygen to the fire. Vile hate speech attacking minorities of all types has run rampant online. With technology giants doing little to rein in the hate and bigotry on their sites, one attack has inspired another, then another, with white supremacist "manifestos" boomeranging online from one corner of the world to another—from South Carolina to New Zealand, from Norway to Germany to Texas and Orange County, and back again. Neo-Nazis have exploited the loose enforcement of the websites' protocols to broadcast their hateful message and build their numbers.

"I am simply defending my country from cultural and ethnic replacement brought on by an invasion," Patrick Crusius, a twenty-one-year-old white supremacist from Dallas, wrote in his manifesto before his onslaught at the El Paso Walmart. The attack on a crowd of overwhelmingly Hispanic shoppers was a way to "fight to reclaim my country from destruction." The same words could have been uttered by dozens of other white supremacists in their own violent attacks on the *others*—on Black people, or Jews, or Muslims, or gays, or Asian Americans.

The notion of a white society under threat of extinction from the marauding minorities was once the hateful idea of a few outliers, but no more. The "Great Replacement Theory" has been trumpeted by Trump himself, along with far-right figures like Elon Musk and Tucker Carlson, fueling the mythical and racist narrative. Millions of dollars in political contributions from right-wing racial extremists have been flowing into the coffers of conservative causes to fuel the extremist politics. Extremists determined to stave off their own supposed demise through racial violence and threats had seized the mantle of mainstream America.

The resurgence of America's age-old stain of white supremacy began bubbling up with a right-wing backlash to the election of America's first Black president in Barack Obama in 2008, a milestone that generated a record spike in the number of hate groups. And it escalated to frightening new levels beginning with the election eight years later of its most vitriolic and divisive president in Donald Trump, who would turn time and again to racial bogeymen and angry, violent rhetoric to inflame his base, much to the delight of white supremacists.

America watched, transfixed in horror, as hundreds of white supremacists marched with torches in a deadly rally in Charlottesville, Virginia, in 2017, an image that harked back to a dark and supposedly bygone era in America. Violent, racially fueled extremism reached another nadir on January 6, 2021, with the attack on the United States Capitol, replete with racist and white supremacist symbols proudly displayed by far-right insurrectionists, overwhelmingly white, trying to overturn an election that Trump had lost. And one crisis after another brought with it a painfully predictable spike in hate crimes, as angry white Americans looked irrationally for someone to blame—first with the Covid epidemic setting off thousands of violent attacks against Asian Americans; then with the Israel–Hamas war in Gaza triggering another enormous wave of attacks against both Jews and Muslims. White supremacists were at the center of it all.

Trump regained the White House in 2025 after a presidential campaign that was even more racist and xenophobic than his last two. He lashed out, in grossly exaggerated or sometimes wholly fabricated attacks, against Hispanics, "dog-eating" Haitian immigrants, transgender people, Jews, Blacks, and a myriad of the *others* who felt the sting of violent bigotry unleashed on them from the highest levels. A fresh round of hate crimes soon followed, as Trump opened his second term with a flurry of steps lashing out against "diversity" in

## "The Ashes of Western Civilization"

America—a dirty word in his administration—and taking particular aim at Hispanic immigrants and transgender people. It had become a perilous time to be one of the *others* in America.

"We are all victims now," bemoaned one Haitian woman in Springfield, Ohio, after Trump's false campaign attacks on her community. "They're attacking us in every way."

---

Orange County, the sun-splashed home to neo-Nazi Sam Woodward and his old high school classmate, Blaze Bernstein, mirrored the surge in violent bigotry cleaving America, but in the extreme. With a long, tortured history of entrenched racism, Orange County has emerged as an epicenter of violent bigotry in America, a petri dish for young white supremacists anxious to take back their culture from minorities they see as an existential threat.

It is a place long famous for its pristine ocean shorelines; its opulence and excess; its promise of a fairytale destination; and, as much as anything, its archconservative politics. It is the founding home of Disneyland, "The Happiest Place on Earth," built in the 1950s on what was once a vast expanse of orange groves, and as it grew into a suburban behemoth separated by both borders and beliefs from Los Angeles to the north, it became renowned as a right-wing political oasis—the "Orange Curtain," a conservative island amid a sea of California-style liberalism; a moneyed political playground for Ronald Reagan and native son Richard Nixon where, as Reagan liked to say, "the good Republicans go before they die."

The first sight that greets visitors leaving Orange County's John Wayne Airport speaks to its long-held cultural ethos: a nine-foot-high bronze statue of the airport's namesake: famed Western movie star, longtime Newport Beach resident and yacht owner, and a Republican icon who, later in life, became known for his unapologetic racism. The image of "The Duke" in his cowboy hat and Western apparel, gun holstered, reflected the county's rugged image, its ultraconservative self-identity and, unintentionally, its racial extremism.

Orange County, once dotted with "sundown" towns where minorities knew better than to stay out after dark, was dominated for generations almost exclusively by ultraconservative white men. But Orange County, once among the whitest regions in the country, has undergone a seismic shift in its political and demographic fault lines in recent years, its population diversifying even more quickly than that of the rest of the country. It has become a case study in the coloring of America—and the violent reaction from far-right extremists. Hispanics, Asian Americans, and other minorities now make up about 65 percent of its 3.1 million residents, far higher than the country as a whole. The signs of a changing landscape—the earthy aroma of Vietnamese *pho* at a café in Orange County's "Little Saigon," the vibrant sounds of mariachi singers in the streets of Santa Ana, or the sight of rainbow flags billowing at a gay pride festival on the beaches of Laguna—pierced the "Orange Curtain" of the white-dominated county. With its makeup changing so rapidly, Orange County broke from decades of ironclad Republican control and began electing liberal Democrats to Congress en masse, including Hispanics, Jews, and Asian Americans.

It was a changing of the tide once unthinkable, and the resistance from the old-guard white supremacists in Orange County, fighting for their very identity, has been fierce and violent. Hate crimes soaring. "White power" music thriving. The KKK and other resurgent white supremacist groups rallying publicly in the shadow of Disneyland. Militant, muscle-bound neo-Nazis training in martial arts on the ocean bluffs of San Clemente. A white supremacist prison gang from Orange County spreading to other parts of the nation. High school students in the county filming "Heil Hitler" salutes and Nazi marching songs in viral videos. Another young white supremacist preparing a "kill list" of prominent local Jews and steps for "killing my first Jew."

Many of the extremists shared a common fight; they wanted to ward off the bogeyman of "WHITE REPLACEMENT," as white supremacists declared in big block letters on huge banners hung from an overpass above one of Orange County's busiest freeways, attacking Jews, gays, Muslims, and others. When an offended bystander tried to take one banner down, two young white men who put it up rushed over to confront him. "What are you doing, you fucking Jew?" one demanded.

A shop in Anaheim, selling white-power music and apparel, started its own line of clothing embracing the violent imagery; "Hate Crime Streetwear," it called itself. "O.C. belongs to me," reads the back of one hoodie sold in the shop, quoting from a racist song by an Orange County "white power" band. Down the coast in Newport Beach, Orange County is even home to its own far-right think tank with a long history of Holocaust denial. Funded decades ago by a wealthy antisemite to present a "revisionist" view of the Holocaust, the Institute for Historical Review has challenged, among other things, the fact that Jews were gassed at Auschwitz; it considers attacks on its pseudo-academic brand of antisemitism to be "a badge of honor."

"Hate is here," Orange County's district attorney declared after one spate of violent hate crimes in the county. It had been simmering not far below the surface, but now it was making a powerful and ugly surge at historic levels, in Orange County and around America, and anyone who tried to challenge and expose it risked the wrath of the hate-mongers themselves.

One longtime hate-crime scholar who lived in Orange County, Brian Levin, found that out after he testified before a congressional committee in Washington and warned of the growing violence of white supremacists and their expanding global reach. As if to prove his point, one of the neo-Nazi groups he identified—"The Base"—put together a chilling recruitment video in response, with its members in military gear, firing assault rifles in the woods. It featured a close-up from the hearing of Levin, a Jew, followed by gunfire piercing a target with a Jewish Star of David on it.

Rifles blazing, the video closed with a final pitch for white supremacists to "take back" their country. "We strive to not only survive accelerated anarchy," the narrator said, "but to thrive in it, and rise from the ashes of Western civilization to impose order from chaos. Join us."

Sam Woodward heard the call, and he was among the growing ranks eager to join.

# PART I

# "No One Can Ever Know"

# CHAPTER 1

# "I'M A CANCER"

The two teenagers saw each other day after day at their Orange County high school, almost invisible to one another. Although they shared a few classes, they would pass each other in the bright, open hallways with barely a nod in their four years together.

Their lives would intersect again irreparably in a serene, wooded park in the foothills of Orange County three years later. But for now, in school, Blaze Bernstein and Sam Woodward knew each other mainly by reputation, as antithetical as they were: Blaze, short and slight with an infectious grin and a frenetic, artistic energy about him; and Sam, the sullen, unsmiling teenager with an outcast's image, usually alone in the corner of the classroom with his face hidden under a hoodie.

Sam and Blaze both attended the Orange County School of the Arts, an elite charter school where students competed for admission. Nestled in the county seat of Santa Ana, in a largely Hispanic neighborhood where locals could often be heard speaking Spanish on the streets outside, it was a progressive arts school: the kind of place where aspiring Broadway stars went to study jazz dancing, where would-be chefs made crepes in culinary arts classes, where kids gleefully danced and sang and painted away their lunch breaks, where rainbow-adorned LGBT themes were on bright display, and students of color were everywhere.

In famously conservative Orange County, the arts school was an island of liberalism and diversity for its two thousand students, a sign of the changes sweeping the "Orange Curtain." Blaze Bernstein, a popular, smart-alecky kid with wide-ranging interests in poetry, literature, music, and more, came off as a poster child for the school's motif—a "Renaissance" student in the eyes of the school director. He fit in at the school. Sam Woodward did not.

Sam's hatred of the *others* would take root at the arts school, where he railed against all of its diversity. But the seeds had been planted in him long before that—at his home, inside the Woodwards' A-frame rambler in the posh, largely white suburban enclave known as "the Ports" in Newport Beach. Sam's father, Blake Woodward, didn't like gays, and he made that plain to Sam and his older brother, Clay, over and over again, especially during Sam's time at the arts school.

Sam's mother, Michele, who worked as a family therapist, thought that the arts school would be a good place for him. Sam had done theater in school before that, getting the starring role in a middle school production of *Willy Wonka*. He had always liked drawing, too, and he was good at it, good enough to help get him into the uber-competitive arts school. He had very few friends at his earlier schools in Newport Beach, and he was an awkward kid socially. "Different," other students would always say; he would be diagnosed years later as being on the spectrum for autism. In light of all his social struggles, his mother was desperate for him to fit in. But Blake was skeptical that the arts school was the right place; he worried that "the homosexuals would convert Sam because he was different," he said. "It has a substantial homosexual population, and we knew that would be an influence potentially on Sam."

Blake, a finance executive in the booming commercial real estate sector, considered himself an Orange County conservative to the core, both in his politics as a Republican and in his religion as a devout

Catholic convert. Blake branded homosexuality a sin: evil and unacceptable. Views on homosexuality were changing rapidly in America; gay marriage would become legal in California in 2013 when Sam was just starting at the arts school, leading the Supreme Court to sanction it nationally two years later, and even the Catholic Church was softening its stance, with Pope Francis famously asking that same year: "Who am I to judge?"

But it remained strictly verboten in the Woodward household. Blake drilled that message of intolerance into Sam from a young age, and Sam took it to heart. It was a deep-seated intolerance, passed from father to son, and it shaped Sam. His father was the dominant figure in the home, and Sam, never as close to him as was his brother Clay, craved his approval. Bashing gays was one way that Sam knew to get it; for a birthday card he made for his father, he drew a picture with a homophobic slur on it. He thought his dad would appreciate the gesture.

Clay echoed their father's message. He taunted Sam about being "a fag" for going to the arts school, and Sam, in turn, would lash out later about "letting Mom send me to the gay-ass" arts school. Blake threw around the *fag* word as well, calling the place a "faggot school," friends said, though Michele insisted her husband was always joking when he used the word. When Blake worried for a time about Sam's own sexuality—his son didn't seem to have much interest in girls—he had a long heart-to-heart with him as they did some gardening in the yard to remind him about the evils of homosexuality. Blake feared that his son might be veering that way. That wasn't acceptable.

Could Sam have really been a closeted, self-loathing gay, repressed by his father's homophobia? Sam always denied it, and his stash of pornography showing women certainly suggested otherwise. He said later that for only a brief moment in high school, after seeing something on Netflix about closeted gays, he wondered whether he might be one himself. "I just thought to myself, *Could I be gay?* and I thought, *Huh, no.*"

Whatever doubts may have lingered in his father's mind, or perhaps even in his own, he made his outward disdain for gays clear, and the hatred began to bleed from home to school. Sam would torment one lesbian student in particular, a classmate named Cassandra Branch, calling her "a dike," "a fag," or worse to her face. "I'm going to kill you," Cassandra later recounted Sam muttering to her under his breath as they passed in the hall one day. "What did you say?" she demanded. "Oh, nothing," he replied, then walked on silently.

Sam "felt like a minority" at his school, he bemoaned, "because there were so many gays there." He never felt comfortable at school. His rage started with the gay kids, certainly, but it didn't stop there. It spread like a fungus to include minorities of all types at school—Black people, Hispanics, Jews, anyone who didn't fit the straight, white, Christian mold that was sacred to him. At his school, there were many.

Biracial kids particularly upset him. "You know what's really bothering me now," he said one day at school, apropos of nothing, to one of his few friends, a classmate named Sean Budge, who shared his passion for video-gaming. "There's this mixed race that's becoming real." He would see a kid at school with blond hair and dark skin, and it just wasn't right, he opined. "Everybody's going to look like that in twenty or thirty years if we don't stop all this mixing of the races," he told Sean. "It's going to be disgusting."

Sam began parroting the dogma of racial purity's most infamous proponent: Adolf Hitler himself. Sam had always been interested in history, especially World War II, but his interests were now focused not on the American side, but squarely on the Germans. He surprised Sean by giving him a battered World War II helmet as a token of their budding friendship, and he spoke with alarming admiration for the Nazis. Hitler "took a country in shit and made them a power," he told Sean. "What if they had more time or more manpower? They could have *won*." He laughed as he said it.

Sean sat silent, not sure what to say. All the Nazi talk made Sean a little nervous. He puzzled over Sam's fixation on the Nazis, but he dismissed it as a goofy if somewhat off-putting phase from his teenage friend, and nothing to really worry about.

## "I'm a Cancer"

Sam excitedly showed Sean a picture of a prized possession in his bedroom: a massive Confederate flag displayed over his bed. The gleaming red-and-blue flag, a toxic symbol of slavery and racism for so many others, was a point of pride for Sam. He adopted the flag in class, too. For one assignment in a digital design course, he had to create a movie poster. He designed one for *Rebel without a Cause*, the James Dean classic—but with a large Confederate flag as the background for the poster. His teacher, alarmed, wanted the onerous symbol taken out of the design. Sam stood his ground; it was a free speech issue, a personal choice, he said. The teacher backed down. The Confederate flag stayed, and with it all the symbolic power it conveyed.

He presented an air of defiance in class, spending much of his time sketching military stick figures and war scenes in his notebook instead of listening to the teacher. He was turning his artistic flair to Nazi art. It became hard for his classmates not to notice his doodling. Assigned to work with Sam in a small group for a history class in tenth grade, classmate Raiah Rofsky was struck by all the detailed etchings of guns that Sam was making whenever she looked over at him. The drawings unnerved her. She thought to herself: *If anybody's going to shoot up a school, it's going to be him.*

He was gaining notoriety in the school with every episode. In a theater class, students were reading from *A Raisin in the Sun*, the classic play about an African American family in Chicago in the 1950s. Sam didn't take to the theme. In the margins of the playscript, he had scrawled one word again and again: *n****r*. For one performance that he had to present in class, Sam told the teacher he wanted to play a military leader, so the teacher picked a Brad Pitt monologue for him from Quentin Tarantino's Nazi-themed film, *Inglourious Basterds*. Woodward immersed himself in the part with gusto. In a music class, the song he chose for one project rang out like a raw plea for help: "Hurt" by the industrial rock band Nine Inch Nails, a testimonial to self-destruction and pain.

In acting class one day, the teacher peered over Sam's shoulder and did a double take. In his notebook were more sketches of swastikas and soldiers, apparently Nazis. "What are you drawing?" the teacher asked. "Nothing," Woodward said. "Okay, this needs to stop," the teacher told him. As the teacher walked away, Sam looked over at Sean sitting in his seat nearby and gave him a silent smirk, as if to say: *Who gives a shit?*

He reveled in his image as the simmering outcast, the rebel-without-a-cause motif that he'd adopted for his defiant class poster. When he would do something jarring, the shocked look on the faces of his classmates seemed to energize him. In one class photo, he posed with his hand in the shape of a gun, his face dead serious, alongside his smiling classmates, and for a photo for another costume day at school he wore a full military uniform and helmet, saluting. "Make the cry-babies cry," he would tell Sean if someone complained about him.

He was fixated on weaponry of all sorts. He talked often of guns — he and his father and brother would occasionally go hunting together — and he always gravitated toward the most violent corners of the video games that he played. He had a particular fascination with knives. He collected all types and sizes, from the small pocketknife he used as a Boy Scout in the troop where his father was a leader up through a long saber he kept in a sheath. He would carry a knife with him practically all the time — in his pocket, clipped to his pants, or in his backpack. One held a special place for him: a wooden-handled model with his father's name etched on the blade. Blake had given it to him — a prized possession.

Blaze Bernstein was his opposite. Like his name, Blaze had a spark about him. He was a friendly, vivacious kid — funny and entertaining, always curious, quirky, with a rapier-sharp wit and a deadpan sense of humor. His tongue could get him into trouble sometimes, but he could usually manage to laugh it away with his boisterous smile. He looked like a young Matthew Broderick in the film *Ferris Bueller's Day Off*, with Bueller's moxie and mischievousness to go with it. On a field trip from school up in Los Angeles, he ventured off with some friends without permission — to attend a poetry reading, of all things. His teacher was not happy about the escapade, poetic or not.

## "I'm a Cancer"

Blaze had started writing poetry when he was just eight or nine years old, and he was reading his first Steinbeck novel not long after that. His mother, Jeanne Pepper, dubbed him her "unicorn" child, because she found his boundless creativity so unique. He played piano and performed in musicals. Creative writing became his love—that, and fine cuisine. When he managed to combine the two —writing about some delectable dish or other that he had made—that made it all the better.

Writing became Blaze's lens into the world. For hours after classes, when he wasn't practicing for a Science Olympiad or another school activity, he could often be found working on his prose in the basement sanctuary of the school's creative writing program. "I write until I can't write anymore, until the page is bursting with so many words and letters and syllables that if I were to fit one more period into the end of a sentence, the entire page might just burst," he wrote.

But his artistic side also brought a certain torment in how other kids saw him. Middle school, before his time at the arts school, was the worst of it. Blaze would come home with stories about being bullied on the bus just for being a bit different. Blaze was smaller than most of the other students, a Jewish kid with a softer side that could make him a target for the bigger kids. "They called me gay on the bus and were throwing trash at me and yelling stuff at me," he told his mother, Jeanne, a lawyer. She agonized over how to protect him.

After she moved to Orange County as a child, Jeanne herself had felt isolated as a Jew, part of a tiny minority in a county that was overwhelmingly Christian. It was a place where Christianity loomed large. Televangelist Rev. Robert H. Schuller built one of America's first megachurches, the Crystal Cathedral, in the late 1970s out of what had started as a small drive-in church. With ten thousand windowpanes, the cathedral rose from the ground as a shimmering shrine to Christianity where Schuller beamed his message around the world every Sunday for decades in his *Hour of Power* television show. Schuller called the cathedral a "twenty-two-acre shopping center for God," a garish and hard-to-miss symbol of the county's religious fervor.

But to minorities who didn't fit the mold of a white, conservative

Christian, Orange County could be a cruel place. "Don't say you're a Jew," Jeanne's own mother had warned her after their family moved to Orange County. Jeanne saw the county as a "simmering pot," a place with a long history of extremists targeting the *others*.

Jeanne's own children grew up with a keen awareness of their Jewish identity — and their vulnerability as targets. Blaze's grandmother, Leah, was a Holocaust survivor from Romania who had emigrated to America, and Blaze gave a sobering speech at the family's synagogue in Orange County about the Holocaust and "six million people systematically murdered throughout Europe in concentration camps," as he related it. He and his family traveled to Israel to celebrate his Bar Mitzvah when he was thirteen, marking his passage to Jewish adulthood, and he carried with him the emotional remnants of his grandmother's experience as a victim of hatred — targeted for being different.

Blaze never really came out as gay to his parents or schoolmates in those years—not directly, at least. Walking on the beach one day in eighth grade with one of his oldest friends, Raiah Rofsky, the ocean splashing in the distance, he hinted at his feelings. There was a boy at school. "I think he kind of likes me and I kind of like him," he told her. "I think I'm bi." He didn't seem sure. It was about the closest he came to any formal acknowledgment at the time. He never got involved in the arts school's gay–straight alliance, or any other LGBT activities. By high school, most of his close friends just assumed he was gay, though Blaze himself seemed conflicted about acknowledging it. "Do I have that *voice*?" he asked his good friend Liam one day. He resisted saying the word *gay*, but Liam knew what he was implying: He didn't want to be seen that way, even if no one else at the Orange County arts school really cared, Liam decided. It was too vulnerable a place.

But Sam Woodward cared, and he was working on new ways to show his disdain for gays, with a scam to lure them into thinking he was gay, a ruse that would eventually pull in Blaze himself.

The original target of the scam was another student at the arts school named Gabe García Combs Morris. Gabe had been out as gay from practically the moment he set foot in the arts school in seventh grade.

## "I'm a Cancer"

His mother was a teacher there, and it was there that he found refuge after being bullied repeatedly at his public school in nearby Long Beach, just up the coast from Orange County; the worst of it came when a group of other kids threw him in a trash can and called him a "faggot." He then transferred to the Orange County arts school, a "gay haven," as he called it. The world just outside the school walls could still be a tough place for a young gay student, no doubt; a couple of anti-gay protesters made that clear when they showed up outside the school one day with a bullhorn, screaming at students on their lunch break that "Homos will go to hell!" and demanding that they repent to Jesus. But inside those walls, Gabe felt like he could be himself. He became a school leader on gay issues, and other kids in school came to him to talk.

The last person Gabe expected to hear from was Sam Woodward— *that* Sam Woodward, the dark, brooding classmate. Yet there was Sam, sending him deeply personal messages on Facebook and Snapchat, asking him questions about what it was like to be gay, how he knew, what he did for fun. Sam's texts became more flirtatious, more explicit, and more sexually charged as time went on. "Sometimes I just lie awake thinking about you," Sam wrote late one night. "OMG...Seriously?" Gabe answered. Sam would pass Gabe in silence in the hall without so much as a glance, then begin another furious round of messages at night. He hinted at wanting to meet up in person, but Gabe, wary about what might happen, put him off.

Sam reminisced with glee in his "Diary of Hate" years later about the ruse of his dalliances with Gabe. "Damn forgot how fun it was back then...to get that one faggot Gabriel interested in me and then just 'cuck' him all the time. Take that fags," he wrote, with a smirking emoji.

Gabe was convinced that Sam was serious. He was flattered by all the messages, but confused and a little worried. Was Sam in the closet, conflicted about his own sexuality and looking to Gabe for help, and perhaps more? Or was this some sort of trap he was laying for Gabe to embarrass him, or something worse? He had certainly heard stories about kids posing as gay just to bait and attack their victims. After all, Gabe wasn't just gay; he was Jewish, too, and Latino on his father's side. Yet here was Sam—a known homophobe and a bigot besides, coming on to him.

Nervous, Gabe decided he needed to tell someone about the strange overtures, so he confided in a close friend: Blaze Bernstein. He didn't show him the actual exchanges, but he told Blaze how Sam had been sending him sexually charged messages for months—and not only that, but was pushing to take things further. Blaze was astounded. Sam Woodward? "Bullshit," Blaze said. It seemed too wild to be true. He didn't know what to think.

Sam's dalliances with Gabe went silent for a while, but then, toward the end of their sophomore year, he contacted him out of the blue with some news. He wasn't returning to the arts school in the fall, he said, "so I just wanted to say good-bye." Gabe asked him why he was leaving. The question prompted a rare moment of raw self-reflection from Sam. His few friends at school had left, Sam wrote, "and now the only people in school hate me, treat me like a ghost, or scorn me, and I can't stand anyone there.... To them, they're a body and I'm a cancer."

Later on, after what happened with Sam and Blaze in that Orange County park, Gabe would think back often, practically every day, about all those messages from Sam. "That could have been me," he said. The mere thought, he said, "was absolutely terrifying."

**CHAPTER 2**

# "THE SKINHEAD CAPITAL OF THE WORLD"

Orange County's reputation as a haven for white supremacists was well-known within the halls of Blaze Bernstein's high school. The kids knew the places to avoid. Be wary of "Skinhead City," the nickname for Huntington Beach down Route 55, where the young white supremacists with shaved heads would often gather at the boardwalk not far from where the surfers tested the city's famous waves. Up the Interstate-5 freeway to the north sat Anaheim, or "Klanaheim" as some of the kids called it, where white supremacists had scarred pockets of Disneyland's home city with a series of violent episodes. The students at Blaze's school, especially gays and minorities, knew to venture there only at their own peril.

Perhaps the worst-kept secret of all was Orange County's thriving "white power" music scene. Beginning in the mid-1990s, bands embracing neo-Nazism had made Orange County into America's epicenter of white-power music. At hundreds of shows hopscotching Orange County over the years, the bands have blared their anthems of hatred for the *others* in beer-soaked bars and halls, as tattooed young men with shaved heads and Doc Martens boots thrashed about in mosh pits below them. The soundtrack for their rage, cued up by followers worldwide on major online music platforms, inevitably stoked violence, and it would provide the backdrop for the first in a decade-long string of mass killings by white supremacists when a mainstay of Orange County's white-power scene went on a deadly rampage in Wisconsin in 2012.

The names that the bands have given themselves over the years speak to their common agenda: Definite Hate, Blue-Eyed Devils, Angry Aryans, Jewslaughter. If there were any doubts about their allegiances, the assorted paraphernalia on display at the shows—the Third Reich flags, the swastika-adorned T-shirts, the neo-Nazi recruitment fliers, the Nazi salutes—quickly answered them. "*White people awake, save our great race,*" they sang.

What Wagner's operas were to Hitler as musical inspiration, "white power" music has been for new generations of neo-Nazis around America. It started as a British import: two decades after the original British Invasion brought the Beatles and the Who to American shores, neo-Nazis in the United States in the mid-1980s began tapping into the race-baiting, white-power music championed by influential British skinhead bands like Skrewdriver. The music, with its thrashing, unyielding pulse and its violent, unapologetically racist lyrics, came to embody the neo-Nazis' dire view of America's ethnic decline and the "assault" on the Aryan race.

Orange County became the launchpad for the movement in America, with bootleg cassettes giving way over the years to CDs and digital music. By the 2000s, the ferocity of this music's following led Resistance Records, a leading neo-Nazi record label founded by notorious neo-Nazi leader William Pierce, to declare Orange County, California, "the Skinhead capital of the world." Indeed, Orange County boasted one of the country's best-known Aryan radio stations, an Internet station called "Radio White," claiming 100,000 listeners, and Resistance Records moved its operations for a time to San Bernardino, just across the Orange County border. "Imagine what we could do with these millions of aimless young white people if we owned MTV," Pierce once mused at a white supremacist conference.

But as popular as the recorded music has become to white supremacists around the world, it is the raw, dark energy of the live shows that has drawn thousands of hardcore faithful over the years to a dozen or so Orange County nightclubs in a blaring swarm of unbridled hate. White-power organizers advertise the "whites only" shows ahead of time through underground networks, the locations and dates kept secret until right beforehand.

Sometimes, a small group of unwitting minorities—Hispanics, gays, *others*—will stumble into a club, only to face jeers, fists, or worse from the neo-Nazis in the crowd. Or the neo-Nazis will crash punk concerts and try to assert their dominance. For punk bands promoting an anti-fascist agenda, the so-called surf Nazis crashing their concerts have made Orange County known as a dangerous place to play over the years; punk bands would hire extra security to brace for Nazi salutes and threats of violence from the crowd. At a 2019 punk show in central Orange County, an appearance by a band named Reagan Youth, whose eponymous song featured a chorus of *"We are Reagan Youth...Heil! Heil! Heil!,"* turned to bedlam when a gang of neo-Nazis started hurling racial epithets at non-whites in the crowd and a brawl broke out. "Orange County is a white man's town!" yelled one of the brawlers.

It wouldn't take much to trigger violence from the neo-Nazis; the faintest whiff of racial dissonance, or sometimes nothing at all, could light the fuse. Once, at a bar in northern Orange County, a gang of about a dozen neo-Nazi skinheads beat and stabbed an eighteen-year-old concert-goer so badly that he was hospitalized with a punctured lung. The victim's offense: he was wearing a T-shirt picturing Jimi Hendrix, the Black guitar icon. "What do you have a [racist expletive] on your shirt for?" one of his attackers demanded as he began pummeling him. "'Heil' raisers," the local media called the mobs.

Wade Michael Page, a beefy young man with a shaved head and arms bedeviled with neo-Nazi tattoos, was a frequent sight at many of the shows in Orange County in the early 2000s. He played bass guitar, and sometimes sang, in a motley crew of bands like the Blue-Eyed Devils, whose signature song, "White Power," declared unambiguously: *"Now I'll fight for my race and nation! Sieg Heil!"*

A military veteran who grew up in Colorado, Page cast himself as a political warrior for oppressed whites, using his "white power" music platform to effect change in what he called "our sick society." He was fighting, he insisted, for the very survival of the Aryan race. He told an interviewer for his white-power label in 2010, with no hint of irony, that he wanted to use his white-power music to achieve "positive results in our society.... If we could figure out how to end people's apathetic ways, it would be the start towards moving forward." For Page and others of his ilk, "progress" meant reasserting white dominance.

Wade Michael Page was a longtime member of Orange County "white power" bands before he went on a rampage at a Sikh temple in Wisconsin in 2012, slaughtering six congregants.

At his bands' shows, Page wore a guitar strap decorated with the Confederate flag, just above a large "14" tattoo on his shoulder, symbolizing the "14 words" that were a creed for white supremacists: "We must secure the existence of our people and a future for white children." His band would play at popular white-power venues like The Shack in Anaheim, just a short drive from Disneyland, with a Nazi flag sometimes displayed behind them for maximum effect.

## "The Skinhead Capital of the World"

If word leaked out about an upcoming "white power" night, opposition groups sometimes turned out to picket, waving signs that read "Honk If You Hate Nazis!" and the like, but many club owners let the shows go on anyway. The cash flowed in from beer-guzzling neo-Nazis chanting "*Sieg Heil!*" in the mosh pit; bar owners who agreed to open their doors to the shows framed it as a free-speech issue. A few owners even admitted that they didn't really mind the white-power agenda on display at their venues. "It's obvious the fuckin' Jews are causing so much of the problems in the world; fuck them," insisted the owner of a club in central Orange County that was the site of many white-power concerts in the early 2000s. "If these guys want to annihilate them, I say do it."

The white-power shows have drawn neo-Nazi VIPs from around Southern California over the years. Tom Metzger, the notorious elder statesman of the White Aryan Resistance (WAR) movement until his death in 2020, would drive ninety minutes or so up the coast from his home in northern San Diego County, just across the border from Orange County, to attend.

At one of his appearances at The Shack, a band that Page played in called Youngland dedicated its signature song to Metzger in the crowd; it was called "Thank God I'm a White Boy," an Aryan twist on the old John Denver classic, and it hailed white pride while taunting "money-hungry Jews" and other minorities. Another one of their white-power tunes about the threat of minorities in Orange County, called "White Man on the Move," took aim at "queers," "jigs," "spics," and "n****rs," declaring that: "*When the last White moves out of O.C., the American flag will leave with me… We'll die for a land that's yours and mine.*" Still other songs envisioned a "race war" to rid America of its "mud" and "scum" and to "smash this melting pot." Metzger, whose bald head needed little shaving to fit into the skinhead crowd, smashed himself headlong into his young acolytes in the mosh pit as the white-power music blasted in his honor.

Metzger, a onetime Grand Dragon of the California Ku Klux Klan before starting his own hate group, had long been an icon among the white supremacists. His notoriety had only swelled years earlier, in 1990, after he and his organization were bankrupted by a $12.5 million judgment in Portland for the brutal beating death of an Ethiopian student at the hands of three skinhead followers, who had been dispatched to Oregon by Metzger to incite "racial violence." Undaunted by the verdict, Metzger declared afterward that "the movement will not be stopped in the puny town of Portland. We're too deep. We're embedded now. Don't you understand? We're in your colleges. We're in your armies. We're in your police forces.... We planted the seeds."

Indeed, Metzger, who repaired televisions for a living when he wasn't fomenting "white revolution," recognized early on the appeal of white-power music as a recruiting vehicle for bringing young skinheads to his Aryan cause, organizing the first-ever music festival dedicated to hate music in 1988 in Oklahoma. He saw Southern California, and not the South, as crucial to his lofty goals for expanding the movement's reach in America. "This may not be the Mecca of white separatism," he once said, "but it is the breeding ground."

Metzger saw the potential in Orange County. The place had drawn white supremacists and hard-line political extremists for generations. In the early 1920s, KKK members had served openly on city councils and captured majorities in some cities, pushing a "law-and-order" platform and declaring that "good, law-abiding people have nothing to fear"; in Anaheim, on-duty police officers robed in Klan regalia would sometimes patrol city streets, and in 1924 a throng of some twenty thousand Klan supporters from around the region gathered at a rally in a city park in a show of might, a thirty-foot electronic cross on display before them.

The Klan eventually lost power, but in the 1950s, dozens of branches of the ultraconservative John Birch Society began sprouting up around Orange County, the heart of the group's national base. Dominated by white business executives in Orange County, the John Birch Society pushed an anti-communist and often conspiracy-mongering philosophy that was branded as extremist even by conservatives like California's own Ronald Reagan. The Birchers held strong.

## "The Skinhead Capital of the World"

The county's vast expanse of orange groves and cattle farms began to give way to megachurches, military contractors, Walt Disney's first theme park, and one new suburban neighborhood after another with ubiquitous orange-tiled roofs. The county population grew fivefold by 1960, but it remained overwhelmingly white and Christian—and racist extremism flourished. Even as the county's population was swelling, racial restrictions—both formal and informal—continued to keep minorities out of many whites-only neighborhoods in those years. "If we had a colored or Oriental family here, all hell would be raised," one local realtor remarked after a prominent Korean American, Dr. Sammy Lee, was stopped from buying a house in Garden Grove in 1954. Lee was an American success story: a first-generation American, born to Korean immigrants, a physician, a retired army officer, and a gold-medal-winning Olympic diver for the United States in the previous two Olympics, but he and his family weren't welcome in Orange County. "I don't want to sound like a crybaby," Lee said. "I just want a home without bigotry and prejudice."

The cold rejection of an American Olympian made international headlines, a sign that bald-faced bigotry in America reached beyond the Jim Crow South, all the way to the bright shores of Southern California. "The story of Major Lee's reception in Garden Grove," the *San Francisco Chronicle* declared, "will embarrass our country in the eyes of the world."

In 1968, *Forbes* magazine declared Orange County to be America's "nut country" because of its extreme brand of politics, much to the chagrin of the proud locals. Orange County's Republican politicians, with a stranglehold on the county's congressional seats for decades, were notorious as perhaps America's most extreme conservatives, with an unabashedly pro-Christian agenda that often took brutal aim at minorities of all types. Bashing the *others* often seemed like political sport for Orange County's congressmen, whether they were attacking opponents as "lesbian spear-chuckers," likening South African icon Nelson Mandela to infamous Black murderer Willie Horton, or warning, baselessly, that "a large contingent of barefoot Africans" were planning to invade America with help from the United Nations. The racist, sexist, and homophobic rhetoric from one of the county's most notorious politicians, Congressman John G. Schmitz, was so extreme that even the far-right John Birch Society dumped him. The broadsides made clear to minorities in Orange County that they were considered second-class citizens in the eyes of their most extreme political leaders. In 1988, Orange County Republicans even hired uniformed private security guards at polling places on Election Day in heavily Hispanic neighborhoods with signs, in English and Spanish, warning ominously that it was a felony for noncitizens to vote. The strong-arming tactic evidently helped lead the Republican candidate to a narrow win.

With its long lineup of far-right politicians and deep-pocketed donors, Orange County also became the well-funded launching pad for decades of far-right political campaigns lashing out at minority groups. In 1978, a failed statewide ballot initiative originating there aimed to keep gays from working in public schools, and another, the notorious Proposition 187 in 1994, would have denied public services such as schooling and medical care to undocumented immigrants. Federal courts ultimately blocked the measure as unconstitutional.

The fevered pitch of the anti-minority rhetoric only seemed to embolden Orange County's white supremacists, with a series of brazen, unprovoked attacks on minorities—whether Black, Hispanic, Jewish, Asian, gay, or otherwise—punctuating the tension and seizing public attention sporadically throughout the 1990s. A pair of tattooed skinheads were harassing minorities near the pier in Huntington Beach one night in 1996 when they confronted a young Native American man named George Mondragon near a lifeguard tower on the beach. "Do you believe in white power?" they demanded to know. When Mondragon turned and ran, the skinheads gave chase and stabbed him twenty-seven times. "They tried to murder another human being," a police lieutenant said, "because of the color of his skin." Remarkably, Mondragon survived that brutal hate-crime attack, but two years earlier, Vernon Flournoy, an African American mechanic and a grandfather, had died when another pair of white supremacist skinheads accosted him on the sidewalk outside a McDonald's in Huntington Beach, then shot him dead. "My husband was murdered because he was a Black man," Flournoy's grief-stricken widow said.

Politicians didn't like to talk much about the hate crimes or Orange County's reputation over the years as a magnet for neo-Nazis. It conflicted with the image that the county had worked so hard to cultivate as a tourist destination not only for Disneyland, with its staggering revenues estimated at more than $75 million per day, but also for its bucolic shorelines, oceanfront resorts, and luxury shopping malls. Reports of neo-Nazi killings, or of swastikas spray-painted on the car of a Holocaust survivor, didn't foster that image. Just as hate-crime reports were starting to soar in Orange County in 2017, Orange County officials went so far as to temporarily block the publication of an annual report on such episodes by a county-run commission. The report "makes Orange County look bad," one commissioner said. In other words, Orange County should be focusing on all the good things that it was doing, not on hate crimes and bigotry.

---

Neo-Nazi band member Wade Page was instrumental in spreading the message of hate that so energized Orange County's white supremacists, shredding on his bass guitar at white-power shows with his Confederate flag and his Nazi tattoos on proud display. If the white-power concerts were Page's angry, amped-up public declaration of white supremacy, his earlier years in the military in the 1990s had been his indoctrination. "If you don't go into the military as a racist, you definitely leave as one," he once said. Page, who became part of an elite psychological operations unit in the army, carved out a psyche of a different sort when he connected with a group of white supremacists in the military. He railed against what he claimed was the military's discrimination against whites in favor of minorities. He talked of creating a homeland for whites and keeping out all the others—"dirt people," he called them. Black people, Hispanic people, anyone who wasn't white—"he hated them all," said one soldier who served with Page. White supremacy had been entrenched in the military for generations, and Page saw no need to hide his neo-Nazi views from his fellow soldiers; once, while on temporary duty in Germany, troop members spotted him goose-stepping drunkenly down the street, Nazi-style, while singing German marching songs, pretending to be a soldier of the Third Reich.

It was during a stint at Fort Bragg in North Carolina that Page met an ideological compatriot named James Burmeister, a paratrooper in the 82nd Airborne Division who was also in a group of young neo-Nazis at the base. Page and Burmeister bonded over white supremacy. Like Page, Burmeister didn't try to mask his neo-Nazi views in the barracks; he even hung a Nazi flag over his bunk. That wasn't necessarily a problem in the eyes of the military. Under a policy still in place today, personnel weren't automatically banned from the military for membership in a white supremacist group, but could be discharged only if they were found to be "active" in the movement. It was a toothless policy that service members, even active neo-Nazis, had openly flouted for years.

One December night in 1995, Burmeister and two other neo-Nazi friends serving with him at Fort Bragg went out drinking and cruised a neighborhood near the base in his friend's car, looking for Black people to harass. Burmeister had been admiring his friend's spiderweb tattoo, a notorious neo-Nazi symbol "earned" for killing a Black person. "You never know, maybe I'll earn my spiderweb tonight," Burmeister said as he got out of the car with his pistol. Seeing a Black couple strolling on a dirt path, he walked up and fired seven shots at them at close range, killing them both in what the district attorney called "a pure execution."

It was one of the worst hate crimes in the history of the American military, and it prompted a deep reckoning for the Pentagon—and a lengthy internal investigation into the long-running subculture of white supremacy within its ranks, a problem that would persist for decades. Wade Page, however, was stoic about the murders. He saw the brutal, unprovoked violence on the dirt road that night, carried out by his fellow neo-Nazi, as somehow inevitable in a country that he bemoaned for straying from its white-dominated roots. "This is the kind of stuff that happens when you have a society that race-mixes," he said.

Page was ultimately drummed out of the military with a dishonorable discharge—not for his white supremacist involvement, but for his frequent drunkenness. Not long after his dismissal, he threw his few belongings in a backpack and rode his motorcycle across the country, ending up in Orange County and immersing himself in the white-power music scene with Youngland and other bands. For a neo-Nazi looking to make his name in white-power music, Orange County was a prime destination, and Page made it his own.

Living with some of his bandmates in a house they shared in the city of Orange, out of place among the fashionable restaurants and quaint antique galleries nearby, Page opened up about his ideology to a young sociologist from the University of Nebraska named Pete Simi. He was doing fieldwork researching white supremacists in the early 2000s and interviewing as many neo-Nazis as he could find. Simi, a white man himself, wanted to understand what made these young men think—and hate—the way that they did.

When Simi was just nine years old, his mother had introduced him to the reality of racial hatred in America and its long history when she sat him down to watch a PBS documentary on the Ku Klux Klan. He remembered it vividly. The images of the Klan's burning crosses left a lasting impression on the boy. He was a high schooler in Portland when the Ethiopian student there was killed by Tom Metzger's skinhead goons in his own city. The neo-Nazis' violent racism repulsed and gripped Simi, and he ended up making a career in academia out of studying a threat that was clearly growing worse.

For his research in Orange County, Simi would sometimes crash on the couch at Page's house, interviewing him and his neo-Nazi housemates for hours at a time over the course of more than two years. Page and his bandmates seemed smitten by the idea of an academic like Simi finally taking them seriously and trying to understand their "perspective." But one of Page's housemates warned Simi not long after he arrived that "if it turns out you're a cop, I'll personally hunt you down and slit your fucking throat, after I kill your family."

Wade Page became Simi's unlikely companion. On many days, Page's drinking binges left him passed out at the group house, keeping him out of work and giving him plenty of time to speak with Simi for his research. In between white-power concerts and neo-Nazi house parties, he and Simi would go to bars, shoot pool, or get breakfast at Denny's and talk about his ideology—his open disdain for Black people, Jews, Muslims, and other "dirt people," for instance, or his preoccupation with ZOG, the mythical "Zionist Occupation Government," which conspiracy theorists and antisemites imagined was secretly running the world. Even the sight of a Jewish symbol in public would set him off. Occasionally Page would take Simi to a German-themed club in Anaheim called the Phoenix, hoping to run into some authentic World War II–era Nazis. He seemed intent on trying to convert Simi to his side, as futile as that was.

Page, though intense in his racist political views, was reserved by nature, a wallflower compared to his loud, gregarious neo-Nazi bandmates. He was the bass player, not a front-man type. He talked with Simi about violence occasionally, but all of the neo-Nazis did, almost as an article of faith, preaching violence as a means to an end in combating the corruption of the Aryan race. Next to his Orange County housemates, Page never struck Simi as particularly threatening.

---

Simi lost touch with Page after finishing his research and didn't hear anything about him again for a number of years—not until one August day in 2012 when news came of a horrific hate crime at a Sikh temple in a Milwaukee suburb. As early details of the attack were still emerging, Simi began working on a column about the massacre and saw a photo of the shooter. He felt a knot in his stomach. He looked again to make certain: It was Wade Page.

## "The Skinhead Capital of the World"

The neo-Nazi bassist, then forty years old, had driven to the Sikh Temple of Wisconsin on a Sunday morning with a 9mm semiautomatic handgun and high-capacity magazines, just as a few dozen worshippers of Indian descent were arriving for the start of services and preparing a weekly communal Punjabi meal of samosas and poori in the kitchen. Without saying a word, Page opened fire on the worshipers from outside the building, then walked inside and continued his rampage room to room, killing six congregants and wounding four others, including a priest who was left paralyzed in the attack and died of his wounds years later. Leaving the temple, Page fired at the first police officer in the parking lot, Lt. Brian Murphy, and shot him fifteen times in the head and body, critically injuring him, but somehow Murphy survived. Moments later, a second officer shot Page, who then put his gun to his head and killed himself as his victims lay dead and dying inside the temple.

The attack on the Sikh temple by the Orange County white-power band member proved to be the harbinger of a jarring new mode of mass-casualty hate crimes in America: laying siege to targets where minorities were known to gather. Avowed white supremacists had waged smaller attacks on symbolic targets before. In 2009, an elderly white supremacist shot and killed a guard at the US Holocaust Museum in Washington, DC. A decade earlier, a shooting at a Jewish summer camp in Los Angeles left a postal worker dead and three Jewish campers injured—"a wakeup call to America to kill Jews," the shooter called it. But not since the KKK's violent rampage against Black targets in the 1960s had America seen a racial or religious attack on the mass scale of Page's rampage. It wouldn't be the last. It was the beginning of a violent new era for white supremacists targeting the *others*.

There was no note from Page, no video, no explanation for what he'd done. Hate-filled manifestos hadn't yet become the *de rigueur* tool of mass hate crimes. But the FBI labeled the massacre an act of domestic terrorism, and the investigation indicated that Page's long trail of neo-Nazi fervor had only deepened in the months before the shootings. He had moved to the Milwaukee area to be with a girlfriend—a white supremacist herself—and he had earned a "patch," a mark of his status as a full member of the Hammerskin Nation, one of the country's biggest neo-Nazi skinhead clans. He had immersed himself in dozens of online chats on white supremacist forums filled with radical talk and conspiracy theories about minorities and threats of all types. One of the online monikers he was using was "End Apathy"—the same name as one of his neo-Nazi bands in Orange County.

But why the Sikh temple? Police struggled to pinpoint any particular motive for that location. "There was no specific group he was after, or disliked more than the other," said John Edwards, the police chief in Oak Creek, the Milwaukee suburb where the Sikh temple was located. "He could have gone past a Korean church, a black Baptist church, could have gone past a Muslim church. Anyone different, it's a personal hate. He just hated."

The Wisconsin attack came barely two weeks after twelve people were murdered at the midnight premiere of a new Batman film, *The Dark Knight Rises*, in Aurora, Colorado. The back-to-back massacres both relied on high-capacity, semiautomatic weaponry—the common thread running through mass shootings in twenty-first-century America. But the attacks seemed distinct in fundamental ways: one a random act of violence, its victims joined only by a desire to see a brand-new superhero movie; the other one a hate crime carried out by an avowed white supremacist who appeared to be targeting the *others*—in this case, Indian-American worshipers—simply for being different from him. It was a cycle of violence that would play out over and over again in America.

Page's violence was the deadliest attack on Sikhs in American history, and for those in the Milwaukee area, the tragedy was made doubly cruel by the suspicion that Page might not have even intended to target their people in particular. Page loathed Muslims—"towel-heads" and "sand n****rs," he called them. And over the years, Sikh men across America—with their tradition of wearing turbans and long beards—had found themselves mistaken for Muslims in hate crimes. "Just because they see the turban," one local Sikh woman remarked after the Wisconsin massacre, "they think you're Taliban."

After the September 11 attacks, in fact, the very first "revenge" hate killing had come not against a Muslim, but a Sikh, just four days after Muslim hijackers with al Qaeda hit the Twin Towers in Manhattan and the Pentagon. Outside a gas station in Mesa, Arizona, a drive-by shooter shot to death the owner, a bearded Sikh immigrant from India, clad in a turban, while he was planting flowers outside the gas station he owned. The shooter apparently thought he was Muslim; he had announced beforehand that he was going to "go out and shoot some towel-heads" in retaliation for the attacks carried out days earlier by al Qaeda terrorists. It was the first murder in what would become a huge burst of hate crimes after 9/11 against American Muslims—or minorities simply mistaken for them.

Page's deadly rampage in Wisconsin reverberated more than seven thousand miles away in India, home to the biggest population of Sikhs in the world. "It is very shocking that a country like the USA, which says, 'We are the super power of the world,' could not protect their own people in their own country," commented one elderly Sikh man in Delhi. "It's shameful for USA."

Pardeep Singh Kaleka, a longtime congregant at the Sikh temple whose father was one of its founders, couldn't help thinking afterward about how he would have been at the temple, too, that morning—there with his mother and his father—if his young daughter hadn't forgotten her notebook for Sunday religious school. He and his two young children were already in the car en route to the temple when she realized she'd forgotten it. Kaleka turned the car around to go home and get it, then headed back to the temple, only to see a crush of police cars scream past him, sirens blazing. Police were blocking off the road to the temple.

Kaleka, a former police officer himself in Milwaukee, got out of his car at the blockade to find out what was happening. "There's been a shooting," an officer told him. "The scene is not secure." His mother and father were inside, Kaleka explained frantically, but the officer wouldn't let him through; it was too dangerous. Calls started flooding his cell phone from friends and family members who had also heard about the shooting. His wife called him; Kaleka's mother had reached her from inside the temple, hiding in a pantry, whispering that there was a shooter in the building; another woman had been shot and lay bleeding nearby.

His father's phone number flashed on Kaleka's phone. "Dad?" he said. He heard an unfamiliar voice, the head priest at the temple speaking in Punjabi. Kaleka, who had immigrated to America from India with his family as a boy, didn't speak much Punjabi, but he understood enough to realize his father had been shot and was badly wounded. Inside his own temple.

Kaleka heard his two young children whimpering in the back seat after hearing the call. "Dad, I will get the bad guys," his son said. But Kaleka felt powerless. Just the day before, he had been celebrating with his father, Satwant, at a family gathering, sharing a northern Indian whiskey drink to celebrate Kaleka's thirty-sixth birthday. His father, who'd been a farmer in India and bought a gas station and convenience store in Milwaukee that he ran, was president of the temple; he and another Sikh friend from India had pooled their money for a down payment on the land, and he had helped dig the trenches and lug the bricks with his own hands to build it. He was a fixture there at the temple, the sacred *Gurudwara*. Now he was lying wounded inside the temple, his pickup truck still parked out front, and all that Kaleka could do was wait in agony.

Police finally let Kaleka and other anxious family members into a makeshift command center in the parking lot of a bowling alley across the street from the temple. People knelt in prayer. Kaleka found his mother there—unharmed after her evacuation, but hysterical with anxiety about the fate of her husband. "Where is Satwant?" she screamed. No one could tell them.

Finally, more than ten hours after the shooting, ten hours after what was supposed to be the start of another weekly prayer service and the ritual lunch afterward, police and the FBI sat Kaleka and his brother down and gave them the news that seemed both unthinkable and inevitable. "Your father did not survive," an officer told him.

In the aftermath, amid all the grief and the mourning and the glare of the national media spotlight cast on yet another horrific mass murder in America, Kaleka vowed to find out everything he could about the senseless killing of his father and the five other Sikh congregants. He was consumed with anger, but he wanted to know more. He learned of his father's attempts, in his final minutes, to ward off the attacker and protect other congregants; a knife was found at his father's side. He learned of the heroism of Lt. Murphy, who became a revered figure to Sikhs around the world even as he recovered from his grievous wounds. And he learned about Wade Michael Page, the man who had spewed hatred for so long through his white-power music and had targeted his family's temple with violent rage just because the congregants looked different than him.

There was a Sikh quotation that Kaleka had learned years earlier, attributed to the founding Sikh guru in the late fifteenth century: *The tongue is like a sharp knife; it kills without drawing blood.* Kids in America grew up learning just the opposite sentiment, with the old adage: *Sticks and stones can break my bones, but names will never hurt me.* But anyone battered by slurs and insults, the kind that flew off the stage from Wade Page's neo-Nazi bands before his rampage, knew it wasn't true. To Kaleka, the Sikh sentiment about the deadly power of the tongue seemed to reflect all the hatred coursing through America—and now claiming the life of his own father.

It was a time of soul-searching for Kaleka, and he decided to make major changes in his life. He became a licensed therapist working with other victims of trauma, and in the course of his newfound mission, he met with a reformed Hammerskin skinhead, Arno Michaelis—a onetime white-power band member himself. Michaelis had turned against white supremacy and now preached tolerance and compassion. Together, he and Kaleka—a former skinhead alongside the son of a hate-crime victim killed by a neo-Nazi—formed a nonprofit group to bring people together and divert young people from the kind of violent extremist ideologies that had consumed Wade Page for so many years. What Kaleka longed for most of all, he said, was a mutual understanding and compassion for all cultures, no matter their differences.

Wade Page's hateful white-power music, lashing out at the *others*, preached just the opposite, and his hatred would outlive him. Even after he killed himself outside the Sikh temple at the end of his rampage that summer morning, the white-power music put out by his Orange County bands has survived online for years, widely available at major public sites and bringing in new fans. "Thank God I'm a White Boy"—the signature tune of his Youngland band, with its thrashing lines about "white pride" and "money-hungry Jews"—racked up tens of thousands of hits on YouTube and remains online. "Hate speech is not allowed on YouTube," the site declared, but the music has stayed up for years, even so. At the same time, the defunct British band Skrewdriver—the British granddaddies of racist, white-power music, inspiring new generations of white supremacists—attracted millions of views on songs that remained online on YouTube, Spotify, and other sites as well.

Online fans of Youngland's "Thank God I'm a White Boy" used the violent, racist tune to parrot neo-Nazi dogma. "Right on, white on," one commenter wrote in a note about the song. A listener from North Carolina quoted the neo-Nazis' infamous fourteen words about securing "a future for our White children." Others used the neo-Nazi's "88" symbol for Adolf Hitler to voice their approval of the hate-filled message. And another simply quoted one of Youngland's songs about Orange County, celebrating the grip of white power: "*OC Belongs to Me*," they sang.

YouTube was far from alone in giving hate-mongers a global platform to spread their message of hate and minority-bashing. Hate-filled material attacking minorities of all types ran rampant online in the Internet age, fueling real-world hate crimes. As the United Nations said in one report on the sprawling volume of material, "Hate speech has the potential to incite violence" and has been a frequent "precursor" historically to racial crimes and atrocities.

## "The Skinhead Capital of the World"

Because hate speech is legal in America under the First Amendment, it is left to the technology platforms, not the government, to decide what is allowed and to police themselves. Most of them, like YouTube, have policies banning hate speech on their sites, using computer algorithms and reports from their own users to flag offensive material and take it down. But it remains plentiful nevertheless. About a third of all Internet users say they've been confronted by hate speech, despite the safeguards, according to one report, and advocacy groups have given many sites failing grades for keeping hateful material off their platforms. And the cesspool has grown even deeper with some tech giants rolling back their own restrictions.

Since Trump ally Elon Musk bought the social media platform Twitter in 2022 and rebranded it as X, it has become a magnet for racist, hateful postings—"a safespace for hate," as one Jewish advocate called it. Musk, casting himself as an absolutist on free speech, relaxed restrictions on hate speech on the platform, let Trump back on, got rid of most of the content moderators, and used his own account to post objectionable material. In one, he said that he endorsed as "the absolute truth" an antisemitic post claiming that Jews were stoking hatred against whites.

After an anti-hate group reported to X in 2023 that it had found three hundred posts on its site that attacked Jews, Black people, and other minorities, and had violated the company's own standards, more than 85 percent of the posts still remained online a week later. Posts denying the Holocaust, claiming that Black people are violent because "it's in their nature," condemning "race-mixing," even declaring that Hitler was "a hero who will help secure a future for white children!" all stayed up on the site for more than a million followers to see, fueling even more bigotry. The message of hatred lived on. As one of Wade Page's white-power bands declared in a widely available song called "Murder Squad," about wanting to kill minority "filth" and Jews: "A cleansing wind throughout this land. The final solution, the final stand."

## CHAPTER 3

# "SABOTEUR"

Sam Woodward was ready to take his brand of militant white supremacy to another level in his path to violent extremism. He wanted to join up with a neo-Nazi group, in the flesh. He had grown restless with the online world of bigotry and minority-bashing, and he longed for the real thing. "I'm ready to commit myself," he wrote to a neo-Nazi pal he'd met online. "Just tell me what I need to do."

It was the spring of 2017, three years since he had left the Orange County arts school where he had become such a reviled figure. Before his junior year, he had transferred to Corona del Mar High School in his hometown of Newport Beach, much less progressive in its politics than the arts school, and much whiter in its student population, but he still never quite seemed to fit in. He was almost mute in school, save for a forced chuckle or two at another student's joke during a group project. He would usually sit in the back of the classroom by himself, earphones and a hoodie over his head, isolating himself from the world around him.

He was a cipher to his fellow students. If they knew anything at all about him, it was that he was very religious, and very Christian. That much was reflected in the congratulatory note that his parents, Blake

## "Saboteur"

and Michele, placed in his high school yearbook, quoting a Bible passage from Philippians. "Your prayer," they wrote. "I can do all things through Christ who strengthens me."

In front of his classmates and teachers, at least, Sam managed to suppress the demons that had made him such a pariah at his old school—"a cancer," as he had put it. There were no homophobic outbursts in school now, no Confederate flags displayed defiantly in class projects, no Nazi swastikas or racial slurs scribbled in the margins of assignments, no murmurings to classmates about the immorality of biracial couples or the "disgusting" nature of homosexuality. He kept his feelings hidden away from them, buried deep inside.

But the Internet offered him a powerful outlet for his darkest thoughts. Online, he was creating a menacing, outsize persona for himself, remote and largely anonymous. Often so silent and sullen in person, Sam found a home, and a voice, on the Web—in a universe of the right-wing online forums he visited, an invisible world where he found solace with like-minded teenagers bonded by anger, racism, and alienation. Here he could express his true, frightening feelings.

His rage poured out. On the social media sites he frequented, there was the typical teenage banter from Sam, griping about schoolwork, about parents, about sex or the lack of it, and trading tips about video games. But beyond the everyday talk was a much darker stream of vile hatred. Adopting war-tinged screen names—"Saboteur" was his favorite—Sam could voice his enthusiasm for Nazi-style fascism, and his disdain for gays and Jews—"fags and kikes," as he called them. "All fags and fakers are in for it, get ready to die," he wrote in a pseudonymous account he created on Grindr, the gay dating site. He could talk of wanting to rape African American women and "force them to carry around the spawn of their master and enemy." He could lash out at then-President Obama as a "spineless socialist" and, like many conservative white men of his generation, voice his support for Donald Trump's budding candidacy for president in 2016, with all its raw, race-baiting rhetoric. He wasn't just a "generic" Trump supporter, he said, but a fervent one. Trump enthralled him, and he adopted some of

Trump's rhetoric as his own, using his drafting skills, for instance, to draw a cartoon under the banner of "Fake News."

He could post a menacing photo of himself on one social media site, smirking as he stood in front of the Confederate flag in his bedroom while flashing a long, jagged knife. Below it, he wrote: "If you're a race mixer comment your address so I can kill you."

He could show off his dual commitments to both God and guns in his online persona; if he were stranded on a desert island, he wrote on one site, the only things he'd need would be a .45 Colt firearm and a Bible. "Anything is possible through the Lord who strengthens me," he wrote, a variation of the same Biblical verse his parents dedicated to him in his yearbook.

And he could grin mischievously in another jarring photo he posted as he pretended to stomp another boy's head against a sidewalk curb, reenacting a notorious scene played out by a neo-Nazi skinhead in the 1998

Sam Woodward in a post threatening "race mixers" on a social media site called iFunny.

## "Saboteur"

film *American History X*, starring Edward Norton. The film was based on real-life violence by white supremacists in Orange County. During production, news of a violent attack by a gang of skinheads on employees at a grocery store in coastal Dana Point prompted the filmmakers to rewrite one bloody scene to give it more gritty reality. Now Woodward was claiming the violent neo-Nazi imagery from the film as his own.

"You are violent. And it scares me," a user wrote to Sam after one outburst on a website called *askFM*. Yet nothing was done about even his most violent and threatening posts. The guardrails that the social media companies promised to put in place to prevent such violent content and hate speech again proved paper-thin, just as they had with the violent "white power" songs on YouTube from Wade Page's neo-Nazi band in Orange County and countless other violent, hateful postings. Sam was free to keep spreading his hateful declarations, and spreading fear; the shock value only seemed to energize him.

His parents were growing alarmed about how isolated and dark he was becoming in those high-school years. Blake, seeing Sam head to school in his typical black, goth-style clothing, told him he "looked like a school shooter." Sam would spend hours and hours alone in his room after school playing violent video games or surfing far-right extremist and neo-Nazi sites—"educating" himself on fascism, as he described it. His parents seemed oblivious. He went long stretches barely speaking to them; they sometimes resorted to communicating with him down the hall via email or handwritten letters. They figured it was that or nothing.

But they did see flashes of his growing rage, enough to be worried. Bagging groceries at a Bristol Farms grocery store, one of the short-lived jobs he churned through, Sam got into a series of fights with customers and co-workers, including a Hispanic supervisor. Angry, he came home after one testy exchange and used one of the knives from his collection to stab a mattress again and again, practically shredding it. Another time, his brother said that Sam had pulled a knife and stabbed him during one of their frequent fights (Sam insisted he'd only brandished the knife), and he smashed a bathroom mirror in still another episode. The outbursts were piling up. Michele flagged his temper in a long letter she wrote to Sam laying out her concerns about his violent behavior. "Don't rage against us," she wrote. He would apologize, then rage again.

After high school, Sam tried college for a bit at California State University Channel Islands, a small, newer state school about a hundred miles up the coast from Newport Beach, but it didn't last. He made a few friends at school, unusual for him, and he started smoking a lot of pot. He did poorly in his classes, blaming the bad grades on all the time he was spending to educate himself on neo-Nazi websites. While immersing himself in all things neo-Nazi, Sam told one confidante, he was having trouble "balancing that with classwork time." He dropped out of school before the end of his freshman year and moved back home with his parents in Orange County. He thought about joining the military as a way to get tactical training that he could put to use in his neo-Nazi ambitions, as many others had done before him. But he was hesitant because he said that military service could mean aligning himself with Israel and "ZOG," the mythical, all-powerful Zionist Occupation Government; he said he didn't want to help "the kikes."

That was the time when he began keeping a journal on his cell phone, writing emails to himself chronicling all his rage and bigotry. His "Diary of Hate," he called one section. He lashed out at Jews, Blacks, and a slew of other minorities, but his disdain for gays, in particular, was a driving fixation. He laid out his *modus operandi* for targeting them. He wrote of luring gays — "sodomites," as he called them — on online sites like Grindr and Tinder only to humiliate them, or worse. "This is fucking hilarious. I tell sodomites that I'm bi-curious, which makes them want to 'convert' me. Get them hooked by acting coy, maybe send them a pic or two, beat around the bush and pretend to tell them that I like them and then, Kabam, I either un-friend them or tell them they have been pranked. Ha Ha," he wrote, followed by a string of laughing-face emojis. "That's what they deserve for being fags, LOL." If he were really gay or bisexual himself, as his homophobic father feared, he was hiding it behind a wall of rage toward gays.

In his journal, Sam later reflected on "how fun it was" back at the Orange County arts school to "get that one faggot Gabriel interested in me" by convincing him he was gay, and then just ditching him. "Take that fags," he wrote. More emojis—smirking this time.

It was on Tinder, where he'd indicated he was either gay or bisexual, that Sam reconnected with another ex-classmate from the Orange County School of the Arts that May in the midst of all his angry journal entries. It was Blaze Bernstein.

It had been three years since Blaze and Sam had had any contact, and their lives had diverged dramatically since their time together at the arts school. Blaze had just finished his second year at the University of Pennsylvania. Always an ambitious kid, he had known almost instantly that he wanted to attend the school after visiting the campus while on a tour of East Coast colleges. His tour left him smitten by Penn's Ivy League pedigree and its historical roots, practically palpable to him as he stood in the quad in front of the statue of founder Benjamin Franklin.

When a recruiter for Penn's writing program later visited his high school in Orange County, Blaze cornered her afterward to introduce himself and let her know how eager he was to apply. He highlighted his passion for writing in his admissions essay for Penn. "When I write, the world around me stops," he said.

He flashed his brash side at one of his very first orientation sessions at Penn. The new freshmen all had to discuss the classic film *Citizen Kane*, and when one student made a comment about the film that didn't ring true to Blaze, he shouted out: "That didn't happen! You didn't watch the movie!" His verve made such an impression on another freshman there that day, Amy Marcus, that she introduced herself to him afterward, and the two became fast friends. Blaze, always working on his creative writing, would send Amy snippets of poetry and short stories that he'd written at all hours, usually with the same urgent query: "What do you think of this?"

While Blaze worked on his creative writing and joined the Penn food magazine, he also started a dual degree program combining bioscience and business. He had always done well in science, in addition to his artsy side, and he was thinking about medical school. The program imposed an intensive course load, and that first semester drained him; he was questioning whether it was too big a grind, and his confidence was waning. He decided to take the spring semester off and went home to Orange County to try to clear his head. His father, Gideon, encouraged him to think about leaving the dual program altogether if it was making him miserable.

He did, and by the time he started his next semester at Penn in the fall of 2017, he had a new academic target in mind, this one focusing on the psychology of "happiness." Blaze's new pursuit seemed to reflect his new mindset as he tried to balance his schoolwork and his other passions—chiefly, writing and cooking. He detested the dining hall food on campus, and during his sophomore year, after run-ins with his roommates, he got his own apartment with a decent kitchen, where he cooked lavish feasts for his friends.

Blaze Bernstein

## "Saboteur"

He decided to stay on campus that Thanksgiving, and Liam Williams, one of his best friends from the Orange County School of the Arts, was coming to visit from college in Boston. He wanted to cook him a Thanksgiving feast, of course, but not the traditional fare. "Roast turkey sucks," he declared. So he made a pasta bolognese from ground turkey, with homemade garlic bread and other delicacies. He talked about his classes for the spring at Penn, and how he was excited to be moving to a new apartment. He had just been elected managing editor of *Penn Appétit*, the school's food magazine, for the spring semester. After the malaise of his freshman year, he seemed energized. He seemed happy.

He was also becoming more open about his sexuality after years spent with one foot in the door, one foot out. His mother, Jeanne, had long thought that Blaze was probably gay, and she and Gideon had tried talking with him about it starting in his middle school years after Gideon found romantic texts with another boy on his phone; Blaze had shut them down each time. Jeanne tried again as he was packing to leave for Penn as a freshman, letting him know that she loved him no matter his sexuality; it didn't matter if he was gay or not so long as he was happy, she told him. "You don't need to worry about me," he said. That was the end of the conversation.

At Penn, however, he had become more open about dating men on campus and going on websites like Tinder to look for potential meet-ups. It was on Tinder that Blaze, home in Orange County on summer break from Penn, saw the photo of Sam's face, aloof and unsmiling, staring back at him on his screen as he scrolled through dating matches for gay men. He recognized him immediately. Sam Woodward: the bigoted, homophobic school outcast.

Blaze was stunned. Back in high school in Orange County, he was skeptical when Gabe García told him about the online come-ons Sam had sent him. Blaze thought Gabe might be exaggerating, maybe even making it up. Sam was the last person the kids at school might have imagined as gay. But now he himself had matched up with Sam on Tinder, and he was seeing firsthand Sam's apparent interest in men.

Blaze had to tell someone. He took a screenshot of Sam's profile and sent it to another close friend from the arts school, Alex Tomlinson. "OMG WE ALL KNEW IT," Blaze wrote to her. Gabe "was telling the truth for once holy shit."

Blaze and Sam began messaging each other that same night. Blaze told Sam he thought he was cute, and Sam replied, "You're not too shabby looking yourself." The flirting went on from there. It all seemed like a game for Blaze, dangerous but thrilling, as he suddenly was reconnecting with a notorious name from the past. Sam, the Southern Californian with the chiseled chin and tortured history, was practically the archetype of the young Hollywood bad boy, and here he was seemingly interested in Blaze Bernstein. As the messages continued coming in, Blaze would forward screenshots of them to his friends Alex and Liam, still unsure what this new online exchange was all about.

Sam blurred his intentions to Blaze at first, and he made grandiose, bigoted claims about his sexual prowess. "I'm on this app mainly because of women, I've got jungle fever and fucked like 5 black chicks since I got here a month ago," he wrote to Blaze. "In terms of men," he wrote, "I'm looking for an outdoorsy person to be a spotter and assist me in deer hunting."

Sam asked Blaze if he was gay. "Very gay," Blaze answered. "My boyfriend literally dumped me today," he confided; he was smarting over the breakup. Sam expressed some sympathy, and his messages became more boldly flirtatious, just as they had with Gabe and other young gay men he'd targeted online. Sam, the avid outdoorsman, was reeling in his line.

Blaze had to admit that he liked the attention; hooking up with Sam would be "legendary," he wrote to Alex in one text message even as he was in the midst of an online session with Sam. Almost in real time, he kept her apprised of Sam's advances. "Oh shit, he's about to hit on me," Blaze wrote her in another text. "He had me promise not to tell anyone...but I have texted everyone. uh oh." The whole situation struck Alex as outlandish. "Hahahahahaha Fuck Sam Woodard [sic]," she answered. "I'm having to coax it out of him," Blaze told her. "I had to stroke his ego to get him to tell me he thinks I'm hot please hold," he wrote.

Sam offered to come over to his house that night. Blaze put him off; it would be too difficult with his whole family there, he said. Once Blaze made it clear that he wasn't going to meet up with him, Sam backpedaled, letting out his reel and doing an abrupt reversal. He wasn't really gay, he told Blaze. "I pretended to be gay because I was curious what gay people do when they're into each other," he wrote. "Which is why I asked you what you were into. I'm sorry for lying to you, man." Blaze was more confused than ever by the sudden turn. "Fair enough then," he wrote back. "So you really are looking for hunting partners."

Sam ended the conversation there. He quickly "unmatched" Blaze on Tinder and left him alone. For now.

---

Sam Woodward had other pursuits in mind. He had started thinking about joining up with a real neo-Nazi group that summer and taking his extremism to the next level. It was an online neo-Nazi friend named Tristan Evans from the fascist *Iron March* online forum who introduced Sam to a group he'd joined: the so-called Atomwaffen Division.

Evans was a construction worker from East Texas who was a few years older than Sam. He went by the online moniker of "Kruz," or sometimes "KKKruz" in tribute to his white supremacist sympathies. Sam hadn't met "Kruz" in person yet, and he didn't even know his real name until months into their online friendship, but the pair bonded over their love of Nazi-style fascism and white supremacy, exchanging hundreds of messages on Twitter about their shared cause that spring and summer.

They talked excitedly online about Aryan resistance, "lone wolf" violence, racial revolution, and "the Jewish question." They lashed out in tandem at people who were gay, transgender, Jewish, Black, or minorities of any type; "our entire society is polluted with decadence and lack of identity," Sam wrote to Tristan. And they bemoaned the lack of real commitment to "The Movement" at a white supremacist group they had each been involved in called American Vanguard. It wasn't militant enough for either one of them; they considered its members to be "alt-right" posers and pretenders. Sam had met up a few times with some white supremacists from Vanguard in Southern California, going up to Los Angeles to plaster neo-Nazi propaganda on buildings at UCLA and tear down LGBT posters. Petty hate-crime stuff. It wasn't enough for Sam. He wanted something more aggressive, more militant.

Evans told Sam that he'd moved on from Vanguard to Atomwaffen Division—"a hardcore group," he said, based on the violent, "revolutionary" mindset laid out in neo-Nazi ideologue James Mason's collection of essays, *Siege*. Sam said he wanted to join the neo-Nazi group, too. "I've been considering joining Atomwaffen if they'd let me," Sam wrote back excitedly.

Out of college and uncertain about the military, he told Evans that he was searching for something. "I'm just so lost in my life and don't know where to go," Sam wrote. He thought neo-Nazism—fighting for the Aryan race—offered him a way and would, somehow, fill the void. "I genuinely want to serve The Movement, you know" he said.

Evans encouraged him. *Come out to Texas and join up with the Atomwaffen clan,* Evans told Sam. Atomwaffen Division was planning a "hate camp" in the countryside that summer: guns, booze, and bigotry. He could get him a job in construction, too, Evans said. Sam loved it.

Sam was so engrossed by the idea that he told his parents about his plans, not via email or letter, as they had often communicated, but in person. He'd given them glimpses lately of his growing extremism, going into angry diatribes about Jews and all the bad things he claimed that they'd done throughout history, based on all the bigotry and misinformation he'd devoured online. For his father's birthday card, he drew Blake a self-portrait with the numbers "88" and "14" on his collar—neo-Nazi symbols for "Heil Hitler" and the white supremacist's sacred fourteen words. "Revolution is not a spectator sport; action must be taken," he had told his father, quoting a white supremacist mantra. Now, to prove his commitment, he said he wanted to go off to Texas to join up with a band of fellow "national socialists"—his preferred term for neo-Nazis.

His parents were alarmed. They were plenty conservative, and Blake himself had planted the seeds of Sam's hatred for gays, in particular, but their son joining up with a band of neo-Nazis was too much for them. All of Sam's radical talk lately and the specter of violence scared them. They didn't want him to go. They thought about putting a tracker on Sam's car without telling him, or maybe getting a UCLA fraternity brother of Blake's in Texas to check on him while he was there. They didn't do either one, though. Their son was nineteen years old, and they figured there wasn't much they could do to stop him. Blake told Sam he was worried that he would end up hurting someone, a minority of one type or another, in the name of his passion for Nazi ideology. Sam could wind up in prison, Blake told him prophetically; it wasn't worth it, they said.

Sam didn't say anything. He had made up his mind.

In Texas, Tristan Evans also wanted to make sure Sam knew what he was doing before he left Orange County to join up with Atomwaffen. He gave him an out. "This movement is for real men," Evans wrote. "I don't want to discourage you from joining," he said, but he cautioned that "it's not easy. We joke around, but we're serious."

Sam said he understood. His tone was reverent. "All aspects of my life have pointed towards the embrace of National Socialism," he wrote to Evans. "I've been struggling to find so many answers.... Atomwaffen/*Siege* has laid out a path for me. It would be against all instincts and intellect to not walk down it."

## CHAPTER 4

# "THE WHITE RACE IS BACK IN THE GAME"

America's white supremacists, isolated on the fringes of American politics for decades, had been giddy with glee in the early morning hours of November 9, 2016, when it became clear that Donald Trump had pulled off perhaps the biggest political upset in American history.

"This is one of the most exciting nights of my life," tweeted David Duke, the onetime Ku Klux Klan grand wizard in Louisiana, who had endorsed Trump's longshot presidential bid. "Make no mistake about it, our people have played a HUGE role in electing Trump!"

On the *Daily Stormer*, which described itself as the "pro-genocide web site" catering to "angry white men," Andrew Anglin declared that: "We won, brothers. All of our work. It has paid off. Our Glorious Leader has ascended to God Emperor.... The White race is back in the game."

Neo-Nazi leader Matthew Heimbach sent a foreboding note to a journalist just after 3:00 a.m. that morning, once Trump had garnered the final state needed to put him over the electoral threshold: "Wisconsin goes to Trump! Everything you love will burn! LOL."

## "The White Race Is Back in the Game"

And in Orange County, local KKK leader William Hagen, who had organized what turned into a violent "White Lives Matter" rally in Anaheim earlier in the year, celebrated Trump's election win at a Klan-sponsored "Victory Parade" for Trump across the country in North Carolina—and promptly got himself arrested in a stabbing.

Now that the white supremacists had "their man" in the White House, Trump's win would give them a momentum and legitimacy they had never had before, and it ushered in a period of surging hate crimes and racial violence across America, with the deadliest attacks being committed by avowed white supremacists. With his coarse racial rhetoric from the White House and barely disguised dog whistles— coded messages of support—to extremists, Trump poured kerosene on the fire—all but ensuring that the climate of violent bigotry would outlast his presidency.

---

The story of violent bigotry in America is older than the nation itself, dating back to the mass killings of Native Americans on their ancestral lands and the enslavement and lynching of generations of African Americans. It's a story of brutal attacks punctuated with powerful symbols: a hanging noose, a burning cross, a Nazi swastika, a vile slur, or a raging manifesto, all meant to send the message that *your kind is not wanted here*. And it's a story that continues today with unremitting regularity, surging to frightening new levels in the last decade.

The attacks are pernicious, taking aim not at a single victim, but at whole groups of the *others*: victims who do not look like the white majority, who do not come from the same places, who do not pray to the same God, who do not love the "right" people, who are somehow seen as less "American" than their attackers. The ripples of violent hatred and bigotry roll over an entire people. "Each offense victimizes not one victim but many," a Justice Department report said after a rash of attacks in the early 1990s. "A violent hate crime can act like a virus, quickly spreading feelings of terror and loathing across an entire community."

The attacks have ebbed and flowed throughout American history—brought to a fever pitch in times of economic woes or political upheaval, as violent passions are stirred; and sometimes eased, at least briefly, when politicians, police, and judges have pushed back in fits and starts. But through it all, that original virus has lived on, toxic and intractable, feeding off intolerance, fear, and misinformation to spread and multiply, breeding new hatred from the darkest original strands of the country's DNA, beginning with the first ill-fated attempt to scale it back.

What amounted to America's first law outlawing hate crimes came in 1871, six years after the Civil War. It lasted just twelve years. No one called them *hate crimes* then; that term, with all its emotional wallop, wouldn't take hold for more than a century, in the 1980s, amid a wave of laws by dozens of states to punish crimes against people based on their race, ethnicity, or religion. But the aim of that first Reconstruction-era measure, just one legal prong in the Ku Klux Klan Act passed after the war, was unambiguous, making it illegal to target newly freed Blacks with violence simply because of the color of their skin.

Just as the KKK was mounting its fiery crusade to restore white "pride" in the South, the federal government was taking a forceful stand against the plague of racial terrorism—lynchings, whippings, mass assaults, and church arsons—that had made life so treacherous for Blacks for much of American history, even after the Civil War and the adoption of the Thirteenth Amendment outlawing slavery. President Ulysses S. Grant personally marched down Pennsylvania Avenue to Capitol Hill, with practically everyone in his cabinet in tow, to push for the Klan Act's approval and implore members of Congress to combat the scourge of racial violence carried out by "bands of disguised marauders."

Grant pledged that, in the face of resistance by the former Confederate states, Washington had "the duty of putting forth all its energies for the protection of its citizens of every race and color." With Grant using the new law to declare martial law and sending in the military to protect Black people, the intervention from Washington worked to slow the violence, giving hope to freed slaves that they might survive another day. "Peace has come to many places as never before," Frederick Douglass, the famed Black abolitionist leader, wrote optimistically. "The scourging and slaughter of our people have so far ceased."

But the short-lived law met its end in 1883, consigned to the history books by a Supreme Court that was damningly successful in dismantling equal-rights protections for Blacks enacted in the wake of the Civil War. The pivotal court case toppling the law arose out of bloodshed: a white lynch mob seized four African American men from a jail in Tennessee and beat them senseless, killing one of them. The newly created Department of Justice in Washington brought charges against the mob members under the anti-Klan law—one of more than 3,400 prosecutions under its newly unleashed powers to protect minorities. But the Supreme Court threw out the verdict, and the enforcement law along with it, ruling it unconstitutional and giving white assailants an unfettered path once again to murder and racial mayhem.

It would be another eighty-five years before Congress enacted a new federal hate-crime law. And it would take more than another half century—as well as more than two hundred proposals that were rejected by old-guard defenders of the status quo—before Congress finally approved a law in 2022 making lynching illegal in order to expunge what Vice President Kamala Harris called "a stain on the history of our nation since our founding."

In the bloody interim, the threat of lynching and racial violence once again became the tragic backdrop of life for Blacks in the decades after the Supreme Court struck down the anti-Klan law, with many thousands of Blacks victimized—not only in the South but increasingly in Northern cities, where Blacks arriving in the "Great Migration" were met with violent resistance from whites who didn't want them there. Fabricated or flimsy accusations against the victims—often involving purported assaults against the "honor" of a white woman—became a favorite pretext for lynching. Claims of the most minor transgressions, or sometimes none at all, could lead to hanging. One Black man in Georgia was lynched in 1899 by a gang of white assailants for simply "talking too much" about the murder of another Black man burned at the stake.

Politicians and civic leaders, then as now, often led the bloodcurdling cries of racial violence. In North Carolina, it was Alfred Moore Waddell, a bearded ex–Confederate colonel and a washed-up former congressman striving for relevance, who urged bloodshed against Blacks in 1898 before a deadly Election Day rampage. Rather than "surrender to a ragged rabble of Negroes," he vowed, whites must rise up, even "if we have to choke the Cape Fear with carcasses" to do it. In Mississippi five years later, it was the governor himself, a silver-tongued racist named James K. Vardaman, who declared in 1903 that "If it is necessary, every Negro in the state will be lynched. It will be done to maintain white supremacy."

For Black people, the years after World War I were perhaps the most violent yet, with whole communities practically wiped out, from the "Black Wall Street" in Tulsa, Oklahoma, to Elaine, Arkansas, and Rosewood, Florida, in the scorched earth of white supremacy. Black Americans had the worst of it, no doubt, but the racial and ethnic violence wasn't limited to them. Immigrants, native-born Hispanics, Jews, gay people—the *others*—all fell prey to violent bigotry as well.

The single bloodiest lynching of the era, in fact, came not against Blacks, but against Italian immigrants in New Orleans, where a white mob stormed the jail and lynched eleven of them to shouts of "We want the Dagos!" after a jury had found them innocent in a local murder. The vigilante justice brought cheers far beyond Louisiana. "Lynch law was the only course open to the people of New Orleans," the *New York Times* declared in an editorial tirade against "those sneaking and cowardly Sicilians," a batch of unwanted immigrants who had "transported to this country the lawless passions... of their native country."

As America spread its borders westward in the second half of the 1800s and opened its shores to millions of immigrants, the scourge of racial violence spread with it. Immigrants new and old became fresh targets. Mexicans, Chinese, Japanese, Germans, Irish Catholics, European Jews, Italians, Poles, Slavs, and more all flocked to America and worked to help build the railroads, sew the garments, mine the coal, and plant the fields in the burgeoning new land of promise and opportunity. But inevitably, each group faced a violent backlash from many of the descendants of white European settlers—and from many white European immigrants, too—declaring themselves America's real "natives." To them, the foreign interlopers were an existential threat.

In the newly minted province of Orange County in Southern California, Chinese immigrants met with some of the worst treatment at the dawning of the twentieth century. A bustling Chinatown had sprouted up next to City Hall in the county seat of Santa Ana, made up mostly of redwood shanties, where hundreds of Chinese laborers and their families lived. But tensions with the white city leaders ran high. When a supposed case of leprosy was reported among the Chinese residents in 1906, it became a pretext for destruction.

"Purge that plague hole once and for all! Burn the damn place down and do it tonight," a councilman implored. Fire officials eagerly complied. As many as a thousand white residents gathered on a drizzly night to watch the torching, as residents fled with the few belongings they could carry. For many locals, the wanton destruction was an event to be celebrated—"as picturesque an event as could be imagined," like a July Fourth celebration, one newspaper exulted.

From a once-thriving community, only a lone Chinese resident remained. The Chinese had helped build Orange County's seat of government, but they weren't welcome there anymore. The destruction was largely forgotten to history, until the city formally denounced it a century later as "the racist and xenophobic actions of our predecessors." Up and down the western frontier, Chinese immigrants from Los Angeles's own Chinatown to Seattle and Wyoming all met with deadly rampages and destruction, too, but law enforcement officials rarely did anything. California's highest court, in fact, had ruled that a Chinese person, or any other "inferior" person "not of white blood," couldn't testify as an eyewitness against a white person, throwing out the murder conviction of a white man who shot a Chinese miner fifteen times near Sacramento.

Mexican laborers in Orange County didn't have it much better. In a region with a long, rich history of settlement by Spanish missionaries dating to the 1700s, thousands of seasonal orange-pickers who came up the coast from Mexico—the *naranjeros*—were the backbone of Orange County's hallmark, multimillion-dollar orange industry, which boasted some five thousand growers in the early 1900s, exporting countless crates of well-known labels nationwide. But labor strife and violent ethnic tensions between white farm owners and low-paid Mexican workers were rampant, and these tensions exploded into international headlines with the "Citrus War" of 1936 after unionizing workers threatened to strike.

The white growers, playing off ethnic fears, stirred anxieties about a "little Mexican Revolution" in their backyards, and the Orange County sheriff, an orange grower himself, deputized guards and gave them shotguns and ax handles to quell the Mexicans. "'SHOOT TO KILL,' SAYS SHERIFF," read the banner headline in the *Santa Ana Register*; the sheriff labeled the workers "radical agitators" and "Communists," as the weeks-long standoff roiled relations between Mexico and the United States. "All law has been suspended in Orange County in an effort to terrorize and starve strikers into submission," a union official wrote, as hundreds of Mexican laborers were jailed and racial hostility flared.

Minority enclaves around America—Hispanic immigrants, Asians, Italians, Blacks, Jews, and others—all bore the scars of the violent backlash from white America. Still, lawmakers in Washington shrugged, even as one episode of racial and ethnic violence blurred into the next. In 1946, the savage beating of a Black soldier named Isaac Woodard Jr.—permanently blinded by a South Carolina police chief as he returned home from fighting overseas in World War II, still in his military uniform—wasn't enough to get Congress to act against racial violence. "My God, I had no idea it was as terrible as that," President Truman explained after learning details of the beating. "We have got to do something!" But Congress didn't. With the help of a newly formed bloc of segregationist Southern Democrats calling themselves the

"Dixiecrats," it again blocked legislation to bring the power of the federal government to bear against racial violence.

The murder of fourteen-year-old Emmett Till nine years later, his bludgeoned Black face visible through a glass-topped casket, wouldn't be enough to prompt Congress to act, either. Nor would the 1963 killings of four Black schoolgirls in the 16th Street Baptist Church in Birmingham in a bombing by the Klan. Or the murder that same year of Medgar Evers, an NAACP leader in Mississippi shot in the back at his home by a sniper, or the hundreds of other high-profile attacks on Black people and other minorities, most never prosecuted, at the hands of Klansmen and extremists.

Not until 1968 did Congress approve the first official hate-crime law in American history, putting back in place much of what the Supreme Court had stripped away after the Civil War. The provision came as part of that year's landmark Civil Rights Act, expanding on the first stage enacted in 1964 under President Lyndon B. Johnson. In addition to the creation of new fair-housing protections, the measure made it illegal to use force, or the threat of it, against anyone because of "race, color, religion, or national origin" to interfere with constitutionally protected activities. Federal protection for gay people wasn't covered; that would have to wait another half century. But once again, the federal government had a powerful tool to combat the racial and ethnic violence so endemic to America.

The promise would prove elusive, though. On the eve of the final passage of the landmark civil rights law, the country was rocked on April 4, 1968, by its most crushing racial murder yet, when escaped convict James Earl Ray, a young white Southerner known for his hatred of Blacks, fired a high-powered rifle toward the second-floor balcony of the Lorraine Motel in Memphis, where a delegation of Black activists was staying to support a local sanitation workers' strike. Civil rights icon Martin Luther King Jr. was killed, and America's long history of racially fueled violence was brought, once again, into jarring relief.

Almost half a century later, Donald Trump's ascension to the White House in 2016 for his first term would help bring the grim American tradition of violent white supremacy to new prominence. The embers of racial hatred had already been smoldering for eight years before that during President Barack Obama's time in office. Obama's election as the first Black president in 2008—a milestone that Trump himself had tried to thwart with his false and racist "birtherism" claims—was a landmark event that many far-right extremists couldn't stomach.

The violent pushback began on the very night of Obama's election. A gang of four young white men went on a violent hate-crime spree in a mostly Black neighborhood of Staten Island, New York, "in retaliation for an African American man becoming president," prosecutors would later charge. Screaming "Obama!" and racial slurs, the attackers beat several of their victims with a metal pipe and ran over another one with a car, leaving him in a coma. That same night in western Massachusetts, three white men doused a predominately Black church with gasoline and burned it down—their way, prosecutors said, of demonstrating their anger over the election of America's first Black president. Two weeks earlier, a pair of white supremacist skinheads, armed with an assault rifle and a sawed-off shotgun, had been arrested in Tennessee in a plot to assassinate Obama and to shoot and behead dozens of Black schoolchildren at a local school. The skinheads planned to kill eighty-eight victims in all, prosecutors said—the glorified "88" number signifying "Heil Hitler" for white supremacists. They weren't ready for a Black president.

It was just the start. Indeed, Obama's presidency became a rallying cry used by white supremacists to stoke racial fury, with the number of hate groups tracked by the Southern Poverty Law Center surging above one thousand for the first time ever during Obama's third year in office. Fledgling neo-Nazi groups like Atomwaffen Division, more radicalized than their predecessors, were using his election to recruit eager new members online. And threats against Obama himself spiked three or four times above anything the Secret Service had seen before, with some extremists threatening to "lynch" the president and his family.

(Michelle Obama decided to keep her hair straightened, she said, because Americans were "not ready" to see a first lady with braided Black hair.)

The warning signs about America's racial powder keg were stacking up in intelligence circles, only to be ignored or rejected out of hand in many quarters in Washington. Daryl Johnson saw the troubling trend lines from his perch as the senior analyst in an obscure intelligence unit within the Department of Homeland Security (DHS) at the start of Obama's presidency in 2009, focusing not on foreign, Islamist-inspired extremists but on homegrown domestic extremists. The intelligence from Johnson's unit rarely got much attention from top DHS leaders, who were focused squarely on al Qaeda and Islamist terrorists at the sprawling new department created in the wake of the 2001 terror attacks. But what Johnson was seeing from newly sprouted groups like the Oath Keepers—an extremist anti-government group with a violent streak—unnerved him. The biggest threat, he realized, was coming from within.

Johnson, a soft-spoken Mormon who had been a registered Republican his entire adult life, worked with his small team for months on a confidential analysis at DHS warning of the "resurgence" of potentially violent "right-wing extremism" in the United States. His nine-page report cited a combustible mix of "drivers" fueling the surge: the election of the first Black president and the backlash from white supremacists; the economic recession in America; and the wave of "disgruntled military veterans" returning home from Iraq and Afghanistan, who represented prized recruits for extremist groups because of their combat experience, just as the FBI itself had also noted in recent reports. Johnson's analysis concluded soberly that "lone wolves" and small cells "embracing violent right-wing ideology are the most dangerous domestic terrorism threat in the United States."

Just as DHS began circulating Johnson's intelligence report confidentially to law enforcement officials nationwide in April of 2009, another round of threats and violence by white supremacists only seemed to validate Johnson's fears about the growing danger. A white supremacist—active duty in the Marine Corps—was charged in yet another plot to kill President Obama. And a week after that, Pittsburgh police officers answered a 911 call about a domestic disturbance between a mother and her twenty-two-year-old son, a white supremacist named Richard Poplawski. It wasn't a typical domestic call. Poplawski, recently discharged from the Marines after attacking a drill instructor, was upset about Obama's election and had turned virulently anti-government. As officers arrived at his mother's home, he strapped on a bulletproof vest under his Pittsburgh Penguins hockey jersey, grabbed his assault rifle and a cache of other weapons, and began firing hundreds of rounds at them; three officers were killed and a fourth was wounded in a standoff lasting more than three hours. Poplawski, shot in the leg, ultimately surrendered and was convicted and sentenced to death for one of the deadliest attacks on police officers in decades.

Three days after DHS began circulating Johnson's confidential report on the growing threat of such far-right extremists, the analysis leaked out to a conservative radio host, and soon it was being discussed on Alex Jones's far-right *InfoWars* conspiracy site, Rush Limbaugh's radio show, Fox News, Pat Robertson's televangelism TV show, and beyond. Johnson had just gotten home from helping at a Boy Scout fundraiser one night when he first learned that the report had leaked out publicly; before long, it seemed as if practically every conservative talking head in America was discussing his report—and not in a good way. Conservatives seized on the findings as evidence that the Obama administration was out to smear everyday political opponents as "right-wing extremists"—"this is an effort to criminalize political dissent," Limbaugh declared—and to besmirch all veterans as security threats. That wasn't what the report actually said, but amid the backlash, irate Republicans in Congress were demanding its withdrawal, along with the resignation of DHS secretary Janet Napolitano.

After a brief scramble to contain the political firestorm, DHS retreated. Napolitano withdrew the report and apologized to veterans for what she said was a flawed report. Johnson's team was quickly split up and "reorganized," with Johnson and other analysts who had been working on far-right extremism moved off to unrelated assignments in what felt to him like a bureaucratic Siberia.

Johnson had sent up a warning flare, and it had blown up in his face. Washington politicians, particularly Republicans, didn't want to hear about right-wing extremism or growing numbers of military veterans turning to white supremacy. The government's highest priority remained the threat of Islamist-based terrorism inspired from afar, not the rising threat from within that the United States was facing from right-wing extremists.

---

The country didn't have to wait long after Trump's election in 2016 to witness the escalation in violent bigotry that many law enforcement officials feared. In just the first ten days after the election, there were nearly nine hundred reports of violent hate crimes and episodes of "hate speech" in the United States, with many of the attackers citing Trump by name as inspiration.

In Sarasota, Florida, a seventy-five-year-old gay man was injured after an attacker pulled him from his car and threw him on the street, yelling: "You know my new president says we can kill all you faggots now." In New York City, vandals wrote "Trump!" across the door of a Muslim prayer room. Schools, in particular, were becoming a breeding ground for bigotry. The day after the election, students in one school in Washington State were shouting, "Build a wall!" in the cafeteria at lunch, a teacher reported. In her own classroom, she heard students telling classmates that "if you aren't born here, pack your bags." In Colorado, a boy approached a twelve-year-old Black girl in school and told her, "Now that Trump is president, I'm going to shoot you and all the Blacks I can find," the girl's mother reported. In Southern California, a Muslim professor reported walking into class and finding a note on his desk that read: "This is not your country, this is Trump's country." A gay couple in North Carolina received a note that said: "Gay families = burn in hell. #Trump2016." And an Oklahoma University student was suspended for sending violent and racist messages—along with photos of hangings and a "daily lynching calendar"—to some 150 Black students at the University of Pennsylvania, Trump's alma mater. "Trump Is Love," he wrote mockingly.

Their inspiration, Donald Trump himself, had been trumpeting his racist tropes for decades, long before he decided to run for president that first time. "Laziness is a trait in blacks. It really is," he reportedly told a senior casino executive working for him. In the early 1970s, the Justice Department brought a massive housing discrimination lawsuit against Trump and the family company he led, charging that they systematically discouraged Black renters at their apartment buildings. In 1989, after five Black and Hispanic teenagers were accused of brutally beating and raping a white woman in the "Central Park Five" case, Trump took out full-page ads to "bring back the death penalty"; all five suspects were later exonerated, but Trump expressed no regrets over his racially fueled attacks against the young men. Trump even had a copy of Hitler's collected speeches, *My New Order*, which a lawyer for his then wife, Ivana Trump, said he kept in a bedside cabinet and would pull out to read occasionally.

Obama, in his eight years in the White House, was the target of some of Trump's most blistering racial attacks, as the then-reality TV star seized on the false and racist "birther" claims that Barack Obama was actually born in Africa and wasn't the legitimate president. Trump pushed the birther lie relentlessly for years and fueled a racist backlash from his ardent followers; he called Obama's birth certificate a "fraud" and claimed to have evidence that he never actually produced, before finally grudgingly acknowledging Obama's citizenship only at the end of his own presidential campaign in 2016, years after he had begun pushing the lie.

Once he became a presidential candidate in 2015, Trump lobbed one racially explosive grenade after another, beginning on the very day when he began his long-shot bid. Announcing his candidacy after riding down a gold-tinted escalator at Trump Tower in Manhattan, he railed against Mexican immigrants as "rapists" and criminals, and he never let up. During the campaign, he promised to "build the wall" with Mexico and attacked the loyalties of an American-born judge of

## "The White Race Is Back in the Game"

Mexican ancestry, saying the judge couldn't impartially hear a massive fraud case against Trump University because of his "Mexican heritage." He called for a complete ban on Muslim travel to America, belittled the Muslim family of an American army officer slain in the war in Iraq, and repeated his oft-debunked claims that he had witnessed "thousands" of Arab Americans "cheering" on a rooftop in New Jersey as the World Trade Center fell on September 11, 2001.

And he repeatedly encouraged violence against protesters, often minorities, at his raucous rallies in Orange County and elsewhere, even promising to pay the legal fees for anyone who would "knock the crap out of" people who disrupted them; "maybe he *shoulda* been roughed up," Trump told Fox News after one Black protester was beaten, kicked, and choked at a rally in Alabama. Indeed, researchers in Texas found that the rate of hate crimes more than tripled in the counties where Trump held some 275 campaign rallies in 2016, with racial and antisemitic attacks rampant.

Trump threw out such a barrage of racially incendiary rhetoric during the campaign that he came under attack even from fellow Republicans, who defied Ronald Reagan's so-called Eleventh Commandment about not speaking ill of other GOPers. "He's a race-baiting, xenophobic, religious bigot," South Carolina senator Lindsey Graham, who would become one of Trump's most loyal supporters in the White House, said of him in 2015 when they were both vying for the Republican presidential nomination. Likewise, Republican rivals Ted Cruz and Marco Rubio—both of them Southern senators and future allies of his—blasted Trump during the campaign for his refusal to denounce David Duke and the KKK's violent racism after the former grand dragon endorsed his presidential bid, telling white supremacists on his radio show that voting for anyone but Trump was "really treason to your heritage." J. D. Vance, the best-selling conservative author who went on to become Trump's vice president in 2025, even suggested to a law school classmate during Trump's first campaign that he might prove to be "America's Hitler."

Trump's rhetoric, so often divisive and race-baiting, set the tone for his angriest followers. But Trump himself claimed ignorance about the acts of violence that were being enacted in his name. In his first television interview as president-elect in 2016, less than a week after the election, Leslie Stahl at CBS's *60 Minutes* asked Trump about all the reports of supporters harassing and attacking minorities since his win. Trump claimed to know nothing about it. "I am very surprised to hear that," he said, shaking his head, his eyes narrowing. "I *hate* to hear that. I mean, I *hate* to hear that."

Stahl was incredulous. "But you *do* hear it. You're not seeing this?" she asked.

"I don't hear it. I saw one or two instances, but I think it's a very small amount," the president-elect insisted.

Stahl continued to press him. "They're harassing Latinos, Muslims—"

"I am so saddened to hear that," Trump told her, "and I say, 'Stop it.' If it helps, I will say this, and I will say right to the cameras: 'Stop it.'"

But his followers didn't stop, and neither did Trump.

Less than two weeks after the election, hundreds of adherents of the newly minted "alt-right" movement—overwhelmingly young white men—gathered in Washington for the annual conference of the white-supremacist National Policy Institute just a few blocks from the White House and celebrated their rising influence in a city that was about to be recast by Trump. Richard Spencer—the fresh-scrubbed young face of the alt-right movement, nattily dressed in a three-piece suit—bemoaned threats to "the continued existence of White America" and led a chant of "Hail Trump! Hail our people! Hail victory!" Young men in the crowd answered with Nazi salutes.

As video emerged from the event showing the Nazi-themed imagery and rhetoric from his supporters, Trump met with a roomful of reporters and editors from the *New York Times*. Trump was asked whether he thought his campaign rhetoric had "energized" people like the alt-right leaders at the Washington convention, who were angry about the changing racial lines in America. Again, Trump denied any connection to the young men chanting Nazi slogans in his name. "I'm not looking to energize them," Trump said. "I don't want to energize the group, and I disavow them."

## "The White Race Is Back in the Game"

Yet as president, Trump seemed to embrace comparisons to the Third Reich—to the shock of his own aides at the White House. In an argument with John Kelly, the retired general who served as his longest-tenured chief of staff, Trump expressed admiration for the obedience of Hitler's Nazi generals in World War II—a trait he saw as lacking in his own military leaders once he became president. "You fucking generals," Trump said, "why can't you be more like the German generals?" When Kelly pushed back, Trump said that Hitler's generals "were totally loyal to him." Even more eye-popping was a comment that Kelly said Trump made on multiple occasions: "You know, Hitler did some good things, too." (Trump denied making the statements.)

Many of his supporters in Washington hoped that Trump would tone down the race-baiting rhetoric he employed as a candidate and adopt a more "presidential" tone once he was in the White House, maybe even shut down his Twitter account altogether. It didn't happen; the incendiary attacks only escalated throughout his first term. He went after a wide swath of perceived "enemies," but his most frequent and impassioned targets, publicly and privately, were often women and members of ethnic minority groups, employing racist, sexist, and xenophobic tropes to degrade them all. There were attacks on immigrants from "shithole countries" in Africa and Latin America, and on Haitians, who "all have AIDS." Attacks on four liberal congresswomen of color—three born in the United States—whom he said should "go back" to the "crime-infested places from which they came." Attacks on Jews who might vote for Democrats as being "very disloyal to Israel." Attacks on "stupid" Black critics and celebrities, like basketball star LeBron James and newscaster Don Lemon, whom he called "the dumbest man on television." Attacks on women as dogs, horses, "lowlife," "crazy," or "low IQ." Attacks on Senator Elizabeth Warren as "Pocahontas" over her claims of Native American ancestry—uttered while standing at the White House next to a group of Navajo code talkers. There was no group Trump wouldn't attack with often dehumanizing broadsides.

When a supporter at a Florida retirement complex screamed "White power!" at protesters in one video posted on Twitter, the president quickly shared it with his millions of online followers, before taking it down under a torrent of criticism over his seeming endorsement of the racist rhetoric.

All the while, he minimized or dismissed altogether the evidence of growing numbers of violent white supremacists around the world. The threat was confined to "a small group of people," he said after a white supremacist's savage, live-streamed massacre of fifty-one Muslims at two mosques in Christchurch, New Zealand, one of the worst in a series of bloody attacks by white supremacists globally and a morbid inspiration to other violent bigots.

While Trump always denied any suggestion that his ugly, racist rhetoric was fueling violence, dozens of his supporters made that connection explicit in unprovoked hate crimes that invoked his name and mimicked his language, just as they had done in the weeks after his election. "This is for Trump!" a young white man in northern Florida announced as he punched and beat an unsuspecting Hispanic worker who was cleaning a parking lot.

"Why did you come here and invade my country?" a Trump supporter in Milwaukee demanded of a Peruvian American outside a restaurant, as he threw acid on the man that left second-degree burns on his face.

After a white supremacist stabbed a Black man and his Cuban-Asian girlfriend on a busy street in Olympia, Washington, for no apparent reason, he told police he "planned on heading down to the next Donald Trump rally and stomping out more of the Black Lives Matter group."

"Get out of my country!" a white man yelled as he shot dead an Indian engineer and wounded a second one at a bar near Kansas City after demanding to know their immigration status.

"President Trump will cleanse America... of all Arab American terrorists," a retired US Foreign Service officer named Patrick Syring wrote in one of hundreds of messages, including a number of explicit death threats, that he sent to a prominent Arab American think tank.

The attackers believed that they now had a man in the White House speaking their language, understanding their rage, sharing their grievances. The links between Trump's angry persona and the surge in hate crimes became so common, in fact, that years before Capitol rioters in the January 6, 2021, siege began invoking the tactic, some defense attorneys began citing Trump's fiery rhetoric as a way to explain their clients' violent actions and to appeal for leniency, usually unsuccessfully. Christopher Hasson, a white supremacist in the Coast Guard, was arrested in Maryland in 2019 in a purported terrorist plot to "establish a white homeland"; his defense attorney compared a "hit list" that Hasson had compiled, filled with liberals and "leftists," to something Trump himself might have written one morning after watching Fox News. "It is hard to differentiate it from the random musings of someone like Donald Trump, who uses similar epithets in his everyday language and tweets," the lawyer told the judge.

Defense attorneys also raised the specter of Trump in another thwarted terror plot in rural Kansas, where three white militia members were accused of plotting to kill Somali Muslim refugees by bombing an apartment complex where many of them lived. "Trump's brand of rough-and-tumble verbal pummeling" had pushed people like their client to the edge, wrote the lawyers for one of the militiamen, an avid Trump supporter, asserting that someone like the defendant, "who would often be at a 7 during a normal day, might 'go to 11.'"

On the world stage, Trump led the rhetorical warfare against ostracized minority groups — the "rough-and-tumble verbal pummeling" — but he had his allies. He came to power alongside a wave of other far-right, populist leaders, including Britain's Boris Johnson, Hungary's Viktor Orbán, the Philippines' Rodrigo Duterte, India's Narendra Modi, and Brazil's Jair Bolsonaro, and with them came a crescendo in the coarse language — and policies — of bigotry targeting minority groups in each of their countries. When the UK's Johnson, a beloved ally to Trump, before becoming prime minister wrote a newspaper column that compared Muslim women with face veils to "bank robbers" and "letter boxes," the violent response on the streets of Britain was immediate: attacks on Muslims increased nearly fourfold the very next week, with twenty-two Muslim women wearing face veils targeted, according to one analysis. Many of the attackers cited Johnson and his rhetoric as justification—just as they did in America amid Trump's rhetorical thunder. In Hungary, Orbán stoked comparisons to Nazi ideology himself in 2022 when he warned against allowing Europeans to become "peoples of mixed race." (Trump welcomed Orbán to his resort barely a week later.)

Trump used the White House bully pulpit, and his Twitter account, as a cudgel against minority groups, against the *others*, in a way that America had never seen before. "No president has ever gone there," bemoaned Michael Yaki, a member of the US Commission on Civil Rights during Trump's administration, who watched the corrosive rhetoric with growing dismay during Trump's time in office. Even in the tensest of times, Trump's recent predecessors had usually used the White House's powerful platform as a calming influence against violent bigotry—for political optics, if nothing else. President George W. Bush, for one, appeared personally at the Islamic Center in Washington just six days after the September 11 attacks in 2001. "America counts millions of Muslims amongst our citizens," he said, "and Muslims make an incredibly valuable contribution to our country.... And they need to be treated with respect." The surge in anti-Muslim hate crimes soon slowed, and Bush earned plaudits for his appeal.

Trump took a much more polarizing tack, fueling hatred and bigotry one moment, then officially disavowing it the next. The nadir came in August of 2017, seven months into his presidency, with the infamous "Unite the Right" rally in Charlottesville, Virginia, when hundreds of white supremacists, Klansmen, and neo-Nazis converged on the city armed with burning torches in a nighttime scene eerily reminiscent of fiery Klan marches a half century earlier.

Richard Spencer, ten months after his infamous "Hail Trump!" convention in Washington, led the throng. Historically, neo-Nazis were a notoriously fractured bunch, with rival groups fighting against each other almost as often as against minorities. Factions would split over whether they revered the Nazis and Hitler himself, or just white supremacy; whether they favored shaved heads and Doc Martens boots, or a cleaner image; whether they indulged in drugs and booze, or not; or whether they built their extremist views around "Christian Identity," or some other religious inspiration.

But Spencer and other organizers, through months of underground networking on far-right media platforms, managed to do something at Charlottesville that his predecessors had never achieved: bringing together several dozen neo-Nazi and white supremacist groups from all over America in a common agenda of hatred. "Jews will not replace us!" the mass of torchlit marchers chanted during their first night in Charlottesville—and, in a refrain straight from Nazi Germany, "Blood and Soil!"

The neo-Nazis from across the country—from New York to Orange County—had talked of waging violence at the rally for weeks ahead of time, according to internal chat logs that would later become public in a major lawsuit. They made good on the talk in Charlottesville, beating up scores of non-whites and counter-protesters, often after provoking confrontations as a pretext for violence. In a street crowded with counter-protesters, James Fields, a young white supremacist, plowed his car into the throng of people, killing Heather Heyer, a thirty-two-year-old paralegal from Charlottesville, and injuring more than thirty others. Fields was there with American Vanguard, the group Sam Woodward and Tristan Evans had abandoned as too passive. Fields ultimately pleaded guilty to hate-crime charges and got a life sentence.

Spencer celebrated the spectacle the next day in a vile rant against Jews and Blacks at a secret meeting with his neo-Nazi supporters. "Little fucking kikes. They get ruled by people like me. Little fucking octoroons" (a slur for people of mixed Black lineage), Spencer said in an audiotape leaked out of the meeting. His vulgarities put the lie to the clean-cut, intellectual image he had tried to hone in public. "My ancestors fucking enslaved those little pieces of fucking shit. I rule the fucking world. Those pieces of fucking shit get ruled by people like me."

The violence in Charlottesville, a throwback to something out of the 1960s in the Jim Crow South, generated shock and condemnation from much of America. But inside the White House, Trump saw it differently, equivocating over the mayhem and putting the neo-Nazis on the same moral plain as the counter-protesters. "You also had people that were very fine people—on both sides," Trump told reporters at Trump Tower just a day after Heyer's killing. He went on to blame the media, always a favorite target, for treating the white-power groups "absolutely unfairly."

A reporter asked Trump the next day if he still believed there were "very fine people on both sides" at the rally. He did. He continued to insist, all evidence to the contrary, that the neo-Nazis with their torches, chanting "Jews will not replace us," were there that day simply to protest the removal of a statue of a "great general"—Robert E. Lee, the commander of the Confederate Army—and Trump wasn't backing down now. "That question," Trump said, summoning one of his favorite phrases, "was answered perfectly."

Trump's remarks were a gift to white supremacists. "Thank you President Trump," David Duke wrote on Twitter afterward, "for your honesty & courage to tell the truth about #Charlottesville & condemn the leftist terrorists in BLM/Antifa." The sight of the president praising "the very fine people" on both sides at the neo-Nazi march would prove an enduring flashpoint of Trump's presidency, one that he would attempt to defend for years. And it gave powerful new ammunition for violent bigotry, with reports of hate incidents targeting Jews spiking by 182 percent to more than four a day in the weeks after Charlottesville.

Trump's moral equivalency upset even some of his most stalwart senior aides. The White House architect of his tax overhaul, Gary Cohn, a Jew who had stood at Trump's side at the press conference as he talked of the "very fine people" on both sides, was so disgusted that he drafted a letter of resignation, though he never delivered it. Nikki Haley, Trump's ambassador to the United Nations and later his rival for the Republican presidential nomination in 2024, called Trump at the White House to tell him that she, too, was disturbed by his

## "The White Race Is Back in the Game"

sympathetic tone toward the neo-Nazis. Haley, an Indian American, had been governor of South Carolina two years earlier when white supremacist Dylann Roof killed nine Black churchgoers in her state in Charleston, and she wanted to let Trump know that his incendiary remarks had the potential to cause real damage in a country already rupturing from racial divisions.

"You need to realize your words matter," she told him. "You have to understand that people can take that and hurt people with it."

Trump wasn't buying it. "Nikki, Nikki, this isn't Charleston," he said.

"I'm not saying this is Charleston," she answered. "I'm saying that I know that certain people hear your words and will react to that, and you have to be careful with that."

But "careful" was out of character for Trump. He wasn't about to start watching his words now.

## CHAPTER 5

# "THEY WANT TO BUILD A FOURTH REICH"

Everything about Atomwaffen Division, from its name to its ethos, spoke to its desire for violence. *Atomwaffen* meant "atomic bomb" in German, and in the ever-more-crowded field of hate groups in America, numbering more than a thousand at their height, Atomwaffen's band of perhaps a hundred or so young men was spreading across America, from California to Florida and beyond, and was building a brand for itself as one of the most violent white-power blocs.

Unlike some of their fellow white supremacists, Atomwaffen didn't pretend to be anything other than what it was: a movement for violent, Nazi-loving revolutionaries like Sam Woodward. Its followers wore their brutality like a badge of honor among their white supremacist peers, with online posts declaring their vision of an Aryan country rid of minorities who were tearing down its heritage. The original Nazis were their beacon, and their enemies were the Blacks, Jews, gays, immigrants, liberal "commies," and anyone else who smeared that vision.

Atomwaffen Division grew out of an underground neo-Nazi forum called *Iron March*, which went online in encrypted chat channels in 2011, drawing angry young white men from all over America to its web of online fanaticism. *Iron March*'s slogan laid plain its intentions: "Gas the Kikes! Race War Now! 1488! Boots on the ground!" It had some sixteen hundred users, perhaps more, and over its six years of life, they posted more than 150,000 messages—many of them as dark and brutal as their slogan.

In 2015, a nineteen-year-old *Iron March*er in central Florida named Brandon Russell wanted to take their ideas operational, so he founded an offshoot group and named it Atomwaffen Division. The name combined two of his passions—Nazism and nuclear physics, which he was studying at the University of South Florida—and he thought that combining the atomic bomb imagery in German would sound "fucking edgy" to other angsty teens in the white-power scene. With a few dozen or so followers in tow, he made himself the leader. Florida was in the midst of feverish political and cultural battles that would ultimately generate huge support for Trump's nativist brand of politics, and Russell made it the de facto headquarters for his nascent white-power bloc.

Outwardly, Russell was a quiet kid, reserved and a bit awkward socially. To his acquaintances in college, he seemed like the stereotypical science nerd buried in his studies, a kid out of TV's *Big Bang Theory*. But to his underground followers—who knew him mainly by his online pseudonym of "Odin," referencing a mythological god of war and death associated with Nazism—he revealed a dark, alpha-male obsession with fascism, Nazism, and white supremacy, and a hatred for anyone who rejected his creed.

There was no clear fuse that lit his hatred, nothing in his past that might readily explain it. Yet something drew him to the Nazis. Russell, who grew up in the Bahamas before moving to Florida as a teenager, chafed at the "blatant lies" he remembered being taught in school about the Nazis and World War II. All he ever heard in school about the Nazis, he complained, was "evil, evil, evil; murder, murder, murder… Why is there only just one side of this story?" he asked. "Why aren't I learning what they actually did?"

He came to admire the Nazis' supposed achievements, like what he liked to call "the great economic miracle of 1933" in Germany, a myth of Hitler's own making. He started rummaging online on far-right sites, where a trove of fabricated and distorted material from Holocaust deniers awaited him. The more myths he found, the deeper he sank. He knew that his mother and his father, who was a deputy sheriff in West Palm Beach, didn't like his newfound ideology, but Russell professed that he was who he was—a budding neo-Nazi, or as he preferred to call himself, in keeping with the original Nazi party name, a "National Socialist."

Russell described the fledgling Atomwaffen Division to would-be recruits as a "very fanatical, ideological band of comrades who do both activism and militant training," with "the goal of ultimate uncompromising victory." This would be real-world stuff, he promised; anyone simply interested in "keyboard activism," he said, "need not apply." He made clear that he only wanted members for his fledgling group who were "committed to their beliefs," as one recruit said. Russell had a three-pronged tattoo on his shoulder with the warning symbol for radiation, which became one of the group's emblems. It warned of danger ahead.

Russell had a keen interest in all things military, and he liked firing guns of all types—paintball guns, airsoft guns, BB guns, and the real ones, too, including a Romanian-style AK-47 assault rifle that he owned. So he enlisted in the Florida National Guard in early 2016 for a six-year commitment in an infantry division. The National Guard screeners who vetted new personnel noticed his "radiation" tattoo, but no one thought it was suspicious at the time. Nor did they discover that just months earlier, he had founded Atomwaffen Division and had started personally screening the dozens of young neo-Nazi wannabes who tried to enlist through encrypted chat channels.

The military had been a magnet for white supremacists for decades, especially in the South, and Russell had little fear of getting caught; he felt free to be a neo-Nazi, he said on *Iron March*, even as he was reporting for duty at the Guard. "Are you worried at all about being found by your mates or someone, now being in the U.S. military?" one *Iron March* user asked him; wouldn't he be "fucked" if they found out? Russell wasn't worried. "I was 100% open about everything with the friends I made at training," he responded. "They know about it all."

Russell's National Guard supervisors noticed his vitriol. It was hard to miss. He "vocalized his hatred for homosexuality and 'faggots,'" a National Guard review later found, and his supervisors pulled him aside repeatedly to warn him that the hateful rhetoric was "unacceptable." Still, they let Russell remain in the Guard, just as the military had done with Wade Michael Page and many other avowed white supremacists before them, and Russell managed to use his status in the Guard as a recruiting tool, trying to lure other young military members to the neo-Nazis. His training with the American military, prosecutors later wrote, helped him "in fulfilling his neo-Nazi mission."

Atomwaffen Division's ranks grew, but it stayed in the shadows—until the heat of the 2016 presidential campaign, when a twenty-one-year-old member in San Antonio named Steve Billingsley, in camouflage pants and a skull mask, gave a "Heil Hitler" salute at a public vigil and declared his allegiance to a group that few people had ever heard of before. That vigil was a prayer service at a San Antonio park for the forty-nine victims—most of them gay—killed days earlier in Orlando at the Pulse nightclub in what was then the worst mass shooting in American history. The massacre, at a well-known gay venue, looked at the outset like a clear-cut hate crime targeting gay people, but the FBI didn't end up classifying it that way; officials regarded it instead as an act of foreign-inspired terrorism, concluding that the mass murderer, Omar Mateen, the American-born son of Afghan immigrants, was driven by Islamist extremism and his fealty to the Islamic State, not a hatred of gays, and that he may not have even known that the Pulse catered to gays. The conclusion infuriated many gay advocates, who saw what seemed like an obvious hate crime against their own kind ignored once again.

Whatever the true motive, Brandon Russell in Tampa cheered the Pulse massacre and made his disgust for the gay victims known privately to fellow Atomwaffen members in an encrypted conversation; "faggots in body bags," he called them. In San Antonio, Atomwaffen member Steve Billingsley wanted to make his own hatred known more publicly. At the vigil for the Orlando victims there, he displayed a sign that read "God Hates Fags" to stunned onlookers. One attendee grabbed the sign and ripped it up, as Billingsley gave a Nazi salute. In a chilling statement declaring his intentions to a local reporter, Billingsley said: "I am a member of the Atomwaffen Division, a new and rising US-based National-Socialist movement... This was my first action taken on behalf of the Division and our first public action—you can expect to hear more of us in the future." The statement ended just as threateningly: "We must preserve the purity of our race, oppose the intrusion of foreign religions, and do away with homosexuality for good. Heil Hitler!"

---

The violence began months later, in the spring of 2017 at a high-end condo in Tampa that Russell was sharing with three other young men, all of them neo-Nazis like himself. It was an upscale, Mediterranean-style gated complex called the Hamptons; Russell had to get his grandmother to cosign the lease when he rented it barely a month earlier. Inside their second-floor apartment in building 37, Russell's home was a shrine to Nazis and violent extremism: A flag with an SS insignia hanging from the wall. A Nazi helmet on the shelf, along with copies of Hitler's *Mein Kampf* and *The Turner Diaries*, the opus dedicated to race war and white supremacy. A framed photo of Timothy McVeigh, the infamous Oklahoma City bomber, sat on Russell's dresser.

Russell's three roommates in the second-floor apartment were all Atomwaffen members as well, young men who had met online and were joined by their admiration for the Nazis. Russell had persuaded two of them, eighteen-year-old Andrew Oneschuk and his friend, twenty-two-year-old Jeremy Himmelman, to move down to Tampa temporarily from the Boston area, where together they had started up Atomwaffen Division's fledgling Massachusetts "chapter." Oneschuk didn't like the liberal direction he saw his generation heading. Like Russell, he had descended deep into a rabbit hole of dark Internet conspiracies and fantasies, telling his shocked parents and his older sister, Emily, that the Holocaust never really happened, that man never landed on the moon, and that the schoolchildren at Sandy Hook Elementary School had never been massacred by a deranged gunman, among the many long-debunked claims trumpeted by far-right propagandists like *InfoWars* podcaster Alex Jones and others.

"Are you serious? Do you really believe that?" his mother would ask him. Yes, he did. "We're on the path to ruin," he told his father, and for Andrew, this new neo-Nazi outfit called Atomwaffen Division was, somehow, the answer. Emily came home from college during break to find a Nazi swastika flag hanging from Andrew's door and a Nazi SS banner tacked above his futon. She started screaming at him and tried to muscle past him to tear down the Nazi artifacts. "How can you believe in this?" she yelled. "Do you know what this stands for? This is evil! When people think of evil, *this* is what people think of!"

Her brother just stared back at her stoically as Emily finally burst into tears. "Emily, you really shouldn't cry. That's why people don't respect women when they get so emotional." There was no reasoning with him. Andrew stood his ground, telling his sister that she needed to respect his beliefs. She stared back at him as if he were a stranger, a sociopath.

Oneschuk was becoming ever bolder in his newfound love for the Third Reich, even making an appearance from Boston as a guest on a far-right Ukrainian radio show with the Azov Brigade, a fascist, militant white supremacist group in Ukraine. At the young age of fifteen, Oneschuk was playing the part on the show of an enthusiastic political commentator abroad, offering his support for then-candidate Trump for his fascist audience. Trump is "the most far-right politician we've had in a long time," Oneschuk said, and "many people have come out and supported him." He acknowledged that he did have some hesitations—Trump's daughter, Ivanka, was married to "a Zionist," a definite taboo, and Trump himself did business with many of them, he said. Oneschuk opined on how the "Zionist propaganda scheme" was corrupting America through gay marriage. And he talked on white supremacist sites about the imperative for violence, identifying himself in one posting as "Breivik V.2" in honor of Anders Breivik, the Norwegian neo-Nazi who had slaughtered seventy-seven people, most of them teenagers, in his native country in 2011. The Massachusetts teen identified with the mass murderer.

Oneschuk got himself thrown out of a private boarding school after the school learned of his racially inflammatory views online. Walking off campus for the last time after his expulsion, Oneschuk gave a "Heil Hitler" salute. He stood by his radical beliefs.

The teenager made plans to go to Ukraine himself and join up with the Azov Brigade. He even secretly bought a one-way plane ticket to Kyiv and secured a passport, emptying his bank account, before scuttling the plan. Instead, he threw himself into homegrown fascism, finding Atomwaffen Division online as easily as if he were searching for a new pair of sneakers. He offered to start a Massachusetts "chapter" for the neo-Nazi group with his friend Jeremy Himmelman, and after establishing his bona fides through an online screening—proving his commitment to racism, homophobia, and antisemitism, among other essentials—he and Himmelman were both in. They took on their new leadership roles with abandon, papering racist, neo-Nazi fliers around Boston, and Brandon Russell and his best friend, Devon Arthurs, who also was his top "deputy" at Atomwaffen Division, drove all the way up the coast from Tampa to Massachusetts to meet their two new branch leaders face to face.

Within months, Oneschuk and Himmelman were heading down together from Massachusetts to Tampa to stay with Russell at his condo. Oneschuk did have some hesitation about where Atomwaffen might lead him, telling Himmelman that he was worried about "all the shit we can get dragged into." But lured by the promise of free rent at a posh condo with a pool, a temporary job he had lined up at a recycling plant, and plenty of time for fishing along with neo-Nazism, he went down anyway.

In Tampa, Russell and his roommates talked national socialism and went out paintballing and target-shooting together. Tensions were soon brewing among the neo-Nazis, however. Devon Arthurs, who grew up in a suburb of Orlando, had recently undergone an abrupt and odd conversion to Islam—and to violent Islamist extremism. Jobless, he would watch violent jihadi videos at the apartment and try to convince the others to join him in his newfound conversion. He wanted to remain a neo-Nazi, too.

It was a strange, combustible mix of political extremes—Nazism and jihadism—and his roommates teased Arthurs about his new, helter-skelter brand of radicalism. Over the years, there had been a few cases of collaboration between neo-Nazis and Islamist jihadists, but not many. Whether Arthurs could be a Muslim jihadist and a white-Aryan, neo-Nazi simultaneously was a matter of some dispute among his colleagues, and Russell would mock Arthurs ("ball-busting," he called it) about his newfound religion.

Their differences about Islam and jihad aside, Russell and Arthurs were still joined by their shared enmity for the United States: they would tear down an American flag that their roommate, Oneschuk, had put up on his wall—a gift from his father, a retired US Navy pilot, who brought it home from an overseas deployment—and then stomp on it and use it as a doormat. The disrespect riled Oneschuk. He became so frustrated by all the drama in the condo that he called his father in Massachusetts and told him he wanted to end his Florida neo-Nazi jaunt after just a few weeks and return home. "I'm ready to get out of here," he said.

Days later, on a hot, overcast Friday afternoon in May, Devon Arthurs walked into the Green Planet Smoke Shop in an airy suburban strip mall a few blocks down Amberley Drive from their apartment. A woman was restocking items behind the counter, with a couple of customers milling about the shop. Arthurs announced that his name was "Khalid," and he pulled a Glock semiautomatic pistol out of his waistband and waved it at them. "Do me a favor and get the fuck on the ground!" he yelled. "Why shouldn't I kill you?" he demanded of one customer. Another customer walked in during the tumult, and Arthurs ordered him to the ground, too.

For the next few minutes, as his hostages cowered on the floor just a few feet away from him, Arthurs went on a wild rant—about the corrupt state of the world, about American bombings of Muslims in the Middle East, about how he had just shot someone in the head. Arthurs said he was Muslim. The woman behind the register, hoping to calm him, told Arthurs that she was Muslim, too, but that only seemed to make him more agitated. He angrily swiped some of the glass pipes off the shelf, shattering them on the floor, and demanded that one of his hostages get him a bottle of Coke from a cooler.

There was a splattering of blood on his clothing. He pointed his gun up at the closed-circuit camera on the wall and boasted that he was going to get all kinds of publicity for what he was doing. He'd be on the news; he'd be famous.

Minutes later, two police officers were at the door of the shop, their weapons drawn. "Put the gun down!" yelled Officer Katie Thanasas. "I'm not going to shoot anyone," Arthurs answered, his gun still at his side. "I was never going to shoot anyone. I just want to tell my story." Thanasas was still screaming at him to drop his gun; she didn't want to have to shoot him, she said. Arthurs bent his head toward his gun ever so slightly, and she thought for a moment he might try to kill himself. Finally, he placed his gun on the glass counter and raised his hands above his head. There was no struggle, no resistance, no fiery exit or gunfire from the police. His one request, he said politely enough, was that he'd like to finish his Coke before the police handcuffed him.

In custody, Arthurs began repeating all his wild claims and more—about American bombings, about shooting people, about neo-Nazism, and about feeling disrespected for his new Islamic faith. He lived in an apartment full of neo-Nazi white supremacists, he said; he had been one himself, at least until his conversion to Islam, he told the officer. "Allah Mohammed," he said, using an Islamic expression of faith, "I had to do it. This wouldn't have to happen if your country didn't bomb my country." An officer asked if anyone was hurt. "The people in the apartment," Arthurs said. "But they aren't hurt; they're dead."

The police summoned medics to Arthurs's condo as soon as they heard that. They would need to tend to the victims. "Oh no. They are definitely dead," Arthurs said. With Arthurs in the back of the squad car, the officers rushed to the neo-Nazis' home at unit #3723 in the Hamptons complex. Just as they pulled up, they heard screaming from inside the apartment, and a young man in full National Guard camouflage uniform came running out of the apartment, screaming uncontrollably. "They are upstairs!" he screamed. He dropped to his knees, still sobbing.

It was Brandon Russell; he had just gotten home to the condo after spending the weekend on Guard duty. Earlier in the day, he had found time during a break to post on *Iron March* a 443-page tactical handbook on "Muslim combat methods" as a guide for how neo-Nazis might wage war. For all his "ball-busting" about Arthurs's religious conversion, he seemed to think there was something the neo-Nazis could learn from violent jihad. Now, however, he seemed stricken by the scene he found back at his home.

Police handcuffed Russell on the spot, unsure what they would find inside. "That's my roommate," Arthurs told the police matter-of-factly. "He doesn't know what's going on and just found out, like you guys did."

Inside, what the officers found was a scene of carnage. The odor of burnt gunpowder still lingered in the air the moment they opened the door. Slumped on a futon in a back bedroom was the motionless body of a young man, bloody from gunshots to his head and chest. It was Jeffrey Himmelman. Nearby was a second young man in similar shape, lying face up on the floor and wedged next to an air mattress. It was Andrew Oneschuk. As Arthurs had promised, both young men were dead—killed, as forensic examiners would determine, from multiple gunshots fired at close range from an assault rifle. Shell casings were strewn on the floor, and blood and human tissue had splattered the walls. Almost as alarming was the decor around them: the Nazi memorabilia everywhere in the apartment, the photo of Timothy McVeigh on a dresser, symbols of hatred everywhere, along with a semiautomatic rifle under a blanket, and other guns and ammunition scattered about the apartment. In a closet, police noticed two Geiger counters and what looked like bomb-making material.

Searching Russell's garage, police found another jarring surprise: a massive cache of explosives and bomb-making materials, including detonation devices, components for pipe bombs, ammonium nitrate and other bomb-making chemicals, radioactive material, and a cooler filled with a white, cake-like explosive material called HMTD. Brandon Russell's name was scrawled in magic marker on the cooler. Nearby were stencils used for spray-painting swastikas and hate-filled slogans such as "God hates fags," the same message that Steve Billingsley had delivered in San Antonio at the vigil for the shooting victims in Orlando.

Arthurs, locked in the back of a squad car in the steady rain as investigators searched the condo, squirmed in his handcuffs and tried to make everyday conversation with the officers in the front seat. He was only eighteen, but his boyish, freckled face and his schoolboy green polo shirt made him look even younger. He chanted Muslim prayers occasionally—*"Allahu akbar"* ("God is greater")—and mused aloud about his time as a neo-Nazi, his conversion to Islam, his family, and the wrong path he thought the world had taken.

The officers didn't say much in response except to offer him some water and see if his cuffs were too tight, but he kept talking anyway in a jumbled stream of consciousness. He endorsed the killings of the forty-nine victims in Orlando. "Those people were sodomites in the massacre.... Leviticus says that sodomites should be killed," he said, his voice flat and unemotional. The Orlando shooter "was still treated as if, like, he had done a terrible thing, or something like that, when he clearly hadn't. He was killing people who make up a highly disproportionate amount of crime, when it comes to pedophilia, when it comes to, like, AIDS, and stuff like that.... They're clearly being corrosive elements."

He ruminated about what he'd done inside the condo in killing his two roommates. "Shit, I shoulda, like, just hijacked some truck" and then run people over with it, Arthurs said. He was struck by all the police cars at the condo complex, and keenly interested in what media coverage he might attract. "Is this on the news anywhere?" he asked. And he thought about his own death, almost wishing it on himself. "I don't suppose you could shoot me in the back of the head?" he asked. The officer declined.

It was after 1:00 a.m., more than six hours after Arthurs had staged the kidnapping at the smoke shop, when he sat down at the Tampa police station for his first interview with two detectives. After the explosives had been found at the scene and with the specter of a terrorism plot foiled, an FBI agent had come to the station and was listening in from another room. The lead Tampa detective, Kenny Nightlinger, read him his *Miranda* rights, but Arthurs kept talking. He didn't want a lawyer, he said. He would admit to everything.

Nightlinger, a former college baseball player in his early forties with glasses and closely cropped blond hair, had become a homicide investigator because he liked putting the puzzle pieces together, but there didn't seem to be much to put together in this case: Arthurs was willing to tell just about anyone who would listen—his hostages in the smoke shop, the cops in the squad car, the investigators at the police station—that he had killed people. He had called his father right after the killings, hinting at something he'd just done. "I screwed up really bad," Arthurs told his father.

Sitting across from the Tampa detectives in the interrogation room, Arthurs seemed anxious to unburden himself. "I'll tell you exactly what happened today," he said at the outset. He started off by telling the investigators all about Atomwaffen Division. It was a group that few law enforcement officials—not even in Washington, much less Orlando—had ever heard of.

"Atomwaffen Division is a terrorist organization," said Arthurs, using the German pronunciation: Atom-*vaffen*. The detectives weren't familiar with it. He spelled the name for them. "It's a neo-Nazi organization that I was a part of before I converted," he said flatly. He had started getting into the neo-Nazi movement when he was just fourteen, Arthurs explained. There were sixty or seventy people in Atomwaffen in all, he said, scattered around the country but linked by encrypted communications on sites like *Iron March*. Brandon Russell was their leader.

Russell venerated Timothy McVeigh, keeping that photo displayed on the dresser as an homage to the Oklahoma City bombing. "He *loved* McVeigh," Arthurs said. "He said that the only thing McVeigh did wrong was that he didn't put more materials inside the truck to bring the whole building down."

All the chemicals and the explosive materials the police had found in the garage—those belonged to Brandon Russell, Arthurs said, and it wasn't part of any college science project or anything. "None of that. It's all literally there specifically to kill people," he said. "The things that they're planning were horrible. They're planning bombings and stuff like that on countless people, they're planning to kill civilian life." Russell had taken him and the other two roommates to the Ocala National Forest to train them in paramilitary operations, he said, and they had specific targets in mind for bombings. "Power lines, nuclear reactors, synagogues, things like that."

"I prevented the deaths of a lot of people," Arthurs said in his rambling monologue. Asked why his roommates would plan such an attack, he responded: "Because they want to build a Fourth Reich." He said it as if it should be obvious. He said his own allegiance now was mainly with ISIS and the Muslims, with his rage redirected to what was happening in the Middle East—what "we" hoped to do there against the American oppressors. Still, he admitted that, his newfound religion notwithstanding, he kept living with his Atomwaffen peers, kept working with them, kept hanging out with them. He took part in hacking operations to help white nationalists in Ukraine with the Azov Brigade, the same fascist group that had attracted Andrew Oneschuk. In hindsight, Arthurs said, the whole neo-Nazi thing was "kind of stupid."

He answered all their questions in a cordial, even friendly voice, as if he were interviewing for a job as a server at Applebee's. After nearly an hour, Arthurs ended the interview on an ominous note. He said he was terrified by what the neo-Nazis might do—not just to him, but to other people, too—if they found out about everything that had happened. "I'm not trying to be an ass or anything," he told the investigators. "Your lives would be in danger, too."

Not long after Arthurs's interview wrapped up, Brandon Russell was in a police interrogation room himself, sitting in handcuffs across from Detective Nightlinger and an FBI agent. He was still in his military uniform. It was about 3:30 a.m., some nine hours since Russell had come home from weekend National Guard duty to the murder scene, and now the detective and the FBI agent were asking him all sorts of questions—about the two young men shot to death in his condo, and about all the Nazi flags and memorabilia on the walls, and about all the explosives in the garage. And what exactly was *Atomwaffen* anyway?

Nightlinger uncuffed Russell after a few minutes. The detective had heard Devon Arthurs's whole confession, and he told Russell he considered him a witness, not a suspect in the murders. "My understanding," he said, is that "you may not have even been there when all this happened." But he said they did have some concerns about whatever was going on in the condo—like that framed photo of Timothy McVeigh on Russell's bedside dresser. "Devon had said that you had admired that guy," Nightlinger said. "Can you explain about that a little bit?"

"He was just someone who, um, I don't know...," Russell said. His voice trailed off, meek and mumbling. He sounded nothing like his firebrand online persona.

"Some people would look at him as a domestic terrorist," Nightlinger said.

The FBI agent interjected. "Yeah, we're kind of concerned, Brandon," he said. Combined with all the explosives and other memorabilia they'd found in the condo, it created a worrisome picture. "What were you doing with that stuff? What were you planning to do?" the agent asked.

"I'm not planning to do anything," Russell mumbled. "I was

planning to go back to school and get my business degree," maybe combining it with physics. He talked of wanting to become a sergeant in the army eventually, after his stint in the National Guard was over.

Atomwaffen Division was really just "a club," he said, a way for like-minded guys around the country to "talk about National Socialism." As for the cache of chemicals and explosives in the garage, Russell said that was all for his model rocketry hobby. "Collector's stuff," he said. He bought most of it online on eBay and Amazon—nothing illegal, he insisted. And he said he had made the HMTD explosives material—a particularly volatile mixture—as booster fuel for his rockets, though he hadn't actually used it for a while.

The investigators remained skeptical; no one had found any rocketry equipment at the condo. But strangely, they let him leave anyway. They even arranged to get him a lift back to his condo, the scene of the murders, so he could pick up his car.

Russell was gone from Tampa within hours after police took him home. He headed south along the coast in his blue Dodge Nitro SUV, and he picked up a friend of his, William Tschantre, another Atomwaffen member with a shaved head who had also been planning to move into the condo with Russell and the other young men.

Russell told him what had happened the night before at his condo. The twenty-year-old Tschantre quickly grabbed three thousand dollars in cash, and the two of them headed out for an impromptu road trip. On the way out of town, Tschantre called in to quit his job at a fast-food restaurant; he wasn't sure if he'd be returning home.

Together, Russell and Tschantre kept driving south another three hundred miles toward the Florida Keys. Along the way, they stopped at a sporting goods shop where they picked up two rifles—one of them an assault-style weapon—along with more than five hundred rounds of ammunition and four high-capacity magazines, which Russell promptly loaded.

Back in Tampa, FBI officials soon realized, belatedly, that they had a problem. Within hours of Russell's release, an ATF bomb expert confirmed that the HMTD found in the cooler was a potential "destructive device" that was illegal for Russell to store. FBI officials determined, only now, that they had enough evidence to bring criminal charges against the neo-Nazi leader. The problem was that they didn't know where he'd gone. They put out a "BOLO" alert to other law enforcement agencies—"Be On the Look Out"—with Russell's name, photo, and vehicle information. "RUSSELL should be considered armed and dangerous," it read.

They quickly caught a break from a sharp-eyed sheriff's deputy some three hundred miles away. The next morning, a police digital license-plate reader in Key Largo picked up Russell's vehicle on a busy highway, and Monroe County sheriff's deputies trailed him as he pulled off the highway, parked at a Burger King, and went inside. When Russell and Tschantre emerged from the front door a few minutes later, Deputy Deanna Torres was waiting with handcuffs and ordered him to put his hands behind his back. Russell, now in street clothes but with his military dog tags still around his neck, looked stunned to see the police. He began shaking and sweating.

"What's wrong?" he asked Torres.

"You know what's wrong," she answered, as she cuffed his hands.

Locked in the back seat of a sheriff's squad car, Russell kept twisting and squirming, and the deputies had to put him in leg and arm restraints to keep him still. Torres tried to calm him down. "My life's over," he kept telling her.

"What are we going to find in that car?" another deputy asked Russell.

"Guns, ammunition," Russell answered.

Inside the SUV, police found the two newly bought rifles, still in their boxes, along with the high-capacity magazines, ammo, and military gear—all sitting in the vehicle of a man wanted by the FBI for his involvement in possible violent extremism. Tschantre told deputies that they bought the guns and ammo in case they decided to go hunting. Except it wasn't hunting season anywhere in the area in southern Florida. "When we found all the weapons," Deputy Torres said, "we were convinced that we had just stopped a mass shooting."

Russell was soon on his way back to Tampa and, ultimately, on to federal prison on illegal explosives charges that would net him a five-year sentence.

For Atomwaffen Division's followers, the national headlines from Florida on the killings and Russell's arrest were a moment of reckoning. Two of the group's neo-Nazi members were dead, a third member had confessed to killing them, and the group's leader was in jail on explosives charges.

The whole situation was "a complete tragedy," one neo-Nazi leader wrote in a long posting to his "comrades" on an *Iron March* forum the day after Russell's arrest in Key Largo. The two dead neo-Nazis were "heroes who stood for their brothers," he wrote, and Arthurs — once one of them — was "an unhinged, duplicitous scumbag." He urged the members to stay strong and press on with their campaign of terror and neo-Nazism. "The harder the storm rages against us, the clearer [we] will all see our banner," he wrote. "SIEG HEIL!"

## CHAPTER 6

# "HATE CAMP"

Beneath a scorching summer sun in the rugged, rolling terrain of South Texas, Sam Woodward finally made it to the ranks of neo-Nazi soldiers in his long march to extremism. He had long fantasized about the life of a militant fascist—in his violent online persona, in his video war games, in his school outbursts. Now he was living it.

For three days that summer of 2017, Sam and nine other members of Atomwaffen Division, dressed in military uniforms and skull masks, camped out on a remote hillside about an hour's drive south of Austin for what they called their "hate camp." They fired bursts of gunfire into the woods from assault-style rifles. They drilled in hand-to-hand combat and survival skills to prepare for coming racial violence. They engaged in Atomwaffen's *de rigueur* trashing of the "subhuman" gays, Jews, Blacks, and other minorities, and they talked of the need for violent "wolf" resistance by young white men and violent revolution. They drank and smoked a lot. And they shot garish photos, weapons in hand, to be used as neo-Nazi propaganda to terrify the public.

There was Sam posing for a photo by the scrub brush with a skull

Sam Woodward gives a "Heil Hitler" salute in a propaganda photo for Atomwaffen, the neo-Nazi group he joined.

mask over his face, thrusting his right arm in a "Heil Hitler" salute as he crouched alongside Tristan Evans, the Atomwaffen member who had gotten him involved with the hardcore hate group. Gone were the days of Sam doodling swastikas and Nazi troopers in his school notebook, or plastering a propaganda poster on a wall. Now he considered himself a soldier, fighting with his comrades for white power. The "brotherhood" of Atomwaffen Division appealed to him, he said later. In his neo-Nazi comrades he also found new role models, filling the space that his father had once occupied. "I admired these men," he said.

The leader of the crew at the hate camp that weekend, and the de facto chief of as many as a hundred other Atomwaffen members nationwide, was John Cameron Denton, a skinny twenty-three-year-old from a tiny one-stoplight town an hour north of Houston. After the Atomwaffen killings in Florida just a few months earlier, the group's power base had moved west to Texas. Brandon Russell, the group's founder, was now in jail in Tampa on charges of stockpiling illegal explosives. And Devon Arthurs, once his right-hand man, was in jail facing charges in the killings of their two Atomwaffen roommates. Denton was eager to fill the void.

Denton brought an even more violent face to the group—"a darker, more satanic type of vision" than before, as one member put it. While Brandon Russell could present a firm, respectful handshake and a docile front to outsiders, Denton, with long, stringy brown hair that fell below his shoulders and a cold, steely scowl, didn't try to disguise his rage. "I'm a misanthrope with zero sense of humor," wrote Denton, a mortuary worker by day. The only time he felt really connected, he said, was when he was "going to black metal concerts, getting drunk, and finding a hot piece of ass." The Nazis' connections to the occult held a strange fascination for him. The online monikers that Denton used to message with other neo-Nazis—"RAPE," "DEATH," and "TORMENTOR"—spoke to his violent bravado. "We must maintain a public image of strength and uncompromising ruthlessness in dealing with the enemies of our race," he wrote.

Denton, like Brandon Russell before him, indoctrinated members through an adherence to their own perverse bible, a blueprint for white supremacy and race war called *Siege*, written decades earlier by longtime neo-Nazi leader James Mason. Russell had made the 552-page tome required online reading for his Atomwaffen followers, and Denton carried on the tradition by using the book as a guidepost for fledgling white supremacists. He called his own web channel for neo-Nazis "SiegeCulture" in honor of Mason's book.

Atomwaffen Division now had followers in more than twenty states, and it was growing. Just as they had under Russell, Atomwaffen members fixated on explosives as a tool in their nascent terror campaign, posting instructions on bomb-making for members to peruse. They honed their use of anonymized and encrypted communications on dark websites like *Tor* to give them cover for possible hacking attacks on their enemies and on infrastructure targets like power plants and electrical grids. Most chilling of all, they began organizing paramilitary training sessions—the hate camps—at remote, rural spots around

Illinois, Nevada, and Texas where young men in skull masks and camouflage uniforms might not attract much attention as they fired assault files at wooden targets.

"Bring your uniform, rifle/sidearm, and whatever camping gear you need," wrote an Atomwaffen member organizing one such hate camp planned in the Nevada desert near Death Valley. It was a site chosen partly for its dark symbolism because, decades earlier, Charles Manson, one of the group's perverse inspirations, had hoped to forge a post-apocalyptic settlement at this same spot after fueling a race war between whites and Blacks with the infamous "Helter Skelter" murders in Los Angeles in 1969.

The Texas hate camp took place that summer just weeks before white supremacists from around the country were preparing to descend on Charlottesville, Virginia, for the violent and very public "Unite the Right" protests. Denton and his men weren't interested. They saw themselves as "off the grid" subversives, operating in the shadows, and they didn't want the attention. So they held their own covert gathering dedicated to white resistance. Sam Woodward was the newest recruit that weekend, and an eager one.

He'd arrived in Texas just a few weeks earlier. He had driven halfway across the country to meet Tristan Evans for the first time in person after all their months of online exchanges about national socialism and white resistance. They were practically inseparable from that point on. Evans had brought Sam to Texas with talk of neo-Nazi rebellion and construction work. The neo-Nazi activity was plentiful, but the work was not. He had little money. His parents, unhappy about his decision to go to Texas, had "cut me off" financially before he left Orange County, he told Evans, and he'd been reduced to "begging" people he knew for cash just to make the trip. Jobless in Texas, Sam had to sleep in the back of Evans's truck for weeks on end, and he and Evans would scrounge for meals at a church food pantry.

But they still had Atomwaffen Division. Sam's initiation into the neo-Nazi group came soon after his arrival in Texas at a meeting that Evans organized at a state park outside Austin with a more senior

## "Hate Camp"

member named Brenan Duffy, who was in his mid-thirties. Duffy was an active-duty service member in the US military, another in the long line of white supremacist soldiers, and he ran the neo-Nazi group's computer security for its encrypted online conversations. He was vetting Sam for a spot. The Florida killings had made the group nervous about interlopers and undercover informants, and Duffy wanted to verify Sam's extremist pedigree before the group would let him in.

The trio talked as they hiked through the park—"just three Nazis getting together to go hiking," Duffy said—and he quizzed Sam on the tenets of neo-Nazism, starting with James Mason's *Siege*. Sam had obviously read it. He quoted from it at length and, in his wordy, circular manner of talking, spoke of its racist, violent teachings as a matter of faith. Duffy was also impressed when Sam went beyond *Siege* and spoke of works by far-right extremists like Julius Evola, a twentieth-century Italian philosopher with Nazi ties. Sam struck Duffy as "pretty sharp, intelligent," he said. In a group where few other members had gone to college at all, Sam liked being considered a real thinker. He'd devoured all the racist, fascist writings he could find, and showing off his knowledge and intellect to the others was a point of pride. "I do have an IQ of 121, if that means anything," he'd told Evans.

The three young men took some propaganda photos in the park and told racist jokes and "horrible" stories about minorities—standard fare for a meeting like this, Duffy said—and soon the interview was over. Duffy liked what he saw in the new Orange County recruit. Sam was now formally a member of Atomwaffen Division. Duffy added his name in yellow to the group's internal database, marking him as a junior member in the neo-Nazi hierarchy.

Sam earned a nickname, too: "Sab," short for "Saboteur," his violent online nickname. He and Evans went to regular meetups that summer with other Atomwaffen members, usually at shooting ranges or bars around College Station, Texas. The clan of young neo-Nazis, six or eight at a time, would drink and smoke, then find minorities to harass—anyone who was gay, Black, or Hispanic was considered "less than human," Duffy said—and sometimes start fistfights. Or they would vandalize buildings by plastering them with Atomwaffen propaganda meant to terrify their targets. Once, they made a video of the group burning a Koran to put out on the Web. The common theme that united them, Duffy said, "was hatred of different kinds of people."

Sam began collecting enormous amounts of racist, threatening Atomwaffen material on his phone and reposting it publicly on extremist sites and even some mainstream ones. "Atomwaffen Division, No kikes, no fags, no tolerance," read one of thousands. But Duffy noticed that "Sab," even as a brand-new member, seemed anxious for more aggressive and violent tactics. Atomwaffen Division's call to action was to further the white race by creating racial "chaos," but Sam signaled that he wasn't sure that they were "serious" enough about their commitment. He wanted more.

The hate camp and his summer in Texas burnished Sam's credentials as a member. He was already making plans to go to another Atomwaffen hate camp scheduled near Las Vegas. But he made another trip that summer that would mark a further rite of passage in his descent into extremism. He and Evans went to Denver in search of the *eminence grise* of the modern-day neo-Nazi movement. Sam wanted to meet James Mason himself.

---

James Nolan Mason, then in his mid-sixties, was the guru and mentor to a new generation of neo-Nazis, an elder statesman who had been preaching hate, violence, and white supremacy for more than a half-century. He talked of "lone wolf" resistance and longed for "spectacular" attacks. After fading into obscurity in the neo-Nazi movement decades earlier, Mason had undergone an unlikely revival online as a man of mythic influence to angry, young white supremacists, his rebirth a twisted sign of the times in twenty-first-century America.

He idolized Hitler—"the greatest man that ever lived," Mason said with his typical bombast—and considered himself a full-fledged Nazi, a descendant of the vanquished Third Reich. The whole notion of so-called neo-Nazis was "bullshit," Mason said, as if you could separate the "new" Nazis in America from the originals. "I'm not a *neo*-Nazi," he said. "I'm a *Nazi*."

The FBI has had James Mason in its sights for years. It has wiretapped his communications with neo-Nazis, used undercover operatives to gather evidence on him, and named him as an unindicted adviser in criminal filings against neo-Nazi followers. But the FBI has never arrested him—stymied, apparently, in its efforts to prove that he has crossed the legal line from preaching violence to actually directing it. He dares them to keep trying. "The closer they watch me, the better I like it, because they know positively that I am clean as a whistle," he said. "I hope they record all my calls." In the meantime, his toxic influence has only expanded.

Born in a small city in southern Ohio in post–World War II America, Mason became a proud card-carrying American Nazi at the age of just fourteen in the 1960s. His mother and father had each served in the American military in the war, fighting against the Nazis, yet Mason came to embrace their enemy—the Third Reich. Maybe it was his father's unbridled racism at home that first sent him down that path. His father, a guard at a Veterans Administration hospital, would spit out the word *n\*\*\*\*r* at home like chewing tobacco into a spittoon; when the racist venom rushed out of him, which was often, James's mother, a nurse, would whisper nervously to the boy not to use that word himself—"they're just as good as you and I," she told him—but James didn't believe her. He eagerly followed his father's lead; Blacks were a people to be loathed, he learned at his father's knee. Like Sam Woodward decades later, however, he put his father's preachings into practice in ways that his old man might never have envisioned—absorbing the hatred, using it to mold his entire identity.

Mason was an angry kid, by his own admission—angry and isolated. Skimming a paperback about extremist groups that he'd found, he learned of the 1960s-era American Nazi Party, the postwar brainchild of another World War II veteran, George Lincoln Rockwell, who proudly coined the term *white power* and wanted Blacks and Jews either deported or killed. Mason dashed off an excited letter to the Nazi headquarters in Arlington, Virginia, just outside Washington, volunteering to enlist in the Nazi Party's fledgling youth brigade. Something about their violent, fascist rhetoric appealed to him. Even his father, racist as he was, became worried at all the neo-Nazi literature arriving for James in manila envelopes; when his father started intercepting his mail and confiscating the Nazi propaganda, the teen went down to the local post office to rent a box for himself and keep the mail coming.

Growing up in the 1960s, Mason liked the far-right politics of Barry Goldwater and avowed segregationist George Wallace, but he thought even those conservative icons were too ingrained in the political establishment for his extremist tastes. He wanted to shake things up, to disrupt the system. Millions of fellow teens in his era did too, but they were agitating on the streets for civil rights for minorities and an end to the war in Vietnam. Mason wanted nothing to do with the long-haired hippies or their liberal causes. His aims were just the opposite. All the change and tumult in America enraged him. He was agitating for a return to the way things had always been, at least to his mind — a white, Christian America.

In high school, Mason's anger spilled over into constant fights and disciplinary problems. The boy thought about swiping a .44 magnum revolver from his father's well-stocked arsenal to settle his scores with the principal and the other administrators at school. He set out to be the very first school shooter long before such tragedies had become rampant, he bragged later. Mason made a call to his new mentors at the American Nazi headquarters and floated his plot to William Pierce, a prominent leader of the group. He expected an eager endorsement, but Pierce persuaded him to abandon the idea; he was of more use as a soldier than a martyr, Pierce said. Instead, Mason dropped out of high school in Ohio and took a bus four hundred miles away to suburban Washington to work full-time for George Rockwell and the American Nazi Party.

Not long after the teen's arrival in northern Virginia, Rockwell was

## "Hate Camp"

assassinated by one of his neo-Nazi protégés, who, after being expelled from the party a few months earlier over his purported "Bolshevik leanings," shot Rockwell to death in his car outside a laundromat. Mason's mother, worried that James was going to get himself killed too, tried to get him to move back home to Ohio, but he stayed on. "I guess I'll take my chances," he told her. The teenager slept on the floor at the large house that served as the group's headquarters—locals called it "Hatemongers Hill"—and took over operations of the Nazis' printing press, earning fifteen dollars a week. His career as an American Nazi had begun.

With Mason surrounded by his fascist idols, his views on the world metastasized into shards of bitter hatred that would come to fill his entire life—hatred against Jews, against Blacks, against gays, against communists, against white "race traitors," against anyone who threatened the existing white-power structure. The "colereds" should move back to their own country, he bristled. "Breeding" between races was repugnant to him—"the ultimate sin," he called it.

He denied that the Holocaust had occurred, even as he called for the genocide of the surviving Jews. "It was indeed a damnable shame that Hitler did not, in fact, kill at least six million Jews during the War," he wrote. "A healthy state will expel—or kill—the Jew." Mason longed for a violent revolution that would return America to his distorted vision of a pure, Aryan society. "Good ole' Amerikan apple pie, but with teeth!" he wrote. "No one can stop it," he predicted—"no one."

Mason quoted Hitler and *Mein Kampf* fondly, and his racist ideology would sometimes turn to actual hate crimes. At a Dairy Queen on a trip back home to Ohio when he was in his early twenties, he and a neo-Nazi friend attacked a group of Blacks in the parking lot, spraying them with mace for no other reason than their race; the victims, including a fourteen-year-old girl, were a "slothful group" of "down-home Negroes," he sneered afterward with disdain. The attack landed him in jail for six months for racial assault. He came out of jail more hardened than ever.

Ohio authorities came after him again years later over another of his dark proclivities—his interest in underage girls. They raided his house twice and found hundreds of explicit photos of a fifteen-year-old girl he had met; he ended up pleading guilty to child porn charges. "Underage girls are sheer dynamite," he said. He deemed it his right—ordained in the Bible, in fact—to take underage girls as his own. His relationship with another underage girl in Colorado led to another stint in jail there after he found her with a Hispanic teenager and threatened the pair with his pistol; Mason accused the girl, who was white, of being a "race traitor" for dating a Hispanic boy, thus committing the ultimate sin, in his eyes, of race-mixing.

Writing fascist Nazi propaganda became Mason's stock in trade, first for the American Nazi Party and then for offshoot neo-Nazi groups that he joined and helped lead. Beginning in 1980, he wrote a dystopian newsletter he called *Siege*, envisioning an "Amerika"—he always spelled it in Klan style with a *k*—in which whites would rise up in violent revolution and start a race war to regain control of the country. He would type out his screeds on his typewriter and send out photocopies in the mail to his followers every month. As much as he hated minorities of every variety, he considered his biggest foe to be the American government itself—"the most evil thing that's ever existed"—for allowing the country to become so bastardized in the first place. In 1993, six years' worth of Mason's vile rantings in his *Siege* newsletters were compiled into a book of the same name, a playbook for fomenting a violent racial revolution. Along with *The Turner Diaries* by his old Nazi Party mentor William Pierce—an inspiration to Oklahoma City bomber Timothy McVeigh—*Siege* became a must-read for neo-Nazis across the country.

In the early 1980s, Mason also became an acolyte and friend of another notorious white supremacist, Charles Manson. He considered Manson "a prophet" who was "ahead of his time" for having used violence to sow racial strife as ringleader of the 1969 "Helter Skelter" murders. The swastika that Manson had carved into his own forehead in prison, repulsive to most everyone else, enthralled Mason. He wrote to Manson in prison, and the two men, bonding over their shared roots in southern Ohio and their racist linchpins, became devoted pen pals, joining together to form a new neo-Nazi organization.

But his alliance with Manson made him something of a pariah among some of his fascist comrades. The act of aligning himself with the generation's most famous mass murderer was a bridge too far, even for many neo-Nazis. The rift forced him out of one of the offshoot groups that he had led — the National Socialist Liberation Front. Mason moved off to a small town in rural Colorado in the early 1990s, largely forgotten by the neo-Nazi movement that he had helped build.

Indeed, James Nolan Mason might well have remained a vestige of another age had a young neo-Nazi in Georgia not read his book and decided to publish a new edition of *Siege* in 2003, hoping it would serve as a "clarion call" for followers to emulate the deadly path of Timothy McVeigh. The online exposure of his racist writings gave Mason a global audience he never had before.

A postmillennial generation of extremists — in America and overseas, from Britain to Finland and Estonia — embraced his words of racism and revolution with a newfound rapture. To his new wave of racist followers, Mason's voluminous writings on the racial inferiority of nonwhites, the perversion of gays, the evil of Jews and the mythical "ZOG" (the "Zionist Occupation Government"), and the need for violent insurrection to upend the system were all grist for the extremists. His violent racism knew no limits.

By 2016, Mason's followers in Atomwaffen Division had created their own radical sect named after his book — "Siege Culture." The phrase *#ReadSiege* began trending on neo-Nazi sites. Followers adopted "James Mason" as their own screen name on neo-Nazi chats and started using it to threaten nonbelievers. "What we are creating here," one follower wrote on an underground site, "is something that James Mason attempted to put into form.... Those of you who are in here, perhaps, will create history. That is our intention." Old videos of Mason's racist, hate-filled talks became popular on underground Nazi websites, as well. On one trip to Poland, Mason filmed himself visiting Auschwitz, where he gave a mocking guided tour of the Nazi concentration camp to a group of supporters. "There's that big, bad gas chamber. Glad I got to see that, very glad!" he said with a sarcastic smile. Commenters on the site cheered him on; "I wonder," one viewer asked, "if you can [buy] little pouches of Jews ashes in the gift shop. lol."

Mason became an unofficial adviser to his new protégés at Atomwaffen Division. He had never used a computer, but with help from a few tech-savvy followers who came to his apartment, he would log on to the encrypted group chats on Atomwaffen's "Graveyard" channel, urging them on in their pursuit of a whites-only nation. Whenever Mason was scheduled to make an online appearance, John Denton expected all the members to log on. James Mason's name and his racist, violent quotations from *Siege* were emblazed in bold type on the Atomwaffen fliers that members would plaster on college campuses, right underneath a swastika and an urgent command: "Don't Prepare for Exams! Prepare for Race War!"

---

Today Mason is a man in demand once again. More than a half century after he became a neo-Nazi, James Mason has become a lodestar for generations of angry young souls, an aging rock star to a band of new groupies. His acolytes now flock to see him in person, usually two or three at a time, at the old brick apartment building in Denver where he'd relocated. Members of Atomwaffen Division had tracked him down and contacted him; it was a momentous event for the group when word spread that they had found Mason and he was willing to meet with them. So many young male visitors trudged up the staircase at all hours to apartment number 10 on the second floor, in fact, that one neighbor suspected he might be using his home to have illicit relations with underage boys.

Instead, though, he was holding court for members of Atomwaffen and other budding neo-Nazi groups—more than a hundred young visitors, by his count, in the last several years. He had become a rarefied elder, and he would pose for photos with his visitors, wearing a Nazi uniform and the radiation patch. Sometimes a visitor would bring along a copy of *Siege* for him to autograph.

## "Hate Camp"

All the newfound attention and relevance, after his decades in exile, have reinvigorated Mason with grandiose visions of his own toxic, racist legacy. He has outlived most of his neo-Nazi contemporaries from the 1970s and 1980s. "I survived," he says. "My life has *gone* for something. I will be remembered!" His own racist world views, he believes, will live on long after his death with a new generation of extremists he helped birth.

Sam Woodward and Tristan Evans, part of that next generation, had called ahead to ask Mason if he was up for a visit. He was. When it came to aspiring young neo-Nazis, he always was.

Mason lived alone, with a cat he unironically named Sunshine, in a gritty apartment complex just a few blocks from the state capitol — Section 8 housing, subsidized by the government that he so loathed. Mason's renewed popularity and the re-publication of *Siege* hadn't translated into riches; he claimed he didn't want any money from it. He had worked for a time at a Kmart store before filing for bankruptcy. Sometimes he ate at a government-sponsored soup kitchen; on other occasions, he used the food stamps he received to pay prostitutes. The man who railed about overthrowing the "evil" menace of government was now relying on its largesse to support himself and his habits.

Mason saw no contradiction in his lifestyle, taking handouts from the government while calling for its destruction. He could "compartmentalize" his own vile racial views from his personal life, he said. He could call for the expulsion of Blacks from America, on the one hand, all while becoming friendly with an elderly African American woman named Lady Clark in the complex next door; she thought he was a nice man and appreciated how he always fed the squirrels outside their building. There were lots of minorities in his neighborhood, but Mason would walk past them placidly on the sidewalk, with no outward signs of his contempt for them or his calls for their expulsion or death. Even a Nazi needed to maintain "civility," he said.

The buzzer at the front gate was broken, so Mason had to go down to the front door and let in Sam and Tristan, his latest visitors, when they arrived for their pilgrimage to meet the notorious neo-Nazi. They trudged upstairs. Sam was measured in his words. He was nervous about offending Mason. He'd read about Mason becoming upset and going "ballistic" when another young neo-Nazi visitor had spoken too exuberantly to him, and too indiscreetly, about violent revolution. That wasn't the "lone wolf" way, and Sam didn't want to find himself in that same situation now; he wanted to stay on Mason's good side. He wanted to talk to him about *Siege*. He had reread Mason's blueprint for race war and marked the important passages, filling pages of a notebook with his handwritten notes about its teachings on lone-wolf resistance, violent revolution, the evils of minorities, and evading police. "Act alone or in small numbers," Sam wrote in his notebook. "Pray for victory and not an end to the slaughter."

He and Tristan took the obligatory selfies, with Mason standing between the two of them. It was a ritual for his young admirers. Mason showed them his prized possessions: a shrine to the Third Reich spilling over into three rooms, with hundreds of Nazi artifacts, war medals, black-and-white photos, banners, and books—including copies of his own racist screed, *Siege*—on display from floor to ceiling. A bright red Nazi banner with a swastika atop it hung down prominently from one shelf, with an SS lightning bolt banner just below it and a smaller

Tristan Evans, James Mason, and Sam Woodward

## "Hate Camp"

Confederate flag perched above. A German war helmet and a sword hung on the wall near a disarmed Nazi hand grenade, German military statuettes, and rows of German beer steins. The mementos, collected over the decades from Ohio to Colorado, overflowed into an office in the next room, where Mason kept some of his favorite Nazi war medals under glass and stashed his original American Nazi Party uniform in a box in the closet, pulling it out for special occasions.

Sam and Tristan slept on the floor, and Mason served them steaks for breakfast when they awoke. They talked about Hitler and the Nazis, about all the non-white, non-Christian, non-heterosexuals who were desecrating America, and about the race war Mason foresaw coming because of it. It was mostly Mason talking and his two young disciples listening. He told them a story about a young American Nazi attacking Martin Luther King Jr. at a speech he gave in Birmingham in 1962, punching him repeatedly in the head before he was arrested and jailed. It was a shame, Mason said, that it had become so tough to get away with something like that today. Like a student with a perverse mentor, Woodward hesitantly picked Mason's brain about the Nazis — the original ones and the American neo-Nazis who followed them — and about the teachings of *Siege*. He asked to see Mason's collection of *The Stormtrooper* magazine, the quarterly put out by the American Nazi Party in the 1960s. He was transfixed.

Mason was a master propagandist, not unlike his old friend Charles Manson or another idol, the Nazi propaganda minister Joseph Goebbels, using their words to inspire their followers to bloodshed without dirtying their own hands. At visits like this one with Sam and Tristan, Mason toed a blurry line that he had constructed in his own mind, never explicitly endorsing violence per se but, with a wink and a nod, telling his followers that if they *must* resort to violence, they should do it with a splash and, by all means, make it "spectacular" and memorable. "I basically say, 'Don't do it,'" he explained on another occasion, "but if you're gonna do it, go *big*." Take the violence in Charlottesville earlier that summer at the "Unite the Right" rally, where Vanguard America's James Fields killed a counter-protester with his car. The killing "had to be done," Mason opined, but he lamented that if Fields was going to launch a deadly attack on "a crowd of communists," he should have killed fifty people, not just one. "There should've been more," he said.

Mason just wasn't going to be the one to do it, he said. He had attacked those Black kids at the Dairy Queen in Ohio many years earlier, and he had gotten in his share of skirmishes with minorities since then, but now he was leaving the violence to others. It suited him that way, especially if the FBI was looking for evidence to use against him.

Sam left their meeting in a state of awe. "Guy is full of stories," Sam wrote to his fellow neo-Nazis with Atomwaffen Division afterward. "Was like talking to a walking library." Mason's masterwork, *Siege*, with all its predictions of a Nazi-ruled dystopia, struck him as nothing short of revelation. He used a grainy old photo of Mason from his younger years as the avatar on one of his social media accounts.

Sam Woodward had made an impression on James Mason, too. He came across as "a fine, upstanding young man," Mason said later, and he wished him and Tristan Evans well in their neo-Nazi pursuits as they headed off.

---

James Mason's brand of hatred was spreading—and spilling into violence.

Not long after Sam's pilgrimage to see him in Denver, another follower of Mason—a white teenager in northern Virginia whom the grizzled neo-Nazi might also have considered "a fine, upstanding young man"—bought into his message of bigotry wholesale and came to terrorize a family in the suburbs of the nation's capital.

Nicholas Giampa had never gone to an Atomwaffen Division "hate camp," never committed a known hate crime, never even joined up with a fledgling local chapter. But the teenager, living in the suburbs of the nation's capital, found its racist propaganda online and soaked it up, becoming an avid follower of both Mason and Atomwaffen as a high school student. Soon enough, he was spouting their neo-Nazi tropes himself.

## "Hate Camp"

Under an online pseudonym, Giampa began reposting and commenting admiringly on the extremist propaganda put out by Atomwaffen Division's leaders. A photo of neo-Nazis in skull-and-crossbones masks, giving "Heil Hitler" salutes. Another one of James Mason reading his own racist screed, *Siege*, with Giampa urging people to buy the book. An image of a man hanging from a noose beneath a slur for gays. There were calls for "white revolution," praise for Hitler and the Nazis, and vile attacks on Jews, Muslims, gays, and a slew of other minorities.

Giampa talked of trying to get transgender people to kill themselves, and when someone asked on Twitter how Christian parents should prepare their children for the election of transgender people, he wrote: "Show them how to use a gun and use Jews as targets." Twitter did nothing; the guardrails it had promised to impose for preventing such violent hate speech once again proved practically meaningless.

The teen's online extremism began to bleed into real life. Startled neighbors in his Virginia suburb of Lorton discovered a giant swastika—forty feet long—mowed into the grass in a neighborhood field. The tracks from the riding mower led straight back to Giampa's house. The grass would grow back, but the shock—and Giampa's hatred—remained.

Nicholas Giampa was exactly the kind of follower that Atomwaffen Division targeted online: young and white, angry and isolated, lonely and vulnerable to misinformation, with online social media serving as his dark portal to the world. Diagnosed with autism, anxiety, and learning issues, he had struggled in school for years. Back in elementary school, he talked on a play date about blowing up his school. He called himself a "freak" and a "retard." He shuffled from one school to another—five in eight years—and rarely had any friends as he grew up. A criminal case against him in juvenile court on charges apparently connected to child pornography led a judge to ban him from going online as a teenager. But he managed to get back on the Internet anyway, soaking up material on neo-Nazism, beheadings, bombings, and torture.

While the boy could be practically mute with anxiety in many social situations, he had found an outlet online in neo-Nazism, hateful as it was. He was tweeting in late 2017 that a white Europe, without Jews or Muslims, "sounds like heaven," and he was re-tweeting a meme with a swastika that declared: "Hitler plz come back we miss you."

His mother, Marilyn Giampa, seemed oblivious to his menacing online persona. What she saw, instead, were signs of hope in his life after years of struggle. At the age of seventeen, Giampa was holding down a job at a Papa John's pizza shop, and he had started dating a girl for the first time. He and Amelia, a year younger, both attended a private high school for children with special needs, and the two seemed smitten with each other, taking trips together to the beach and an amusement park. "I found somebody that loves me," Giampa told his older sister. Relief washed over his mother. *Oh my God! He's turning normal*, she thought to herself.

The girl's mother, Buckley Kuhn-Fricker, was much more wary about the budding relationship. A bright red flag sprang up almost as soon as the two started dating. Amelia told her mother that Giampa knew a lot about history, and she began repeating some of the things he'd told her. "Did you know that the Jews are partly to blame for World War II?" she asked her mother. Startled, Kuhn-Fricker tried to correct her. She looked for documentaries on the war and the Holocaust to educate her daughter about the truth, but she learned that such disturbing, antisemitic themes seemed like "an obsession" for her daughter's new boyfriend.

Only months later did Kuhn-Fricker and her husband, Scott Fricker, Amelia's stepfather, discover the dark depths of that obsession. That December, Kuhn-Fricker found on her daughter's cell phone the Twitter account that Giampa appeared to be using to post all his twisted praise for Nazis and white supremacy, and his ugly slurs against minorities of all types. She and Scott were aghast. "We can't allow her to see someone associated with Nazis," Kuhn-Fricker, a lawyer who was passionate about social justice issues and civil rights, told a friend after the jarring discovery. "We don't associate with hate groups in our house."

## "Hate Camp"

Amelia's parents were desperate to get her out of Giampa's grip. This was supposed to be a festive time for them; they had recently moved their family into a bigger house in a serene, wooded area in their Virginia suburb, near a neighborhood pool and tennis club, and in a few weeks they would be celebrating their first Christmas in the new house. They had decorated the home with wreaths and snowflakes, and Scott's parents were coming to stay with them for the holiday.

Instead of celebration, though, they were now planning an intervention for their sixteen-year-old daughter. At a tearful family meeting, they warned her about the relationship and forbade her from seeing Giampa anymore. Amelia did not take the edict well. Kuhn-Fricker called Giampa, too, and she told the teenager to stay away from their daughter and their house. "Don't see her again," she said. She reported to the school what she had learned about his violent neo-Nazi postings. "He is a monster, and I have no pity for people like that," she wrote in an email to the school administrator. "He is spreading hate."

Giampa was distraught and angry about the breakup. His mother tried, unsuccessfully, to put him in an in-patient psychiatric hospital a few days later. He wasn't sleeping, and that same night, she let him stay overnight in her room to keep an eye on him, hiding the car keys under a pillow to keep them away from him. She dozed off, only to awaken sometime after 4:00 a.m. to realize that her son was gone. So were the car keys.

Frantic, she texted Kuhn-Fricker to see if she knew where Giampa was. "He is here," she texted back. "We are calling police."

Giampa was already inside the house, upstairs in her daughter's bedroom. Amelia's parents heard something down the hall around 4:30 a.m. and went to investigate. They banged on the door, but it was locked, according to a police account. Amelia refused to let them in at first, but after they tried to force open the door, she finally unlocked it.

That was when Giampa took out the gun. It was his father's handgun; Giampa had found it in the cellar, where it was kept unlocked despite the teen's long history of mental health issues, and he had taken it with him to the Frickers' home inside a bag, along with a knife and a hammer. Giampa was a skilled shooter—a photo that his mother posted on Facebook showed him at a firing range, gripping an older-style submachine gun—and he put his experience to use now. First, he shot Scott Fricker—once in the head, and again in the back, according to the police account. Then he shot Buckley Kuhn-Fricker, who fell to the hall floor by the stairs.

The shots awakened Amelia's ten-year-old brother down the hall. He raced out of his room to find his parents on the floor—his father motionless, his mother still moving—and Giampa with a gun in his hand. "There was an intruder," Giampa claimed to the boy.

The next call to the police came from Amelia. "Caller advising her mother and father were shot," the police dispatcher said. "Caller is still upstairs with her boyfriend."

Fairfax County police arrived to a scene of carnage: bodies on the floor upstairs, blood splattered on the walls, screams in the early-morning suburban air. Officers could hear shots still being fired upstairs as they entered the house. Giampa, after shooting the two people who had kept him away from his girlfriend because of his neo-Nazi devotion, had turned the gun on himself and fired it into his forehead, the bullet lodging in his brain. He would survive. Buckley Kuhn-Fricker and her husband would not.

As Giampa was being rushed to a nearby hospital, Amelia gave a detective at her house a chilling account of the killings and what led up to them. She had given Giampa the electronic code for the home's security system many weeks earlier, she said, and he had been using it to come in the front door and visit her secretly in the middle of the night, usually sneaking in after 2:00 a.m. and leaving by 5:00 a.m., before everyone else was up, according to the police account of the interview. Giampa had shown her the gun several times before, she said, and they had made a "suicide pact" weeks earlier, with the idea of "wounding" her parents if they tried to keep them apart, she said.

The girl told the detective how her parents heard her with Giampa in her room that morning and tried to get in; how she finally opened the door and Giampa shot them each in quick succession; and how he took her to an office down the hall to follow through on their "suicide pact."

Giampa put the gun to her head and she closed her eyes, according to the police account. She heard the trigger click, but the gun didn't fire. Expecting to die, instead she opened her eyes to see Giampa shooting himself in the head.

---

At a church memorial service a little over a week later, an overflow crowd of stunned, glazed-eyed mourners heard the pastor speak about overcoming hate, while Scott Fricker's father alluded to the "deranged adolescent" whose actions had brought them all there that day. It was hard for the mourners to imagine that the violent hatred of neo-Nazism had struck their placid suburb.

The killings generated a very different response from Atomwaffen Division's leaders. They used the violence at the hands of one of their followers to push their own perverse marketing. The group put out a foreboding photo montage not unlike the threatening posters they delivered to people of color and Jews. This one showed an unsmiling Giampa staring straight ahead, his long brown hair falling in his eyes and peach fuzz on his face, flanked by images of a swastika and a rifle.

"Love Conquers All," the graphic read mockingly. "The Atomwaffen Division."

## CHAPTER 7

# "RIGHT-WING DEATH SQUAD"

Sam Woodward had traveled to Colorado to pay homage to James Mason, and to the remote brush country of South Texas to train in secret at an Atomwaffen "hate camp." But Orange County beckoned him back: a place where Sam had unfinished business, and where a long-standing culture of intolerance and hate was transforming into something more frightening, and more militant. Just as Sam had done in Texas, young men from another budding group of rabid white supremacists were beginning training of their own at a public park in Orange County—and eager for all the attention it would get them. Like Sam and his comrades in Atomwaffen Division, the hatred that they espoused would turn to violence in the name of their "cause"—aimed at left-wing opponents and, often, minorities, from coast to coast.

On a normal day, Marblehead Park is a bright oasis sitting serenely atop an ocean bluff at the southern tip of Orange County. With views of the glistening beaches of San Clemente in one direction and rugged canyon walls in the other, giggling children from the elementary school next door and from the million-dollar homes in the neighborhood play on the brightly colored jungle gym and hang from monkey bars, rope ladders, swings, and a climbing wall.

But for the group of young neo-Nazis, Marblehead Park became a destination with more ominous purposes in mind: as a training ground for martial arts and combat drills in furtherance of their own violent brand of "white unity" around America.

They called themselves the "Rise Above Movement," or RAM, and they cast themselves to their growing legions of followers as "a combat-ready, militant brand of a new nationalist white supremacy and identity movement." What Atomwaffen set out to do with assault rifles and bombs, these young white men wanted to achieve with clubs, fists, and muscle.

At the park in San Clemente beginning in 2017, young men from RAM wearing skeleton masks trained for months in martial arts, kickboxing, and hand-to-hand combat to ready themselves for violence—or "security," as they called it euphemistically—at upcoming political events that they planned to crash. They were readying themselves for combat. "Training is a go. Saturday at 11 am. Marblehead Park, San Clemente," one of the group's leaders texted a new recruit. "We'll probably have equipment for shield and stick training and our formation tactics ready."

The monkey bars and the playground equipment, symbols of youthful innocence, were put to quick use for RAM's training drills, and the masked men—many of them shirtless, their chests covered with white-power and neo-Nazi tattoos—ran up a set of stairs Rocky-style to test their stamina. They posed for photos and posted highlights from their training sessions on recruitment videos on public websites, along with posters and graffiti targeting immigrants, Jews, Muslims, and other minorities. They hoisted a banner from a highway overpass nearby and spray-painted graffiti with their logo on the walls of the underpass— promising to defeat their non-Aryan enemies "by any means necessary"; "#RightWingDeathSquad" read the caption for one photo on the group's official Instagram account. It was the kind of violent rhetoric that should have gotten them kicked off the popular site, but for many months, it didn't.

The young men reveled in the attention. Unlike their neo-Nazi counterparts at Atomwaffen Division, who preferred to operate mostly underground in plotting their own violent agenda, the RAM members wanted to make as public a statement as possible, whether it was online on Facebook, Instagram, and Twitter, or in person, in daylight hours in the middle of a well-known Orange County park, as if to say: *We're not hiding.* At the close of one of their public recruitment videos, RAM laid out its priorities in large, white block letters on a black screen: "FATHERLAND. HONOR. FIGHT. LOYALTY. WHITE. UNITY. REVOLT."

The unquestioned leader of the gang was Rob Rundo, a New York City transplant who lived for a time a few miles away from Marblehead Park in an apartment he rented in San Clemente. Rundo, trained in martial arts, had a history of violent crimes dating back to his days as a teenager in Queens, an Italian kid who described himself as "a troublemaker, a hooligan type." A street brawler, he wound up at the age of fifteen in juvenile custody, and by nineteen, as the leader of a street gang called the "Original Flushing Crew," he was convicted in New York of stabbing a Hispanic man multiple times after confronting him in a store and chasing him down in the street; Rundo earned himself the nickname on the streets of *El Diablo Blanco*—"The White Devil"—from rival Hispanic gang MS-13. He was a menace to be feared.

Nearly two years in a New York state prison hardened Rundo's racial extremism even further, especially against Blacks, whom he blamed for bringing "chaos" and "anarchy" to his cell block.

He moved to Orange County in 2016 after his release and got a job in construction. The conservative politics that he found there suited him. "There were a lot of like-minded people there," he said, and he spoke wistfully of his life in Orange County. "I had a good apartment in Huntington Beach, right on the beach. I had a fiancée, I had a good union job, everything was going good for me," he told followers in one video he recorded.

In Orange County, Rundo became more intent than ever on waging a fight that he saw in starkly racial terms: the white man, under siege, fighting against the *others*. "We have a long history," he said, "of fighting for the white race." It was a fixation fueled by what he said were his many hours spent "constantly consuming videos of fucking Blacks just beating people up." The specter of violence by Blacks against whites, grossly exaggerated by right-wing misinformation, had driven many a white supremacist before him, most notably Dylann Roof in his massacre of nine churchgoers in South Carolina. Rundo admitted that watching all the violent, racially fueled videos "is going to mess with your psyche." He called it "toxic."

He became a follower of Hitler, and he pledged his support for the white supremacists' canonical fourteen words: *We must secure the existence of our people and a future for white people.* "I'm a big supporter of the fourteen, I'll say that," Rundo remarked.

So Rundo, with help from another white supremacist, Ben Daley, a redheaded tree trimmer in Los Angeles, started a white-supremacist crew in late 2016 that became the Rise Above Movement. Orange County, with its long history of conservative, white political control, held an obvious appeal for Rundo as the birthplace of his "movement"; the county catered to white nationalists like himself, he said, "simply because we haven't been replaced yet." By *we*, he meant whites, and he predicted that any place with a "healthy white community," such as Orange County, would ultimately wage a racial war of its own—"the struggle," he liked to call it. He contrasted Orange County with its neighbors up the 405 freeway in Los Angeles—a place that, in his distorted view, was ridden with nothing but "mass homeless, gang wars, its virtually nonexistent white population, and all the other vices that run rampant there."

Rundo and Daley found many of their first recruits at local gyms—fitness buffs and martial arts aficionados joined by their angry grievances over how whites were being treated in America by the liberal body politic. Rundo had grievances even with other white supremacists in their tactics and approach. He didn't like the image of the cerebral, "suit-and-tie politics" of "alt-right" leader Richard Spencer, and the more radical, "antisocial" approach of groups like Atomwaffen Division turned him off, too. He preached fitness, discipline, and masculinity for alienated young white men, along with what he called a more "moderate" and less in-your-face brand of bigotry. "You don't always need to be naming the Jew every five minutes," he said.

Most of the young men under him liked Trump and the extreme racial politics that had just helped put him in the White House; their main gripe, though, was that Trump, if anything, didn't go far enough; they wanted to see the influence of minorities smashed altogether, not coddled.

They weren't racists, Rundo insisted—just guys tired of seeing white Americans pushed around and degraded. "I care about my race. That's the only thing that made me, I guess, an outlaw of society," Rundo once said. There were blue-collar workers like Rundo and Daley among those early members, side by side with active-duty Marines and even an aerospace engineer at a major defense contractor in Southern California. They also drew from local neo-Nazi skinhead groups in "O.C.," including one member of the notorious Hammerskin Nation who had gone to prison years earlier for robbing and badly beating up a Jewish man in another Orange County park while screaming antisemitic slurs at him. Scrawled on the concrete near the Jewish victim's blood were a swastika and the words "White Power."

RAM members in the region numbered a few dozen or so at the start, but Rundo had bold ambitions for growing bigger and broader. He personally handled the group's Twitter account—@RiseAbove Mvmt—posting recruitment videos that showed its members at rallies, beating up people like something out of *Fight Club*, the cult film classic, and he even started the group's own clothing line, calling it Right Brand Clothing. Like Atomwaffen Division, which had recruited members in Europe and ultimately made the UK's list of banned groups, Rundo wanted his gang of neo-Nazi street fighters to go international. In 2018 he and Daley, along with a third RAM leader, went to Europe to celebrate Hitler's birthday closer to the Fatherland, visiting Germany, Ukraine, and Italy, and meeting with members of European white supremacy extremist groups, including a leader of the Azov Brigade, the same Ukrainian white supremacist group that Atomwaffen's Andrew Oneschuk had tried to join from his home in Massachusetts. "It was an honor to meet...the patriot," RAM said in an Instagram posting with a photo of their get-together.

Far-right extremism was on the rise in Eastern European nations, just as it was in America, and Rundo saw an opening for his "right-wing death squad." He posted photos and videos from each of their stops, a running travelogue of their dalliances with white-nationalist extremists that included a stop at a torchlit supremacist rally, a scene that Rundo said "warms the heart." He found time to do some martial arts fighting while he was in Europe, too. In one video, Rundo, muscle-bound with his hair closely cropped, was shown in the ring fighting against a white supremacist ally, and in another, his partner was seen giving a white supremacist salute.

---

To make a name for their militant group among other far-right extremists, Rundo and RAM wanted to put their street-fighting skills to use, and they had a distinctive target in mind: political rallies and protests. The events became a fertile target for the white supremacist group in a prolonged nationwide spree of violence against minorities, liberal "commie" protesters, and anyone else who opposed their icon: Donald Trump.

The coming-out for Rob Rundo and his band at RAM—their first appearance on a public stage—came two months after Trump's inauguration as president in 2017 at a raucous "Make America Great" rally in Orange County. The event was one of several dozen rallies around the country designed to show support for the embattled new president, and organizers were billing it as a "family-friendly" event in Huntington Beach.

Rundo and his band, however, came looking for a fight; they had been training for it, in fact, meeting up at the park in San Clemente again ten days earlier to go over combat drills. Among a crowd of hundreds of Trump supporters marching along the beach, the young men, most of them with shaved heads and wearing sunglasses and athletic gear, stood out as they displayed a huge banner that read: "Defend America." A smaller sign above the banner displayed a Christian cross on it and read: "Da Goyim Know"—an antisemitic dog whistle among white supremacists connoting the Jews' supposed world domination over the *goyim*, or non-Jews.

A small group of counter-protesters gathered at the beach to voice their opposition to Trump, along with a throng of journalists covering the event. As the pro-Trump crowd marched south along the beach, Rundo and his men stayed back to confront the counter-protesters. That's when the violence broke out. One of the RAM men, twenty-two-year-old Tyler Laube, slugged a Hispanic intern for the *OC Weekly*, the alternative weekly in Orange County, hitting him three times in the face, according to video later pieced together by the FBI. One of the counter-protesters used pepper spray in apparent self-defense to try to quell the assault, as a number of the other counter-protesters fled in the other direction to escape the fighting.

White supremacist leader Rob Rundo, surrounded by other members of a street-brawling extremist group in Orange County called the "Rise Above Movement," was convicted in 2024 over violence and rioting at political rallies.

Rundo and his men chased after them, attacking them from behind with a flurry of kicks and punches. Rundo slugged one counter-protester in the back of the head, then grabbed the back of his neck and threw him to the sand, landing on top of him and continuing to pummel him as RAM members cheered him on. Another man slipped brass knuckles on his hand in the midst of the melee. Meanwhile, a Trump supporter with a flag reading "Trump, Make America Great Again" chased after the counter-protester who had pepper-sprayed the attackers, then bragged about battering him with his flag when he caught him. "I hit him five times with the flag over his head," he said, casting the Trump supporters as the victims of wrongful attacks. "We're not xenophobic. We're not racist. We're just proud Americans."

For RAM, the day at the beach was a rousing success. Photographs of Rundo pummeling the counter-protester, along with violent shots of other members of his crew, made it into the news coverage of the rally nationwide—not just in mainstream news outlets, but in leading neo-Nazi websites like the *Daily Stormer*, which takes its name from the original Nazi publication, *Der Stürmer*, and includes a clock continuously counting down the years until it predicts that whites will become a minority in the United States. "Trumpenkriegers Physically Remove Antifa Homos in Huntington Beach," the *Daily Stormer* declared after the violence. Rundo and his men crowed with delight. "Front page of the stormer we did it fam," Daley texted another member later that same day. "Celebrity status...well done," another member wrote. RAM went on to use the violent imagery in its own marketing, too, with the image of Rundo beating up his victim under the headline "Physical Removal." RAM bragged in another post, with a photo of Rundo and other members in combat gear, that "antifa was btfo"—*blown the fuck out*—"in Huntington Beach." Still another post demanded "a shout-out to the only alt right crew that actually beats antifa senseless and wins rallies."

Rundo and his gang weren't done. Weeks later, after more training at the San Clemente park, about a dozen members drove a rented van some 375 miles up the California coast from Los Angeles to Berkeley, and crashed another political rally there alongside far-right Trump supporters from better-known extremist groups like the Proud Boys and the Oath Keepers. Berkeley had become ground zero for violent rallies between political protesters on both sides, and for this one, the crew arrived with their hands taped like martial-arts fighters and their faces covered with skeleton masks and goggles.

Rundo and his men crossed over an orange police fence meant to separate the protesters and began attacking Trump opponents en masse, punching and kicking them while other crew members held them down on the ground. Daley kicked one counter-protester from behind, then sprayed him with a chemical irritant. The RAM members were "wrecking" and beating the counter-protesters so badly that there was "not even room to get a hit in," one crew member complained with bemusement. "I was like alrite, u guys got it handled then lol."

Berkeley police tried to end the melee. An officer ordered Rundo to stop punching a defenseless protester, but he ignored them; the officer knocked Rundo to the ground, but Rundo punched the officer twice in the head before police could arrest him, according to an FBI account. Even then, the other RAM members kept chasing the Trump opponents from the park and beating them, finally brandishing a left-wing banner they had seized from a well-known liberal teacher and activist, a Filipino immigrant named Yvette Felarca, who had led anti-fascist protests in the area. They kept the banner as a war trophy and hung it on the wall of a garage they used for boxing, alongside their white supremacist signs. And in the chilling Jim Crow–era language of lynching, they talked about what they wanted to do to Felarca, the "subhuman" minority whose banner they'd seized. "She needs the rope," one crew member texted Daley. "Yep lol," he answered.

Just as they had in Huntington Beach, the neo-Nazis celebrated the violence afterward with a buffet of self-congratulations online. RAM crew member Michael Miselis was one of the heroes of the day. The bearded young man worked in aerospace engineering with a security clearance at Northrop Grumman in Los Angeles and was getting his PhD at UCLA. But on the side, he was a secret white supremacist and brutal street fighter, and after the Berkeley brawling, he bragged of punching a counter-protester so hard that he had broken his own hand, despite all the athletic tape wrapped around it; the pain was worth it to him. "I've been dealing with my hand all day," he texted another RAM member right after the rally. "Just found a video...where you can see me breaking it on a guy's head lol."

The other crew member, who hadn't made it to the brawl but watched all the violent videos afterward, was duly impressed by RAM's performance. "There's a grey-shirted trooper at the fucking front every, single, time. You guys were lions."

Miselis, the aerospace engineer, responded with just three chilling words, a familiar mantra to their crew: "Total Aryan Victory."

---

There were still more weekly training sessions to be held at the Marblehead Park in San Clemente, complete with drills on how to use "palm strikes" and elbows in attacks to avoid breaking a hand with a punch the way that Miselis had. Two months after the Berkeley brawl came another California protest, this one a conservative, anti-Muslim event protesting Islamic law in San Bernardino, just east of Orange County, and RAM members were there again to beat up counter-protesters. Three of them were arrested in the violence. "We smashed some antifa as they were leaving," Daley told another member in a text afterward. "If it wasn't for the white nationalists, nothing would ever get done," his friend answered. "This is true," Daley said; there "would've been no victory in Huntington or Berkeley."

But the RAM crew was already setting its sights on its biggest target yet: the massive "Unite the Right" rally that August, which would bring hundreds of white supremacists from groups around the country to Charlottesville for a spectacle unlike anything seen in decades.

RAM members were anxious to attend, preparing for months. What seemed to many outsiders at the time as a spontaneous outburst of violence had been planned long ahead of time. The aim of RAM members was clear, federal prosecutors later concluded: to provoke violence with counter-protesters so they could justify their own brutal force and "shield them from prosecution" if they got caught. Weeks before the event, in fact, Daley offered his combat bona fides on Discord, a favorite underground chat channel, to other white supremacists who would also be going to Charlottesville; he and other RAM members "were experienced at these events" and "all were in Berkeley riots," he wrote, saying that one in particular was "an excellent fighter" and he was "stoked" to join up with them for the rally.

As the day approached, rumors were circulating online among the white supremacists that the city of Charlottesville might pull the permit for the rally. Daley was undeterred, letting other white supremacists know that he and his men would be there one way or the other. "I'm flying out from CA with a handful regardless," Daley texted another member. "Fuck those Jews."

Rob Rundo himself didn't make it to Charlottesville; he said he had to work. But RAM was well represented without him. Miselis, the aerospace engineer, was assigned to help gather supplies ahead of time; he brought baseball helmets with him in a backpack for all the brawling that RAM planned to do. Careful not to use a credit card, he got cash at a Walmart in Charlottesville so he could buy torches for the surprise torchlit ceremony the night before the actual rally, where white supremacists marched, eerily lit by flames from their torches, and screamed "Jews Will Not Replace Us!" and "Blood and Soil," a favorite Nazi slogan from the Third Reich.

At the fabled statue of Thomas Jefferson at the University of Virginia rotunda, students were gathering to protest the surprise arrival of the white supremacists, and the marchers quickly surrounded them and started brawling. Miselis and Daley, along with at least two other RAM members in full combat gear, were in the midst of it, slugging and beating protesters with abandon. "Come and get it!" Miselis yelled. Daley bragged on Facebook that he "hit like five people," and he racked up even more "hits" at the daylight rally the next day, as he and RAM crew members were seen punching and kicking defenseless protesters at a university park, throwing one woman off a sidewalk and grabbing another by the throat and tossing her to the ground.

## "Right-Wing Death Squad"

Although Charlottesville police officials knew of the potential for trouble well ahead of the weekend, police on the scene were ill-prepared for the widespread violence and did little to intervene in the brawling; the police's passive and inept handling of the mob scene produced "disastrous results," an independent review afterward would conclude. The Charlottesville city manager said he was "profoundly sorry" for all the shortcomings.

The one regret for RAM's men, though, was that they hadn't racked up more victims in all the bedlam. In one video that Miselis shared with another crew member afterward, he was seen struggling to punch a counter-protester perched at the top of a flight of stairs. He saw it as a missed opportunity.

"You should have ran in [and] chest kicked that faggot down the stairs," his friend told Miselis.

"Yeah, massive regret after watching that footage," Miselis answered. "Next time he's going flying."

---

To prosecutors, Rob Rundo and his Orange County crew were violent extremists who belonged in prison over the havoc they wreaked from California to Virginia. The young men "were essentially serial rioters," the federal prosecutor in Charlottesville declared, with the targets of their white-supremacist agenda usually minorities.

But to other right-wing extremists, they were martyrs. Rundo and his band brashly cast themselves as "political prisoners," even garnering donations for a legal defense fund. They were being persecuted for their political beliefs, they insisted. "These are small little fistfights," Rundo said, mocking the idea of him as some sort of "neo-Nazi Jason Bourne." Their appeals resonated; to many supporters, they were fighting for the survival of the white race.

Robert Bowers, a white, middle-aged truck driver in Pittsburgh, would become their most notorious supporter in 2018. And his violent bigotry would snowball to frightening new levels with the deadliest antisemitic attack in American history.

Bowers, a stocky man with closely cropped gray hair, had led a nondescript, blue-collar life for most of his forty-six years. He dropped out of high school and worked as a delivery man at a bakery before becoming a trucker. He liked beer, action movies, Hooters restaurants, and guns, with twenty-one registered in his name. Never married, he lived with his grandfather for many years. Neighbors rarely saw him. He didn't have much of a presence.

He seemed affable enough to co-workers at his job stints, but he mainly kept to himself. Some did notice his fierce anti-government streak on display at times—he made clear that he didn't like paying taxes—but it wasn't until his forties that he began descending into the extremist world of angry white nationalism, fed by his fascination with right-wing radio shows and online sites such as Gab, a favorite neo-Nazi gathering spot. Only then did the extent of his simmering rage become public.

In a fusillade of online postings, Bowers leveled his ugliest rhetoric at Jews, his disgust becoming an obsession. He would post three or four memes a day attacking "filthy EVIL jews," as he described them; "jews are children of satan," he declared in his profile. He distrusted even Trump, who he believed, in keeping with some antisemitic conspiracists, was secretly controlled by Jews through his Jewish son-in-law, Jared Kushner. "There is no #MAGA," Bowers wrote, "as long as there is a kike infestation."

After Rundo and the other RAM members were arrested on rioting charges, Bowers rallied to their cause, reposting a twisted take-off on the famous anti-Nazi poem *First They Came For.* "Then Trump came for the Rise Above Movement but I kept supporting Trump because he is better than Hillary Clinton," his posting read.

Driven by bigotry and misinformation, Bowers was especially riled up by a right-wing conspiracy theory that combined his revulsion for both Jews and immigrants. With President Trump putting out tweets, wildly exaggerated, about a "caravan" of Central American immigrants en route to America, Bowers became convinced that a refugee resettlement program run by the Jewish humanitarian group HIAS (originally the Hebrew Immigrant Aid Society) was a ruse for bringing violent "invaders" into the country. Not long after voicing his support for the neo-Nazis at RAM, Bowers posted a link to the Jewish group's site listing hundreds of synagogues nationwide that were hosting services to support new refugees of all religions; one congregation hosting an event was in Pittsburgh, near Bowers—a small congregation called Dor Hadash that met at the Tree of Life building.

"Why hello there HIAS!" Bowers wrote on Gab. "You like to bring in hostile invaders to dwell among us? We appreciate the list of friends you have provided."

---

Brad Orsini's main job was to keep people safe at the dozens of Jewish synagogues and facilities in Pittsburgh. With bigotry surging, he realized his task was becoming much more difficult.

Orsini wasn't Jewish, but he knew about security from his twenty-eight years as an FBI agent, which was why the Jewish Federation in Pittsburgh had made him its first-ever director of security in 2017. For his last fourteen years at the FBI, Orsini, a burly white ex-Marine, worked on civil rights and hate crimes in Pittsburgh, and he watched with alarm the resurgence of extremists at home—not foreigners sent by al Qaeda or ISIS, but white supremacists.

One challenge had been simply to get police to take hate crimes seriously. When three young white men, shouting racial slurs, burned a six-foot-high cross in the backyard of a Black teenager about sixty miles outside Pittsburgh, the local police wrote it off as "a prank gone bad" until Orsini and the FBI stepped in and brought a hate-crime case, he recalled.

In his new security post in Pittsburgh, Orsini tracked with alarm the rising flood of antisemitic threats coming into local Jewish groups—hate mail to synagogues, swastikas spray-painted on buildings, violent neo-Nazi literature left at Jewish homes. One notorious neo-Nazi in Pittsburgh, Hardy Lloyd, was back out on the streets after another stint in prison for violent bigotry, and the threats were only growing.

Synagogues were "soft targets"—places of powerful symbolism with little or no security. Orsini began leading more than 130 security training sessions at Jewish sites to prepare for the worst-case scenario: a violent armed attack. At a training session in September of 2018 at the Tree of Life synagogue in Pittsburgh's tree-lined Squirrel Hill neighborhood, the cornerstone of the city's Jewish community, Orsini laid out for congregants and staff what to do if a shooter attacked, from finding the best exits to calling 911. Rabbi Jeffrey Myer, who led the synagogue, interjected. As an observant Jew, he explained that he didn't carry his phone on the Sabbath. "Rabbi, it's a different world," Orsini told him. "You need to carry it."

---

Weeks later, on the drizzly Saturday morning of October 27, 2018, Robert Bowers posted one last comment on Gab. Cryptic to anyone reading it at the time, its meaning would become painfully clear hours later. "HIAS likes to bring invaders in that kill our people," Bowers wrote. "I can't sit by and watch my people get slaughtered. Screw your optics, I'm going in."

At about 9:45 a.m., Rabbi Myers began Shabbat services in the sanctuary. Prayer services were also underway for Dor Hadash and a third congregation using the building. People were milling about nearby in the kitchen for the day's activities. A baby-naming was scheduled.

It had already been an unusually fraught few days of political and racial violence nationwide. A day before, the FBI had arrested a Florida man, his van plastered with photos promoting President Trump, for sending sixteen homemade pipe bombs to Barack Obama, Hillary Clinton, and other liberal targets in a weeks-long crime spree. Two days earlier, an armed white supremacist, unable to get past the locked doors at a predominantly Black church outside Louisville, had gone instead to a grocery store nearby and shot to death two Black shoppers. Spotting a white man with a gun outside as he fled, shooter Gregory Bush told him: "Don't shoot me, I won't shoot you. Whites don't shoot whites." As police arrested him, the bald, bearded killer shouted

"Dylann Roof!"—an homage to the white supremacist mass murderer at the South Carolina church.

Now, just a few minutes into the Tree of Life service, Rabbi Myers heard what sounded like a loud crash outside the sanctuary. Two congregants went to investigate. Moments later, a volley of *pop-pop-pops* made clear that the worst-case scenario envisioned at Orsini's trainings had come to pass: there was an "active shooter" in the synagogue.

"Drop to the floor!" Myers yelled. "Do not move! Don't utter a sound." Myers scurried to hustle those congregants sitting up front out of the room. As he went back into the sanctuary to look for those in the back, another volley of gunfire stopped him. It was the sound, he realized later, of the other congregants being executed.

The rabbi raced to a choir loft and reached into his jacket for his cell phone, the one he'd started carrying only after Orsini's admonition. He called 911 and, in a panting whisper, reported that the synagogue was under assault. He was praying. At that moment, he was expecting to die.

The first officers to arrive, from an outpost just a few blocks away, got there minutes later to find a middle-aged white man standing by the doorway and firing away at them with an AR-15. Robert Bowers had just unleashed the deadliest attack on Jewish people in American history, going room to room to hunt down the congregants with deadly precision, stepping over the bloodied bodies of his victims as he went. Eleven congregants were killed in all—husbands and wives; fathers and mothers; a pair of inseparable brothers; a doctor, a dentist, and a retired accountant. It was a slaughter, the head of the Anti-Defamation League said, that was "unthinkable...in the United States of America in this day and age."

When it was all over—after Bowers had shot and injured four of the arriving police officers, one gravely; and after he was shot and cornered and finally gave himself up, his hands in the air—he gave the police an unvarnished motive for the killings. "All these Jews need to die," he declared. They were "committing genocide" against his people, Bowers said. He had a look of satisfaction on his face.

Hate crimes often come in waves, one violent bigot inspiring another. Sure enough, six months to the day after the Tree of Life massacre, a copycat killer struck at a Jewish synagogue in northern San Diego, just down the coast from Orange County, and just a short drive from where a nineteen-year-old college student named John Earnest lived with his parents.

Earnest, a young man with a broad smile and thick, wavy brown hair, was no brooding Sam Woodward. He had always been an overachiever: he earned top grades in school, he swam for his high school team, and he had trained since the age of four as a classical pianist. Earnest was studying nursing at a California state college and, as he himself wrote, he seemed to have everything ahead of him in life—a promising and well-paying career in nursing, plenty of friends and family, a church that he liked, and the prospect someday of "a happy family of (my) own."

To his peers, Earnest didn't seem like an angry kid, much less a violent white supremacist. But in recent months, through the lure of his own batch of far-right extremist online forums, he had become fixated on violent, conspiratorial notions about "the destruction of my race"—the white race. And like Robert Bowers in Pittsburgh and others before him, Earnest was determined to act on those dark obsessions.

Earnest had been working on his plan for weeks, and he wrote a long, vengeful manifesto detailing all his hatreds—an "open letter" that he planned to post on 8chan, a popular site for far-right extremists. The online forum had become, as its own founder acknowledged, "a receptive audience for domestic terrorists." Even more than Gab, the far-right site of choice for Bowers, 8chan was the go-to forum for extremists who wanted to broadcast their violent intentions widely to a like-minded audience and then go on a rampage.

Brenton Tarrant, a young white supremacist in New Zealand, had done just that a month earlier on March 15, 2019, writing a seventy-four-page manifesto called "The Great Replacement" on 8chan, before he shot to death fifty-one Muslim congregants at two mosques in Christ Church and live-streamed his attack on Facebook. Patrick Crusius would post his own bigoted screed on 8chan that same year, writing of "a Hispanic invasion of Texas" before mowing down twenty-one mostly Hispanic shoppers at a Walmart in El Paso. And Dylann Roof had posted a two-thousand-word manifesto he had written before murdering the nine Black congregants in South Carolina.

And so John Earnest turned to 8chan to publicize his own manifesto—a step that had now become almost *de rigueur* for violent extremists.

In his manifesto, seven pages in all, Earnest traced what he called the "magnificent bloodline" of his white European ancestors. He wrote with disdain about Blacks, Muslims, and gays, but like Bowers in Pittsburgh, he saved his most violent vitriol for Jews—an "evil" group that he said was "sealing the doom of my race." He repeated one antisemitic trope after another—from the killing of Christ to their supposed control of the media, Wall Street, and Hollywood, and their alleged role in pushing immigration in America to "displace the European race." The Jews, in his warped, conspiratorial view, were the root of virtually every "evil" facing the world, and he was committed to stopping them. In his own mind, he was a savior of the white race.

"I'd rather die in glory or spend the rest of my life in prison than waste away knowing that I did nothing to stop this evil," he wrote. "I would die a thousand times over to prevent the doomed fate that the Jews have planned for my race." Earnest was a regular churchgoer, the son of a church elder, and he quoted Scriptures frequently in his manifesto to justify his maniacal hatred. "My God does not take kindly to the destruction of His creation. Especially one of the most beautiful, intelligent, and innovative races that He has created," he wrote. "I feel no remorse. I only wish I killed more. I am honored to be the one to send these vile anti-humans into the pit of fire—where they shall remain for eternity."

Among his inspirations, he listed Hitler, Bowers, and Tarrant in New Zealand, putting the three mass murderers alongside Jesus and

Beethoven as models for himself. "To my brothers in blood," he wrote, "make sure that my sacrifice was not in vain. Spread this letter, make memes, shitpost, FIGHT BACK, REMEMBER ROBERT BOWERS, REMEMBER BRENTON TARRANT." Earnest bragged of how, just a week after Tarrant's attack in New Zealand, he had set fire to a San Diego mosque with gasoline, then spray-painted "For Brendon [sic] Tarrant" in the parking lot. "They never found shit on me," he wrote.

On a Saturday morning, Earnest posted his rambling manifesto to 8chan, just as planned, and hours later he drove his Honda Civic to the Chabad of Poway synagogue near his home. It was Shabbat, as well as the final day of Passover, and Jewish worshippers had gathered at the synagogue for prayer and celebration. Earnest, wearing a military-style vest with ammunition in the pockets, came armed with a Smith & Wesson assault rifle, which he had picked up at a local gun shop for $963 just the day before—illegally, as it turned out, since he did not yet have the active hunting license required in California for anyone under twenty-one to buy a gun.

The synagogue had received $150,000 in grant money just weeks earlier to install new gates and security measures at its doors, but it hadn't scheduled the work yet. Earnest raced up the steps of the building toward a front door propped open with a planter and started firing into the lobby before he was even inside, hitting four people, including the rabbi and an eight-year-old girl. One longtime congregant was killed: a sixty-year-old woman, Lori Gilbert-Kaye, who the rabbi said tried to shield him from the sudden gunfire, only to be shot twice herself.

The death toll might have been far higher if Earnest's new rifle didn't apparently jam; he ran toward his car across the street, with an Iraq war veteran and an off-duty border patrol officer in the congregation both giving chase. Earnest fled in his car just as the two men caught up with him. Then he called 911 to report what he had done. "I just shot up a synagogue," he told the dispatcher excitedly as he raced toward the freeway. He wanted the dispatcher to hear what he thought of Jews. "They're destroying our people," he said. "I'm trying to show them that we're not going to go down without a fight. I'm defending my nation against the Jewish people, who are trying to destroy all white people."

After he pleaded guilty to both federal and state charges, Earnest was ultimately given multiple life sentences in prison. At the federal courthouse in San Diego in late 2021, he declined to say anything to the judge before hearing the judgment rendered against him. The young white supremacist had written reams in his manifesto, thousands of words of vile, hateful bigotry, and he had continued ranting to the police dispatcher after the shooting about his hatred for Jews. But now he simply sat in silence in the courtroom, staring at a wall. He had nothing left to say.

## CHAPTER 8

# "TEXT IS BORING BUT MURDER ISN'T"

Blaze Bernstein was back in Orange County, home on winter break from Penn his sophomore year in 2018. He'd been spending time with his family and seeing old friends from the Orange County School of the Arts. He and his close friend Liam had met up for lunch and gone to a Goodwill store together for Blaze to pick out a gift for his family's annual "white elephant" gift-exchange party. He found a garish candle holder shaped like a witch's head. It was ugly. Blaze loved it, and he bought it.

The day after New Year's was a typically balmy one in Orange County. It was a lazy day at the Bernsteins' home, which sat on a cul-de-sac in Foothill Ranch, a lush, wooded patch of southern Orange County tucked between the Santa Ana Mountains to the east and the Pacific Ocean fifteen miles to the west. His grandparents, who lived in the area, were coming over that night, and Blaze wanted to make dinner for everyone. After staying in Philadelphia, where he'd made his turkey bolognese in place of the usual Thanksgiving fare, he now wanted to roast a turkey with all the traditional fixings for his family.

He and his mother went to a nearby Costco to shop for food, but they got split up amid the holiday crowd. Jeanne went to her GPS tracking app, Life360, to figure out where he was; it was a rule that all three of the kids needed to keep the app on, even for Blaze away at college. But his location didn't show up. That's when she realized that he must have turned his off. That concerned her; if something happened and he went missing, they might have no way of finding him. Reconnecting with him a few minutes later, she made him promise to turn it back on.

The meal was a hit—a delicious feast, his mother said, that left her "blown away." Few things made Blaze happier than cooking for his family and friends. Blaze's grandfather, Richard Bernstein, asked Blaze at dinner what his friends at college thought of his unusual first name. Some kids would ask about it, Blaze said, but he had to admit that he couldn't remember the origin. Jeanne and Gideon explained it to him: the name was inspired in part, they said, by Blaise Pascal, a seventeenth-century French mathematician, scientist, and philosopher who invented one of the earliest calculators, among other innovations. His parents told Blaze, always bursting with novel ideas himself, that they were expecting great things ahead for him, too, just like his French namesake.

Blaze smiled, a bit humbled by the story. Great things ahead. After his struggles in the spring, when he'd decided to take the semester off because of the strain of his course load, he was in a good place now. His mood was upbeat, even buoyant; he was excited about returning to college in a few days—especially about becoming the managing editor at *Penn Appétit*, the student magazine for foodies. He talked about a psychology class he was looking forward to taking with a renowned Penn professor. He'd even been getting along well at home with his little sister, Beaue, five years his junior, after years of typical big brother/little sister sniping.

Finally, the leisurely dinner wound down. Blaze said good night to everyone and went upstairs to his room. His parents left not long after to take Beaue to a sleepover at her friend's house.

That was when Blaze heard, once again, from Sam Woodward.

"Well there's a face I haven't seen in a while," Sam wrote to him on Tinder. It had been six months since Sam's first flurry of messages to Blaze on Tinder, pretending to be gay and then pulling back; "pranking" him, as he wrote in his hate journal, out of a long-simmering desire to scare or humiliate young gay men.

Sam was back in Orange County now, too. After his eventful summer of joining up with Atomwaffen Division at the Texas "hate camp" and making his pilgrimage to meet *Siege*'s neo-Nazi author, James Mason, he'd moved back to Newport Beach. Jobless, he'd run out of money to keep living on the road, and he'd moved back to his parents' home, back to his old room.

But Sam certainly wasn't done with Atomwaffen. He was still active in many of the neo-Nazi cell's encrypted online chats about violent white resistance, and he and Tristan Evans, who'd come to California with him, were starting up an Atomwaffen branch in Orange County, with ambitions of taking it statewide. They wanted to spread the gospel of violent neo-Nazism to America's most populous state, with an image different from other such groups in existence. The image of Rob Rundo's white supremacists at RAM training down the Orange County coast—brawny, public street fighters—didn't mesh with Atomwaffen's covert, blow-things-up mindset, and RAM's brand of white supremacy didn't idolize Hitler and the Nazis the way Atomwaffen's did. Sam and Tristan wanted to make their own mark.

Sam's violent online postings and his "pranking" of gays online were only escalating. He'd posted one particularly eerie image on Snapchat just two weeks earlier. It was a photo he'd taken of a drawing he made on a napkin; a knife dripping with blood and a skull with a pair of eyes popping out. With it were the words: "Text is boring but murder isn't." Like his violent postings before, it wasn't flagged or taken down. He also created a new Twitter account under an alias, declaring: "A man has begun to truly live only when he has found something he is willing to die for." And he took a menacing photo of himself, in his home in

Newport Beach, wearing his Atomwaffen skull mask and holding his father's revolver.

On a fake account on Grindr the LGBT dating site, Sam posted a threat to kill "fags," along with a photo of Charles Manson, one of Atomwaffen Division's notorious heroes. At the same time, he reached out to more young gay men online, indicating that he was gay himself and looking for meetups. The same day he messaged Blaze, in fact, he'd contacted another young gay man named Jackson who had also attended the Orange County arts school with them. He used the very same line he'd sent Blaze: "Well there's a face I haven't seen in a while."

Jackson didn't answer him. Blaze didn't either, not at first. Sam messaged him again. Still no response. On his third try, Sam wrote: "Well, this is awkward. I think I owe you an explanation for why I unmatched with you, LOL."

Blaze answered him this time, but curtly. "Fine," he wrote. Sam explained: "I was going through a weird time in my life. I think I figured things out now."

"Okey dokey then," Blaze answered. "Glad you figured things out. Good for you, Sam."

"I'm sorry I didn't really tell you anything," Sam said.

Blaze wasn't impressed. "I literally do not care but woohoo, congrats," he wrote.

After a few more messages, Sam began reeling in his line once again, flirting a bit as he reflected on their Tinder exchange six months earlier. "Can I ask just one question?" he wrote to Blaze. "Why did you 'like' me if you didn't care? I'm confused."

"I must have not even noticed who I was liking," Blaze wrote. "Or I thought you were hot and forgot that I knew you, LOL."

"Damn, knowing me is the biggest turnoff," Sam said. He joked that "you were interested until you realized it was me. LOL."

"Well, you're straight," Blaze said.

Sam reeled the line tighter. He asked Blaze if he was alone. "I might make an exception," he wrote.

Blaze was dubious. "We've already done this prank, Sam," he said. "Remember?"

Sam tried to assure him this was not another prank. Blaze was curious enough to believe him, to imagine that Sam Woodward, the notorious homophobe and bigot from their days at school in Santa Ana, was actually coming on to him. So when Sam told him he'd like to get together that night to hang out and asked him to send his address on Snapchat, Blaze agreed.

At 10:37 p.m., Blaze sent Sam his address on Pallazo Circle in Lake Forest. Within a few minutes, Sam was in the car for the drive from Newport Beach to meet up with Blaze.

Roughly twenty minutes later, Blaze slipped out of the house. No one inside heard him leave. Sam was parked nearby on the street, waiting for him. Blaze didn't expect to be gone very long; he had left his wallet and his glasses in his room. Wearing sweatpants and a striped T-shirt in the warm Orange County night air, he got in the car and they started driving down the hill toward a nearby park.

Not long after they drove away, Blaze texted Liam, whom he'd told about Sam's first overtures to him months earlier. He didn't say now where he was or what he was doing, and he didn't mention anything about seeing Sam. But out of the blue, he wrote: "I did something really horrible for the story... But also no one can ever know."

Liam was baffled by the cryptic message. He knew Blaze could be a bit dramatic sometimes; this seemed like one of those moments.

"What story," he texted back. But Blaze never answered.

# PART II

# "No Turning Back"

## CHAPTER 9

# "THE SPIGOT IS ON FULL BLAST"

America's white supremacists had begun surging to their highest numbers in decades in Trump's first term, fueled by the race-baiting rhetoric of the president himself. Neo-Nazis had always come and gone over the years, but for every one of them who left, there now seemed to be two more eagerly waiting to take his spot—another foot soldier like Sam Woodward in Orange County, another platoon leader like Johnny Denton in Texas, or another online acolyte like Nick Giampa in the suburbs of Washington, DC. The swell was hard to miss.

"The spigot is on full blast," said Christian Picciolini, the onetime skinhead leader in Chicago and front man for a white-power band called Final Solution. Picciolini himself had left white supremacy after experiencing pangs of remorse over beating up a Black teenager outside a McDonald's in Chicago, and he began working to lead young people away from the movement's grip. But that was becoming more difficult than ever, he found, with the political climate ignited by Trump. Eager new recruits were sprouting up faster than his group could extract the old ones. "This environment," Picciolini said, "has created a never-ending queue of people."

The number of white-nationalist hate groups tracked by the Southern Poverty Law Center in Alabama reached a record height of 155 halfway into Trump's first term. Atomwaffen Division, RAM, the Proud Boys, the Oath Keepers, the Ku Klux Klan—they were all in the game now. The specter of the torch-wielding neo-Nazis in Charlottesville in 2017 had proven to be a recruiting boon for white supremacists, drawing in new members from Orange County to Virginia, and nearly two years later, Trump was still defending his assertion that there had been "very fine people on both sides" that day. Joe Biden launched his 2020 presidential bid with a video condemning the display at Charlottesville; the scene had convinced him to seek the White House again, and he declared that Trump's jarring reaction had "shocked the conscience."

If Trump's words set the tone for further racial strife in his first term, his policies at the White House cemented them in practice. Trump himself "almost seemed to have an affinity for these alt-right groups," said Elizabeth Neumann, a top homeland security official in his administration, and his directives reflected that. During his first week in office in 2017, he ordered the controversial "Muslim ban" on foreign travelers that he'd promised during his campaign, with the Supreme Court ultimately upholding a third version of the order that civil rights advocates called discriminatory and unconstitutional. His administration gutted funding for an Obama-era program aimed at countering violent extremism and the radicalization of Americans, and the White House frowned on even using the phrase "domestic terrorism" in official intelligence reports when referring to right-wing extremism. It cut too close to Trump's base, and administration officials knew that they risked the wrath of the president if they veered in its path. At the Justice Department, federal prosecutions for hate crimes in Trump's first term slowed to a trickle, with prosecutors rejecting the vast majority of referrals sent to them by the FBI. Prosecuting hate crimes wasn't a priority for his administration.

With the conflicting and often discouraging signals from the White House under Trump about how to handle the growing threat of domestic extremists, the federal intelligence bureaucracy seemed fractured, even paralyzed. A buried report prepared by the National Counterterrorism Center warned bluntly in 2020 that, when it came to domestic extremism, "there is no whole-of-government threat picture." The myriad federal agencies couldn't even agree on what to call the homegrown threats, much less what to do about them in any cohesive way. Were they "domestic extremists"? "Terrorists"? "Militants"? Or even, in the view of some on the far right and Trump himself, actual patriots? No one seemed certain, or willing to say.

The white supremacists lapped it all up. With their numbers surging, they were becoming more brazen and violent in their tactics. So it was that a Florida truck driver named Burt Colucci—"Commander," as he always wanted to be called—seized the reins of one of the country's most infamous neo-Nazi groups, the National Socialist Movement, which took its name from the original Nazi Party under Hitler, and pushed to make it even more fearsome.

The National Socialists had always reveled in their notoriety. They had become known over the years for staging loud, racist, and often violent marches in full Nazi stormtrooper uniforms, and they had dispatched their members to Charlottesville with shields and rods, attacking counter-protesters arm-in-arm alongside Orange County's Rise Above Movement and others. But the National Socialists' longtime leader, Jeff Schoep—long one of the most recognizable faces of neo-Nazism in America—abruptly quit the group two years later in 2019. After two decades spent mercilessly bashing Jews and Blacks, as well as a range of other minorities and "multiethnic scum," Schoep (pronounced "Scoop") claimed a change of heart and declared that he was ready to give up white supremacy for good.

It was a tumultuous time for Schoep's neo-Nazis, hit with a series of setbacks in their backward quest to promote their Aryan agenda. The National Socialists were named as a defendant in a massive federal lawsuit over the violence that day in Charlottesville. One of its Missouri members died in a shootout with the FBI after allegedly plotting to bomb a hospital filled with Covid-19 patients and other possible targets, including a school filled with Black students, a synagogue, and a mosque. In the strangest twist of all, Schoep signed over legal control of the neo-Nazi group—unwittingly, he claimed—to a Black preacher and activist from Southern California; the preacher, James Stern, convinced Schoep that turning over control could help protect his group from all the outside legal threats it was facing. Instead, in a bit of bait and switch, Stern made plans to use the neo-Nazi group's notorious name and its website to air anti-hate material and Holocaust movies like *Schindler's List* in order to mute the group's decades-long message of hate. Then Schoep himself quit the group.

From his home outside Orlando, not far from Disney World, Burt Colucci eagerly stepped into the void. Colucci, then in his early forties, was a burly Italian American with a goatee and the customary shaved head of a neo-Nazi. His hatred of minorities had taken root early. When he was growing up near Niagara Falls, a few isolated interactions he had with Black schoolchildren bused into his area first turned him against an entire race of people, he said, and his hatred ultimately ballooned into a violent, blatant strain of racism targeting virtually all minorities, leading him to the neo-Nazi movement. He wore his hatred on his sleeve. He loathed Blacks as "animalistic and barbaric," Jews were all "liars" and "toxic," and he found Trump "fearless and inspirational," a politician finally willing to stand up for white men. He was anxious to take over the remnants of the National Socialists, even with all its legal and organizational baggage. After another legal fight with Stern, Colucci tweaked the name of the group slightly, moved it from Michigan to his home state of Florida for legal reasons, and worked to bring back its hard-core image as "true" neo-Nazis.

Schoep had tried to blur that image before his exit, removing the swastika as the group's symbol and replacing it with a more obscure Aryan hate symbol, and he tried, implausibly, to repackage the group as a "white civil rights group," rather than simply the virulent, bigoted neo-Nazi clan that it had always been. In hindsight, Schoep later laughed off his own rebranding efforts as naive. "It sounds ridiculous or stupid now," he said in an interview. "What kind of idiot thinks he can turn the Nazis into a civil rights organization?"

## "The Spigot Is on Full Blast"

Colucci certainly didn't. The Florida trucker hated the rebranding; he thought it had cost the group members from their loyal base and "alienated a lot of good members," and he wanted to appeal once again to "traditional" Nazis. He quickly brought back the swastika, with all its ominous power; not only would he display it on large banners at public events, but sometimes he would construct huge wooden swastikas and light them on fire to produce a glowing testament to terror.

"We embrace the swastika. We obviously love Hitler," Colucci declared unapologetically. "Why are we trying to reinvent the wheel here? There's nothing you could improve on." The swastika "was perfect," Colucci said, and it was a sign of fear and defeat for the National Socialists to ever back away from it. "Fear no one, that's what Hitler said, and that's what I say," he declared.

With so much minority-bashing from neo-Nazis now pouring out online, Colucci and his men took to the streets to demonstrate their rage the old-fashioned way—in person. He drove his truck up to Michigan to crash a big Gay Pride festival that was being held in Detroit. He led a small cadre of about a dozen National Socialists in full Nazi uniform, including the reclaimed swastika armbands, as they marched on the outskirts of the festival, shouting slogans from the Third Reich, anti-gay slurs, and other ethnic broadsides against all the dreaded *others*—Jews, Blacks, immigrants, and other minorities. Five of the men carried rifles or pistols—perfectly legal under Michigan's open-carry laws. "America is for whites, and whites only! Everyone else get the fuck out!" one member shouted as they marched. "*Sieg heil!*"

One of his neo-Nazi followers urinated on an Israeli flag, and Colucci himself shoved a female counter-protester down to the pavement from behind after she walked in front of him without ever touching him. "Touch us again and I'm going to fucking put you out!" he threatened as she picked herself up off the street. None of the police patrolling the area did anything, as Colucci continued ranting. "Fuck you, n****r!" he yelled at another counter-protester minutes later. "Fucking monkey motherfucker."

None of the neo-Nazis were arrested, even though Detroit police chief James Craig, an African American, acknowledged afterward that Colucci and his men came looking for violence in an effort to produce a "Charlottesville Number 2." His handling of the neo-Nazis sparked a backlash from local activists and politicians. The police gave the neo-Nazis their own police escort for their march to keep them away from counter-protesters, and Craig declared that "both sides were wrong," even as videos circulated showing Colucci and his men assaulting and threatening counter-protesters. It was the same kind of moral equivalency heard two years earlier from President Trump himself after Charlottesville and, again, the neo-Nazis were thrilled.

For Colucci, the day was a win in his efforts to reclaim the group's notorious status. As the courts had long held, the First Amendment protected even the most offensive and repugnant "hate speech" in the public square, so long as it didn't threaten to incite imminent lawlessness. It was Colucci's neo-Nazi forebears with the National Socialists of America, in a landmark Supreme Court case in 1977, who had won the right to march through Skokie, Illinois, in a neighborhood filled with Holocaust survivors forced to witness the revival of the Nazis. Colucci and the modern-day National Socialists were now determined to squeeze every drop of free speech that they could from America's broad embrace of First Amendment protections. The revulsion that Colucci met at every street corner only seemed to embolden him, further fueling his rage.

Leading small groups of one or two neo-Nazis at a time, Colucci kept on marching anyplace he could—in the streets in Michigan, in Pennsylvania, in Florida, in Arizona. Journalists and outraged protesters would flock to the events, sometimes outnumbering the neo-Nazis themselves. Colucci would hurl racial epithets at every turn and threaten to fight the protesters, sometimes pushing or shoving them in what he always claimed were acts of self-defense, but he never got arrested for it—not until a trip to Phoenix for a neo-Nazi rally there in 2021.

At the parking lot of a hotel in suburban Phoenix where he was staying for the rally, Colucci confronted a carload of Black visitors from Milwaukee, two men and two women, who were staying at the same hotel. They were celebrating a family birthday in the area. As usual, Colucci came looking for a fight. He claimed he saw them dropping some garbage in the parking lot, a claim no one else could verify. He angrily began chucking trash and bottles on the windshield of their Mercedes SUV and spewing racial slurs, calling them "apes," "monkeys," and "n****rs," and telling them to leave the country, according to witness statements. Another neo-Nazi pal with Colucci, wearing a "White Power" T-shirt with a gun holstered on his right hip, joined him in the tirade.

After the Milwaukee visitors began throwing the trash back at Colucci and swearing at him, Colucci grabbed a pistol from his front pocket and began waving it wildly and pointing it at them, according to one witness interviewed by police. "Come on n****rs, I'm gonna kill all y'all monkeys," he yelled, according to one woman in the Mercedes. Then he grabbed a container of pepper-spray from his pocket and doused the passengers in the car with it, the witnesses said.

Officers from the Chandler, Arizona, police department arrived to break up the fracas, but they didn't arrest Colucci—not then, at least. He was a walking hate crime, broadcasting his violent, racist intentions to anyone who would listen, but police gave him a pass.

Just a few hours later, though, Colucci and his neo-Nazi pal confronted the same group of African Americans yet again when they spotted the group returning to the hotel parking lot; Colucci pulled out his gun again, holding it menacingly at his side, and began spewing racial expletives at them anew, witnesses said. "You fucking monkeys never learn, do you?" Colucci yelled, according to a video that police reviewed. "I'm the leader of the largest neo-Nazi organization in America!" he boasted. "You better get in the car and fucking leave!"

No one was injured in the fracas, but the Black visitors from Milwaukee were still visibly shaken when police returned to the hotel parking lot for a second time that morning. They had just been confronted by a gun-waving neo-Nazi telling them that their type was not welcome. "Today just changed my whole entire life. I never had something like this happen to me in my life," one of the visitors told police. Colucci and his friend were defiant. Even as police were interviewing witnesses at the scene about what had happened, officers spotted the pair giving a Nazi salute to the Black visitors in the Mercedes across the parking lot.

Police finally slapped two sets of handcuffs on Colucci and arrested him as he stood next to his pickup truck, charging him with aggravated assault and disorderly conduct. He denied pointing a gun at anyone during the confrontation. But he readily admitted that he was the "commander" of the National Socialists Movement and warned ominously that, as a result of his arrest, "Chandler is about to become 'Ground Zero' for their movement," according to the police report.

Arizona, unlike most states, doesn't have a hate-crime law that would allow prosecutors to bring charges for targeting the victims because they were Black. Instead, Colucci faced criminal charges that would net him, at most, only three years in prison. Ending up in cuffs didn't leave Colucci with any second thoughts about his extremist path, though. He would never become one of "the formers," like Jeff Schoep, who renounced white supremacy, he vowed. When he was asked if he ever saw himself leaving the neo-Nazi movement, Colucci began railing anew against "Blacks burning down our cities," against "Mexicans invading our country," and against "Jewish supremacists" dominating the world economy.

"As long as things stay the way they are," Colucci vowed, he would remain a neo-Nazi.

---

Jeff Schoep was trying to distance himself as much as he could from his own quarter century as the fiery leader of the National Socialists. After quitting the group and allowing Colucci to succeed him, Schoep began a *mea culpa* tour around America, warning about how dire the climate of hatred had become. He sat for interviews, including one with the Jewish newspaper in his home city of Detroit, to discuss "the burden and the shame from my past and the things that I've done." He traveled to a synagogue in Skokie, Illinois—site of the infamous neo-Nazi march of Supreme Court lore four decades earlier—to tell Jews of his new attitude, ask their forgiveness, and even exchange hugs with them. And he went to Southern California in 2020 to appear at special hearing on the "State of Hate" organized by the California State Assembly.

Schoep was coming for forgiveness, but Brian Levin wasn't willing to give it to him so quickly. Levin, a longtime Orange County resident who led a research center on hate and extremism at the state college in nearby San Bernardino, helped to organize the hearing and was speaking alongside Schoep, but he was skeptical of the neo-Nazi's sudden conversion. He suspected that it might have as much to do with Schoep's legal troubles—chiefly the threat of the coming lawsuit over his group's role in the Charlottesville violence—as with any sudden epiphany or moral compulsion, as Schoep insisted. Levin didn't want to let Schoep off that easy.

Levin, a lawyer and a professor, was a Zelig-like figure when it came to hate crimes and extremists, popping up in myriad roles in four decades of rising racial tension in America.

During a stint as a street cop for the New York Police Department when he was just out of college in the late 1980s, he sat down to talk with a girl who had left a swastika at the apartment door of an elderly Jewish woman, counseling her about the gravity of what she'd done rather than arresting her. As a law student at Stanford, before he'd even taken the bar exam, he wrote a legal brief before the Supreme Court arguing in favor of what became the high court's unanimous landmark verdict in 1993 affirming the use of hate-crime laws for stiffer sentences. As a young lawyer, he won a $1.1-million verdict against a neo-Nazi in Pennsylvania for terrorizing a local housing rights activist with racist postings branding her a "race traitor" who should be lynched.

From his small research center in San Bernardino, Levin surveyed major police departments around the country regularly on hate-crime reports and often identified the national trend lines—all on the rise of late—before the FBI itself. Going back to the vitriol of the 2016 presidential campaign, Levin had tracked how each attack from Trump on one minority group or another—Mexican "rapists," Muslim "terrorists," and the like—preceded another round of senseless hate crimes against the *others*. He could track the triggers like clockwork. And it was only worsening.

Levin had testified regularly before Congress about the culture of hate infecting America, leading neo-Nazis to post the clip of him in one of their chilling recruitment videos juxtaposed with their own members firing assault rifles at a Jewish Star of David. And he also showed up at many white supremacist events himself to monitor their activities, earning him occasional notoriety. At a Ku Klux Klan rally in Orange County in 2016, with supporters shouting Trump's name, he found himself standing between a fallen Klansman and a rush of angry counter-protesters, holding out his arms to keep the counter-protesters at bay. "Get away, get away!" he shouted at as he perched over the Klansman. "Don't hurt him!...That's not what Dr. King was about!" As loathsome as the Klan's racist views were, and as brazen as the white supremacists had become, Levin didn't think violence was the answer. Video of the incongruous scene led the *Daily Stormer*, the notorious neo-Nazi website, to label Levin "the Jewish Batman." He hated the nickname.

Levin was passionate about combating hate crimes as an insidious threat to the country, yet here he was on a panel sitting side by side with Jeff Schoep—who, for so long, had been "America's poster boy for Nazism," as Levin called him. It was hard for him to reconcile.

Before the event began, as the speakers gathered over cheese and grapes for a reception, Levin spotted Schoep across the room. Apart from the shaved head, Schoep held little resemblance to the fiery neo-Nazi who had appeared at so many hate-filled demonstrations over the years, denigrating Jews and Blacks and immigrants as vile and subhuman. Instead of his old Nazi uniform, Schoep now wore a conservative black suit, with a black-and-purple tie and a matching pocket square. His voice, booming and bombastic in his neo-Nazi oratories, was now halting and nervous as he mingled with the assembled guests. His tone was reserved.

Levin wasn't the confrontational type, and he didn't swear much, but as he looked over at Schoep munching on some grapes, he couldn't help thinking back on all the hateful, violent rhetoric he'd heard from him over the years, and all the hate crimes it had fueled in Orange County and beyond. He walked over to him angrily. "I don't care what the fuck else you plan to say, but the first thing out of your mouth better be an apology," Levin said, "because you don't know the damage you wreaked on my community."

Schoep seemed taken aback. "Absolutely," he said.

When the event itself started and it was Schoep's turn to speak, he began by displaying for the audience an ominous sight: a photo of a huge wooden swastika in flames at one of the many National Socialists rallies that he had led. After just a few moments, though, he began to stammer and cut away from his notes. "Before I get on to this, though," he said, clearing his throat, "I'd like to apologize to the local community for the part my organization had in some of the incidents that took place here over the years." A few people started clapping, then more joined in, with Brian Levin, a few seats down from Schoep, among them.

"It's not easy," Schoep continued, "to get up here and after twenty-seven years in a movement to admit that you were wrong, that the life that you lived, my entire adult life, was wrong and incorrect, so bear with me."

He talked of how easy it was to get sucked in, and how difficult it was to get out. He knew that even with him gone, there would be more young men willing to take his place—more than ever before, in fact. Neo-Nazi groups were like a cult, he told his audience—a "bubble" where angry young white men listened only to the vile things that their leaders wanted them to hear and see online, isolated and shut off from the rest of the world by their own bigotry and bias. Trump's racial rhetoric and the growing cesspool of violent, racist material online had made the task easier to accomplish than ever, he said.

Neo-Nazi leaders like Schoep knew the buttons to push to bring in recruits, either online or in person: identifying a kid victimized by a

Black person or an immigrant and playing off his fear and anger; highlighting the myth of Jewish world "domination" and denying that the Holocaust had really happened; or telling young Christians that "the White race is the Chosen People of God."

The neo-Nazis—or "we," as Schoep still called them out of habit—boasted a veritable playbook for recruiting young people, complete with video games, social media videos, podcasts, and leaflets all stressing different parts of their "commonality" as whites in their fight against the *others*. That was how they hooked them. "If we get 'em in the door," Schoep said, "that's all we were trying to do." And in an era of such intense racial divisions in America, more young neo-Nazi recruits were now coming in the door than ever before.

## CHAPTER 10

# "WHO'S SAM WOODWARD?"

Blaze was missing. He was supposed to be meeting his mother, Jeanne, at the dentist's office that afternoon, and they were going to get lunch together afterward. But he hadn't shown up at the dentist. That wasn't like him; Blaze was a punctual kid, always on top of his schedule. He didn't just miss appointments with no explanation.

Jeanne couldn't reach him on his cell phone, so she tried Gideon at his office. Did he know where Blaze was? Had anyone even seen him today at home? Gideon tried calling Blaze, but his calls went straight to voice mail, too. A house cleaner checked inside Blaze's closed bedroom door, but she told Jeanne he wasn't there. She was growing panicky now.

She and Gideon both rushed home, but there was no sign of Blaze. His Prius was sitting outside, right where he'd left it. In his bedroom, Jeanne and Gideon found his wallet, his eyeglasses, his phone charger, his medicine—just as he had left them. It didn't even look like Blaze had been home the night before. His bed hadn't been slept in. In fact, they realized no one had seen him since he went upstairs to his room after putting together his feast of a dinner the night before for his parents, his siblings, and his grandparents. And the location tracker still wasn't finding him; he hadn't turned it back on after the episode at the Costco the day before.

So began a heart-wrenching search for Blaze, a drama that Gideon later likened to a surreal episode of a crime procedural on television, except that he and Jeanne now found themselves at the center of the real-life drama. All the events blurred past them, an out-of-body experience, as if these things were happening to someone else. Pacing, waiting, praying, hoping. Filing a missing-person report with the Orange County Sheriff's Department. Making hurried calls to Blaze's friends to see if they knew where he was. Trying to get into his computer and social media accounts for any hints. Gideon combing the neighborhood and a nearby park and screaming Blaze's name, thinking about his son—short and slight, not terribly athletic, a bit clumsy—lying injured or worse in the woods. Calling out his name over and over.

Gideon kept turning over possible explanations in his mind: Blaze was just having cell phone problems, or maybe he was doing something that he didn't want his parents to know about. Kids do things like this sometimes, a sheriff's deputy told him reassuringly after responding to the missing-person report; they decide they don't want to go back to college, the deputy said, then they just buy a plane ticket to escape somewhere, before turning up safe and sound. Gideon listened—hopeful, wanting to believe that his son was okay—but that didn't sound like the Blaze he knew.

Blaze's friends were growing worried, too. Liam Williams hadn't gotten any response from Blaze after his cryptic text late the night before about doing something "horrible." He tried Blaze again the next day after learning of his disappearance. "hey I'm really worried about you," he said in a text. "please text me." Still no response.

But Liam did hear from Blaze's sister, Beaue, with an urgent query later that night. Beaue, five years younger than Blaze, had managed to get into Blaze's Snapchat account and some of his other social media accounts on his laptop after he went missing. Among all the messages between Blaze and his usual group of friends, Beaue noticed an exchange with someone it looked like Blaze was planning to meet the

## "Who's Sam Woodward?"

night before, the night before he'd gone missing. It was a name she didn't recognize, so she texted Liam to ask about it.

"who's sam woodward," Beaue asked him.

---

Gideon had never heard his son mention anyone named Sam Woodward either, but now he was on the phone late that night trying to reach him. Jeanne and Beaue were with him at their home, and they taped the call. Just in case.

Sam picked up his phone.

Gideon, his voice remarkably calm after a day of panic, told Sam that he'd seen the messages between him and Blaze. "He's been missing and we haven't heard from him all day," Gideon said. "You're the first clue to the puzzle." Gideon wanted to know: Had Sam seen him?

Sam seemed frazzled, his voice halting and breathless as he launched into his account of what had happened the night before. Yes, he had seen Blaze, he told Gideon; they'd hung out for a while in the parking lot at the Hobby Lobby a few minutes' drive from the Bernsteins' house, he said, and Sam had a cherry Coke. Blaze didn't want anything to drink, he said. Then Blaze announced that he wanted to meet up with "a third friend" — apparently another student from the Orange County School of the Arts, Sam said; no, he didn't catch his name — but Blaze was planning to meet up with the other friend outside the local library right up the road, less than a mile away. It was almost midnight, maybe earlier, maybe later. Sam wasn't sure because he said his watch had broken. He sounded more confused. Sam said that he'd driven Blaze up there in his car and then watched him walk off toward the library, next to a heavily wooded park, expecting him to come back soon. But he never did, Sam said.

"I searched all over for him," Sam told Gideon. "I couldn't find him anywhere." He tried calling him, he said. No answer. Sam said he thought something might have happened to Blaze. "I'm scared now," he explained. He hoped maybe Blaze would contact him in the morning, Sam said, but he didn't hear anything more from him.

If Gideon suspected that Sam was lying, he didn't let on. He appealed for Sam's help in doing anything he could to find their son. "This is becoming kind of an urgent issue, trying to figure out what really happened to him at the park, and we really need your help on this because you're the last person that probably saw him," Gideon said. "You're a nice young man, and I'm asking for your help on this."

Sam said he would do anything he could to help. "I wanna find Blaze as much as you do," he said. They hung up.

"I think he did it," Jeanne declared flatly. "He did something to Blaze. Let's call the police."

---

The police were on the phone with Sam themselves soon after he spoke with Blaze's parents. That night, just before 11:00 p.m., Orange County Sheriff's Deputy Patrick White was at the Bernstein home in Lake Forest, and Gideon and Jeanne led him through the day's events—Blaze's no-show at the dentist, the wallet and other items left in his room, all the unanswered calls to his cell phone. They reached the part about the messages from the unfamiliar name. Gideon gave the deputy the phone number, and White went straight out to his patrol car to call Sam Woodward from the car.

Sam picked up right away. He seemed calm and matter-of-fact now as he answered the deputy's questions, running through the same drill he had gone through with Gideon: how he had picked Blaze up at his house; how they went to the Hobby Lobby to "catch up" and then to Borrego Park before Blaze abruptly announced that he was going off to meet another friend in the park; and how Sam waited at the park for an hour for Blaze to return. But he never did, Sam said, so he went to his girlfriend's house. He thought maybe Blaze was "pranking" him, he told the deputy; or just "being a jerk." Hours later, around 3:40 in the morning, Sam said, he became worried, so he returned to the park and roamed around the woods calling Blaze's name into the darkness. No answer. So he went home to his parents' place in Newport Beach.

The account, as full of holes as it was, didn't strike the deputy as suspicious. For the moment, the Sheriff's Department regarded Sam merely as a witness, not someone who might be involved in Blaze's disappearance. But his account did give investigators a place to focus their search: Borrego Park, the area where their newfound "witness" said he had last seen Blaze. The park sat next to the elementary school that Blaze had attended and an athletic field where he'd played soccer, butting up against a sprawling wilderness.

For days, search teams scoured the area by foot, with police dogs trying to pick up a scent, and by air, with volunteer drone operators taking aerial footage. The Sheriff's Department put out fliers and public notices pleading for help. "Help us find Blaze Bernstein," urged a Facebook page set up to help in the hunt.

Almost overnight, Blaze's disappearance became a Southern California–style mystery, with celebrities like cast members of *The Real Housewives of Orange County* and Los Angeles Lakers' basketball star Kobe Bryant—who happened to belong to the same Newport Beach church as Sam Woodward's family—tweeting out their support publicly, and media across the country, from ABC's *Good Morning America* to Blaze's campus newspaper at the University of Pennsylvania, picking up on the story of the search for the missing Ivy Leaguer.

A few possible sightings called in by tipsters produced nothing. Psychics sent in leads about Blaze's supposed whereabouts, too. For Gideon and Jeanne, hope was turning to dread with each passing day, even as more than a dozen friends and family members packed into their home to do whatever they could to help in the search. Six computer stations were set up atop their dining room table, an ad hoc command center, for the volunteers to track all the online leads. Gideon and Jeanne pleaded for the public's help, their anguish laid bare. "I can't figure out why anybody would want to hurt my son," Jeanne told one interviewer. There was a direct plea to Blaze himself, if he could hear her: "If there's any way you can come home, whatever has happened, wherever you've been, whoever you've talked to—it doesn't matter," Jeanne said. "We love you so much that we would give up everything. We have to have you back."

Sheriff's investigator Dylan Jantzen was at Borrego Park to help in the search two days after Blaze's disappearance. Jantzen was a homicide investigator; this was still a missing-person case for now, not a homicide, but if it turned into something worse, he knew he would likely be the one in charge. He wanted to be ready.

Walking through Borrego Park in search of clues the deputies might have missed, he noticed a young man in a dark hooded sweatshirt walking near the restrooms by the entrance. He recognized him; it was Sam Woodward, the kid who had spoken with a sheriff's deputy by phone about hanging out with Blaze that night. He noticed that Sam had gotten a new look since Blaze's disappearance, dying his hair jet black on top and buzzing it on the side in a skinhead-style. It was a curious place for Sam to be, back at the very spot in the park where he had told the deputy he'd last seen Blaze. And it was strange to see him wearing a hooded sweatshirt on a hot California afternoon with the temperature near eighty degrees. Jantzen took note, but he didn't approach him—not yet.

Hours later, Jantzen spotted Sam again—still in the park, still wandering around, still looking out of place. He approached him this time with another investigator and began chatting him up, telling Sam they just had a few more questions about the night he'd seen Blaze.

At first, Sam stuck largely to the account he had given the deputy on the phone, but this time, he seemed nervous: breathing heavily, talking rapid-fire. Jantzen noticed him shaking as they spoke. Then Sam's story began to veer from his initial account, adding brand-new details, contradicting others. He talked about a moment in the car when he said he and Blaze were parked outside the Hobby Lobby: Blaze started to kiss him, Sam said this time. On the lips. Sam said he pushed him back and moved away from him. He had the urge to call him a "fucking faggot," Sam told the detectives, clenching his jaw and his fist as he uttered the words. It was the first sign he revealed to law enforcement of his feelings about gays.

Homosexuality was "gross" and "disgusting," he said, before abruptly changing his tone, as if he suddenly realized the ugliness of his words. "Well, who am I to judge?" asked Sam, now echoing the refrain about tolerance for gays made famous by Pope Francis years before.

The officers' suspicion only grew as they steered the questioning toward Sam's earlier statement about going to see his girlfriend at her home after Blaze disappeared into the park. Her name was Donna, he told Jantzen. No, he didn't know her last name, he said. No, he didn't know her address, either. He hadn't actually gone to her house, he said now; they had met up at another park in Orange County sometime after 1:00 a.m. and they "made out underneath the gazebo," Sam told the detective.

Sam and the investigators began walking through the park, retracing the steps that Sam said he took to look in vain for Blaze in the dead of night. Down a footpath that led from the park toward the wilderness trail, past a basketball court, near a set of green metal benches. The investigator noticed that Sam kept his hands jammed in his pockets almost the whole time. As they walked, Sam mentioned in passing that he'd spent the past summer in Texas, working in construction. There was no mention of his new friends at Atomwaffen Division, or his time in the Texas brushlands at the neo-Nazi "hate camp." That was better left unsaid. Jantzen asked Sam if they could go back to the Orange County sheriff's headquarters in Santa Ana and talk some more. He agreed.

At the station, Jantzen got a good look at Sam's hands for the first time, no longer jammed in his pockets; there were cuts and scrapes all over the fingers and knuckles on both of his hands. No wonder he didn't want the detectives to see his hands. Jantzen asked him what had happened. He was in a fight club, Sam explained, and his sparring opponent the day before had clawed at him, scraping him up a bit. The detective noticed dirt caked underneath his fingernails, and he asked Sam how they had gotten so dirty. He had an explanation for that, too: he'd fallen into a puddle during his sparring match, he said.

Sam's story was unraveling. Officially, at least, he was still considered a mere "witness" in the investigation into Blaze's disappearance, but slowly, Orange County investigators were beginning to look at him as something more than that.

---

A week after Blaze went missing, Detective Jantzen wanted to go back with his investigators to Borrego Park. They'd traced the last known signal from Blaze's cell phone to the north end of the park, but they still hadn't found any sign of him in their prior canvassing. Jantzen thought they might have missed something. It had been pouring much of the day, and the rainfall had dislodged some of the dirt and terrain since they had last searched there. Another investigator noticed some debris they hadn't seen before, and he used a wooden tree stake to poke at the dirt. He called out to Jantzen searching nearby. Jantzen sensed instantly from the urgent tone what it was.

There, in a shallow grave only a few inches or so below the surface, was a body. It was a young man wearing sweatpants and a striped T-shirt, with a hoodie covering his head. The deputies turned the body

The park near Blaze Bernstein's home in southern Orange County where he was stabbed to death.

over in the makeshift grave, laying him on his back. His eyes were still open. The victim's face and neck were riddled with stab wounds. They would need to await official confirmation from the coroner, but even at first glance, they were confident it was the young man they had been trying to find for a week now. It was Blaze. Their search was over.

Investigators went to the Bernsteins' home to deliver the news; they thought they had found Blaze's body. "Stay away from the park," one of the investigators told them, "and don't talk about it."

For Jeanne and Gideon, after a weeklong search, the moment was excruciating and surreal. Blaze was really dead, barely a mile from their home. Gone, at the age of nineteen. "Suddenly a big piece of who we were," Gideon said, "had disappeared."

The next day, the Sheriff's Department scheduled a news conference at the sheriff's station in Lake Forest, and Jeanne and Gideon decided, despite all the trauma of the last twenty-four hours, that they wanted to be there. "Our family is devastated by the news," Gideon told reporters. "We, like so many of you around the world, love Blaze and wanted nothing more than his safe return." Tearfully, he grabbed hold of Jeanne.

More than three hundred people turned out that same night for a candlelight vigil at the park, not far from where Blaze's body had been found in the shallow grave. There was still no one in custody for the young man's violent death. Yellow ribbons were wrapped around trees and light poles to memorialize Blaze. Gideon and Jeanne brought Blaze's two younger siblings and his grandfather, Richard, who choked back tears as he spoke. There was relief, at least, in finally knowing his grandson's fate, he said; "We thank God for this hard rain that exposed his grave."

---

Even as his friends and family were burning candles for Blaze, with his case now escalated from a missing person to a murder, Orange County sheriff's investigators were trailing Sam Woodward's every move. From an undercover police vehicle, they videotaped him as he parked his car around the corner from his parents' house in Newport Beach, out of sight; he used a rag and a spray bottle to wipe down the vehicle and, on another trip, removed a bulky bag.

Electronic surveillance of his computer would give investigators a glimpse into his frantic Internet searches after Blaze's disappearance, as he queried "can DNA get you arrested?" and "how long is security footage kept?" at Borrego Park. He also reached out to his fellow Atomwaffen members on their encrypted Discord channel; he didn't say anything about Blaze's death, but he spoke stoically about "the passing of life" and, reflecting back on his time in Texas, he told the other members that he was "truly grateful for our time together." And he talked of going to Atomwaffen's next "hate camp" scheduled in Nevada.

Two days after the vigil, a team of more than a dozen investigators raided Sam's home with a search warrant in the dead of night, just before 3:00 a.m. They combed through the home for hours, inside and out. In the front lawn, shoved behind some shrubbery by a fence, they found a sleeping bag. An investigator eyeballed it and called over a colleague to take a look at the staining on it. It looked to both of them like dried blood. They bagged it as evidence for the lab personnel to examine. A search of Sam's silver Nissan, seized by sheriff's deputies, would turn up four more traces of blood stains on one of the sun visors. And the investigators found something else in the car: a stained piece of fabric with a ghoulish skull on it. They put that in an evidence bag as well, its significance not apparent until months later. It was Sam's Atomwaffen mask, the one he'd worn at the Texas hate camp as he posed for "Heil Hitlers."

Inside the house, in Sam's large, cluttered bedroom, the investigators found knives from Sam's collection scattered around the room. One in particular, tucked inside a desk drawer, stood out. It was a folding knife with the name of Sam's father, "Blake Woodward," etched into it—the prized knife that his father had given him. On both the wooden handle and the tip of the metal blade, they noticed staining. It looked, again, like blood.

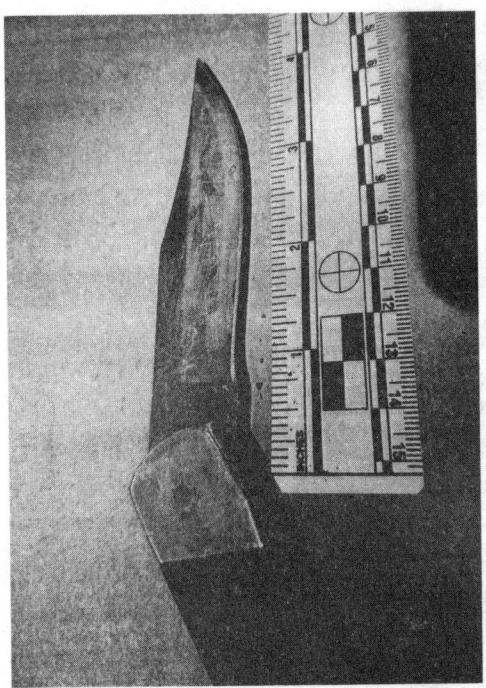

The knife used to stab Blaze Bernstein more than two dozen times.

It didn't seem as though Sam had made much of an effort to hide the knife, or to discard it. His attempts all along at an alibi—explaining Blaze's sudden disappearance at the park to go meet a friend; or the girlfriend whose last name he couldn't remember; or the scratches on his own hands at a fight club—seemed equally half-hearted. Now there was a knife with apparent blood stains on it, sitting in his drawer. It was almost as if he wanted to get caught.

Forensic scientists at the Orange County crime lab soon found in the blood traces what they described as a near-certain match to Blaze's DNA; the odds of the DNA belonging to someone else were "more rare than one in one trillion unrelated individuals," according to one forensic examiner. The blood on the sleeping bag and on the car visor came back as matches, too.

Sheriff's investigators now had enough evidence from the raid of the Woodwards' home to move against Sam. Two days after the candlelight vigil, sheriff's investigators trailed Sam's silver Nissan as he drove off with his mother, Michele, from their home in Newport Beach.

Sam Woodward's mug shot following his arrest on charges of murdering Blaze Bernstein.

After just a few miles, the officers pulled him over, handcuffed him, and placed him under arrest on suspicion of murdering Blaze Bernstein. He was wearing a T-shirt with a message strikingly at odds with the situation in which he now found himself. "Keep the Peace," it read.

The Bernsteins buried their son three days later. The rabbi at their synagogue, Rabbi Arnie Rachlis, who had watched Blaze grow from a student at religious school to a bar mitzvah, a classroom helper, and an Ivy League student, spoke of Blaze's "unforgettable smile," his endless potential, and the numbness, anger, and inexplicability of his murder. The rabbi had attended college at the University of Pennsylvania himself decades earlier, and he recalled Blaze sitting in his office, looking at the Penn diploma on the wall, and saying: "In a few years, I'll have one too." Tragically, the rabbi said, that would no longer happen.

That same day, a sealed search warrant affidavit in the case, leaked to the hometown *Orange County Register*, showed just how violent the murder was: Blaze had been stabbed some twenty times, the affidavit

## "Who's Sam Woodward?"

said. The report also noted Sam's claim, unverified and self-serving, that Blaze had tried to kiss him in the car and that he had pushed him away.

The timing of the leak was especially unnerving for Jeanne and Gideon: on the day they were burying their son, they were learning new details about the sheer violence of his death—along with the salacious claim that he had somehow pursued his attacker. It made an already traumatic day doubly difficult for a family mourning their eldest child.

But within the ranks of Atomwaffen Division, the neo-Nazis were hailing the murder. "I love this," one member wrote in an encrypted chat on Discord after learning of the arrest of "Saboteur," their fellow member. Sam was "a one man gay Jew wrecking crew," wrote another. "Samuel 'Gay Jew Wrecking Crew' Woodward," chimed in Kaleb Cole, an Atomwaffen leader in Washington State. "That's his new name."

## CHAPTER 11

# "THE SWORD HAS BEEN DRAWN"

Blaze Bernstein's murder, and his suspected killer's ties to the shadowy group known as Atomwaffen Division, would bring new scrutiny to the once-obscure band of extremists—from the FBI down through local law enforcement in Orange County. But the attention didn't deter the neo-Nazis. With their numbers and influence expanding both in the United States and abroad—cells were springing up in Canada, Britain, Germany, Russia, the Baltics, Australia, and elsewhere—Atomwaffen was able to escalate its campaign of racially fueled terror, even with a number of its original leaders now behind bars.

From within the walls of the federal prison in Atlanta, the hate group's founder, ex–National Guardsman Brandon Russell, managed to put out a public call to arms to his fellow neo-Nazis in the spring of 2018, mere months after Blaze's killing. Earlier, Russell had sounded a note of contrition when he stood before a Florida judge and received a five-year prison sentence for stockpiling illegal explosives at his condo, where his two fellow neo-Nazis had been murdered. "I'm sorry for what I have done," he told the judge that day in a soft voice.

## "The Sword Has Been Drawn"

But there was no hint of regret in the threatening video message that he put out from federal prison with the help of Atomwaffen's newly empowered Texas branch, despite all the security restrictions on inmates aimed at preventing such material from getting out. Instead, Russell raised the specter of racial violence and terrorism anew, apologies aside.

Russell quoted two of his sadistic role models in the video—Adolf Hitler and Charles Manson—and he thanked the "loyal comrades who've stuck around through thick and thin." But the video, with a montage of violent Nazi imagery, was aimed as much at Atomwaffen's ex-members—the ones Russell said had "abandoned ship" and were suspected of snitching to authorities or journalists—as it was at the group's current followers. Russell mentioned three turncoats by name, in fact. To them and their ilk, he vowed retaliation. "There is no room in this world for cowardly people, so there is certainly no room for you in the Atomwaffen Division," he said. "The sword has been drawn. There is no turning back."

The imprisoned neo-Nazi leader also had a message for "outsiders who are trying to hinder our efforts." To them, he said with an air of grandiosity: "I created something beautiful. Beautiful things scare you people. You don't like it because it doesn't like you."

---

A. C. Thompson, an investigative reporter in California with ProPublica, was one of the "outsiders." As much as any other journalist in America, Thompson had been shining a spotlight on the resurgence of white supremacists in America during the Trump era, exposing secrets that Russell and other neo-Nazis didn't want to see revealed.

Thompson, who played in punk rock bands before turning to journalism, had first written about neo-Nazis in the 1990s, then moved on to other topics. But he turned back to them the day after Trump's election in 2016, dropping another project to focus instead on what felt to him and his editor like a foreboding moment in American history. There was plenty to cover. He went to Charlottesville to report on the huge white supremacist rally in 2017, tracking down hidden participants in the violence months later. The next year, he and his colleagues discovered Sam Woodward's secret identity as a neo-Nazi with Atomwaffen Division after Blaze Bernstein's killing, and they published a cache of documents they obtained exposing the group's violently racist internal dialogues. Among a string of scoops, Thompson also identified an aerospace engineer in Southern California, Michael Miselis, as a violent neo-Nazi with Orange County's own "Rise Above Movement," leading to his firing from Northrop Grumman and his eventual arrest.

Thompson's forceful reporting often put him far ahead of other journalists and even federal law enforcement agents—and made him a target of the white supremacist groups he was investigating, who prized secrecy and loyalty above all else in their operations, much like the Mafia ethos. Each story he wrote would bring more online death threats; white supremacists attacked Thompson, an olive-skinned man who is part Arab and part Anglo, as a "mongrel," and other reporters at ProPublica as "kikes" and "antifa terrorists," threatening to shoot them and blow up the news outlet's office. "There's not enough rope in the world to bring these scum to proper justice," one user wrote on Gab, a popular site for far-right extremists. "Why even bother arguing with these jews. FUCK THEM UP," wrote another.

The neo-Nazis, in a so-called doxxing operation, hacked into private online information and financial documents of Thompson and his family and posted the information on white supremacist forums. From there, they were able to siphon thousands of dollars from the credit cards of Thompson's father-in-law and seize his digital accounts for ransom. "I'm gonna take your digital life," a blackmailer warned his father-in-law.

It was a harrowing time for Thompson and his family. He contacted the FBI to report the hacking, but he was feeling increasingly guilty about all the threats and harassment that his reporting had rained down not just on him, but on his family, too.

Their life would become still more harrowing one rainy February night in 2018 at his suburban home in the San Francisco Bay area.

Thompson and his wife, Lori, were watching a documentary on Netflix, and their eight-year-old son had come to sleep in their bed after waking from a bad dream. Thompson's mother was downstairs in her basement apartment. Thompson drifted off to sleep with the television still on, only to be jolted awake around midnight by his wife's frightened voice.

"Get up! Get up!" Lori yelled. The police were outside, Lori yelled. Thompson ran to the door as a booming voice on a police bullhorn commanded him: "You need to immediately come out of the house with your hands up!" Thompson went out to the front stoop, with his son clinging to his side and his wife behind him, to the sight of a phalanx of police cars and officers from the sheriff's SWAT team, with the lead officer and others behind him all pointing rifles at him.

Thompson sent his son scurrying downstairs to his grandmother, as he stepped out from the stoop. A moment later, officers were handcuffing him and leading him to a patrol car in the street. Then they were handcuffing his wife as well, putting her in a second patrol car. "We have an active shooter situation," an officer told him in the midst of the bedlam, and it soon became clear to Thompson that he was the suspected shooter.

His mother was texting him frantically from the basement. "What is happening?" she asked.

What was happening was a sophisticated "swatting" operation carried out by members of Atomwaffen to terrorize one of their main antagonists. A caller, identifying himself as A. C. Thompson, had phoned the local police to report that he had just shot his wife with an M16 rifle, warning that he was ready to kill any officers who approached the house. The team of heavily armed officers had stormed Thompson's home, bracing for violence.

Swatting had started as a reckless "prank" among young video gamers to send police SWAT teams scurrying to fake reports of violence at the homes of unsuspecting strangers. But it had become a powerful tool for extremists, and the consequences could be deadly, not only wasting police resources and creating scenes of panic, but putting unwitting victims in harm's way. In one swatting in Kansas a year earlier, an officer shot and killed a twenty-eight-year-old father in front of his house after police rushed there in response to a hoax called in by a video gamer in Southern California.

Thompson had already feared that the neo-Nazis might try to "swat" his home, especially after the breach of his family's private information, but it was surreal even so to find himself and his wife now both in handcuffs as police stormed their home. He had written about violent criminals for decades, but now police thought he was one himself. The police believed he had killed his wife, who at that moment was sitting, very much alive, in the other patrol car.

"I didn't kill her, I didn't kill anybody," he protested. "This is a swatting hoax; this is likely being perpetrated by white supremacists who are not very friendly to me." In the blur of the moment, his mind raced through images of what might be going on inside his home. His young son, who had been training in jujitsu and boxing, might try to fight the police and get himself shot. His elderly mother might have a heart attack. The police might not believe his story. He couldn't predict everything that might go wrong. "Please don't kill them," he implored the officers.

With no sign of anything amiss inside the house, the police eventually realized that Thompson was a victim, not a killer, and they let him and his wife go back inside their home. "The victim and his family were left shaken by these events," an FBI agent would later write in a bit of understatement. The night had traumatized Thompson's whole family. His son began having nightmares about his home being raided and his family kidnapped, and he feared that the white supremacists were going to kill his father. "What's going to happen next, Mama?" he asked. The agony on his son's face tore at Thompson. So did the knowledge that the people who had done this to them would likely strike again.

---

For Atomwaffen Division, creating fear had become its modus operandi. The neo-Nazi crew was in the midst of a campaign of threats and harassment against people of color, Jews, journalists, federal officials, and anyone else they considered an enemy, and Thompson was at the top of the list of targets in one of hundreds of swatting operations across America, Canada, and Britain.

Relying on an elaborate system to leave few digital fingerprints, the neo-Nazi group called in desperate reports of mass murders, kidnappings, bombings, and mayhem to more than 130 police departments in all, masking the true origin of the calls through multiple layers of communication and using voice-altering software to disguise the caller's voice. Two Atomwaffen members living abroad would call in most of the threats to help blur the trail.

Sometimes, crew members were even able to hack into a city's street cameras to post live video of the police raid along with their own racist commentary on their internal chat networks, a virtual play-by-play account of the panic they caused. The scenes gave the neo-Nazis a rush of adrenaline confirming their power to terrorize their enemies; they became a lurid source of "entertainment and bragging," as an FBI agent put it in one account.

"Who did you swat," an Atomwaffen member asked in one encrypted online conversation.

"N*****s," came the answer.

A swatting in New Hope, Pennsylvania, brought the small town to a standstill for hours one afternoon in the fall of 2018 because of reports of a brutal murder and multiple bombs. Atomwaffen members delighted in the frantic response. The "whole town shut down, the citizens all shook and [scared] now," one wrote. "This was the best by far tho," said another. "This was hilarious yeah," said a third member.

In a splinter operation, Atomwaffen members developed another scheme to terrorize minorities with threatening, swastika-laden posters delivered to their homes—by mail or sometimes in person. The aim, one Atomwaffen member wrote to three other participants, was for the targets to "all wake up one morning and find themselves terrorized by targeted propaganda." One Jewish journalist in Phoenix, the editor of a

Jewish publication, woke up one day in 2020 to find a macabre poster with swastikas and violent imagery on it glued to a bedroom window, with the message: "YOU HAVE BEEN VISITED BY YOUR LOCAL NAZIS."

Some of the people "visited" by the neo-Nazis in Arizona, Florida, and Washington State quickly bolstered their home security, or moved out of their homes altogether, even as Atomwaffen leaders talked among themselves about escalating their campaign to more-violent levels. Atomwaffen members should go "full McVeigh," Cameron Shea, a participant in the scheme from the Seattle area, wrote in reference to Oklahoma City bomber Timothy McVeigh. They needed to find political and economic "targets" that would help Atomwaffen "build the social tension that will accelerate the collapse of the system," he said.

Shea was talking about "accelerationism," the radical notion championed by Charles Manson, Atomwaffen Division mentor James Mason, and younger generations of white supremacists to sow racial violence in hopes of triggering a full-on civil war. It was a concept that went hand in hand with "the Great Replacement Theory" threatening white power. White supremacists feared that time was running out for them to push back against the creeping diversification of the American body politic, and that nothing short of societal collapse would achieve the goals outlined in their cherished fourteen words: "We must secure the existence of our people and a future for white children." Now Atomwaffen was planting the seeds.

---

For all the high-tech security measures that Atomwaffen Division took, the neo-Nazis' plans first began to unravel for the most callow of reasons: one member, a bearded college student in Virginia named John Kelley, wanted to get out of going to class. Kelley was studying cybersecurity at Old Dominion University in Norfolk and, according to the FBI, was putting his computer skills to use on the side as Atomwaffen's technology guru for many of its swatting attacks, using the online "graveyard" channel he'd created, which had become a gathering spot for Atomwaffen members to launch their swats. Putting aside their usual racial and religious targets for the moment, Kelley wanted to turn Atomwaffen's cyber-weapon against his own school because, as he wrote to his neo-Nazi partners, "I dont want togo [sic] to class Wed."

So at around 2:00 a.m. one morning in late 2018, using the group's usual methods to mask the source, Kelley called Old Dominion twice to report that he had an AR-15 rifle and had planted multiple bombs on campus. The school went into full emergency mode, calling in all campus officers and nearby agencies, sweeping every campus building, ordering students to stay in their dorms and—as Kelley had hoped—canceling classes for the day. A gunman at another Virginia college, Virginia Tech, had killed thirty-two people in a campus rampage in 2007, and security administrators at Old Dominion weren't going to ignore any possible threats.

Just a few hours after calling in the original swat, Kelley phoned campus security again. This time, though, he didn't mean to do it; he explained to the dispatcher on the line that the call was "an accident," an apparent misdial, and he apologized. He sounded nervous. It was a break for campus police; Kelley's phone number wasn't blocked this time, and police used it to match the latest call against the earlier threats and trace it back to Kelley. Police raided his room and, after finding illegal drugs there, arrested him and moved to expel him.

His partners in crime at Atomwaffen Division were irate when they learned what had happened, blaming Kelley, known online as "Carl," for the sloppy security breach. "Carl fucked himself over," one Atomwaffen member wrote in an internal chat. They worried about the heightened scrutiny from law enforcement that the screwup seemed bound to bring. Sam Woodward's arrest in Orange County had already drawn national attention to Atomwaffen Division, with the swatters remarking in one of their chats that a court hearing was coming up in Orange County for him, and now Kelley's arrest threatened to bring even more heat. "FUCK ITS GONNA GET REAL," one member wrote. "shit got seized," a friend of Kelley's chimed in.

When Kelley himself resurfaced in an online chat a few days later, his cohorts mocked him for his carelessness. "First step, DON'T BOMB THREAT YOUR OWN SCHOOL," one told him.

But Atomwaffen's crew kept swatting away, even after the scare. A few months later, it targeted the home of Trump's Homeland Security secretary, Kirstjen Nielsen (whom Trump had accused of being soft on illegal immigration), prompting a formal federal investigation into the online attack.

The threats against Old Dominion and a sitting cabinet member had given FBI agents a glimpse of the neo-Nazis' terror campaign and one of its key operators, but they were slow to peel back the curtain. It was not until nearly a year later, in early 2020, that the FBI was able to trace the cyber trail back to its leader: John Denton, a.k.a. "RAPE," the young mortuary worker who had taken over many of Brandon Russell's duties after Russell's imprisonment and helped him to put out his video message to neo-Nazi followers past and present.

From his home in rural Texas, Denton had overseen many of the swatting operations and carried out some of them himself, FBI

John Denton, a mortuary worker in eastern Texas, became a leader of Atomwaffen in waging cyberattacks against minorities and other groups.

investigators concluded. He had picked at least two of the targets personally because of his deep scorn for them: A. C. Thompson in California and the office of his news organization, ProPublica, in New York City. In one news story about Atomwaffen Division in early 2018 in the aftermath of Blaze Bernstein's killing, Thompson and other reporters at ProPublica had identified Denton as a leader of the neo-Nazi group and named other key members as well, publishing many of their internal chat logs. "Politics are useless," Denton said in one of the chats that was exposed. "Revolution is necessary."

Four months later, Thompson personally confronted Denton at a "black metal" concert held at a bar in Houston. He had gotten a tip that Denton might be at the bar, and he went there with a camera crew for an investigation he was doing for PBS' *Frontline* with ProPublica. The journalist, an ex-punk-band member with a shaved head and tattoos up and down his arms under a metal-music T-shirt, looked like he could easily fit into the metal scene himself. Thompson approached Denton—a.k.a. "RAPE" in the group's encrypted communications—who was sipping a beer at a back patio with his brother and a third Atomwaffen member.

"Hey Rape, I'm A. C. Thompson," he said, "and I wanted to come out here and talk to you about Atomwaffen."

"No comment," said Denton, his long brown hair falling onto a black T-shirt with a large skull on it.

"Are you worried about going to prison?"

"Nope," Denton said curtly. He stared stone-faced at Thompson, betraying no emotion. He seemed frozen on his barstool, small and unassuming; nothing like the monstrous, angry neo-Nazi persona he'd adopted online as "RAPE," "TORMENTOR," and "DEATH."

Afterward, though, Denton began plotting his revenge. He was "furious" with Thompson and ProPublica for exposing his role with Atomwaffen Division, according to the FBI, and for confronting him about it at the black-metal concert. He wanted hackers to get into Thompson's private information. The swattings months later against Thompson's home and ProPublica's office were part of Denton's retribution. He added a personal touch for the ProPublica swat, identifying himself as "James Mason," the group's *eminence grise* in Colorado, in reporting a murder, bombs, and a kidnapping that led police to swarm the office.

Afterward, Denton told a confidant all about the two swatting operations against Thompson and ProPublica. With evident glee, he talked of how he would use a voice changer to call in the threats, how other Atomwaffen members would listen in with their microphones silenced, and how he could watch and record some of the swattings on street cameras as they unfolded. And he told how Atomwaffen Division planned to escalate its cyber tactics with denial-of-service attacks on corporate targets.

Denton didn't seem worried about getting caught. Even if he was arrested, he said, it could actually be good for Atomwaffen because it would be seen as a "top-tier crime," a mark of status for the fledgling neo-Nazi group in the eyes of other extremists.

What Denton didn't know, as he talked on and on about all of Atomwaffen's cyber successes in going after Jews, Blacks, journalists, and other enemies, was that his supposed confidant was an undercover FBI agent who was working to help build a federal case against him. Another Atomwaffen crew member had introduced the man to Denton and vouched for him as a trusted and like-minded white supremacist, but it was all a ruse. Denton was furnishing the FBI with recorded evidence that would be used, line by line, in his own indictment.

---

The FBI was growing much more aggressive in infiltrating white supremacist groups as the scale of the danger became clear. Undercover agents like the one who built the case against Atomwaffen's Denton were now a growing part of the FBI's arsenal against them after years of inattention.

The focus after the September 11 attacks had been squarely on foreign-inspired terrorists. After the attacks on the World Trade Center and the Pentagon, the Justice Department had loosened the standards for using undercover methods in terrorism investigations, and the FBI devoted the bulk of its undercover agents to rooting out suspected Islamist extremists, sending hundreds of them into Muslim communities in an aggressive but controversial campaign that often generated protests of entrapment and racial profiling from law-abiding Muslim Americans. Many Muslims came to assume that the new visitor at their mosque might be an undercover FBI agent.

Investigations into extremism at home had often gotten short shrift after the September 11 attacks. But that was changing with the acknowledgment from top intelligence officials, including FBI Director Chris Wray, that white supremacists and domestic extremists—homegrown terrorists—were now a rising threat on par with Islamist terrorists. Undercover agents at the FBI were now burrowing more deeply into white supremacist groups like Atomwaffen Division in an effort not just to prosecute past crimes, but also to head off future plots.

That meant relying on some unsavory characters as well-paid informants. In its Atomwaffen investigation, the FBI relied on a longtime informant—a white supremacist who published neo-Nazi propaganda—and paid him more than $80,000 beginning in 2018 for information on one of the neo-Nazi group's leaders in Seattle, according to court documents. It was the price that FBI officials believed they had to pay in order to infiltrate violent neo-Nazi groups and head off the rising threat.

Atomwaffen's Denton—who had been so brash online with his fiery rhetoric and violent *noms de guerre*—went quietly; he agreed to plead guilty to conspiracy charges, and he was sentenced to about three and a half years in prison. He and his cohorts at Atomwaffen had "caused irreversible trauma," a federal prosecutor said, "to the victims of these hate-based crimes." John Kelley, the former Old Dominion student, pleaded guilty and was sentenced to nearly three years in prison, and at least a half dozen other members of the neo-Nazi crew were convicted as well.

Some of them actually seemed remorseful. Days before he began a sixteen-month prison sentence, Johnny Roman Garza, a twenty-one-year-old Atomwaffen crew member from Arizona, apologized to one of the victims, a Jewish reporter for a Seattle TV news station named Chris Ingalls, whose family had gone into hiding at a hotel and received round-the-clock security after finding a threatening Nazi poster at their home. Unlike Brandon Russell, the Atomwaffen Division founder whose brief courtroom apology in Florida was soon followed by more violent threats from prison, Garza seemed sincere in his regret. The Nazi threats seemed to him like just a "minor petty-crime thrill" at the time, he said, but he came to realize they weren't.

"It's simply just evil and I didn't realize how evil it was, you know?" Garza told his victim. "Professing to be wise, I was actually a fool."

# CHAPTER 12

# "IMPUNITY TO VIOLENT BIGOTS"

Prosecutors had plenty of physical evidence linking Sam Woodward to Blaze Bernstein's murder when they arrested him, but they had little in the way of a motive. Nothing was stolen; Blaze's shattered cell phone, in fact, was found buried near his body. So why would Sam, who had not seen Blaze in over three years, meet up with him out of the blue and turn on him so violently? The news stories after Sam's arrest described him and Blaze as "friends" from high school, but the truth was that they barely knew each other there. Even if Sam's latest claim about Blaze trying to kiss him were true—and there was certainly no confirmation of that—would that explain the horrific act of violence?

The DA's office didn't rule out a hate crime, but investigators had little evidence so far to back it up. They tried, without success, to get into Sam's phone to see if it provided any answers, but the PIN code locked them out, and getting into it could take weeks, if not months.

A key break came two weeks after Sam's arrest—not from investigators, but from the media. An investigation published by ProPublica revealed the startling news that Sam was "an avowed neo-Nazi" and a member of Atomwaffen Division, the notorious white supremacist group. A. C. Thompson and his colleagues at ProPublica had gotten ahold of a cache of internal messages from Atomwaffen members showing not only that Sam was a member of Atomwaffen, but that he had gone to one of its "hate camps" in Texas for paramilitary training. They even had a photo of Sam giving a "Heil Hitler" salute. The revelations raised Blaze's death from a random killing to something much more chilling: a murder at the hands of an avowed neo-Nazi.

A month later, ProPublica produced another story about a cache of 250,000 once-encrypted messages from Atomwaffen's internal chat logs that it had obtained. The chat logs included messages not only from Sam himself, railing against "mongrels and jews" and gays, but also from other neo-Nazis in the group hailing Sam as "a one-man gay Jew wrecking crew."

Another member bemoaned the killing—not because a young man was dead, but because he wasn't worth the long prison sentence Sam was facing if he were convicted. "Sam did something stupid. Not that the faggot kike didn't deserve to die. Just simply not worth a life in prison for." The callous words echoed the mantra that James Mason, the group's elder statesman, had long preached to his young followers: *If you're going to kill the enemy, you have to go big.* Mason himself, tracking it all from his apartment in Denver, was disappointed, too. He wasn't "a damn bit sorry" about the death of a gay Jewish teenager, he said, but in his warped view, killing him wasn't worth a one-for-one swap, with the victim dead and "a fine young man" in jail on murder charges. Sam had been sitting in Mason's living room just a few months earlier, surrounded by all his Nazi artifacts, and listening to him wax on about the Aryan race under threat and the need for violent resistance. If Sam had told him what he was planning that day, Mason said, "I'd have told him, 'For God's sake, don't do that.'" If Sam was going to commit murder and risk prison, Mason would have told him to "go bigger."

The leaks of Atomwaffen Division's chilling internal communications didn't come from an outside hack or from law enforcement, but from a secret source deep inside the neo-Nazi group: Brenan Duffy, the senior Atomwaffen member who had first vetted Sam Woodward for a spot in their hike in the hills outside Austin with Tristan Evans ("just three Nazis getting together to go hiking," as he'd said). Duffy had deployed to Kuwait with the US military three months after the Texas hate camp that summer, and he had begun souring on his role in the group. It was "destroying my marriage," he said, and he came to realize, only several years into his involvement with the hate group, that its ethos conflicted with the Eastern Orthodox Church values that he'd been raised on in Texas. Then there was the fact that being an active member of a hate group violated military code and, theoretically at least, could have gotten him court-martialed. But the existence of many active white supremacists in the military, including Atomwaffen Division's own founder, Brandon Russell, made clear that official military policy was enforced only sporadically, if at all. A "paper tiger," one expert on extremism called it.

Duffy began to distance himself from Atomwaffen, logging on to fewer group chats on the encrypted Discord system he'd set up. Learning of Sam Woodward's arrest on murder charges finally convinced him of what he needed to do, he said. He decided it was time to cut ties completely—and to turn against Atomwaffen. Blaze Bernstein wasn't the first person to die in the name of Atomwaffen, but something about the brutal killing of the gay Jewish student finally turned Duffy after years as a neo-Nazi and spurred him to act.

Covertly, he went to reporters at ProPublica, not only disclosing Sam's role in Atomwaffen Division but also turning over a huge collection of internal hate-filled communiques and photos that formed the crux of the news organization's reporting. "I wanted to see Sam behind bars for good, and I want to see justice for Blaze," he said. He ultimately went to the Orange County Sheriff's Department as well, becoming a main source of information for the investigators in tracing Sam's ties to Atomwaffen. Dylan Jantzen, the Orange County investigator who'd spotted Sam lurking around Borrego Park and was now leading the murder investigation, wished Duffy had come to him before going to ProPublica to give investigators the chance to digest the material before the public storm hit. Stories in the media about the case "didn't help at all," he told Duffy. But it was too late to do anything about that now. The story of the accused neo-Nazi killer was already out there.

The revelation of Sam's ties to Atomwaffen, to say nothing of the internal chat logs that went with it, was a huge break for investigators in establishing Blaze's killing as a hate crime. But they were still struggling to find out what was inside Sam's phone—and whether it might provide more evidence of his motives. One of Jantzen's colleagues, a computer forensics specialist named Craig Goldsmith, decided to take the phone to a technology company in New Jersey called Cellebrite, flying there to deliver it personally.

Cellebrite had become one of the go-to companies for law enforcement officials locked out of suspects' electronic phones and devices. The stronger security measures that tech companies like Apple had placed on each new version of their products, while a boon for users' privacy, had created growing headaches for law enforcement, even at the highest levels and in the biggest cases. The conflict between Apple and law enforcement officials had reached a crescendo in Southern California in early 2016 after an Islamist-inspired terrorist attack carried out by a husband and wife at a holiday party in San Bernardino, neighboring Orange County, left fourteen people dead and nearly two dozen more injured. The FBI couldn't get into an iPhone 5C model used by one of the shooters because of its built-in encryption and, in a standoff with Apple, went to court to try to force the company to allow it access before paying a private contractor as much as $1 million to successfully hack into the phone.

For weeks, technicians at Cellebrite waged a high-speed computer guessing game to hack into Sam's phone, using a method the company had developed for a "brute force attack," trying thousands of possible password combinations without tripping the security measure that would erase the data after ten unsuccessful tries. Ten weeks after Blaze's killing, Cellebrite finally succeeded, allowing investigators to extract all the data inside.

The results proved worth the wait for Goldsmith and Jantzen. Inside the phone was a trove of evidence pointing to a motive for the murder: Sam's "Diary of Hate," laying out his disgust for gays, Jews, and other minority groups; his history of "trolling" gays online and threatening them to the point that "they think they are going to get hate-crimed"; thousands of neo-Nazi images and documents excoriating minorities; proud photos of James Mason and Charles Manson; his encrypted chats with other Atomwaffen members about neo-Nazism and their plans for another "hate camp" in the Death Valley desert. Even the wallpaper that Sam used as the background for his phone was from Atomwaffen Division; it was a shot of the neo-Nazi group's radiation logo, a warning of danger. Unlocking his phone had revealed a bottomless well of hatred.

The investigators also went back to some of the original evidence they'd gathered from the search at the Woodwards' home. The ghoulish mask they'd found in Sam's car was still sitting in an evidence bag, unexamined. It hadn't meant much to them at first, but now they realized that it was the same Atomwaffen skull mask that Sam was wearing in his neo-Nazi propaganda photos. Jantzen sent it to the Orange County crime lab for testing. It came back showing two blood stains—and a possible match for Blaze Bernstein's DNA.

Prosecutors had seen enough. Sam was already facing a murder charge that could net him twenty-six years in prison if convicted. Now, after digesting all the neo-Nazi material and homophobic hatred that they'd found, prosecutors added another charge months after the killing: a hate-crime count that would likely land him in prison for the rest of his life without the chance of parole if he were convicted.

"We will prove," Orange County district attorney Tony Rackauckas said in announcing the decision at a press conference, "that Woodward killed Blaze because Blaze was gay." There was ample evidence from his own words that Sam hated Jews as well as gays, but prosecutors weren't certain they could prove, beyond a reasonable doubt, that Blaze's religion was a driving factor in his killing. They were confident, though, about Blaze's sexuality as a motive, and they brought a so-called hate-crime enhancement charging that Sam Woodward had murdered Blaze Bernstein because the latter was gay.

Rackauckas had never shown much personal interest in hate crimes, but after twenty years in the powerful DA's post, he was in the midst of a tough battle for reelection because of a scandal in his office over the use of jailhouse "snitches," and he wanted to announce the hate-crime charge himself before a throng of reporters. The district attorney pointed to the mountain of evidence found on Sam's phone; it was "graphic and chilling" imagery that he said "spews hate" toward virtually every minority group—blacks, Jews, women, and most pointedly, gays. "All of this revealed the dark side of Woodward's thoughts and intentions," he said.

For months, Gideon and Jeanne had been hoping that prosecutors would bring a hate-crime charge against Woodward. When it finally came, they were there at the district attorney's office in the Orange County main courthouse, sitting in the front row in front of Rackauckas for the announcement before the glare of the television cameras. But seeing Blaze's name attached to an official hate-crime designation—the latest in the growing list of hate-crime victims nationwide—provided little satisfaction now that the moment was here, only another brutal reminder of the loss of their eldest child and the hatred that spurred it.

"Today, we suffer an added layer of pain," Gideon said in a soft voice, "from learning he was likely killed because of who he was as a human being."

---

While Sam Woodward was locked up in the Orange County jail in the summer of 2018, facing hate-crime charges that were still years away from a trial, another avowed white supremacist sat in a nearby cell block awaiting murder charges of his own in a brutal killing that would prove yet another flashpoint in the county's surge in hate crimes.

His name was Craig Tanber, an Orange County native then in his late thirties. With a clean-cut look and thick brown hair parted neatly to the side in a boyish cut, at first blush Tanber looked more like an accountant than a neo-Nazi. But his tattoos gave him away. There were the "8"s inked on each of his buff arms—Aryan code for "HH," or

## "Impunity to Violent Bigots"

"Heil Hitler"—and the phrase "PEN1" tattooed on his neck, short for "Public Enemy Number One," a violent white supremacist street gang based out of Orange County, with deep ties to prison gangs, white-power music, drug trafficking, hate crimes, and an assortment of other street thuggery. The tattoos were a testament to Tanber's identity as a white supremacist, a fixation for most of his adult life.

Tanber grew up in a wealthy Orange County household, raised for much of his childhood by his grandmother and grandfather, who was a well-heeled stockbroker and a big Republican donor. His own mother, who gave birth to him when she was just a teenager, was often absent. He lived with his grandparents by the ocean in the picturesque seaside community of Dana Point, with a pool in the backyard and all the trappings of luxury. But trouble always seemed to find him, with frequent disciplinary problems getting Tanber kicked out first from a private high school in southern Orange County, then a public school, then finally a school for troubled youth.

Tanber began doing a lot of hard drugs and hanging out with white supremacist gangs. In his mid-twenties, he and a group of other PEN1 gang members beat to death one of their own with a claw hammer in southern Orange County, hiding the battered body in the back of a Ford pickup truck under some scraps of wood and carpeting. The killing was payback, investigators said, because the victim was accused of stealing money from another gang member's girlfriend. Loyalty and trust were always prized by the white supremacist gang; "we were a group of fuckin' white boys that formed together to protect each other gang-style," one member said, describing PEN1's ethos. The dead gang member had betrayed that trust.

Tanber's role in the killing landed him in prison for six years for manslaughter. His time behind bars only seemed to solidify his devotion to white supremacy. Prison officials put him in solitary confinement for a while because he was deemed to be a leader of the Nazi Low Riders gang in prison, his family learned, and he managed to get new white supremacist tattoos while he was incarcerated to show off his affinity for white power.

Soon after his 2015 prison release, Tanber attended a picnic in Orange County at an oceanside park with some family and friends. Bare-chested, he blithely showed off all his tattoos. "Proud as a peacock," one family member described him. His turn toward white supremacy mystified family members. He had never shown much interest in politics or ideology as a kid. The irony was that Tanber was of mixed heritage himself, though people wouldn't have known it from looking at him; his grandfather was Lebanese, and quite active in an Arab American club in Orange County.

Tanber didn't advertise his mixed family heritage; he was, to any outsider, a proud white man through and through. Tanber was careful not to talk much about his racist views around his family members, but there it was, inked on his chest for all to see. Even out of prison, he showed no signs of wanting to break from his neo-Nazi allegiances.

One thing that Tanber did seem to want to change, however, was his longtime drug addiction. Even among white supremacist gangs, PEN1 was known for its deep culture of drugs—smoking them, snorting them, injecting them, and trafficking in them. Tanber, addicted to both heroin and methamphetamine, fit the profile all too well. Between his drug addictions, his stints in prison, and his involvement with white supremacist gangs, Tanber had never held a steady job, with the money he got from his grandparents often going to buy himself more drugs.

Out of prison, Craig Tanber called his uncle, Paul Tanber, with whom he'd been raised practically as a brother in his grandparents' home in Dana Point, and said he finally wanted to get clean. "I'm in trouble," Tanber told him. He had started to use drugs again right after getting out of prison, he said. "I'm not a good person on drugs," Craig told Paul. "You wouldn't like me on drugs."

Together with Tanber's grandfather, they arranged to get him into a drug treatment facility. A bed came open at a facility in Laguna Beach, and they scheduled Tanber to be admitted. He missed his first appointment after storming off in the midst of a family fight, but they scheduled another one for a few days later, and he seemed determined to go and check himself in this time.

## "Impunity to Violent Bigots"

He never made it there, though. The night before his appointment, Tanber met up with an old girlfriend, Elizabeth Thornburg. They went to a brewery in southern Orange County, then on to another bar, an Irish pub called Patsy's. It was a popular neighborhood bar in Laguna Niguel with live music and a pool table, and a twenty-two-year-old college student named Shayan Mazroei was there that night with some friends, too.

Mazroei was a regular at the bar. A goateed Iranian American immigrant, he wore a white fedora hat and a brightly colored, button-up shirt, and he was playing pool. He lived just a few minutes away from Patsy's with his parents, and sometimes all three of them would go there for dinner; the pub served a good prime rib. More often, though, he would come later in the night with friends to hang out and work on his pool game, a favorite hobby.

He had gotten to know the employees at Patsy's by name. He felt comfortable there; that was important to him, because he hadn't always felt comfortable in America, his adopted country.

His parents had come to the United States with him from Iran sixteen years earlier when Mazroei, an only child, was six years old, settling first in Oklahoma. His parents moved him out of his school in Oklahoma after a science teacher began picking on him over his Middle Eastern heritage and telling him how "hairy" he was. The family finally left Oklahoma altogether for Southern California—a place they saw as multicultural, an international destination—and Mazroei enrolled at a community college in southern Orange County to study mechanical engineering. He'd always had a passion for cars and motorcycles—working on them and driving them. His father owned a used-car business, and he helped manage the auto lot. He talked of wanting to design turbocharged engines once he got his engineering degree.

For now, though, he just wanted to shoot some pool. So did Craig Tanber and Elizabeth Thornburg, a blonde woman in her mid-thirties who was a white supremacist herself. With Tanber in the bathroom, she walked up to the pool table and asked Mazroei about the sign-up list for the table. That's when the tensions began to flare. She didn't like the way the young man answered her. Thornburg felt disrespected, and she called him a "son of a bitch."

She and Mazroei saw each other again standing outside the bar a little later, both smoking cigarettes. Thornburg saw a tattoo on Mazroei's arm with the Persian word *eshgh* on it and asked what it was. "It means love," he answered. Witnesses heard her snap at him and go on a rant about Middle Easterners. She told Mazroei that she didn't like them. "You're all the same," she said, calling him a "terrorist" and telling him to "go home."

Then she spat on him — three times. Mazroei spat back and flicked a cigarette at her. Soon, an irate Thornburg was chasing him back inside the bar, and he was darting around the pool table to keep away from her and yelling out to a bouncer to get her away from him.

The bouncer threw both Thornburg and Tanber out of the bar over the ruckus, and Tanber began yelling outside in the parking lot and spewing racial epithets over his expulsion. He called Mazroei, still inside the pub, a "fucking sand n\*\*\*\*r" and "a rag head," according to witnesses. The anti-Muslim venom poured out as he readied for a fight. "No one spits on my woman," he said. "No one fucking disrespects me like that." He warned that he had a knife and threatened to hurt the kid. Minutes later, Tanber poked his head back in the bar and called out angrily to Mazroei. "You!" he said, motioning toward him and walking back outside.

No sooner had Mazroei started walking out the door than Tanber belted him, according to video captured at the scene. "A bar fight," a local TV newscast called it afterward, but it wasn't really much of a fight. Tanber punched him once in the face. Mazroei staggered backward and then tried punching back vainly at his attacker before Tanber pulled out his knife — the one he'd been threatening to use — and stabbed him once in the heart and again in the back. Mazroei crumpled to the ground, blood pouring from his chest. Tanber and Thornburg took off into the night as the young man lay dying on the ground.

Tanber disappeared for nearly a week after the killing, as police searched for him. They finally found him only with the help of an informant, another old girlfriend of his named Adrian Volz. Like Tanber, Volz was a drug addict who hung out with white supremacists and had a history of run-ins with police. That made for the pair's improbable, real-life connection to *The Real Housewives of Orange County*, the hit TV show that played off the county's opulence and excess and, occasionally, its conservative politics.

Tanber and Volz had a young child together, and when Tanber was in prison on another bust, she was arrested for running a massive, million-dollar-a-year meth lab in Orange County, alongside three members of the Nazi Low Riders; the profits went toward financing the white supremacist gang. The setting for their meth lab was the unlikeliest part of their whole story: It wasn't run from a rural farmhouse, a gritty cellar, or a mobile home in the desert as on TV's *Breaking Bad*, but instead from an ornate, 5,000-square-foot home in a gated coastal community in Laguna Niguel. Practically every room in the mansion was filled with meth laboratory equipment.

Tanber's toddler with Volz, along with her other young son, were often in the mansion with her while she and her neo-Nazi accomplices were cooking the meth, police said. Volz had the run of the place only because her mother and stepfather, George Peterson, a wealthy Orange County developer, were splitting up and had each moved out; her stepfather went on to marry a cast member on *Real Housewives* in a "fairy tale courtship" that became a main storyline of the reality TV show. Her mother, meanwhile, dated former NBA star and Orange County homeowner Dennis Rodman, the basketball bad boy and occasional emissary to North Korea, as the show brought together unlikely Orange County bedfellows.

With Tanber on the run after killing Mazroei at the pool hall, Volz agreed to surreptitiously help police find her fugitive ex-boyfriend. She arranged to meet him at the Motel 6 up the freeway in Westminster in central Orange County where he was hiding out, and a SWAT team stormed in to make the arrest. Orange County prosecutors charged him with murder in the killing at Patsy's bar, but Mazroei's parents, bereft, wanted more: they wanted him to be charged with a hate crime, and Muslim American advocacy groups rallied around their cause. Trump, then a candidate for the White House, was already taking frequent jabs at Middle Easterners and suggesting that Obama himself was a secret Muslim, and Arab American leaders were beginning to see a frightening rise in crimes against Muslims—and a return to the violent anti-Muslim climate in America in the immediate aftermath of the September 11 attacks.

To the Mazroeis, a hate-crime charge would not only mean more time in prison for their son's killer, but it would send a powerful message, in Orange County and beyond, about the deadly threat that white supremacists posed to America's minorities.

Mazroei's murder had wrecked them; they wanted their son to be remembered among the tragic victims lost to senseless hate crimes. They had never imagined Orange County as a place where white supremacy thrived, despite its long history as a wellspring for hate and extremism, but now their only child was one of the casualties. "We lost everything," Mazroei's mother, Shahzad, told a judge. Tanber stared straight ahead, unflinching, at the defense table. "The only justice," Shahzad said, is "that no other parents go through what we went through."

Orange County district attorney Tony Rackauckas's office wanted to bring the hate-crime charge, though. California has one of the strongest and broadest laws of any state. There seemed to be ample evidence from both Tanber and Volz, in their own words, of their hatred for Middle Easterners, and a California appeals court would later note that the "ethnic slurs" Tanber hurled just before stabbing Mazroei were evidence of his "motive and attitude" toward the victim. But the district attorney's office didn't think it was enough, despite all the fervent appeals from the Mazroeis' advocates reaching as far as Washington and Tehran. The jury didn't even hear evidence of Tanber's long history as a white supremacist, as Tanber was convicted of second-degree murder and given a sentence of fifty-six years to life in prison.

---

One man who disagreed vehemently with the decision not to bring a hate-crime charge against Tanber was Todd Spitzer, a fiery Orange County politician and former prosecutor himself who favored cowboy boots in court over the traditional dress shoes. Spitzer was running for district attorney against Rackauckas, who had held the office for twenty years. The two men, once friends, were now bitter adversaries: Rackauckas had been a mentor to the younger Spitzer when he worked as a prosecutor under him in the DA's office years earlier, but after a nasty personal rift between the two men, Spitzer was now trying to unseat him, and he was using his ex-boss's lackluster record on hate crimes as one of the main issues in his campaign. "Make no mistake, Mazroei was stabbed to death because he was Iranian American," Spitzer declared flatly during his run for the DA's seat in 2018. He called Rackauckas's record on hate crimes "deplorable and dangerous." With hate crimes surging, Spitzer pointed to the low number of cases where hate charges had actually been used, and he charged that the DA, his old boss, cared more about touting high conviction rates in easy cases than about bringing important prosecutions.

Rackauckas's office had just brought the hate-crime charge against Sam Woodward in Blaze Bernstein's killing, one of the few high-profile cases in which it was used. But in Mazroei's case and in many other less-high-profile crimes, prosecutors had begged off on hate-crime charges, despite what seemed like reams of evidence showing the attacker's motives. That indifference, Spitzer charged, was granting "impunity to violent bigots."

Lowell Smith, a longtime Orange County probation officer who focused on white supremacists, was glad to see the push for tougher sanctions. He had tried for years to get the higher-ups in law enforcement to pay more attention to neo-Nazis. He kept warning about how prevalent and dangerous they had become in Orange County over the years, with card-carrying members of almost every white supremacist group imaginable: Aryan Brotherhood, Nazi Low Riders, PEN1, and more. The typical response he heard from higher-ranking officials was that Latino and Asian gangs were a much bigger problem, and that he didn't need to spend so much of his time chasing down neo-Nazis. This seemed ridiculous to Smith, given the threat they posed. So when he heard Spitzer clamoring to make hate crimes and white supremacy a higher priority, it resonated with him. Someone finally seemed to be listening to what was going on.

Spitzer won the race for district attorney, unseating his old boss in an upset. His aggressive stance on hate crimes proved more than just campaign rhetoric; he made it a central priority once he took office. Spitzer had felt the sting of persecution and harassment himself, and it gnawed at him. Raised Jewish before converting to Christianity, he remembered as a boy being threatened with a knife in school because of his religion. And when he was first running for elected office in Orange County years earlier as a single man, he remembered bitterly how his political opponents had tried to smear him with insinuations that he must be gay. (He isn't.)

As a member of the Orange County Board of Supervisors, Todd Spitzer had fought—unsuccessfully, in the end—to protect the independence of a county commission credited with combating hate crimes. Now he was seeing the damage created by the rising tide of violent hatred. He was a lifelong Republican, but he bristled whenever Trump would go after a particular ethnic or minority group, seemingly indifferent to the impact his words had in fueling bigotry on the streets. "Hate is out of control in this country," Spitzer said. "It's now okay to hate. It's almost a badge of honor to hate." As DA, he created a special unit of prosecutors and investigators just to handle hate crimes, and it began investigating as many as two hundred cases a year, with the number of hate-crime prosecutions doubling in Orange County.

Spitzer was determined to send a message that "we won't tolerate hate in Orange County," and he ultimately found a medium for that message in the fearsome figure of Tyson Mayfield, a local transient with a shaved head and steely blue eyes who, like Craig Tanber, had spent years running with neo-Nazis and had become a serial hate-crime offender in Orange County.

Mayfield had fallen in with the skinheads in Huntington Beach as a teenager, not long before he wound up in juvenile hall for beating a young man to death with a golf club. When he wasn't in jail, Mayfield usually lived out on the streets of Fullerton in northern Orange County, just a few miles from Disneyland. But that wasn't often, because Mayfield was usually in jail. He had spent most of his adult life behind bars, racking up eighteen criminal convictions in the span of twenty years for a string of increasingly violent and random attacks on strangers; random, except for the fact that the targets were usually minorities—the *others* for whom the neo-Nazi felt particular disgust.

There was an unprovoked attack on a biracial couple at a gas station that left a man with eight stitches in his lip. And another one a year earlier on a man Mayfield approached outside a liquor store, asking for a light for his cigarette. The victim, a Turkish man with dark skin and dreadlocks, told him politely enough that he didn't smoke. That was enough to set Mayfield off. He became irate, screaming that the man was a "fucking n\*\*\*\*r" and pounding him with his fists.

The assault netted Mayfield a year in jail, and he was back on the streets of Orange County in the fall of 2018, hanging out one afternoon at a bus station in Fullerton with a couple of other men. He was shirtless, his bare chest displaying a tattoo of a swastika on his right shoulder and another of a Nazi SS lightning bolt. It was a menacing sight to onlookers.

Mayfield spotted a young Black woman waiting outside the station. Her name was Jasmine, she was eight months pregnant, and she was expecting her boyfriend to pick her up momentarily. She could hear Mayfield talking animatedly nearby with some other men; he seemed to be talking about her. He motioned toward her and she heard him telling his cohorts that he hated Black people, especially pregnant Black women, and that he got his "kicks" by hurting them. Something about the thought of another Black life seemed to trigger him. That was when Jasmine saw the shirtless man with all the Nazi tattoos walking right toward her.

"I don't like pregnant n****rs like you," Mayfield told her. "I'm going to make sure you drop your baby." She told him to stay away from her. He ignored her and continued spewing racial epithets. Jasmine could feel her legs shaking. She reached for the pepper spray she carried in her bag and sprayed him with it. Blinded for a moment, Mayfield swiped her backpack and began running away. Jasmine caught her breath and called the police. Then she looked up to see her assailant rushing back toward her, even angrier than before. His hands were balled up into fists now. "You're going to pay now, you n****r. I'm going to make sure you really drop this baby." Jasmine, shaking almost uncontrollably now, managed to run to a nearby café to escape Mayfield before he could hit her. All she could think about was her child.

With Mayfield soon behind bars once again after the assault, the Orange County judge assigned to the case, Roger Robbins, brokered a proposed deal that would have allowed the habitual criminal to plead guilty and face the prospect of a two-year sentence in prison. Under California's "three strikes" law, Mayfield could have been looking at far more — as much in thirty years in prison if he was convicted of another felony in the attack. Mayfield pleaded guilty in exchange for the lesser sentence, but privately the white supremacist grumbled that even that was too harsh: "They've just drummed up some charges and went and shot the moon," he said. "No one got hurt." The terror he had caused the pregnant young Black woman meant nothing to him.

The case might have ended there, with an unrepentant Mayfield on his way to another brief stint through the prison system's revolving door for chronic offenders, had it not been for Orange County's new district attorney. "Hate is here, and it is becoming more and more frequent," Spitzer warned in an op-ed piece in the *Orange County Register*, citing the alarming spike in hate crimes in the region. Just a week after the attack on Jasmine, in fact, came another attack that was hauntingly similar: another middle-aged white man, at another bus stop in the city

### "Impunity to Violent Bigots"

of Fullerton, assaulting another Black victim while spewing racial epithets—only this time the attacker was wielding a knife, not just his fists, before he was arrested.

Spitzer had been in office as district attorney for only a few months when he heard about the proposed deal that Judge Robbins was considering for Mayfield. To Spitzer, the assault on Jasmine seemed like the very definition of a hate crime, and he believed it deserved a much stiffer punishment: Mayfield, a known white supremacist with Nazi tattoos on his chest, had picked out a woman at random because she was Black, then proceeded to terrorize her in menacing and explicit ways and threaten her fetus. Yet here was the judge ready to deliver what Spitzer saw as another slap on the wrist for a habitual criminal.

Irate, Spitzer walked into Judge Robbins's chambers to let him know what he thought of the deal the judge wanted to broker. District attorneys don't typically plead their cases personally before a judge alone in a courtroom, much less alone in a judge's chambers, because of ethical and legal restrictions. But Spitzer wanted to let Robbins know just how furious he was over the idea of Mayfield getting another short prison stint for his second hate crime in just over a year.

He brought a copy of the recent report from Orange County's Human Relations Commission, the anti-hate-crime panel, showing the upward spiral in hate crimes. "Are you aware that the county issues a hate-crime report?" Spitzer asked the judge, waving the report. The judge looked at him blankly. He didn't seem to know anything about it, as far as Spitzer could tell. "Hate is out of control in this country," he said. "You have to be part of the solution."

The judge seemed swayed. He withdrew the two-year offer, and when it came time for another court hearing a month later, he came down harder on Mayfield with a sentence of five years. Spitzer was still not mollified. He went back to court himself for the hearing, bringing civil liberties leaders from the community with him for the sentencing. He thought Mayfield deserved far longer than even the five-year sentence after his long record of offenses against minorities.

"He is a dangerous person... There is just no question he is a racist,"

Spitzer told the judge. "He is indiscriminately picking out people on the street because he doesn't like the way they look and using violence against them," he added. "Is a five-year sentence going to protect society against someone so evil?"

Spitzer's office appealed the decision, and a California state appellate court eventually handed down a stinging rebuke of the judge's legal rationale for the light sentence. "We've seen enough to make it difficult to shock us. But not, as it turns out, impossible," the judges wrote regarding Mayfield's criminal history and the handling of his latest hate-crime case. Given Mayfield's history of violence against minorities, the judges wrote that: "Everything about [his] crime and his record shouts for application of the Three Strikes law." Moreover, "his unrelenting criminal behavior" over the years "demonstrates him to be an unchanged man, with a stubborn character and no discernible prospects for reform." The court threw out Judge Robbins's sentence and kicked the case back down to the trial court to reconsider it.

The decision left some defense attorneys in Orange County seething. They thought Spitzer was a "grandstander" who had attracted media attention by personally appearing in the courtroom, then leveraged the attention to help win over the appellate court. "I just think it's wrong," grumbled one defense attorney.

Mayfield, the serial hate-criminal with two Nazi tattoos, ultimately received a whopping new sentence of twenty-seven years in prison. For Spitzer, the outcome was a vindication that signaled a new attitude toward bigotry and hate. That was important, he said, "but we still have a long way to go." As it turned out, Orange County was undergoing a seismic political shift that would bring more racial tumult than anyone had predicted.

## CHAPTER 13

# "WHITE REPLACEMENT"

In the midst of the wave of hate crimes sweeping Orange County, the unimaginable happened, and it would trigger a backlash from angry whites that pushed violent bigotry to even greater heights. Democrats won all six open seats in its congressional districts in 2018, as their party regained control of the US House in Washington midway through Trump's first term. The upset victories gave Orange County Democrats a clean sweep in a county that for decades had been synonymous with archconservative Republican politics. The famed "Orange Curtain" had fallen, swept away in a blue wave driven by the county's liberal Latino and Asian voters in a place where minorities now made up a majority and were making their political voices heard.

The sweep was a tide-turning event that even the most jaundiced political strategists thought they would never live to see. Long dominated by conservative white men, the congressional delegation now included, remarkably, a Hispanic man, three women, and even a Jew. Democrats hadn't held so much as a majority of the county's congressional delegation since the Depression. "The Republican wipeout in Orange County," the *Los Angeles Times* called it.

At the same time, the city of Irvine, the master-planned community at the heart of Orange County, elected the first-ever Muslim woman to the city council, with Farrah Khan becoming the first to lead any major city when she was elected mayor two years later. Issues of racial strife had first driven her to run: Khan, who immigrated from Pakistan with her family as a toddler and ran her own catering business in Irvine, was enraged to see the city's mayor falsely describing Black Lives Matter activists at peaceful protests as violent and disruptive, echoing the rhetoric of Trump himself. The rhetoric didn't reflect the changing community that Khan saw around her, or the one where she wanted to live, so she decided to take on the mayor in the race. She won.

The rapid changes in Orange County's political makeup, bringing minority faces to power as never before, enraged Orange County's white supremacists. "White Lives Matter" banners began appearing on an overpass high above the 405 freeway in her city, bemoaning "White Replacement" and attacking Khan and her Muslim "mosque," along with "JEWS," Black Lives Matter, and a variety of other minority causes. One racist banner would come down from the freeway, and the white supremacists would put another up. Khan received anonymous death threats attacking her as a Muslim woman. To Khan, it was all a dismaying sign of the powerful grip of hate and intolerance from the county's growing cadre of white supremacists. "They know that they have people here, and they're trying to get to them," she said. "That's why they keep coming back."

Reported hate crimes in Orange County were surging to record heights, nearly tripling in the span of five years, with Black, Jewish, and gay victims consistently the most frequent targets. A young white supremacist in Orange County with a "kill list" he'd compiled for local Jews was prosecuted for threatening a Jewish synagogue and other religious institutions. White supremacists were plastering racist slogans on the doors of Orange County's Democratic party headquarters. And one viral video after another showed bigotry leeching into the community. At a high school basketball game in Laguna Hills, a student in a video could be heard taunting a Black player from nearby Irvine at the

## "White Replacement"

free-throw line with a torrent of racist attacks. "Where's his slave owner?" the student shouted. "Chain him up, chain him up!...Who let him out of his cage? He's a monkey!"

Mayor Khan was repulsed when she heard about the episode targeting a student from her own city. It wasn't a hate crime, but even so it was shamefully public, casting Orange County, once again, as a home to bigots. The school district denounced the episode as "unacceptable" and took unspecified steps to discipline the student, but in Khan's eyes, this was mere lip service. Hatred was left unchecked.

As unabashed as Orange County's bigots were becoming, it was Sam Woodward who had emerged as the face of uncurbed hate in Orange County—an avowed white supremacist jailed on charges of killing his gay, Jewish high school classmate, Blaze Bernstein. News crews from across the country would pile into the courtroom on the eighth floor of the aging, gray-brick Orange County courthouse for all his hearings in the months after his arrest, hoping to get a glimpse of the young man who had joined up with a neo-Nazi crew and kept a "Diary of Hate" on his phone. Sam would sit in the prisoners' lockup at the side of the courtroom, unsmiling and unflinching, casting an occasional glance at his parents, who attended many of the hearings and always sat near the front, sometimes with their pastor, a Catholic priest, at their side.

But for all the attention cast on Sam Woodward and on Blaze's killing, justice was maddeningly slow, as the murder case against him ground on in court month after month, then year after year, with no trial in sight. The covid epidemic shut down Orange County courtrooms and delayed trials. Sam cycled through four different lawyers, one of whom even questioned Sam's mental competence to stand trial—only to have two psychological experts declare, after monthslong reviews, that Sam was indeed competent. The lead prosecutor left the case and became a judge, delaying the case still further. It looked like justice might never come.

Sam remained in the Orange County jail as the case wore on, denied bail because of the danger that a judge found he posed on the outside. Inside his dank cell, Sam was still professing his allegiance to Atomwaffen

Division — and he was becoming a martyr to outside sympathizers. Deputies searching his cell found drawings he had made of scenes and symbols from Atomwaffen, white supremacy, and "The Lion Rises," a neo-Nazi meme. They also found letters that extremist supporters had written to him in jail, including a prison inmate who said he was "pulling for you, man" and cited *Siege*'s Mason: "I never forget my brothers and true family, as James Mason put it," the supporter said. A young woman in Canada, who called herself a fellow "national socialist," wrote affectionately to tell him she had the same skull mask as his.

Others inside the jail, though, weren't so welcoming of the young neo-Nazi whose murder case had made headlines. Sam got in a slew of fights with other inmates, and one cellmate, a person of color, attacked him because he said Sam had refused to stop chanting "satanic" and "demonic" expressions in their cell. Sam ended up in a neck brace afterward. His stature in jail as a man from wealthy Newport Beach made him a target, too; other inmates were "extorting" him for money for the jail commissary, his lawyer said, threatening violence if he didn't pay up.

The delays were agonizing for Jeanne and Gideon Bernstein. They usually stayed away from the courtroom at the outset; it was too difficult to see the case being kicked down the road again every few months. "Delay, delay, delay," Jeanne said with anger after yet another court hearing led nowhere. Blaze's two younger siblings were growing up without a brother, his parents without a son, and the court system seemed indifferent to their pain. "If you're gay and Jewish in Southern California, I guess it's okay to let the family linger. It's outrageous," she said.

At one court hearing that Gideon and Jeanne attended, Sam's mother and father approached them outside the courtroom. "We've been praying for you," they said. The Bernsteins didn't like the sound of that, or of the letters that Sam's parents sent them with the same tone-deaf message. The parents of the young white supremacist accused of murdering their son were now praying for them? Jeanne and Gideon didn't want their prayers. The judge stepped in and urged the Woodwards to stop contacting Blaze's family. They did.

## "White Replacement"

The tensions between the two families ran deep. With no media attention, the Bernsteins quietly brought a wrongful-death lawsuit in Orange County civil court against Sam's parents, Blake and Michele, over the murder of their son. It contained some explosive charges, alleging that Sam's parents not only financed and "actively supported" Sam's involvement with neo-Nazis, but also knew of his desire to kill gays and Jews, including Blaze. The source of the claims in the lawsuit wasn't made clear, and they were never tested in court; instead, the Woodwards agreed to a private settlement with the Bernsteins for what one source called "a significant" sum of money that was paid through their insurance. (Sam's parents were never charged criminally in the case.)

Jeanne and Gideon wanted to think about Sam Woodward as little as they could. They wanted to think about Blaze instead—and to find a way forward for their family. They worked on a project that they'd started in Blaze's name to fight hate, calling it "Blaze It Forward." It was a way to carry on his memory at a time when the kind of violent bigotry that prosecutors said killed their son seemed to be everywhere. They made appearances at community events and on television,

A rock garden created in memory of Blaze Bernstein at the park near the spot where his body was found.

promoting tolerance and speaking out against the latest in what seemed like the never-ending episodes of hatred in Orange County and beyond. At the scenic park near where Blaze's body was found, they worked with friends and supporters to create a memorial garden with hundreds of painted rocks encircling a magnolia tree in his memory, the ocean off in the distance. "Choose Love," read one. "BLAZE."

Gideon threw himself into another new cause in Blaze's memory—giving to charities, and pushing others to do the same. At a Vietnamese café he liked to frequent in Laguna Beach, he bought some coffee and a pastry for a young homeless man from Philadelphia, then gave him a hundred-dollar bill and a #BlazeItForward card. The young man sat stunned. For Gideon, it felt wonderful. He ended up writing a book on charity; the act of giving, he found, was a path to healing and happiness even in the wake of tragedy. He didn't want to stew in his own sadness.

It was an effort he had first started, in fact, during the frantic eight days when Blaze was still missing—"the worst days of my life," as he remembered it. On the seventh day of the search, Gideon decided to use the "Help Us Find Blaze Bernstein" Facebook page to urge supporters to donate to a cause they'd picked, an Orange County charity for at-risk and needy children, and "create something good" out of his disappearance. The public response was immediate: the flood of donations crashed the server at the charity within an hour, but not before $16,000 was raised.

The very next morning, the coroner's office called to tell the Bernsteins that the body found in the park had been positively identified as Blaze. The search was over, even as a new mission for the grieving parents had begun.

---

As the prosecution against Sam Woodward continued to languish in the courts, Jeanne Bernstein was jolted by another setback—this time from Orange County's own elected officials. With Gay Pride Month approaching in 2023, both the Orange County Board of Supervisors and the city council in Huntington Beach, the famous surfside mecca with a staunch conservative leadership, each voted to effectively ban the flying of the rainbow-themed gay pride flag at their government buildings. The flag, a symbol of inclusion to the LGBTQ+ community, was "divisive" and even "sinful," supporters of the ban said. It would no longer be allowed on government property.

After years of civil rights progress for gays, conservative lawmakers across America were taking steps hostile to the LGBTQ+ community, led by Florida governor Ron DeSantis's "don't say gay" policies restricting what could be taught in schools about sexual orientation. But the flag bans in Orange County were seen as an extreme step even by conservative standards, something few if any jurisdictions in America had ever done before, and they drew international attention.

For Jeanne, the votes against the flag were a personal affront, inexplicable and hurtful. Though Blaze hadn't come out to his mother as gay for years, telling her only weeks before his death that he'd been seeing a young man, she had become a vocal advocate for gay rights and tolerance in the wake of his death. It was a way to honor his memory. Her son was killed because he was gay, Orange County prosecutors had charged, and now elected officials were taking a huge step backward, symbolic but powerful, in voting to ban the gay pride flag. Jeanne joined with one of Orange County's state senators, Dave Min, an Asian American, to try to stem what felt to them like an unbridled wave of hatred blessed by elected officials.

Attacks against LGBTQ+ people were soaring in Orange County and across America, with hate crimes against people based on their sexual orientation or their gender identity rising at least 22 percent, according to data from the FBI in 2023. LGBTQ+ students were at particular risk of attacks in states like Florida that passed restrictions on gay rights and education, with attacks in the schools there rising even more quickly than elsewhere, data showed. With transgender people among the most frequent victims, the Justice Department stepped in and secured its first-ever guilty verdict at a trial for transgender-related violence, with a South Carolina man sentenced to life in prison in the brutal murder of a transgender woman. Days after Orange

County's vote to ban the gay pride flag, Huntington Beach residents awoke to find hate-filled fliers at their doors targeting gays and Jews together, with a banner headline declaring that "Every Single Aspect of the LGBTQ+ Movement Is Jewish"; the fliers ominously displayed images of gay people and the Star of David alongside the devil. Hatemongers now felt "emboldened to act on their worst instincts," said Min, a first-generation Korean American. They "feel empowered, they feel socially licensed to go out and be racist or sexist or anti-LGBT, and sometimes in very, very violent ways."

Orange County's decision to ban the gay pride flag resonated in violent ways with Travis Ikeguchi, a young Southern Californian man with a history of homophobic postings on social media. The gay pride flag incensed him like few other things. "Halleujah!" he wrote on Twitter with a photo of the rainbow-colored flag in flames after the Orange County vote to ban it. On Gab and other far-right social media sites, the twenty-seven-year-old Ikeguchi, a vagabond who struggled for money and lived for a time out of his car, vented about a slew of far-right conspiracy theories and trigger points, railing about abortion, pornography, police oppression, and the need for Christian morality and "family values." But he always saved his most incendiary judgments for gays. "We need to STOP COMPROMISING on this LGBT dictatorship and not let them take over our lives!" he wrote.

Two months after the Orange County vote and his posting of the burning flag, Ikeguchi ended up outside a quaint boutique called mag.pi in the Glen, near Lake Arrowhead in the San Bernardino Mountains, just east of Orange County. The owner, a sixty-six-year-old fashion designer named Lauri Carleton, sold handmade clothes, jewelry, gifts, and knickknacks. Ikeguchi had an unregistered handgun on him. Why he ended up at her shop that day was never clear. His family had reported him missing days before, and now here he was near closing time at 5:00 p.m. outside Carleton's shop, which had a rainbow-themed gay pride flag hanging outside the store. The flag was faded from the sun, and Carleton had ordered a new one that was already on its way. Ikeguchi began ripping the flag down.

## "White Replacement"

Carleton spotted Ikeguchi from inside the store and went to the door to see what was going on. Gay-bashers had torn down her flag before, and she had always put another one right back up afterward. Carleton herself wasn't gay; she was a straight woman, a mother of nine, but she had always been a vocal backer of the LGBTQ+ community and "fearless," her daughter said, in her defense of gay rights.

"Why do you need to do this?" she asked Ikeguchi. She seemed anxious to understand his motives, maybe even try to get him to change his mind. He began hurling a barrage of homophobic slurs at her. He railed on about the flag, the target of his rage. Then he brought out his gun, as verified by video footage at the store and eyewitness accounts reported to the police. He seemed to flinch for a moment, as if he was considering what to do next, then he fired twice, hitting Carleton. She crumpled to the ground outside her shop, fatally wounded in a one-sided fight over a flag. She was dead by the time police arrived, and the gunman was soon dead as well, killed by police in a shootout about a mile away from the shop.

A "senseless" killing, the San Bernardino sheriff said, as the department logged its latest hate crime, this one driven by an angry young man's apparent belief that the woman flying the pride flag outside her shop was gay. Carleton's friends, family, and neighbors had a hard time wrapping their minds around what had happened outside her boutique. "It's hard to believe there's that much hate," said a shop owner down the road.

Just as Lauri Carleton's family was mourning their matriarch that summer, federal authorities were building a chilling case against two more young white supremacists nearby in Orange County who had been secretly plotting to violently attack gays, Jews, and other minority targets. The two young men, Chance Brannon and Tibet Ergul, loathed them all, and they talked of starting a "race war" to further their racist ends, the authorities learned.

More troubling still, the twenty-four-year-old Brannon was an active-duty Marine stationed at nearby Camp Pendleton, just across the border in San Diego County. The sprawling oceanside base had been home to entrenched pockets of racial extremism over the years, including a band of more than a dozen white Marines in the Ku Klux Klan who openly harassed and attacked Black personnel in the 1970s. Brannon was only the latest service member there to be drawn down the well-trod path of white supremacy in its ranks.

He had a cache of weaponry, both legal and illegal, including an M70 assault rifle with a handwritten racist message in Cyrillic that said "Total N****r Death," the words written out as part of a violent mantra that had become a catchphrase of white supremacists after the start of the Black Lives Matter protests. On a thumb drive disguised as a military-style dog-tag necklace was a blueprint for destruction, with an operation plan and a list of the gear needed for attacking Orange County targets, including the M70 rifle with the racist credo. Brannon also had a recording of a white supremacist's horrifying 2019 attack on Muslims in Christ Church, New Zealand, as well as neo-Nazi material and an antisemitic cartoon of a soldier shooting a Jewish figure who was holding money. "Thank you for keeping America pure," it read.

Brannon and Ergul had been friends since their days together in high school; they'd attended Corona del Mar High School in Newport Beach at the same time that Sam Woodward was there. Together with a third young man in Florida, Brannon and Ergul began plotting a series of politically inspired attacks against minority targets and others, as the FBI would later determine. They talked of attacking an office of the Anti-Defamation League, the Jewish civil rights group, as well as a location catering to gay customers, before deciding instead on a Planned Parenthood clinic in central Orange County as a convenient first target symbolizing liberal doctrine to them.

In Ergul's garage in Irvine, they assembled a Molotov cocktail—a flammable, orange-colored concoction in a large glass jar with a cloth fuse peeking out the top. Dressed in dark hoodies and wearing gloves, the two men drove up to the clinic in Costa Mesa in Brannon's red Dodge Challenger, grabbed their homemade firebomb, then set it ablaze and launched it at the entrance to the clinic. Fifteen-foot flames began shooting up the walls, forcing the clinic to shut down temporarily after the damage was discovered the next morning.

The arson remained unsolved for months, as the young men continued plotting more attacks. Emboldened by their first strike, they planned another one at a second Planned Parenthood clinic soon after the Supreme Court's historic decision overturning the right to an abortion in June of 2022. The pair assembled another Molotov cocktail in Ergul's garage and cased the second clinic, authorities said, but pulled back from their plans when they spotted tight security near the clinic and feared getting caught.

They plotted a possible explosives attack against an electrical generator in Orange County—a favorite target for white supremacists intent on sowing chaos, in keeping with James Mason's plans for racial "accelerationism"—and they scoped out a substation in the northern part of the county that they wanted to hit in the summer of 2023. "The rifle is in a box in my room waiting to be used in the upcoming race war," Ergul wrote to Brannon. Ergul wrote of his disdain for the political establishment—"godforsaken 2 party fags," he called them—and of the need for action, violent action, to bring changes. "Voting doesn't change anything. If it did, it would be illegal," he said.

Still, no one was on their trail yet. But after the FBI put out a reward offer of $25,000 for information about the original Planned Parenthood arson, investigators got a break. A high school classmate in Newport Beach identified both Brannon and Ergul as the men behind the firebombing; Ergul had admitted to it, the classmate told the FBI. The attack had been too exhilarating for Ergul to keep to himself. He had bragged to his old classmate about it in a text—"Boom," he wrote next to a fire emoji with the clinic's address. He even included a photograph of the Molotov cocktail in the car. Ergul just wished he "could've recorded the combustion," he wrote.

Their former classmate identified both Brannon and Ergul from surveillance video taken at the scene of the firebombing, the FBI said. But just as agents began to close in on the pair, the stakes ratcheted up dramatically.

As agents were quietly building a criminal case against them that summer, the two were plotting ways to attack a Gay Pride Night planned at Dodger Stadium up the freeway in Los Angeles. The run-up to the pride night had generated wide publicity and controversy, with protests from Christian groups over an honor being given to a satirical group of nuns in drag, and the Orange County pair wanted to make their disdain for gays known in violent and dramatic fashion. They talked of using a remote-controlled detonator to trigger an explosion, and they made plans to do a "dry run" at the stadium beforehand to identify their targets.

FBI agents moved in quickly and arrested them both—just two days before the gay pride event took place, drawing nearly 50,000 people for the game. It was a chilling episode, said Martin Estrada, Southern California's top federal prosecutor, fueled by "a hateful ideology."

A potential disaster on a mass scale had been averted. The tip from the ex-classmate following the FBI's announcement of reward money had led FBI agents to the two Orange County men before they could put their plan to attack the Gay Pride Night into deadly motion.

LGBTQ+ patrons at a gay bar called Club Q in Colorado Springs hadn't been so fortunate when, during a festive night of dancing, drinking, and drag shows on November 19, 2022, a young neo-Nazi named Anderson Aldrich, clad in body armor, walked in with an AR-15-style assault rifle and a handgun.

Aldrich ran a website for neo-Nazis and white supremacists, posting videos glorifying mass shootings and hate crimes against minorities. There had been ample warning signs. Aldrich had posted an image of a rifle scope aimed at a gay pride parade, and after Aldrich was arrested a year earlier with a stockpile of weapons and explosives in an alleged kidnapping, a Colorado judge had warned that the defendant seemed intent on carrying out "some sort of shootout" and that "it's going to be so bad." Yet the case was dismissed, and the local authorities never followed up or sought to confiscate the weapons under Colorado's "red flag" law.

Unimpeded, Aldrich bought thousands of dollars of additional

## "White Replacement"

weaponry, made multiple trips beforehand to case Club Q—one of the few gay bars in Colorado Springs—and had a rainbow-colored gun target at home. Just before midnight that November night at the club, Aldrich opened fire for six terrifying minutes, killing five people and shooting and wounding seventeen more in an attack that was "fueled by hate," as Attorney General Merrick Garland described it. The death toll no doubt would have been even worse if two men at the bar, both with military experience, hadn't wrestled the blisteringly hot rifle away from Aldrich and stopped the onslaught.

Aldrich was ultimately sentenced to multiple life sentences in prison, avoiding the prospect of the death penalty by pleading guilty to federal hate-crime charges. US District Court Judge Charlotte Sweeney, the first openly gay judge to serve on the federal court in Colorado, noted how fitting it was to hand down the sentence during Gay Pride Month. The gay community was under assault, said Judge Sweeney, but it would not buckle: "This community is stronger than your armor, stronger than your weapons, and stronger than your hatred."

A memorial for five people killed at a gay bar in Colorado Springs in 2022, one in a slew of mass shootings by white supremacists targeting minorities in America.

## CHAPTER 14

# "GO BACK TO YOUR OWN COUNTRY"

The sheer beauty of Orange County was what first lured Haijun Si—the rolling hills, the lush green landscaping, the glimmer of the Pacific Ocean in the distance. The Chinese-born businessman found the balmy climate soothing, and four years after he and his wife and three children left their native country for California, he bought a $1.1-million brick-façade house in the tony neighborhood of Ladera Ranch, a planned community in Orange County built on a former cattle ranch. They moved into their new home on Mocha Lane in the fall of 2020.

Si had left behind the rigors of authoritarian China for what he saw as a new promised land. A businessman who ran his own medical supply company, he imagined a bucolic existence where the couple's three children could attend top-tier schools amid a booming population of fellow Asian-American faces living side by side with people of every ethnicity.

But there were storm winds coming that Si couldn't foresee. His new neighborhood, like much of America, was being roiled by violent racial and political tensions, and the Covid pandemic of 2020, reaching its peak just as the moving trucks pulled into the driveway of his new home, was unleashing an epidemic of its own: a wave of violence, harassment, and hate crimes against Asian Americans at record levels across America, from the shorelines of Orange County to the streets of downtown Manhattan. Instead of the calm and serenity that Si imagined he'd be greeted by in his new neighborhood, what awaited him instead were months of stinging racial slurs and harassment, futile calls to police, sleepless nights, and paralyzing anxiety for him and his family.

It started with the chiming of the doorbell one fall night in 2020, just a few weeks after Si's family moved into their home on a corner lot across from a skateboarding park, right near the neighborhood pool. Si scampered to the door to find out who was ringing the bell so incessantly, only to see a figure running away in the distance. He didn't think much of it, not that first time.

But the intrusions went on for days, then weeks, then months, escalating to a full-on campaign of harassment, with teenage boys ringing the bell late at night, when everyone in the house was asleep. They banged on doors and windows at all hours, laughing and screaming obscenities; they threw rocks at the house; they dumped garbage on the lawn; and perhaps most offensive of all to Si, they left a framed lewd picture of a young Asian woman propped up by the front door just a few feet from his young daughter's pink-and-white bicycle.

"Go back to your own country!" one teenager yelled at Si, mimicking the rallying cry of xenophobia that had become so rampant during the pandemic in the Trump era.

"Chink!" another called out to his wife, Yixin, as she drove home with the kids one day from pickup at the elementary school nearby.

It went on for weeks. Si called the Orange County Sheriff's Department. There was nothing they could without more evidence, a deputy told him. Put up a video camera by the door, the sheriff's department suggested. So Si did, gathering many hours of video showing his teenage tormentors rushing up to his doorstep—on foot, on bicycles, or on skateboards—to taunt the newcomers, some of them with their faces shrouded by their hoodies.

From the videos, it looked to Si as if a dozen teenagers were involved, maybe more. All of them white. Still, the police told Si they didn't have enough evidence to do anything. Si put his oldest daughter, finishing high school, on the phone with the sheriff's department; he figured that her English was better than his and that maybe she could better explain the torment the family was experiencing. She didn't get anywhere, either.

Try putting up a fence, another deputy told them. So Si did, spending $3,000 on a new wrought-iron gate, only to see one of the kids slip over it easily on his way to the front door. Si hung a heavy chain across the driveway, along with a sign announcing: "Private Property: No Trespassing." Still, the torment continued. Sometimes, Si would give chase out to the street, yelling at the teenagers in his halting English as they disappeared into the night. "Who are you?" he yelled as he ran out the front door, with his son and daughter walking not far behind him. He heard only laughter in the night. Nothing seemed to deter them.

The Sis' two younger children were too afraid to fall asleep or leave the house. They started sleeping in the back end of the house, away from the street, and Yixin would stay with them for hours until they finally fell asleep. There were frequent nightmares and sleepless nights. Si's son, normally a chatty five-year-old, went suddenly silent, barely speaking a word at home or in class. No one was hurt physically, and there was no significant damage to the home, but the trauma ran deep for Si and his family. His family, he realized, was being terrorized.

The children wondered: *Why are the kids here being so mean to us? What did we do to them?* Si wondered the same thing. *Because we are strangers, newcomers,* he told himself. *Because we are Asian faces in a sea of whiteness.*

---

The onset of the Covid pandemic in March of 2020 brought America to a standstill, but it brought no respite from the hate crimes coursing through the country. The worst public health crisis in a century only shifted the focus, with the attackers now targeting Asian Americans with a frightening escalation of violence and harassment because, as President Trump liked to remind people at almost every turn, the epidemic had originated in China.

The surge in anti-Asian hate crimes started even before Covid became a full-blown epidemic in the United States. In February of 2020, just as cases of the mysterious new illness were first beginning to show up on the West Coast, school officials in Los Angeles reported that classmates of an Asian American teenager beat him up so badly that he wound up in the emergency room. The boy's attackers accused him of bringing the mysterious new disease over from China; as he was being beaten, the boy told them that he wasn't even Chinese, but his pleas held no sway with them. Racial hatred didn't answer to reason. It was a sign, school officials said, of the "racial backlash" that Covid was already generating against Asian Americans.

When a Southeast Asian immigrant named Bawi Cung was shopping for groceries with his two little boys at his local Sam's Club in West Texas a few weeks later, he felt a sudden blow to the back of his head. He turned and felt something slashing his face—from his ear down to his cheek. He glimpsed a stranger running away with a knife, then turning back and heading for his sons, slashing one of the boys in the face and the other in the back. "Get out of America!" the attacker yelled as an employee tackled the man to the ground. It was a refrain that Asian American residents would hear over and over again.

The attacker was driven to violence, the FBI would determine, because he thought the family was Chinese and was "infecting people with the coronavirus."

So began a rash of thousands of violent attacks, threats, vandalism, and harassment against Asian Americans, all born of bigotry and ignorance. Like so many hate crimes, the attacks were often driven by irrational rage—a feeling by the attackers, young and old, that lashing out at random Asian Americans might somehow satisfy their misplaced rage over the pandemic. Asians were killed in unprovoked attacks on subway platforms, in shops and restaurants, and on the streets of major cities from New York to San Francisco. There was an hours-long string of assaults up and down the sidewalks of Manhattan, with a white attacker, an army veteran, punching seven different Asian American women, badly injuring several, as he shouted racial slurs. Then there was a spree of vandalism and property damage at hundreds of Asian-owned businesses around the country, such as the ramen restaurant in San Antonio spray-painted with graffiti reading "Kung flu," "go back 2 China," and "hope you die," or the dim sum restaurant in Seattle's Chinatown vandalized with white-supremacist stickers and shattered windows.

In Orange County, the county's human relations commission catalogued a staggering 1,800 percent increase in episodes of hate and harassment against Asians across the county at the start of the pandemic in 2020. A young Japanese American woman—an Olympic athlete in karate for the United States—harassed and threatened with anti-Asian slurs while exercising at a park in the city of Orange. An elderly Korean American couple attacked and punched in the face at the same park. Asian American students at a high school rehearsal mocked with chants of "Coronavirus!" Fliers left at the home of an Asian American family declaring: "You guys are Chinese Viruses. Get out of our country!!" A Korean American man confronted at a fast-food restaurant by a stranger declaring that "because of you I'm getting sick!"

With new Covid restrictions already in place, Asian Americans began staying home altogether, or looking over their shoulders with trepidation if they had to go out in public. Many had long been aware of lingering hostility against their people, but now it was surging to the surface with shocking regularity. "There's a feeling now that 'hey, it's okay to express all this stuff,'" said Patty Yoo, a Korean American in Orange County who led an Asian American advocacy group. "I've never had this feeling before. There is genuine fear." Some people thought about leaving America altogether. "Every single week, you see a new attack in the news," said Eric Wu, a Seattle native who was studying in London at the start of the pandemic and decided to stay overseas rather than return to a country he felt had turned hostile.

## "Go Back to Your Own Country"

Historically, times of national crisis have brought waves of crime, and the Covid pandemic was creating another huge surge in hate crimes—this time against Asian Americans, with a 73 percent rise in attacks in the United States in 2020 alone, the FBI determined. It was a uniquely American crime wave in its scale; other countries didn't see the same surge. A United Nations report singled out the United States for "an alarming level" of racially motivated attacks spurred by Covid, calling out "the contribution of the President of the United States in seemingly legitimizing these violations" through Trump's rhetoric about "the China virus." The world was experiencing "a tsunami of hate and xenophobia, scapegoating and scare-mongering" during this once-in-a-century epidemic, said UN secretary-general António Guterres, and America, sadly, was at the forefront.

Trump, as he had done after the violent white supremacists' rally in Charlottesville, dismissed any connection between his rhetoric and the violence. At the White House, a reporter for ABC News pressed Trump on why he insisted on calling the illness "the Chinese virus" despite dozens of reports just in the early weeks of the pandemic about crimes of bias against Chinese Americans. "Why do you keep using this? A lot of people say it's racist," the reporter asked him. "Because it comes from China," Trump shot back. "It's not racist at all. No, not at all. It comes from *CHY-nuh*," Trump said, using his distinctive, sinister-sounding pronunciation for the Eastern power.

Nor did he see anything wrong with an administration official reportedly calling it "the Kung Flu," he said. Two months later, Trump again faced accusations of fanning racism for his treatment of a Chinese American reporter at the White House, who asked him about the mounting death toll from Covid. "Maybe that's a question you should ask China," Trump, who had a habit of scorning female reporters of color from the White House podium, snapped at Weijia Jiang of CBS News. "Don't ask me, ask China that question, okay?"

"Sir," she responded, "why are you saying that to me, specifically, that I should ask China?"

Trump said he would give the same answer to anyone who asked him "a nasty question," then abruptly ended the news conference seconds later and stomped off. Trump had a daily soapbox during the Covid pandemic, and he was determined to use it to point the finger at the Chinese whenever he could.

Neo-Nazi leaders seized on the pandemic for their own agendas. They instructed any members who became infected with Covid to go to synagogues and other places where Jews congregate in an effort to infect them, the FBI warned. And though the majority of attacks on Asian Americans were carried out by whites, data showed, the white supremacist groups tried to exploit several widely viewed videos of Blacks attacking Asians, blaming people of color for the violence and pitting them against Asians in an effort to create racial friction to their advantage.

The pandemic raised to a dangerous fever pitch the long-simmering hostilities that had made Asian Americans frequent targets of hate crimes and harassment for decades in America. Blacks and Jews were always the primary targets for white supremacists and neo-Nazis in their campaign of terror, but Asian Americans had long been threatened as well, demonized in racist broadsides for supposedly taking jobs, spreading disease, or attacking white women. In the early 1980s, the Ku Klux Klan, led by their fiery "Grand Dragon," Louis Beam, unleashed a campaign of violence along the Gulf Coast of Texas against Vietnamese fishermen whom the United States had resettled in the area as one-time allies after the Vietnam War; hooded Klansmen firebombed the refugees' fishing boats, burned crosses in their yards, beat them up, and shot at them. "It's going to be a hell of a lot more violent than it was in Korea or Vietnam," Beam promised at one Klan rally. In Orange County, the convictions of four young Vietnamese refugees in the rape and kidnapping of local women gave white supremacists fodder to vilify Vietnamese people as a whole in a new wave of harassment, portraying them as violent invaders carrying infections into white Christian communities in America.

For older Asian Americans, one attack in particular was seared into their memories—not only because of its viciousness, but because of the measly response from the judicial system. It came in Detroit in 1982, when a twenty-seven-year-old draftsman and part-time waiter named Vincent Chin, a Chinese American who was to be married just days later, was celebrating his bachelor party with friends at a strip club. Chin got into a dispute with two white men, both unemployed auto workers in Detroit in the throes of a recession as Japanese car imports were surging. The fight spilled out into the street, and Chin's attackers chased him to a nearby McDonald's, where they pummeled him in the head with a baseball bat while calling him a "Chink" and reportedly shouting other ethnic slurs. "It's because of you little motherfuckers that we're out of work!" one yelled at Chin, according to a witness. After four days in a coma, Chin died.

Both attackers pleaded guilty to manslaughter charges, yet neither one served a single day in prison. Instead, the judge sentenced each of them to three years' probation and less than $4,000 in fines. "These weren't the kind of men you send to jail," the judge wrote. The lenient treatment sparked outrage in Michigan and beyond, galvanizing a generation of younger Asian American activists to push for strong civil rights protections and tougher measures against hate crimes.

Orange County had more than its share of violent attacks on Asian Americans over the years as their presence in the region grew. While the Asian American population had been growing quickly around America, Orange County had become a true mecca. More than one in five residents were Asian American by 2020, according to census data—a whopping 31 percent growth from a decade earlier. Vietnamese immigrants had created their own destination in the center of Orange County, "Little Saigon," where the aroma of *pho* soup, *ban it ram* dumplings, and other delicacies highlighted the fact that Orange County was now home to the largest population of Vietnamese people outside Vietnam itself. Asian Americans were sending people that looked like them to serve on city councils and the powerful Orange County board; nearby, the University of California at Irvine had become a nationwide magnet for Asian American students, who made up a third of all students—twice the proportion of white students.

But with their rising profile had come a violent backlash driven by rage and resentment. One of the most brutal episodes would become a landmark in California hate-crime laws and a trigger for change. At the start of the school day one winter morning in 1996, in the quiet suburb of Tustin in central Orange County, a janitor at the local high school found the body of a young man lying in a pool of blood on the school's tennis courts. The victim, twenty-four-year-old Thien Minh Ly, who lived nearby, had been out roller-blading the night before, doing laps on the tennis courts to work on his technique. Ly had come to America from Vietnam with his family as a boy, a refugee from the war. A top student with degrees from both UCLA and Georgetown, Ly was thinking about going to law school, and he talked of one day becoming the American ambassador to Vietnam, marrying his new country with his old.

He never got the chance. The scene at the tennis courts was a grizzly one. Ly, a slight young man weighing less than 120 pounds, had been stabbed nearly two dozen times, with his throat slashed and his head stomped; the killing was so brutal that police suspected initially it must have been committed in a crime of rage by someone who knew Ly. But they had no suspects for more than a month—not until police were given a copy of a handwritten letter that an ex-convict had written to a cousin in New Mexico. The ex-convict, a white supremacist skinhead in Orange County named Gunner Lindberg, recounted in the letter with morbid nonchalance that "oh, I killed a jap a while ago," as he went on to recount all the gory, blow-by-blow details of his attack on Ly and the victim's vain pleas for mercy. "Here's the clippings from the newspaper and we were on all the news channels," Lindberg, a shipping clerk at a local Kmart, boasted to his cousin. "Having a ball" in Orange County, he said. "Wish you were here."

When an Orange County SWAT team went to arrest Lindberg at his home soon after his casual confession, they found a cache of neo-Nazi and white supremacist literature and memorabilia, including a helmet adorned with a swastika and a poster hailing the assassination of Martin Luther King Jr. "If you're not white you're not right," he wrote in another letter that police found. At the age of twenty-one,

Lindberg already had a long rap sheet, including a violent, unprovoked attack in a strawberry field on a Hispanic day laborer he derided as a "wetback." He admitted the pleasure he got from beating people up, especially minorities. Killing Ly gave him "a rush...like a high," he told his cousin, and he saw his act as part of a "racial movement." The murder was "a thrill kill, a bravado murder," his own lawyer said.

Lindberg became the first person in California sentenced to death for a hate crime, and the state's highest court upheld the death sentence against him in 2008, an important step in the evolution of hate-crime laws. "The evidence overwhelmingly showed," the high court ruled, "that defendant was a racist who regarded non-Whites as subhuman and who, by his own admission, callously murdered victim Ly 'for racial movement' because defendant thought Ly was a 'jap' or a 'Chino.'" Gunner Lindberg remains on death row today.

---

One year into the global Covid pandemic, many Asian Americans were already on edge amid the crush of ugly hate crimes around the country. But the worst violence was still ahead. In March of 2021, a young white man from Georgia went on a shooting spree at three massage parlors in the Atlanta area, killing eight people. Six of them were Asian American, all of them women who worked at the spas.

It was the worst mass killing of Asians in America in decades, and it sparked immediate fears of another escalation in the growing violence against them. Early missteps by local police only deepened suspicions about how vigorously the justice system would handle the scourge of violence by a white man against a group of minorities.

The shooter, twenty-one-year-old Robert Aaron Long, confessed to the killings in the hours after his capture. A Christian evangelical, he indicated that it was a "sexual addiction," not the race of the victims, that drove him to kill because the spas represented a "temptation" he wanted to eliminate, according to a police account. Some police officials seemed quick to accept that explanation — too quick. A day after the shootings, in fact, a sheriff's department spokesman in Cherokee

County, a rural area north of Atlanta where the first spa shooting took place, gave what came across as a remarkably empathetic account of Long's possible motives for the massacre. "He was pretty much fed up and kind of at the end of his rope," Captain Jay Baker told reporters. "Yesterday was a really bad day for him, and this is what he did."

The seemingly tone-deaf remarks drew howls of protest from Asian Americans and non-Asians alike, and the backlash only worsened after a post surfaced from Captain Baker's personal Facebook page that showed him promoting T-shirts reading "Covid 19: Imported Virus from Chy-na"—language parroting Trump's rhetoric. For generations, sheriff's departments in the South had often sympathized with white offenders over their minority victims, and Cherokee County risked the appearance of doing so once again in the spa massacres. The sheriff's department quickly apologized for Baker's "really bad day" comments and removed him as spokesman on the case.

All the same, Cherokee County wound up bringing no hate-crime charges against Long. Prosecutors charged him with four counts of murder for the killings in their jurisdiction, which led to a life sentence against him after a plea deal, but they brought no additional charges under a new hate-crime statute passed by the Georgia legislature less than a year earlier. But their counterparts in Fulton County, where the four other victims in Atlanta were killed, did.

Georgia had been one of only four states left in America without its own hate-crime statute after the state's Supreme Court threw out an existing measure in 2004. The Georgia legislature rushed to pass the new hate-crime law in 2020 after national outrage over the killing of Black jogger Ahmaud Arbery at the hands of three white men who chased him down on a suburban street in southern Georgia.

Long's murder of the four victims at two spas in Atlanta—all Asian American women—would be the first to test Georgia's new hate-crime law, with Fulton County prosecutors charging that he targeted them based on their race and gender. A conviction against him could result in the death penalty. For a number of the victims' families, the DA's decision to label the massacre as a hate crime was a critical moment—a recognition that they had been killed simply for who they were and an effort, as the lawyer for two of the families said, "to make sense of a senseless act."

---

For months in the midst of the Covid epidemic, Haijun Si and his family lived with the dread of the near-daily harassment at their home in Orange County, just waiting for another teenager to come banging on a window in the middle of the night, or throw more rocks at their house, or toss more garbage on the lawn, or leave another lewd photo by his daughter's bicycle. His pleas for help had gotten him nowhere with the Orange County Sheriff's Department, and the only response from the homeowners' association was to scold him for putting up the new fence to keep the kids away; the association said the fence didn't comply with their community rules. The mood in his neighborhood seemed hostile to newcomers like him. At a rally for Trump in Ladera Ranch's quaint town park, a conservative student speaker echoed Trump in warning that that her generation of students was being "brainwashed by the Kung Flu virus." Neighbors cheered from their lawn chairs.

Frustrated, Si described to a neighbor what was happening one day in early 2021 as she walking past his home on her daily stroll with her two toddlers. The neighbor, Layla Parks, a white woman who'd moved there from Georgia, was one of the friendly ones in Ladera Ranch when the immigrant family arrived; she had noticed the moving trucks in Si's driveway the day the family moved in, and she had walked up and introduced herself right away.

When Si first told her about all the late-night doorbell-ringing, she thought it was probably just a harmless game of "ding-dong-ditch" being played by some thoughtless kids in the neighborhood. Then Si came back to her a few weeks later with more jarring details: the racial taunts and epithets, the escalating menace and physical threats, the trauma to his family. Layla Parks felt sickened. She had never really thought of Orange County, or her own neighborhood for that matter, as a place where racism and xenophobia festered. Now she had to admit that she had been wrong. Haijun Si and his family were evidence of that. Parks wondered where the kids learned this stuff. Was it youthful naivete, or outright bigotry and entitlement? Parks was so disgusted by the whole episode that she contemplated leaving Orange County altogether once her young children started school.

White kids in Orange County behaving badly toward minorities — again. "It's an Orange County ritual as reliable" as another underachieving season from the hometown Angels baseball club, *Los Angeles Times* columnist Gustavo Arellano wrote of the phenomenon. Yet the targeting of the Si family was only the latest in a long string of ugly racial episodes. There was a viral video of a dozen kids on an Orange County high school water polo team giving "Heil Hitler" salutes and marching to a Nazi theme song. Another group in Newport Beach giving Nazi salutes in front of a display of red cups in the shape of a swastika. Kids at a mostly white high school in southern Orange County chanting "USA! USA!" at a football game and displaying a "Build the Wall" sign against a mostly Hispanic team from Santa Ana, prompting the visitors to threaten to pull their team off the field. And in Laguna Niguel, the student yelling racist slurs at a Black basketball player on the opposing team and asking, "Where's his slave owner?"

Videos of the teenagers involved in all the racist episodes would pop up on social media feeds and in local television news broadcasts, even nationally at times, drawing shame and condemnation, then soon to be forgotten. Now it was happening again in the small, largely white town of Ladera Ranch, with a pack of white kids in the neighborhood tormenting a family of Chinese immigrants.

For her part, Layla Parks was determined to do whatever she could to help Haijun Si's family after hearing the details of the ongoing harassment at his home. On a neighborhood Facebook group, she alerted people to what was happening, posting doorbell videos of the recent episodes to see if anyone recognized the faces at the door. And she appealed for help, asking for volunteers to set up a patrol on the Sis' front yard to ward off the young intruders. The aim, Parks said, was "to give this family some peace."

A few of her neighbors might agree to help out, Parks speculated. Instead, more than fifty people quickly volunteered, and Parks found herself leading an impromptu phalanx that formed for six weeks outside the Si family's home, almost every night from 6:00 p.m. to 1:00 a.m. Parks and the other volunteers would plant themselves in folding lawn chairs outside to watch the house, or drive the streets to monitor who was coming and going. So many people signed up for patrol duty, in fact, that it was difficult to find an open slot to volunteer on some nights. The outpouring of support for the immigrant family became a symbol of defiance in the face of hate.

Dave Uemura lived a few blocks away from the Si family but had never met them. As soon as he heard about the harassment, he went over with a box of donuts. On patrol duty, he camped out in front of the house for sixteen straight nights. Uemura, a pharmaceutical representative, was Japanese American himself, born in Hawaii, and he had seen all the rampant news reports about Asian Americans coming under attack during the Covid epidemic. He found himself wondering if he, too, might be a target as he ventured out to public spots in Orange County. *Am I safe here?* he asked himself. Seeing the harassment of the Si family—fellow Asian Americans—tore at him, and he was determined to help them however he could. "You can have a good dinner without being bothered," Uemura promised Si during one evening patrol.

As Uemura, Layla Parks, and the rotating shifts of neighbors stood guard at the house, kids on bicycles would whir down the street and glance their way, then veer off when they saw the assembled crowd patrolling the yard. A few times, teenagers gathered on a nearby hillside and yelled menacingly, throwing rocks down at the crowd. One the size of a golf ball whizzed past Uemura's head as he stood watch, quickly followed by two more tosses. He held his ground.

Not everyone was so supportive. The mother of one ten-year-old boy in the neighborhood, recognizing her son's face in a video on a neighborhood site that showed him rushing to Si's door and shouting graphic sexual obscenities, demanded that Parks take down the video. Parks refused, even when the mother sent her a cease-and-desist letter and threatened to bring a defamation lawsuit because of the "shame and mortification" the episode had brought the family.

A few weeks into the patrols, hundreds of residents gathered on the lawn across the street from the Si home for a traditional Chinese Lantern Festival marking the lunar new year, complete with a lion dance and bright, festive costumes. The idea, said Dave Min, the Asian American state senator who spoke to the crowd, was to show the Si family that everyone was welcome here despite the harassment they had received—that the supporters outnumbered the tormentors in the face of "an epidemic of hate." The failure of the sheriff's department to take more aggressive action infuriated Min. "If these kids were Black," he said later, "they'd be going to jail."

The support overwhelmed Haijun Si. Some five months after the harassment started, it finally stopped; the neighborhood patrols had worked. Where his calls to the Sheriff's Department had failed to deter the neighborhood kids, the support of his neighbors had succeeded. Si grew emotional just thinking about it, struggling to find the words in English to express what it meant to see all those neighbors—almost all of them strangers until now—standing guard on his front lawn night after night. "I'm very grateful," he said finally as he sat on his patio and thought back on all the vigils. "They do too much," he said. "I would tell them, 'Go home, it's quiet; go home.' And they stayed."

---

With violent bigotry the stuff of daily headlines, and police often silent, some neighborhoods started pushing back—not just in Ladera Ranch, but in other communities, too. What happened in Orange County was seen again months later across the country in a quiet neighborhood in Virginia Beach, Virginia, where a Black military family was similarily enduring months of harassment.

Jannique and Joel Martinez and their three children had lived for nearly five years at the end of a cul-de-sac on Jessamine Court when the commotion started. They had little contact with their next-door neighbor—a white man who lived with his mother—until the neighbor set up motion detectors, loudspeakers, and strobe lights aimed at their front door. Whenever anyone walked into or out of the Martinez house, they would be greeted with a cacophony of monkey noises and vulgar, racist recordings filled with the N-word. Scared by the constant torrent of slurs, Jannique Martinez's seven-year-old son asked her what the N-word meant. The scene was "the modern, electronic version of a cross-burning," wrote columnist Petula Dvorak.

It was threatening and intimidating conduct by any measure. Virginia Beach police insisted, however, that "as appalling and offensive" as the white neighbor's behavior was, it "did not rise to a level" of a crime, and police said they had no power to do anything. But Martinez's neighbors and other Virginia Beach residents did; after the story hit the local news, dozens of people of all races and backgrounds turned out en masse at the family's home to march in support of them and picket their bullying neighbor. "SPREAD LOVE, NOT HATE," read one homemade sign.

As with Haijun Si in Orange County, the public shaming succeeded where the authorities had fallen short, and Virginia Beach police reported that the racist intimidation "voluntarily ceased." The Martinez family could once again walk in and out of their home without being confronted by the blare of vile, racist recordings. For Jannique Martinez, it was heartening to see so many community members, many of them complete strangers, come together to support her family and finally silence her racist neighbor.

"It's quieter," she said. That's all she really wanted.

## CHAPTER 15
# "IS THIS AMERICA?"

Haijun Si's family would finally find some peace. But the racial strife in their well-manicured slice of Orange County suburbia didn't fade away; it was only intensifying with Donald Trump's desperate effort to overturn the results of the 2020 presidential election. A smoldering stew of grievances racking America over political and racial fault lines was pitting neighbor against neighbor in Ladera Ranch, and the country as a whole, and it would come bursting to the fore when one of the town's own was arrested as an organizer of the attack on the U.S. Capitol on January 6, 2021, an event replete with symbols of racism and white supremacy.

The racial climate in Ladera Ranch was unnerving for Shereen and Marc Rahming, a Black couple with two young children who had moved there from the Los Angeles area six years earlier in search of the prototypical suburban life and "the white picket fence," as Shereen called it. The couple realized when they made the move, about forty miles south down the coast, that they would be among the few Blacks in Ladera Ranch—or all of Orange County, for that matter. With the county's entrenched history of hostility, the Black population there—unlike the rising numbers of Asians and Hispanics—had remained largely stagnant at a paltry 2 percent of the population. Even money and celebrity were no guarantee of entry: a veteran NFL football player, Brandon Mebane, complained that he and other Black teammates on the Los Angeles Chargers were met with rejected rental applications and discouraging signals in Orange County when the Chargers moved their summer training facility there in 2017 and the players went looking for homes. "You could just tell they didn't want us there," Mebane said. "No matter how much money you have, you're still black."

The Rahmings knew Orange County's reputation, but they were still startled by the icy stares, the snubs, and, occasionally, the outright hostility that they and other minorities faced from some neighbors. Shereen was happy for Haijun Si's family after the neighborhood's nightly patrols shut down the harassment. But she wondered where the outrage was over all the other day-to-day indignities that people of color were facing in her town, like the Confederate flag hanging off a pickup truck parked for days across from the Rahmings' home (police said there was nothing they could do) or all the racist memes circulated by town leaders on neighborhood sites, including one showing Vice President Kamala Harris as a corn-rowed prostitute and Joe Biden as her pimp.

Someone had written "n****r" in big chalk letters on the street, and a neighborhood kid was videotaped apparently screaming the same vile word while skateboarding down the street with a group of kids and waving a Trump flag. There was the large swastika found carved into a tree, with another spray-painted onto a neighborhood school. One resident even reported hearing someone on a public-address system outside a neighborhood restaurant announcing: "Keep Ladera Ranch majority-white." The episodes weren't necessarily hate crimes on their own, but they were jarring reminders of what the Rahmings saw as their status as outsiders in their own suburban, white-picket-fence enclave.

"I never thought I'd see these things," said Shereen, a former elementary schoolteacher. "I thought we were beyond this." The racial hostility she and Marc felt was so upsetting that they moved their two children to a different elementary school and refused to even let them play in the yard outside their home by themselves; they were afraid, Marc said, of "another Trayvon Martin"—a reference to the Black teenager whose fatal shooting by a neighborhood watch captain in central Florida, George Zimmerman, set off outrage and anguish in 2012.

The Rahmings' relations became particularly strained with one well-known Ladera Ranch resident. Russell Taylor, a politically connected businessman, was a tall, beefy white man in his late thirties who was a hard-to-miss sight in the neighborhood, driving his bright-red Corvette and often wearing a matching red "Make America Great Again" cap. Taylor lived with his wife and young children in an expensive home inside a gated enclave within Ladera Ranch, and he displayed an enormous American flag that covered his entire two-car garage door, filming himself driving his Corvette through the flag with the engine revving. He was a popular figure among Ladera Ranch's conservatives and fellow Trump supporters, organizing events and creating a Facebook page called "Patriots of Ladera Ranch." But to the Rahmings, whose son played in the same local football league as Taylor's boy, he was a big part of the problem, and they felt his ire directed at them as one of the few Black families in the area.

Tensions came to a head over the Black Lives Matter vigils that broke out nationwide after the police killing of George Floyd in Minneapolis in May of 2020, when an agonizing video captured officer Derek Chauvin with his knee on Floyd's neck for more than eight minutes. A BLM event was planned in Ladera Ranch, and Shereen Rahming was planning to take her eleven-year-old daughter; with another Black victim killed by police, she felt it was important for them to make their voices heard. Russell Taylor had a different view. He was alarmed to hear of plans for the vigil, and he put out an "urgent" notice to his neighbors on his "Patriots" page, warning of "bad actors" at the event who might be looking to cause trouble in the neighborhood.

Taylor's warning about "bad actors" at the vigil echoed the rhetoric of Trump himself, who portrayed BLM protesters, often in overtly racist tones, as "thugs," lawless marauders, and "radical left, bad people." In fact, the vast majority of the hundreds of Black Lives protests nationwide after Floyd's killing were peaceful—93 percent, according to one study. Much of the violence that did occur came from white supremacists infiltrating the protests; one member of the far-right Boogaloo Boyz, posing as a BLM protester, fired thirteen rounds from an assault rifle into a Minneapolis police precinct; another Boogaloo Boy, a military veteran, ambushed two law enforcement officers near an Oakland protest, killing one of them; and three more Boogaloos plotted to detonate Molotov cocktails at another protest in Las Vegas.

Yet it was the Black Lives protesters who drew Trump's ire. "When the looting starts, the shooting starts," Trump tweeted after a clash in Minneapolis. It was an ominous, racially charged threat echoing the words of segregationist police officials in the South during the civil rights movement decades earlier. Twitter slapped a warning on the president's tweet for "glorifying violence," a step it had never taken before. Trump was so upset by the Black Lives protests that he even asked stunned Pentagon officials privately: "Can't you just shoot them, just shoot them in the legs or something?"

At Ladera Ranch's Black Lives vigil, Shereen Rahming spotted Russell Taylor across the street, watching for "trouble" as he chatted and laughed with local sheriff's deputies on the scene. She felt his glare—and the sting of racial profiling—as he watched the thirty-five or forty protesters, most of them people of color, marching and waving signs. Her own daughter was accosted at the event by a woman screaming at her about the Black Lives protests, she said, but to Taylor, the protesters were the ones causing the problems.

Taylor was no racist, his lawyer said; he simply feared that a Black Lives Matter vigil was going to bring rioting and destruction to their quiet suburb. But to the Rahmings, all the talk of "bad actors" and fears of damage to the neighborhood felt maddeningly familiar—and racist. The climate in the neighborhood became even more heated after yet another racial flashpoint two months after Floyd's murder, this one in Kenosha, Wisconsin. The police shooting there of another young

Black man — Jacob Blake, shot seven times in the back and left paralyzed — sparked another round of national unrest, including a protest in Kenosha where seventeen-year-old Kyle Rittenhouse shot three protesters with an AR-15-style rifle, killing two of them, only to later be acquitted of homicide and other charges.

Shereen Rahming took part in another small vigil in Ladera Ranch for Jacob Blake and the victims killed at the Kenosha protest, but again, Russ Taylor was unhappy to see it unfolding in his town. Soon, he and Shereen were exchanging heated accusations on a neighborhood webpage, with Taylor accusing Shereen of spreading "fake news" about Rittenhouse, who he said had "protected himself in self-defense," and Shereen firing back at Taylor, saying that she "wouldn't expect any other response from the local white supremacist."

Taylor was furious. "I am truly curious why you would publicly call me a white supremacist?" Taylor texted Shereen. "It is appalling to me that you would make such a statement. It's the furthest from the truth and you are publicly slandering me. I expect you to do the right thing and retract that comment." She refused.

Taylor was becoming more agitated by the day about a long litany of third-rail political grievances of the political right that would set him on a path to the Capitol that January 6th day — not just the Black Lives Matter protests, but also Covid restrictions, perceived government overreach, and, most of all, the prospect of Donald Trump not returning to the White House for a second term as the 2020 election neared. Venting his anger, Taylor wrapped himself in the mantle of a "patriot" defending freedoms under assault from the radical left and BLM protesters, and he bestowed the "Patriot" title over and over again — on himself, his allies, his Facebook group, and even on his prized red Corvette, which he dubbed the "C-8 Patriot Missile."

Taylor, a Mormon who graduated from Brigham Young University, ran his own Orange County company customizing cell phones and electronic devices for Apple and other technology companies. But that fall, he was spending more time than ever on conservative political causes. He went out to greet Trump at the airport for a big rally in

Orange County before the election. He hosted a screening of a pro-Trump film that decried what it derided as Democratic-fueled socialism; he led the attendees in a chant of "Four More Years!" And he joined forces with two other Orange County conservatives—Alan Hostetter, a former police officer turned yoga instructor in San Clemente, and Morton Irvine Smith, a fifth-generation scion of the Irvine family, the real-estate dynasty that founded much of Orange County in the late 1800s. Both Hostetter and Smith were followers of "Q," the mythical leader of "QAnon," the wild, conspiracy-minded group that revered Trump for supposedly leading the fight against Satanic pedophiles and the hidden "deep state" in Washington.

Hostetter, a military veteran who served briefly as police chief for another small Orange County city, had started a nonprofit group called the American Phoenix Project months earlier, in the spring of 2020, with Taylor and Smith joining the board to work with him on it. It started as a way for them to combat what they saw as excessive Covid restrictions, but after Biden's victory in the presidential election that November, they shifted focus abruptly to what they now claimed was an election victory fraudulently stolen from Trump. While IRS regulations prohibit such tax-exempt nonprofits from supporting political candidates, the Phoenix Project went at their newfound mission to help Trump with zeal nonetheless—and sometimes with jarring, violent warnings that presaged their efforts on January 6.

As Trump continued to dispute the election results in Washington, Hostetter, Taylor, and Smith organized a "Stop the Steal" rally in Huntington Beach five weeks after the election, with former Orange County congressman Dana Rohrabacher at their side. Hostetter, with an American flag bandanna wrapped around his fedora, declared that "execution is the just punishment for the ringleaders of this coup"—meaning those who had "stolen" the election. "President Trump must be inaugurated on January 20," he said.

Days later, Taylor stood up in front of the Orange County Board of Supervisors during a public session to protest emergency Covid restrictions, warning ominously that "revolution" was coming in the face of government tyranny. "My name is Russell Taylor, and I am a free American," he began, his voice somber. He and thousands of people like him, he said, were protesting week after week "in the streets all up and down the state of California, and do you know what they're saying? Revolution. Storm the capitols. Pay attention and act wisely, as time is transpiring. End this state of emergency before we the people will."

Three days later, Trump put out his latest declaration of victory in the election. At least eleven aides and confidantes had told Trump that there was no fraud. Even Trump's stalwart attorney general, William Barr, told Trump bluntly in December that his claims of fraud were "bullshit." Trump didn't want to hear it. "Statistically impossible to have lost the 2020 election," Trump tweeted. "Big protest in D.C. on January 6th. Be there, will be wild!"

Russ Taylor was listening. "Who is going?" Taylor asked in a post alongside Trump's tweet on an encrypted Telegram chat he called "the California Patriots—Answer the Call Jan 6." He and Hostetter connected online with a number of other ardent Trump supporters from Southern California who identified as members of the Three Percenters, the far-right militia group, and together they began making plans for January 6. Taylor made himself the leader. He had never served in the military, but he adopted the tone and verbiage of a military officer, writing on New Year's Day, five days before the Capitol siege, that he was establishing a new Telegram chat for some three dozen people for "able-bodied individuals that are going to DC on Jan. 6." He told Hostetter: "I truly believe that we were meant to come together to be engaged in this war at this time."

Many of the thirty or so men on the chat had never met in person, but Taylor believed they had one thing in common: "We are all ready to and willing to fight." He sought out people with experience in military or police work and set up the encrypted chats to share "key intell" about their plans. "I am assuming that you have some sort of weaponry that you are bringing with you," he wrote, along with body-armor chest plates. Some talked of trying to sneak guns into Washington, despite the city's tough gun control laws. As for weapons they could legally carry into the city, Taylor suggested a hatchet, a fixed-blade knife, a bat, or a large metal flashlight. He himself would be coming well-armed.

If there was any doubt about his intentions, Taylor laid them to rest when a member of the brigade asked when they should be at the Capitol that day. "I personally want to be on the front steps," Taylor wrote, "and be one of the first ones to breach the Capitol!"

---

A day that would end in historic violence and chaos at the hands of right-wing extremists had begun, remarkably enough, much like any other day in Washington for Harry Dunn and many of his fellow line officers at the Capitol Police Department.

For weeks, warnings had been swirling around Washington — among intelligence analysts at the FBI, at DHS, even inside Dunn's own police department — about the prospect of potentially violent Trump supporters, armed and organized, converging on January 6 for the expected certification of Biden's election win. "Get violent," read one posting circulated by an FBI field office a day earlier. "Stop calling this a march, or rally, or a protest. Go there ready for war."

But none of those warnings reached the people who needed to hear them most: the officers on the front lines like Dunn, a Black officer who was working to protect the Capitol and more than 500 lawmakers inside for what was normally a pro forma process for certifying the election of the next president of the United States. For years, warnings of violence from Muslim or Black groups had generated rapid-fire responses from the FBI and other law enforcement agencies; a brewing rebellion from an overwhelming white crowd did not. For Dunn and his fellow officers, there was nothing to indicate they would face anything beyond typically raucous but peaceful protests, with perhaps some arrests for civil disobedience. Supervisors hadn't passed along any official threat alerts to them, and some of the officers' riot gear still remained locked away in buses far from the Capitol as Dunn took up his post on a stairway leading to the Senate chamber.

Dunn, a six-foot-seven-inch, 325-pound officer who had been an offensive lineman for his college football team, made for a dominating presence as he patrolled the Capitol grounds. His shift started quietly enough that day. But just before 11:00 a.m., he received a troubling text—not through any official channels, but from a friend—with a screenshot showing Trump protesters talking of plans to converge on the Capitol with guns, gas masks, and trauma kits, on what they said were "marching orders" from Trump itself. For the first time, Dunn was worried.

Then came an alert crackling over his police radio about a possible bomb found a few blocks away, then reports of the crowd surging outside the Capitol, and then an urgent dispatch reporting that demonstrators had breached the Capitol fence. Dunn raced to grab his M4 rifle and put on his twenty-pound steel chest protector. The Capitol was under attack.

For the next five hours, Capitol police officers—ill-prepared and vastly outnumbered—engaged in hand-to-hand combat against a mob of some two thousand Trump supporters using baseball bats, flagpoles, bear spray, police shields, metal bike racks, and anything else they could find to force their way onto the gated Capitol grounds and, ultimately, into the Capitol itself. One officer likened the scene to a "medieval battlefield," with five people dying and some 140 officers injured in the brawl. The riot, unprecedented in America history, forced lawmakers to evacuate both the House and the Senate as they were ushered to safety, delaying the vote certifying the next president of the United States and, for a few chaotic hours, derailing democracy.

In the midst of the melee, Dunn knocked down one rioter who was trying to grab him in Statuary Hall in the south wing, and he headed off an onrushing crowd of about twenty rioters near the Capitol rotunda, the ornately decorated dome at the very center of the sprawling complex. Dunn ordered the crowd of rioters to turn around and leave the building. Instead, the rioters began yelling at him. "We're here to stop the steal!" someone yelled. Another rioter chimed in: "Joe Biden is not the president! No one voted for Joe Biden!"

## "Is This America?"

Dunn was trained to keep politics out of the job, but this was a situation he had never confronted before. "Well, I voted for Joe Biden," he said. "Does my vote not count? Am I nobody?" That's when all the racist vitriol started spewing from the white crowd. "You hear that, guys? This n****r voted for Joe Biden!" shouted a woman in a pink MAGA shirt. Soon, other rioters in the crowd were shouting at Dunn and screaming, "Boooo, fucking n****r!" In all his time in uniform, Dunn had never heard anyone call him that word, much less a whole crowd of rioters attacking the Capitol. It was then that he realized, he said, that he was confronting a throng of racist rioters storming the Capitol.

When it was all over, when the rioters were finally cleared from the building hours later, Dunn went back to the rotunda and commiserated with other officers about what they had just experienced. Dunn sat down on a bench with another Black officer, telling him of the ugly racial epithets hurled at him. It felt to him like the rioters hated him not just for his position of authority, but for the color of his skin. He became emotional, yelling and then sobbing.

"How the fuck can this happen?" Dunn asked. "Is this America?"

---

The mob's central aim that day was clear: to stop Congress from certifying Biden's election and, somehow, keep Donald Trump in the White House. But in a sea of overwhelmingly white rioters—93 percent of those arrested—the subtext for the violence was almost as plain: Many of the rioters wanted to make a statement about white America. The sight of this sea of white faces among the rioters, including dozens of former or current members of the military, was not lost on the chairman of the Joint Chiefs of Staff, General Mark A. Milley, who said of the scene afterward: "I want to understand white rage.... What is it that caused thousands of people to assault this building and try to overturn the Constitution of the United States of America?"

Symbols of white supremacy were everywhere. One rioter brought a huge Confederate flag from his home in Delaware, used it to attack a

Black officer, and paraded it proudly in the rotunda—an anachronistic moment that even the original Confederate soldiers who attacked Washington in 1864 hadn't managed to achieve.

There on display on the Capitol yard were nooses and a makeshift hangman's gallows—painful symbols of the lynchings of African Americans, and of the manner some rioters said they favored to murder Vice President Pence for refusing to overturn the election.

One rioter from New Jersey, a US Army reservist and Navy contractor who was an open Nazi sympathizer, donned Third Reich garb at the Capitol, complete with a Hitler-style mustache and comb-over. A bearded Virginia rioter sported a "Camp Auschwitz" sweatshirt with an image of a skull and the Nazi slogan "Work Brings Freedom" on the front and a single word—"Staff"—on the back. Another rioter was seen giving the Nazi salute. The many flags waved by rioters displayed logos for "America First," "VDare," "Kek," Pepe the Frog, and other notorious white-nationalist symbols. And many of the rioters flashed "OK" signs—another symbol coopted by some far-right extremists to mean "white power." And there was the sign, held mockingly by a white man, that read "Blacks for Trump."

And among the rioters there were many—hundreds in all—aligned with a motley crew of notorious white supremacist and far-right extremist groups such as the Proud Boys, the Oath Keepers, the Three Percenters, QAnon, the Boogaloo Boyz, VDare, Groypers, and Aryan Nation.

Among all the extremist and white supremacist groups at the Capitol that day, the Proud Boys boasted the highest profile of any of them, thanks to Trump. Three months earlier, Trump had handed the Proud Boys what amounted to a rallying cry all their own when he was asked at a presidential debate against Biden whether he was finally willing to condemn white supremacists. "Proud Boys, stand back and stand by," Trump answered after prodding from Biden and the moderator, Chris Wallace. The Proud Boys, a violent group who marketed themselves as "Western chauvinists" rather than straight-out white supremacists, were thrilled by the exposure, giving them a legitimacy they had never had before. "So Proud of my guys right now," the group's charismatic if unlikely leader, Henry "Enrique" Tarrio, the son of Cuban immigrants, posted right after Trump's non-denunciation. "Standing by sir."

The Proud Boys were ready to stand up again once it became clear that Trump had lost the election. "No Trump—no peace," Tarrio told his men three weeks after the election, as he warned of a "war" against President-elect Biden and led several protests in Washington that turned violent. He and other Proud Boys leaders created a new branch of hand-picked men, calling them "the Ministry of Self-Defense," to prepare for violence, and they plotted with the Three Percenters and the Oath Keepers ahead of the January 6 certification date in Congress to create what one Proud Boy called a "force multiplier" that would "shut this shit down."

Tarrio directed the Proud Boys to "turn out in record numbers" at the Capitol that day, and turn out they did, with several hundred group members from all around the country gathering at the Capitol. At least three dozen of them would ultimately be arrested for their role in smashing their way into the building and ransacking the place. "Let's take the fucking Capitol!" a Proud Boy from Florida's Gulf Coast, who went on to assault a police officer, was heard on video yelling outside the building, before other members admonished him as "an idiot" for his blunt language. "Let's not fucking yell that, all right?" another member cautioned him. But several of their fellow Proud Boys couldn't help themselves as they tore down fences, broke through windows, attacked police officers, and stole police shields. "Dude, we're right in front of the Capitol! American citizens are storming the Capitol—taking it back right now!" one of Tarrio's deputies was heard yelling in a video seized by the FBI. "Oh my God! This is such history! This is insane. We've gone through every barricade this far. Fuck you!"

The Proud Boys had such a high-profile role in the violence, in fact, that Canada banned the group—originally formed by right-wing Canadian provocateur Gavin McInnes—as a terrorist organization just weeks later. Tarrio himself, for all his fiery bluster, wasn't among the rioters that day, though. He didn't make it out to the Capitol at all; the day before, a federal judge in the District of Columbia had banned him from the city altogether after he was arrested and jailed at a Proud Boys rally for bringing high-capacity weapons and burning a Black Lives Matter banner stolen from a historic Black church in what police investigated as a possible hate crime.

Tarrio's white-nationalist operatives carried on at the Capitol that day without him. "Don't fucking leave," he posted more than ninety minutes after the rioting began. "Proud of My Boys and my country," he wrote three minutes later.

Even as Tarrio was directing his men to hold their ground, lawmakers inside both chambers of Congress were still trying to evacuate, with security officers barricading doors around them and handing out gas masks. After rioters smashed through the glass doors leading to the lobby of the House chamber, a Capitol police officer—screaming "Get back!" at the mob—shot and killed Air Force veteran Ashli Babbitt as she attempted to climb through the broken door. "I know members of Congress, as well as my fellow officers and staff, were in jeopardy and in serious danger," said Lt. Michael Byrd, the veteran Black officer who fired the fatal shot and was cleared of wrongdoing in an investigation. "And that's my job."

For older Black lawmakers in particular, the sight of the overwhelmingly white mob surging into the House chamber brought back painful images of the kind of political violence they thought they had left behind in the Deep South decades earlier during the civil rights movement. "I saw the kind of hatred in the eyes of the people who broke in the Capitol," said Representative Bennie Thompson, the longtime Black congressman. "It was that same kind of hatred I saw in people who wanted to stop people of color from casting a ballot for the candidate of their choice in Mississippi."

At one harrowing point in the melee, with more than thirty lawmakers still trapped in the House gallery, Representative Jason Crow—a former Army Ranger—told his colleagues to take off the lapel pins identifying them as members of Congress in order to make them less identifiable if the mob broke through the doors. The response he got split along racial lines: many of his fellow white colleagues took their pins off right away, but a number of the Black and minority lawmakers trapped in the chamber did not. They worried that as people of color in the midst of the violent chaos, police wouldn't recognize them as members of Congress without their pins and would come after them. They could get hurt either way. "I thought, there's no way I'm taking off my pin," said Representative Pramila Jayapal, a South Asian immigrant and a Democratic congresswoman in the Seattle area. "Because it was either you get recognized by the insurrectionist or you don't get recognized by Capitol Police as a brown woman or Black woman."

---

While the crowd of rioters at the Capitol on January 6 was overwhelmingly white, many of them did not fit the convenient profile that developed around them publicly in the aftermath of the riot. The conventional wisdom suggested that the rioters came from the reddest of red regions, the Republican strongholds from which Trump had always drawn his deepest political support: rural areas, overwhelmingly white, with high unemployment. But as political scientist Robert Pape began to dig into the data for the hundreds of people arrested after the riot, he and his team of researchers at the University of Chicago found something startling. Not only was that commonly held stereotype not borne out by the data, but a very different explanation emerged: Most of the rioters came to Washington that day from places that *Biden* had won, not Trump, and their defining feature in terms of demographics was that they hailed from counties where the proportion of the white population was shrinking rapidly compared to that of non-whites. The more the white population had shrunk, the more likely it was to send rioters to the Capitol, the data indicated. The declining proportion of the white population had "a galvanizing effect" on the rioters, Pape and his team concluded, with the storming of the Capitol driven in part by "racial cleavages and white discontent" with the changing diversity in their hometowns.

Buttressing that idea was polling that Pape's team conducted about Americans' views on the rioting and what drove it. For conservative

Americans who sympathized with the rioters, their fears about people of color driving whites out of the majority, and out of positions of power in America, stood out as a powerful motivator. This "Great Replacement Theory" had burned for generations on the political fringes among white supremacists, but what Pape was seeing suggested that this idea was now playing out on a massive scale, with many millions of right-wing Americans believing not only that whites were at risk of being "replaced," but also that Biden was an illegitimate president and that force was justified to keep Trump in office. The more dramatically the proportion of the white population was shrinking in a particular locale, the more fervent these extremist views became.

Pape and his researchers were talking about places like Orange County—an area that, despite its long history as the fabled "Orange Curtain" of white, Republican politics, had voted for Biden over Trump by nine percentage points and was quickly becoming a place where whites were in the minority. Indeed, Orange County was overrepresented at the Capitol on January 6, with at least sixteen people from the county arrested in the rioting after traveling across the country to Washington by plane, car, or bus.

A number of these locals occupied places of prominence in the events that day. Among them was a graying Orange County law professor who had given Trump the brazen legal imprimatur to try to overturn the election results, as well as a college-student-turned-rioter who claimed the very same chair on the Senate dais where Pence had been sitting minutes before the inrushing mob forced him to flee.

Before his moment of infamy in Pence's chair ultimately landed him in jail, Christian Secor lived with his mother in Costa Mesa in central Orange County and was studying political science at UCLA, about fifty miles up the coast. He was a political outlier there. Like many elite colleges, UCLA is a school where most students lean liberal. Christian Secor did not. He considered himself a white nationalist and a fascist, according to the FBI, and his "extremist ideology" earned him a reviled reputation on campus.

His turn to right-wing extremism was even more puzzling because of his family background: he was half Mexican, and his mother, along with many members of her extended family, had come to Orange County from Mexico as immigrants. Yet Secor himself was vehemently opposed to all immigrants, declaring on one conservative podcast: "No immigration, end it all."

Secor thrived on provocation, and he told of his plan to "fuck with the liberals" at a big political protest over immigration in 2017 in the "lefty stronghold" of Laguna Beach, along one of Orange County's most picturesque stretches of ocean. "Me and my friends, we just decided, 'You know what'd be funny? What if we just walked into the antifa camp with a Rhodesian flag?'" he recounted. The green-and-white flag of the former African nation of Rhodesia, once a white-minority-ruled nation that became Zimbabwe, had become a symbol of Aryan power for some white supremacists. They included, most infamously, Dylann Roof, who wore a patch of the flag on his jacket before carrying out his massacre of nine churchgoers in South Carolina in 2015.

For Secor, the Rhodesian imagery was a way to poke the liberal beast with racist provocations. "We knew we were going to get into trouble with this one," he laughed, and soon enough, liberal protesters were yelling at Secor and his friends about white supremacy and the Rhodesian flag he was waving, and fisticuffs were breaking out. He'd gotten what he wanted.

Secor became part of the "Groyper Army," a newer brand of in-your-face white nationalists who took their name from a cartoon frog popularized online by the alt-right. He became an avid follower of Groyper leader Nick Fuentes, a white supremacist and Holocaust denier who was at both the "Unite the Right" march in Charlottesville in 2017 and the Capitol riot on January 6, 2021. As one of his online aliases, Secor also adopted "Scuffed Elliot Rodger"—a dark homage to another one-time California college student of that name, who killed six people and wounded fourteen others in a rampage in 2014 outside Santa Barbara. The real Elliot Rodger, who left behind a raging manifesto before committing suicide, had inspired other angry young men who considered themselves "incels," or "involuntarily celibate" men angry at women; one of his followers, a young man in Toronto, killed eleven people and injured more than a dozen others when he plowed his van into a crowded city sidewalk four years later. Another "incel" admirer of Rodger's in Ohio, a military trainee, was arrested on hate-crime charges with a machine gun and tactical gear in a foiled plot to "slaughter" women at a college sorority, according to a manifesto he wrote. Now Secor, another blustery college student who looked a bit like the original Elliot Rodger, had adopted the dead mass murderer as his own online persona, too.

Secor's views were too extreme even for conservative students on the UCLA campus. The Bruin Republicans club expelled him for "being radical, reckless, and acting inappropriately," so he founded his own far-right political group at school called "America First Bruins," inviting other white nationalists onto campus to speak. "America First" was a white-nationalist slogan dating back to the pre–World War II isolationism and antisemitism of famed aviator Charles Lindbergh, and Secor's Groyper idol, Fuentes, used it as the name of his own podcast. "America First" became Secor's mantra as well, and Twitter was the megaphone for his rage; he used it to blast out more than twelve hundred politically fueled tweets in the months before the Capitol insurrection, attacking women, gays, people of color, immigrants, and Jews, along with liberals, gun-control advocates, and "anti-racism" activists.

Fascism was "epic," Secor said in one tweet, and the infamous torchlit rally by white supremacists in Charlottesville was an event to be admired. He supported "nationalism everywhere," and when a Hispanic woman on Twitter bemoaned the lenient treatment of white criminals compared to minorities, Secor answered back flatly: "Well America is a white country so..." Of the growing diversity in Orange County, the place where he'd grown up, he said: "This is why Orange County has fallen." As for political feuding: "I don't want peaceful separation with the left. I want holy war. I want to raze. I want to conquer."

The rantings were just the online bravado of a college kid in an age of anything-goes social media, some people close to Secor insisted. But fellow UCLA students took it seriously, especially when they noticed photos he posted showing him at a gun range. They complained to the school administration about what they said was Secor's violent and hateful online rhetoric, only to be told that free-speech protections kept the university from taking action. Nine months before the Capitol insurrection, one student even publicly called out Secor by name in a piece for a Jewish publication at UCLA denouncing the rising tide of fascism on campus. Still, nothing happened.

In the midst of the Covid pandemic, Secor began showing up with other "Groypers" in Orange County to support "Curfew Breaker" protests against Covid restrictions organized by American Phoenix, the group led by Alan Hostetter and Russell Taylor. Covid protests had become magnets nationwide for many white supremacists and right-wing extremists who were drawn to the issue by the racial tensions spurred by Trump's rhetoric about the "China virus," their own distrust of Covid vaccines and restrictions, and their deep-seated anti-government sentiments. The lure of such thinking reached a boiling point in Michigan, where thirteen men—most of them tied to white supremacy and far-right militias—were arrested for allegedly conspiring to kidnap Governor Gretchen Whitmer in 2020 in a plot that grew out of their fierce resistance to her Covid lockdown orders. Orange County itself had become a hotbed of Covid resistance and protest, with the county's top health officer quitting in 2020 in the face of violent threats from anti-masking protesters; some even displayed a photo of her with a Hitler mustache and swastikas, throwing the Nazi label back onto her.

Hostetter, arrested for chaining himself to a fence in one Covid protest in Orange County, was as virulent as anyone in his opposition to the health restrictions. But the sight of Secor and other Groyper white supremacists at their protests—shouting "America First!" and "Groyper! Groyper!," screaming "Go home, whore!" at one woman, and stomping on a gay pride flag—was apparently a bridge too far even for him. He didn't want the Groypers there, for the negative optics if nothing else, and he got into a shouting match with them. Picking up a bullhorn, he accused them of being left-wing "plants" who came to the Covid protests just "to make us look bad." The Groypers, avowed white supremacists who weren't planted by anyone, stuck around anyway.

Secor's path would converge again with the American Phoenix leaders a few months later in another common political cause, this time in Washington, DC, on January 6, 2021.

The day before the Capitol riot, Taylor, Hostetter, and Smith were all featured speakers at a rally in front of the Supreme Court that their group helped finance. Taylor was seething once again, telling the crowd of Trump enthusiasts that he was standing with them "in defiance of a communist coup that is set to take over America." He spoke of patriots, as he so often did, and of antifa and tyranny and "deep state commie actors," and he hinted at the violence that was to come. "We will fight and we will bleed before we allow our freedom to be taken from us," Taylor said. Their opponents "have brought out the patriots' fury onto these streets, and they did so without knowing that we will not return to our peaceful ways of life until this election is made right, our freedoms are restored, and America is preserved."

Hours later, Taylor posted a message just before midnight on one of his encrypted chat groups, along with a menacing photo. "Now getting ready for tomorrow," he wrote, with his equipment laid out on his hotel-room bed: two hatchets, a stun baton, a knife, a helmet, a military-style vest, a walkie-talkie, and other supplies. He had been preparing for this day in Washington for weeks, and now it was here.

Taylor, Hostetter, and Smith all awoke early the next day for the big rally at the Ellipse, featuring Trump himself as the final speaker. They had to listen from a distance in the cold rain; with the knife, the stun baton, and the other weapons that Taylor was carrying, they couldn't risk trying to get inside the secure area policed by the Secret Service. A slew of familiar faces, from Donald Trump Jr. to Rudy Giuliani, got up onstage to declare that the certification of Biden as president had to be stopped. "Let's have trial by combat," declared Giuliani, whose campaign of lawsuits alleging election fraud had already lost more than sixty court cases. The crowd roared its approval for his fiery call to action.

Giuliani had been firing up Trump's followers around the country for weeks with his debunked claims of election fraud, sometimes with ugly racial undertones. The worst came in the hotly contested race in Georgia, where Giuliani made baseless accusations of election-rigging against two Black election workers—Shaye Moss and her mother, Ruby Freeman, who both worked election night in Atlanta at a ballot-counting center and were shown in a video circulated by the Trump campaign. Giuliani accused the mother and daughter by name of bringing in suitcases filled with fake ballots for Biden and of "quite obviously, surreptitiously, passing around USB ports as if they are vials of heroin or cocaine." (What Giuliani pointed to as a vote-laden USB drive in the video was actually a ginger mint that her mother was giving her, Moss said.) Trump joined in the fray, singling out Freeman by name eighteen times in a call with Georgia election officials and accusing her, in racially tinged terms, of being a "hustler" and a "scammer" as he pressed them to "find" him the votes he needed to win Georgia.

There was no truth to any of it; multiple investigations by state and federal officials, including one by the Trump-appointed United States attorney in Atlanta, found no election impropriety. Even so, the lie spread like a virus among Trump's followers. The president's supporters unleashed a slew of violent and often racist threats against the two Black women in online postings and in hundreds of texts and emails to them. "Be glad it's 2020 and not 1920," one told Moss, alluding to the mob lynching of Blacks in that era. "The coon c*nts should be locked up for voter fraud," another Trump supporter wrote on Parler. "Those two should be strung up from the nearest lamppost and set on fire," wrote a reader on another far-right platform.

Moss called 911 for help after angry strangers kept banging on her door menacingly, and her grandmother called her screaming hysterically because people had shown up at her own house and tried to push through the door to make what they claimed was "a citizen's arrest." Freeman moved out of her home for two months after the FBI warned her she wasn't safe there anymore. "There is nowhere I feel safe. Nowhere," Freeman told congressional investigators. "Do you know how it feels to have the president of the United States target you?"

Giuliani had no regrets about his attacks on Freeman or her daughter, and he doubled down on his claims of vote-rigging and a "stolen" election in his raucous remarks at the January 6 rally. To explain "how they cheated," Giuliani introduced the white-haired man at his side, dapperly dressed in a beige coat, a floral scarf, and a wide-brimmed fedora.

John Eastman wasn't a familiar face to most people in the crowd. Back in Orange County he was a well-known conservative spark plug, law professor, and former law-school dean at Chapman University, but in Washington he was still unknown. That would change dramatically, however, after Eastman emerged as the chief legal architect of Trump's audacious plan to overturn the election results—a plan that the law professor himself seemed to acknowledge was illegal.

Eastman, a former clerk to Supreme Court Justice Clarence Thomas, had for years been a strident legal voice in Orange County. Among a long list of conservative legal positions he had staked out, the Nebraska native supported using torture against terror suspects after the September 11 attacks, and he was against allowing gay marriage under California's Proposition 8 or birthright citizenship as a constitutional right for children born in the United States. During Trump's reelection bid, he had moved even further to the right, eliciting charges of racism for a 2020 column in which he falsely argued that Kamala Harris, Biden's pick for vice president, might not be eligible to serve under the Constitution because her parents, immigrants from Jamaica and India, were not yet naturalized citizens when she was born in Oakland.

Eastman's argument about Harris drew howls of protest and derision. Constitutional experts denounced his legal rationale as flawed and shoddy. Amid the backlash, *Newsweek* had to apologize for running a piece that it acknowledged was "being used by some as a tool to perpetuate racism and xenophobia" and had rekindled "the racist lie of birther-ism," which Trump himself had used for years to try to undermine Obama. Trump eagerly repeated Eastman's dubious assertions about Harris' eligibility to be vice president, praising the Orange County professor as "a very highly qualified, very talented lawyer," and he tapped him after his election loss to devise a strategy to overturn the results—and keep Biden and Harris out of the White House.

Eastman would prove critical to boosting Trump's desperate hopes of overturning the election, as he shuttled for weeks between the White House and Trump's makeshift command center at the Willard Hotel nearby in downtown Washington, DC. "A serpent in the ear of the president," Pence's chief counsel, Greg Jacob, called him. As the January 6 certification date approached, Eastman authored two memos for the president amounting to a blueprint for an electoral coup, mapping out ways that he believed Pence could stop Congress from certifying Biden's electoral victory.

"The main thing here is that Pence should do this without asking for permission—either from a vote of the joint session or the Court," Eastman wrote regarding one tactic he proposed for kicking the election to the Republican-led House. "BOLD, Certainly," Eastman wrote in a second memo. "But this Election was Stolen by a strategic Democrat plan to systematically flout existing election laws for partisan advantage; we're no longer playing by Queensbury Rules."

It was right-wing extremism of a different sort—legal extremism. A federal judge in Central California later described Eastman's plan as obviously illegal—"a coup in search of a legal theory," wrote US District Court judge David O. Carter, a former Orange County lawyer himself. "This plan was a last-ditch attempt to secure the Presidency by any means," the judge wrote.

Trump himself, however, loved the plan. He seized on Eastman's ideas to try to pressure Pence, both privately and publicly, and in sometimes humiliating fashion, to stop the routine certification and to get

Republican officials in seven states that he had lost to submit fake slates of electors to tip the election to Trump.

Two days before the January 6 congressional proceedings, in a volatile meeting that Trump called in the Oval Office, he and Eastman met with Pence, along with the vice president's chief of staff, Marc Short, and Jacob, his chief counsel, to press the vice president to send the votes back to the states to review the debunked "irregularities." This would be Trump's last chance to stop the traditional transfer of power, a core democratic process that had gone on unimpeded throughout American history. Eastman laid out the case for Pence taking the brazen step of blocking the election results. Pence and his aides thought the legal pretexts that Eastman was throwing out made no sense. Eastman seemed to acknowledge that he knew it was illegal, according to Jacob, even as he and Trump pressed the vice president to execute the plan. For four years, Pence had played the part of the president's most diehard loyalist, an unflinching sidekick even in Trump's most audacious moments, but the vice president had finally found a line that he was unwilling to cross. He told Trump and Eastman that he didn't believe he had the unilateral authority as vice president to stop the certification of Biden as the next president. Trump fumed. That wasn't the answer he wanted to hear.

Unbowed, Trump directed Eastman to meet at the White House again the next day with Pence's aides, Jacob and Short. They talked for nearly two hours. Eastman went even further than he had the day before. "I'm here asking you to reject the electors," Eastman said pointedly at the start, an idea he himself had rejected in the meeting the day before as too extreme. He appealed to the alumni roots he and Jacob shared as graduates of the University of Chicago Law School, known for its conservative ethos. The answer from Pence's people was still the same. Jacob told him that if the vice president were somehow to do what Eastman was asking, "we would lose nine to nothing in the Supreme Court, wouldn't we?" Eastman hemmed and hawed a bit, suggesting that the vote against Trump might be 7–2, before grudgingly conceding that a unanimous loss seemed more likely.

## "Is This America?"

*The vice president doesn't have the power to overturn a presidential election,* Jacob told Eastman yet again. Jacob pointed back to the 2000 election, when Vice President Al Gore had duly carried out the certification in Congress of his presidential opponent, George W. Bush, confirming his own loss in the tightest election in modern times. "I mean, John, back in 2000, you weren't jumping up and saying Al Gore had this authority to do that," Jacob told him. "You would not want Kamala Harris to be able to exercise that kind of authority in 2024, when I hope Republicans will win the election. And I know you hope that, too, John." Eastman agreed, but only so far as it helped his case. "Al Gore did not have a basis to do it in 2000," Eastman said. "Kamala Harris shouldn't be able to do it in 2024, but I think you should do it today."

Eastman had been pitching his audacious legal ploy for weeks, pressing not only Pence and his aides at the White House, but urging Republican legislators in various states to throw out the electoral ballots for Biden. "You're asking me to do something that's never been done in the history of the United States, and I'm going to put my state through that?" Rusty Bowers, a Trump-backing Republican who was speaker of the Arizona House of Representatives, told Eastman when he called a day earlier to ask for his help. "No, sir."

Jacob, at an impasse with Eastman over his furious lobbying campaign, appealed to reason at the close of their meeting. "John," he said, "in light of everything that we've discussed, can't you—we—just both agree that this is a terrible idea?" Eastman wouldn't agree, but he did realize that his lobbying campaign was at an end. "I see we're not going to be able to persuade you to do this," Eastman said finally.

The next day, with the keenly awaited certification just hours away, Eastman found a much more receptive audience facing the stage at the "Stop the Steal" rally as he made his case to the crowd of screaming Trump supporters. With two American flags billowing in the wind behind him, his fists pumping in the air, Eastman thundered to the crowd about how "secret folders" were buried in voting machines to rig the count, and how "dead people voted," and how the election had been stolen from Trump—all claims rejected as baseless by federal judges in more than sixty cases since the election. Then Eastman turned his attention to Pence, demanding that he send the election back to the state legislatures that afternoon without certifying the vote. Although Pence and his aides had already made clear to him repeatedly that he was not willing to do that, Eastman pressed his case with the rabid crowd. "Anybody that is not willing to stand up to do it does not deserve to be in the office," he told the crowd. "It is that simple."

Then it was Trump's turn to rile up the crowd. Just hours before, he had called Pence and pressured him yet again to stop the certification. "You can either go down in history as a patriot," Trump told his vice president, "or you can go down in history as a pussy." Four days earlier, he had also called the Georgia secretary of state to pressure him to turn in his favor a state that Biden had won, telling him, "All I want to do is this. I just want to find 11,780 votes." Awaiting the speech, Trump had been told that supporters in the crowd had weapons, but he didn't seem to care, telling the Secret Service to get rid of the magnetometers screening for guns, according to testimony from White House aide Cassidy Hutchinson. "I don't effing care that they have weapons— they're not here to hurt me," Hutchinson reported hearing Trump declare.

The election was lost, but Trump, in a typically fiery speech at the Ellipse packed with blame and bravado, went after Pence again in unscripted remarks, saying, "I hope Mike has the courage to do what he has to do," and he urged the thousands of screaming supporters on the lawn in front of him to fight on and "stop the steal."

"We will never give up, we will never concede. It doesn't happen. You don't concede when there's theft involved," Trump declared. In words of aggression that would form the basis for his second impeachment barely a week later on grounds of inciting the riot, Trump said: "And we fight. We fight like hell. And if you don't fight like hell, you're not going to have a country anymore."

The throng of rally-goers was soon on the march down Pennsylvania Avenue toward the Capitol, with Taylor and Hostetter near the front of the pack. Taylor wore an armored chest protector with a knife peeking out of it, and Hostetter had a hatchet in his backpack. Taylor began videotaping himself en route to the Capitol to document what he saw as a historic moment. "We are on the move. Heading up to the Capitol," he announced. At the sound of a police siren and officers nearby, he said: "We'll see who these guys end up working for."

Taylor had always cast himself as a backer of law and order in Orange County, smiling side by side with police at civic events, but now he could be seen in one photo near the Capitol flipping off the police officers who were lined up in riot gear. Along with a mob of other rioters at the west end of the Capitol, Taylor, a bear of a man, pushed his way past the outnumbered police officers who were trying vainly to keep them back. Hostetter followed behind in the path cleared by his "blocking back." An officer pepper-sprayed Taylor, but that didn't stop him. "I was pushing through traitors all day," he bragged in a text hours later. He urged other rioters behind him to do the same. "Move forward, Americans!" he implored the crowd, according to video gathered by the FBI. He then turned back to the officers just a few feet away from him, speaking directly to them: "Last chance, boys," he warned. "Move back!"

Throngs of rioters were soon shattering windows on the side of the Capitol, while crowds outside were screaming "Hang Mike Pence"—a threat that Trump himself seemed to endorse privately from inside the walls of the White House, saying that Pence "deserves" to be hanged. Pence "is nothing but a traitor, and he deserves to burn with the rest of them," a rioter in full military gear said on video.

Using stolen police shields as battering rams, the first throng of rioters shattered windows on the side of the Capitol and climbed inside at 2:13 p.m. Just eleven minutes later, Trump put out another tweet—not to urge calm, as some of his own aides were exhorting him to do, but to go after Pence again for his disloyalty. "Mike Pence didn't have the courage to do what should have been done to protect our Country and our Constitution," Trump wrote. The frontal attack by Trump, coming across Twitter on many rioters' cell phones, only seemed to fuel their anger further, as they surged toward the Capitol Rotunda. Crowds were screaming "Hang Pence!"

With the Capitol in full lockdown, and Secret Service ushering Pence and his team to a secured underground location as the mob moved within forty feet of him, Jacob, the vice president's counsel, sent Eastman a brutally blunt email from their hiding spot. Eastman's legal claims to stop the certification, he wrote, were "essentially entirely made up. And thanks to your bullshit, we are now under siege."

Eastman, hours after his fiery performance at the rally, remained unrepentant. "My 'bullshit'—seriously?" Eastman answered. "The 'siege' is because YOU and your boss did not do what was necessary to allow this to be aired in a public way so the American people can see for themselves what happened."

Taylor and Hostetter reveled in the siege. Another member of Taylor's "brigade" from California had already made it inside the Capitol, along with dozens of other rioters, through one of the smashed windows on the other side of the building. Taylor and Hostetter held their ground amid the rioters occupying the terrace. "We did our part. We are proud of our fellow patriots, our President, and our country," Hostetter wrote with a photo he posted of himself and Taylor smiling buoyantly from the terrace. Because he "had weapons," on him, Taylor said in one of his texts that night, he made the decision not to go into the Capitol building from the terrace; he had already breached the security grounds with the mob, but he was worried about the legal peril of going further inside the complex. Regardless, he felt as though he had already accomplished what he set out to do. "WE STORMED THE CAPITOL," Taylor declared in one text, and the mob had brought a halt to the vote to certify Biden as the next president. Asked what comes next in one thread of texts, he answered: "Insurrection!"

Christian Secor went even further that day. The UCLA student, carrying his blue "America First" flag on a white flagpole as a symbol of his white nationalism, was among a pack of several dozen rioters inside the Capitol who shoved their way past three police officers guarding a

## "Is This America?"

set of double doors into the Senate chamber, pinning officers against the doors as they swarmed in.

"Where the fuck are they?" one disappointed rioter yelled out as the mob entered the chamber, only to find it emptied. "While we're here, we might as well set up a government," another rioter said. "Hey, let's take a seat people!" someone yelled. "Where the fuck is Nancy?" asked another, disappointed not to find House Speaker Nancy Pelosi in the chamber. The so-called QAnon Shaman—Jacob Chansley, a shirtless man wearing a horned, animal-skin hat and carrying a spear—affirmed the mob's faux-Christian foundation with a prayer to "thank you for filling this chamber with patriots that love you and that love Christ!"

Soon, rioters were posing for triumphant selfies and rifling through the small wooden desks of the senators, and Secor was stepping to the upper tier of the dais and seating himself in the presiding officer's brown leather chair. He propped his "America First" flag up against the wall behind him, on display right across from the official American flag. Another rioter made a video of Secor in the chair. With his red "Make America Great Again" cap on his head, he smirked for the camera as if he were about to gavel the election vote to a close without a vote for Biden.

Secor wanted credit for what the rioters had done. Some of Trump's supporters, including Eastman himself, were soon spreading baseless conspiracy theories online claiming that provocateurs from antifa, posing as Trump loyalists, were actually behind the rioting. Secor wanted to set the record straight. He wanted the credit. "It was Trump supporters you losers, and you should be proud," he tweeted the day after the rioting. "One day accomplished more for conservatism than the last 30 years and all the normie [mainstream people] have to say is denial. You boomers will kill our republic."

After returning to Orange County, Secor quickly got rid of his phone and his car, apparently in hopes of avoiding detection, and he "bragged that he would not be caught for his involvement at the US Capitol," according to the FBI.

But he didn't anticipate the slew of tips that the FBI received from nearly a dozen people at UCLA and elsewhere who recognized him amid the flood of photos and videos from the Capitol. Pictured sitting in the chair that Pence had occupied, Christian Secor was hard to miss. Agents trailed him for three days before arresting him at his mother's home in Costa Mesa in a predawn raid five weeks after the insurrection as part of one of the biggest criminal investigations in FBI history. He was charged not only with breaching the Capitol, but with assaulting or resisting officers, too. At his home, the agents also found a cache of weapons and military gear and a video that Secor, a self-described gun lover, had made of himself posing with an assault-style rifle inside his home.

In Ladera Ranch, a team of FBI agents also raided Taylor's home in his gated community with a search warrant early one morning, with his family asleep inside, and the Justice Department ultimately charged him, Alan Hostetter, and four other members of their self-styled "brigade" with conspiracy, weapons charges, and other offenses for their parts in the riot. The FBI raid was a spectacle for the small community in Ladera Ranch, with neighbors shooting video of the scene and trying to get a glimpse of what was causing all the commotion. Once word got out that Taylor was the target of the raid, his supporters in the neighborhood quickly rallied around him, portraying him as a victim of political persecution. Taylor himself sounded the same theme that he had for months, casting himself as a patriot defending his country. "The fbi is fully weaponized against patriots," he wrote in a message to his neighbors circulated on social media. "I never went into the Capitol, no violence no damage to property. All this for waving a flag and singing the national anthem!"

---

For his part, John Eastman kept pushing his debunked claims of a stolen election.

Even after police had cleared the rioters from the building on the night of the January 6 insurrection, Eastman continued looking for ways to overturn the election. At 11:44 p.m. that night, before the vice president and members of Congress had a chance to reconvene to certify the results, Eastman emailed Jacob again to "implore" him to have Pence delay the vote for ten days. Jacob didn't even bother bringing the request to the vice president that night. After everything that had happened, the midnight plea was insane "rubber-room stuff," Pence remarked when Jacob showed him Eastman's email a few days later.

The next day, with the vote finally certified, Eastman was still pushing. He called a lawyer in the White House's office, Eric Herschmann, who had joined Trump's team to help defend him in his first impeachment battle over Ukrainian influence-peddling. Eastman wanted Herschmann's help in pushing the legal case in Georgia claiming election fraud. Herschmann thought that Eastman's ideas for challenging Biden's win, particularly the idea of getting Pence to intervene, were "completely crazy," as he had already told him in one of their conversations. Hearing that Eastman now wanted to continue pushing the case in Georgia struck Herschmann in much the same way. "Are you out of your f-ing mind?" he asked Eastman. "I only want two words coming out of your mouth from now on: *orderly transition*," Herschmann said. He got a halting Eastman to repeat the words back to him: "Orderly transition."

"Good, John," Herschmann said. "Now I'm going to give you the best free legal advice you're ever getting in your life. Get a great f-ing criminal defense lawyer. You're going to need it." Then he hung up the phone.

Eastman seemed to take the advice to heart. A few days later, he emailed Giuliani, looking for an assurance of legal protection — not for his client Trump this time, but for himself. "I've decided that I should be on the pardon list if that is still in the works," he wrote. A pardon "will taint me," he said, but "having that protection is probably the prudent course," he wrote.

John Eastman didn't get it. Trump pardoned more than seventy people in his final week in office, even finding time to pardon alt-right firebrand Steve Bannon, the onetime White House strategist he fired after a bitter falling-out. But Eastman wasn't on the list. He'd had the president's ear for weeks as Trump was trying to overturn the election, using his radical strategy as a blueprint, but with the result now a lost cause, his influence was already waning.

Eastman went back to Orange County, where he had become a *persona non grata* in many circles after all the turmoil in Washington. A week after the rioting, he retired under pressure from his long-held post as a law professor at Chapman University; the school president said that his role on January 6 had "jeopardized our democracy." He faced an indictment in Georgia for election interference and the possible loss of his bar license in California, and he pleaded the Fifth Amendment a hundred times in refusing to answer questions from the House Select Committee investigating the January 6 attack. The *Orange County Register*'s conservative editorial page, which had expressed admiration of his legal work for years, asked: "What happened to John Eastman?" He was, the newspaper said, "a man who has descended into the fever swamps."

## CHAPTER 16

# "PURE EVIL"

Hate struck in the most mundane of places, and on the happiest of occasions. Andre Mackniel just wanted to get his son a birthday cake that hot spring day in Buffalo in 2022. His boy, with wavy brown hair and a perpetual smile, was turning three, and Mackniel, a fifty-three-year-old Buffalo native, wanted to surprise him with a cake, so he headed to the store.

The Tops grocery sat in a mostly minority neighborhood on the city's hardscrabble east side. For two decades, it was the only place locals could find fresh, affordable food — an oasis in a food desert. Mackniel and nearly all the shoppers were Black. That's why eighteen-year-old Payton Gendron, an unabashed white supremacist living 200 miles away, had picked it.

As Mackniel and dozens of shoppers milled about, Gendron drove into the lot, ready for war in body armor, camouflage uniform, and tactical helmet. He'd driven some three and a half hours from his home outside Binghamton, New York. He knew the route well by now: he'd driven it at least twice before on surveillance, sketching the layout, eyeing guards, counting Black shoppers.

His aim, Gendron wrote beforehand in an online journal, was to "kill as many blacks as possible." He "had to commit this act," he wrote, "for the future of the White race."

The teen live-streamed the last minutes of his drive for several dozen other white supremacists he'd met online. An assault rifle he'd bought at a gun shop months earlier could be seen on the passenger seat. The rifle was festooned with racist graffiti he'd scrawled on it—neo-Nazi symbols, racist slogans, the names of white supremacist killers such as Robert Bowers in Pittsburgh and Dylann Roof in Charleston, South Carolina. "Here's your reparations!" he wrote on the rifle.

With the video still running, Gendron grabbed his rifle and got out of his car. He muttered a few final words, seemingly as much for himself as viewers. "I just gotta go for it, right?" he said. "It's the end, right here, I'm going in."

Gendron began firing at the first Black shoppers he spotted in the lot. An employee was helping an eighty-six-year-old woman with her cart; she and two other customers were shot dead, and the employee was badly wounded. Gendron hovered over one body and fired again.

After shooting out a front window, he burst into the store with a hail of gunfire. Customers and employees ran frantically for the exits, while others, trapped in the back of the store, sought refuge in a freezer and a stockroom—anywhere to hide from the teenager with the assault rifle. It was a scene played out in so many American cities, and now it was happening to them at their local grocery—"the worst nightmare that any community can face," the mayor said afterward.

As Gendron surveyed the bloodshed in the midst of his spree, he was upset to see a white employee on the floor, shot in the leg. "Sorry," Gendron told him, moving on to more Black targets. At the checkout area, he killed three more Black shoppers, his last victims before police converged. He surrendered without a struggle; he'd done what he'd set out to do. He stared blankly at the ground, saying nothing, as officers hustled him into a police car. Ten people killed, all Black, eclipsing the grim mark set by his hero, Dylann Roof, in South Carolina—more than any single Black massacre in a century.

## "Pure Evil"

"Pure evil," said the local sheriff, John Garcia. A Tops executive, who left his son's high school graduation to rush to the scene, wondered "how someone could be that filled with rage and hate."

Gendron had laid out the explanation himself in 675 pages of racist tropes and debunked conspiracies. He found the springboard for his violent bigotry online, easily available in a cesspool of racist propaganda on far-right sites. The isolation of Covid led him to them, he wrote. Every post he saw on the "evils" of Blacks and other minorities led him to search out another racist cache. "I only really started to turn racist when 4chan started giving me facts that (Blacks) were intellectually and emotionally inferior," he wrote.

On 4chan, Gendron watched the live-streamed massacre of Muslims in New Zealand not with revulsion, but excitement. "Every time I think maybe I shouldn't commit to an attack I spend 5 min" on 4chan's "politically incorrect" board and "then my motivation returns," he wrote.

Andre Mackniel never got to give his son the birthday cake. Instead, at a memorial two weeks later, his son fidgeted in the arms of his mother, Mackniel's fiancée, as President Biden hugged the boy and spoke of the "poison" of white supremacy at another scene of mass carnage.

The mother, Tracey Maciulewicz, gave voice to her grief in a video she posted months later, her toddler on her lap. "My fiancé was shot and killed on May 14 by a white supremacist mass shooter," she began. The child looked up at his mother. "Daddy?" he asked. She was angry not just at Gendron, but at the manufacturers who made the assault rifle and the body armor that facilitated his deadly attack. "What are you going to do...," she said, breaking down in tears. The child placed his head on Tracey's shoulder consolingly. "It's okay," he told her. "...To make sure," she continued, "that your products don't get into the hands of a mass-shooter white supremacist ever again and will take a child's father away?"

"It's okay," the boy told her again.

## CHAPTER 17

# "HATE WILL NEVER BE TOLERATED"

Sam Woodward slumped in the witness stand, his eyes half closed, his long, bedraggled hair flopping down over his face. He was struggling to answer all the questions that the prosecutor was throwing at him about the violent killing of Blaze Bernstein.

He made for an unsettling sight. It was June of 2024, nearly six and a half years after the killing, and all that time in jail had clearly changed him. With his ragged goatee, his wild-eyed gaze, a wound above his eye, and that long, unruly hair draped down over his face, Sam now bore a striking resemblance to the Atomwaffen Division hero whose picture he kept on his phone—Charles Manson. Everything except the Nazi swastika that Manson carved into his forehead during his own murder trial in Southern California more than a half century earlier.

Sam was finally on trial for murder himself. He was testifying in his own defense in the long-awaited case, and veteran Orange County prosecutor Jennifer Walker, who was looking to put him in prison for the rest of his life, was confronting him about one lie after another that he'd told at the time of Blaze Bernstein's disappearance.

The lies he'd told Blaze himself on Tinder about being gay. The lies he told Blaze's father afterward about Blaze going off to meet another "friend" in the park. The lies he told police about his desperate search to find Blaze. The lies he told police and others about the scratches on his hands and arm—from a coyote, he'd claimed, or a fight at a boxing club.

"Several people saw you with injuries to your hands, knuckles, and arm after the killing, correct?" Walker, a senior homicide prosecutor, asked Sam as he sat on the witness stand.

Sam sighed deeply. There was a long pause before he answered, one of many. "Yes," he said finally, his voice deep and croaky.

"You lied to all of them about how you got the injuries, correct?" Walker asked.

Another long, uncomfortable pause. "Yes," Sam answered.

"And you got those injuries because Blaze was fighting you for his *life* when you were stabbing him to death, correct?" Walker asked, her voice now rising in anger.

Sam sighed heavily, twice now, squirming in the witness chair. Amid the eerie quiet of the jam-packed courtroom, he sat silently for even longer this time, a full forty seconds, and he shook his head slightly before finally answering. "He inflicted all of them on me, correct," he said of his injuries, "but I can't remember at which point, at which time, at which, how..." His voice trailed off unintelligibly, with Sam lost in the moment of Blaze's killing.

---

Sam Woodward's lies had ensnared him. After all the endless delays in the case, the onetime neo-Nazi foot soldier was finally on trial for allegedly murdering his old high school classmate—murdering him out of hatred. Even as the trial seemed on the verge of starting, there had been yet another delay, this one of Sam's making, the result of his own temper. As the court was about to pick the final jurors to hear the case, Sam became upset over something Judge Kimberly Menninger had told them about the Daughters of the American Revolution, a group that had once given him an award in school. He stood up as if he needed the bathroom, but instead threw a Dixie cup filled with water straight at the judge, almost hitting her. The judge, concerned that the outburst might prejudice the jurors, scrapped the whole panel at the request of the defense and ordered the lawyers to start anew, a process that set the start of the trial back by another several weeks.

The trial, lasting nearly three months in the spring of 2024 in Department C-30 on the eighth floor of the main Orange County courthouse in Santa Ana, would cast a harsh spotlight on the scourge of violent bigotry in "the Orange Curtain" and beyond, a swell of hatred that had grown even more potent throughout America in the time since Sam's arrest. Curious onlookers, journalists, lawyers, academics, members of Sam's church, and Blaze's parents and family friends packed the courtroom day after day for a glimpse of the notorious accused killer who had joined a neo-Nazi cell and kept a "Diary of Hate" to chronicle all his bigotries. Hatred was on display.

The trial was never going to be a whodunit. Who killed Blaze Bernstein was never really in dispute. Within a few minutes of starting his opening statement, public defender Kenneth Morrison admitted as much to the jury, saying that "the evidence will show that my client, Sam Woodward, was responsible for that death."

The real question was *why*: Was Sam so consumed by hatred and rage that he lured Blaze to the park and stabbed him to death simply because Blaze was gay? The answer to that question was critical: It would determine whether Sam Woodward would go to prison for the rest of his life at the age of twenty-six, without the possibility of parole, if he was convicted of first-degree murder and a hate crime; or, if not, whether he might see the outside of a prison in his forties or fifties.

Going into the trial, Morrison, a balding, wiry man who was the fourth defense lawyer on the case, recognized the hurdles in public perception that he faced after all the notoriety that the case had garnered. "There is this narrative that's been pushed: Nazi kills gay Jew," he told the judge at a hearing before the trial started. It was a "tantalizing and salacious" storyline, he said, but "from the defense perspective, that's inaccurate." Blaze's sexual orientation and his religion had nothing to

## "Hate Will Never Be Tolerated"

do with what he described as an unplanned act of violence, Morrison insisted.

His client's appearance alone, though, created a fearsome first impression in court. Sam's disheveled, Charles Manson–like look made such an unnerving sight that even one of his old neo-Nazi buddies, Brenan Duffy, recoiled after he walked into the courtroom and got a look at him. "I got upset seeing Sam the way he is," Duffy told Judge Menninger when she asked if he was okay.

During the trial, Sam would sit shackled at the defense table next to his lawyer, with his hair often completely covering his face, his eyes invisible. He would draw on a notepad occasionally, but mostly he sat still and silent, in an almost catatonic state. There were no angry outbursts like the one that had prompted Judge Menninger to dismiss the original jury pool. There was no sign of emotion at all.

With Sam on the stand, Morrison had to prod him repeatedly to pull his hair away from his eyes and look up at him, instead of staring down at the floor. Then there were those long, agonizing pauses. Morrison asked him whether he was "faking" some sort of cognitive condition with his slow, drawn-out answers in order to "deceive the jury."

Sam Woodward on the witness stand at his trial in 2024.

Sam chortled with annoyance at the question. "No," he said, fairly quickly this time. His appearance aside, two psychological experts who had evaluated him—one picked by the prosecution, the other by the defense—had already concluded that he was mentally competent to stand trial. Judge Menninger agreed, and the trial was allowed to move ahead.

It was an important ruling for prosecutors, and in the months before the trial finally started, they would notch a series of other critical wins ensuring that Sam's neo-Nazi ideology would be put squarely before the jury. Some of the most damning evidence of Sam's vile bigotry came straight from his cell phone. Prosecutor Jennifer Walker wanted to show the jury potentially hundreds of neo-Nazi photos, cartoons, and material that Sam had circulated, collected, or in some cases made himself. She was trying to show that Blaze's murder was the tragic, even inevitable result of Sam's long history of bigotry. Morrison, though, argued that much of the "horribly disgusting" evidence—imagery of Hitler, the Holocaust, and hatred of gays, Jews, and minorities—should be kept out of the trial because it would unfairly prejudice the jury and risk portraying Sam "as some sort of monster."

Judge Menninger, who had served on the bench for more than two decades after starting her career as a prosecutor, spent days going over all of the neo-Nazi material with the two lawyers, piece by piece, reading each one aloud before deciding what the prosecutor could show the jury. Some of it was so graphic—propaganda about killing and raping minorities, for instance—that the judge didn't want to read it out loud herself. "Oh my Lord, I'm going to make you read it," the judge told Walker after looking at one particularly offensive meme.

In the end, the judge gave Walker almost everything she wanted. Because Blaze was gay and Jewish, Menninger decided the prosecutor would be allowed to show the jury anything Sam had that was specific to the hatred of gays or Jews, even material praising Hitler or supporting the Holocaust. Anything else—material bashing Blacks or Hispanics, for instance, of which there was plenty—was deemed irrelevant.

## "Hate Will Never Be Tolerated"

And the judge also decided that prosecutors would be allowed to call Duffy, the ex–Atomwaffen member, to testify under an alias about Sam's involvement with the group after he joined up with them in Texas that summer before the killing. The court made Duffy an expert witness of an unusual type: an inside authority on neo-Nazi hatred.

If there was any doubt beforehand, Sam's neo-Nazi ideology would now be a dominant theme at the trial. Being a neo-Nazi wasn't a crime per se, but it did reveal the odious mindset that Walker was trying to convince the jury made this killing a hate crime. It was a motive, and it would mean a much longer stint in prison if Sam was convicted on the hate-crime charge.

---

Soon after Walker began her opening statement on the first day of the trial, a chilly Tuesday morning in April of 2024, she was telling the jurors all about Sam's history with neo-Nazis and Atomwaffen. She displayed the hateful memes found on his phone, and she showed them a photo Sam had taken side by side with *Siege*'s James Mason when he met the neo-Nazi elder on his pilgrimage to Denver. Mason, a thousand miles away from Orange County in his dark, Nazi-adorned apartment, would be a constant presence in absentia at the trial, mentioned dozens of times in testimony as one of the dark inspirations to Sam and other followers of "Siege Culture."

*Siege* "was their Bible, a book written by James Mason, who they revered just like Hitler," Walker told the jurors, a diverse group made up of men and women, whites and people of color, straights and gays. "And in that book, he talks about all the principles of *Siege*, which are getting rid of people that are not desirable, taking down the government, and being ready."

Sam Woodward, a.k.a. "Sab" or "Saboteur" to his friends in Atomwaffen Division, embraced his role as a "lone wolf" in keeping with Mason's twisted teachings, and he began "researching his prey," the prosecutor told jurors before a hushed courtroom. "The prey that the defendant had chosen was gay people," she said. And while prosecutors were charging him with a hate crime for killing Blaze because he was gay, and not specifically because of his religion, "being Jewish could have been another reason... a double bonus for the defendant," she said.

A parade of witnesses took the stand to tell the jury not only about Blaze Bernstein's brutal killing, but also—and just as important in Walker's view—the hatred and rage that she said had driven it. This was not just another violent crime, another murder; this was a hate crime, Walker charged, and she would turn again and again to the motive of hatred to make her case.

A nervous Gabe García, the former classmate of both Sam and Blaze at the Orange County School of the Arts, testified about the monthslong series of sexually charged messages he received from Sam when they were in school together—messages that Sam would later recall fondly in his "Diary of Hate" when he wrote "how fun it was" to prank "faggots" like Gabe into thinking he was gay. Gabe testified about how shocked he was to be getting all the explicit messages from Sam, the school homophobe well-known for his "extreme" conservative views. It was the beginning, Walker said, of Sam's online "catfishing" of gays, a dry run for what was to come.

Duffy, the onetime Atomwaffen member turned whistleblower, testified about Sam's eagerness to join up with the neo-Nazi group that summer in Texas; his clear desire to engage in "lone wolf" attacks, in keeping with *Siege* and James Mason's orthodoxy; and his occasional frustration that the group wasn't doing enough beyond mere propaganda to further its terrorist aims against "degenerate" gays and Jews. "At the root level," Duffy said of the mindset that attracted Sam and other members, "it's hate in the heart of the individual." A few of the jurors grimaced as he described their racist, violent ethos during three days of testimony.

And Craig Goldsmith, a forensics expert for the Orange County Sheriff's Department, testified about the huge cache of incriminating, hate-filled material he'd extracted from Sam's cell phone and from his computer, including more than a thousand Nazi-themed images, the online "Diary of Hate," and entries about his fascination with "trolling"

## "Hate Will Never Be Tolerated"

gays. Most jarring of all was the photo Sam had taken of the drawing he'd made on a napkin: a knife, dripping blood, a skull's eyes popping out, with the handwritten words: "Text is boring but murder isn't."

It was all a grim prelude to the crime itself: Blaze Bernstein's disappearance—just two weeks after Sam made the drawing of the bloody knife—and the discovery six days later in the park of his bloody body in that shallow, muddy grave, partly exposed by a heavy rainstorm.

Blaze's parents, Gideon and Jeanne, each took the stand at the very start of the trial to tell of the agonizing ordeal of rushing home that January afternoon when Blaze didn't show up at the dentist, only to discover that he hadn't been home the night before. "The beginning of hell," Gideon called it on the witness stand. He had vowed to think about Sam as little as possible in the years since his arrest, but now, as he sat on the stand less than ten yards across from the impassive defendant, there was no avoiding it.

Dylan Jantzen, the lead sheriff's investigator, described for jurors the trail that led the authorities to Sam long before the body was discovered. Blaze's family discovering Sam's name in the Snapchat thread. A deputy calling Sam and hearing his strange story about Blaze leaving him in the park, then disappearing. Jantzen noticing Sam as he milled about in the park while searchers combed the area, then talking to Sam, with his injured hands jammed in his pockets. The electronic trail ultimately revealing Sam's flirtatious baiting of Blaze. The round-the-clock surveillance of Sam that showed him scrubbing his car, out of sight from his house.

Not until the investigators found Blaze's body in the rainswept grave, though, were they certain they had a murder case. They finally had a body. An autopsy revealed the sheer savagery of the attack. Blaze's slight frame, barely a hundred and forty pounds, had suffered twenty-eight knife wounds in all—fourteen of them on the left side of his neck alone, the pathologist who examined the body, Dr. Aruna Singhania, told the jury. At the site of one wound, the knife had penetrated his skull. There were defensive wounds on his hand as well, she said, from Blaze trying to fend off his attacker.

Blaze could never have survived that many stab wounds, she testified.

---

Sam's defense lawyer, Ken Morrison, promised the jury what he called a more "nuanced" portrait of his client—as something other than a rageful, cold-blooded, neo-Nazi killer. As he cross-examined the DA's witnesses and called his own string of witnesses to the stand over the course of a month, including Sam's parents and a psychologist hired by the defense, he tried to paint a picture of an antisocial, sexually confused young man who had difficulty relating to people. The aim was to avoid a sentence of life in prison for Sam. To do that, he needed to show that the killing wasn't the result of his hatred of gays, Jews, or anyone else—and certainly not premeditated—but rather a rash, impulsive act by a troubled young man.

The defense lawyer questioned whether Sam, rather than "posing" as gay, was really a closeted homosexual himself, sexually repressed by his father's homophobia. "This young guy was struggling with his sexuality," Morrison told the jury. The defense lawyer insisted that Sam wasn't *posing* as gay in all his online come-ons to Blaze and the other young men online; he really *was* gay, or perhaps bisexual—despite the many times that he'd insisted he was straight, and despite all the pornography of women that investigators had found on his computer. A small portion of the pornography he'd gathered later—about one in ten items, an investigator testified—was of gay material. Orange County prosecutor Jennifer Walker had asserted that Sam was using the gay porn to learn about his "prey" in catfishing his targets, but Morrison maintained it was actually evidence that he was gay. To show that the idea of a gay neo-Nazi wasn't as far-fetched as it might sound, he even put on the stand another former member of Atomwaffen Division to talk about how he had come out as gay after leaving the group.

Legally, Sam's sexuality didn't really matter one way or the other; a gay man could be guilty of a hate crime for killing someone because they were gay, no different than a straight man. But Ken Morrison believed that if he could raise doubts about Sam's sexuality, it might give the jurors an alternative view of his client as something less than a hate-filled monster.

Likewise, the defense lawyer repeatedly raised the issue of Sam's late-diagnosed autism to try to soften the image the DA had presented. He pressed former classmates about how isolated, socially awkward, and "different" he was. And he tried to show that Sam, rather than being an eager neo-Nazi, was a struggling kid who was wooed to Atomwaffen by Tristan Evans and tried to find a home in, of all places, a group of white supremacist revolutionaries.

Two months into the trial, Morrison called Sam himself to the stand to testify in his own defense. It was a risky gambit, something most criminal defendants didn't do, especially not in murder trials. Even Donald Trump, after vowing loudly and publicly to testify in his "hush money" fraud trial going on at that same time in New York, had decided against taking the stand just a few weeks earlier. But Sam, despite the risk of damaging his own prospects, decided with Morrison that he wanted to tell his version of what had happened that night—or at least his latest version.

The jury had already heard all the different accounts that he had given the authorities about what happened, with Blaze disappearing to meet another friend, or Blaze trying to kiss him in the car before they parted ways. Now, as Morrison questioned Sam on the stand, with his legs shackled and a deputy sitting behind him for extra security because of his earlier outburst, Sam told a much different story, dramatically at odds with all the earlier accounts.

He now admitted, after all his earlier denials, that he had killed Blaze in the park that night after the two of them went there together. But it hadn't happened the way prosecutors said it had, he insisted. He'd been provoked, Sam claimed under questioning from his own lawyer. He laid out his improbable story for the jury: he awoke at the park from a drug stupor from two puffs of marijuana, Sam claimed, and he discovered that his belt was unbuckled and Blaze was touching his crotch with one hand and aiming his cell phone at him with the other. He testified that he thought Blaze was trying to take a compromising photo of him to embarrass him. (No photos of Sam were ever found on Blaze's phone.) Sam thought of his homophobic father and "the look on his face if he ever saw something like that," he said. "I couldn't fathom something like that."

Sam tried to get the phone away from Blaze, he testified, then he grabbed his knife on the ground and "I just kept driving and driving and driving the knife down" into Blaze.

He felt "an anger like nothing I'd ever felt in my whole life," Sam said. "I couldn't control myself," he said. "I was disgusted, I was enraged."

As he described the gory scene, with the images of his knife driving into Blaze over and over again, an emotional Jeanne stood up at her seat in the back row of the courtroom and hurried out the exit. The heavy wooden door clanked loudly behind her, heads turning in the courtroom. She'd had to "sit there and listen to lie after lie from this person about what happened the night he killed my son," she said later. She wasn't going to listen to any more.

Sam insisted to Morrison that he never planned to kill Blaze when he picked him up at his house that night; he just "lost it," he said. And no, despite his neo-Nazi loyalties, he certainly didn't hate Blaze because he was gay, or because he was Jewish, he told Morrison. "Not at all."

Then it was Jennifer Walker's turn to cross-examine Sam on the stand. She pressed him on all the lies he told after Blaze's disappearance; all the inconsistencies in his latest version of events on the stand about Blaze supposedly provoking him that night; all the online "catfishing" of gays he had done in the months and years before that; and all the bigoted, homophobic, antisemitic screeds on his cell phone, his public postings, and in his "Diary of Hate."

She asked him about a threat he'd put on the bio he'd created for Grindr, the gay dating site, saying that "All fags and fakers are in for it. Get ready to die."

"Do you remember something like that?" she asked.

"Uh, yes, I think so," he said after another long pause.

She showed him the photo he posted of his doppelgänger, Charles

Manson, and another, shot in Texas, of him wearing an Atomwaffen skull mask while giving a "Heil Hitler" salute for a neo-Nazi propaganda poster. "That's your picture, correct?" she asked him.

"Yes, that's me," he said in a flat, emotionless voice.

Walker wanted to know more about Atomwaffen Division and why Sam decided to join the neo-Nazi group that summer in Texas before he killed Blaze. He had told the psychologist hired by the defense after his arrest that he adhered to the neo-Nazi group's ideals and had joined up with them to "win prestige" among young men he liked and admired. Walker asked him about that comment. There was another long silence. He struggled with his words. It was all about being accepted, he said finally. He did whatever was necessary, he said, to earn "the right to be liked and the higher degree of acceptance." Even among a group of Hitler-loving neo-Nazis.

At the very end of nearly four days of testimony from Sam on the witness stand, Morrison prodded him to explain his feelings about the killing in the park that night.

"Do you have remorse for what you did to Blaze Bernstein and his family?" the defense counsel asked.

There was another long pause, another deep sigh.

"Yes, I do," Sam said finally.

Walker wasn't buying the claims of remorse. When it came time for her closing argument to the jury, she portrayed Sam Woodward as an unrepentant, neo-Nazi murderer responsible for an act of "lone-wolf terrorism," who killed Blaze Bernstein simply because he hated gays. It amounted to a "ceremonial killing," intended to earn Sam prestige in the eyes of his neo-Nazi friends at Atomwaffen Division, Walker said. She took the jury back to the image of his Atomwaffen skull mask, the one found in his car with blood stains on it. She theorized that Sam put on his Atomwaffen skull mask just before he began brutally attacking Blaze with the knife his father had given him. That skull mask may have been the last image that Blaze ever saw. "All of that anger, all of that hate, came out in all of those stab wounds," she told the jury. "And then he hid the crime and lied."

It didn't take the jury long to decide Sam Woodward's fate. On their first full day of deliberations, the day before the July Fourth holiday, word came after 2:00 p.m. that the jury had reached a verdict—a quick one, considering that the trial had lasted nearly three months and involved thousands of pages of documents, social media exchanges, neo-Nazi propaganda, and dozens of hours of tape recordings and interviews.

Onlookers began packing the courtroom in expectation of an announcement of the verdict, with Blaze's parents on one side of the courtroom, along with their daughter and a throng of friends, and Sam's parents, along with some church supporters, sitting on the other.

The clerk, Anthony Villa, read the verdict on the charge of first-degree murder. "Guilty," he said. Cheers went up from the Bernsteins' side of the room, drawing an admonishment from the judge. "I understand that it's emotional, but I cannot have that," she warned. Sam sat emotionless and silent, his hair still covering much of his face, blinding him to the judgment confronting him.

The verdict on the hate-crime charge was the same. "Guilty," Villa read again.

The jury hadn't believed that Sam had killed out of some impulsive panic, as he and his public defender had maintained. This was a first-degree murder—premeditated, the jurors found, and driven by hatred over who Blaze was.

"Thank God," Jeanne Bernstein exclaimed after the final verdict was read. She began weeping. Two weeks earlier, she had been left practically in tears by the anguish of hearing Sam describe stabbing her son over and over. Now she was shedding tears of sheer relief.

Jeanne and Gideon Bernstein each gave Walker a long, emotional hug. One juror could be seen tearing up as well, and another juror later went to Blaze's rock-garden memorial by the murder scene to leave a letter about the trial's deep emotional impact on her. Barring something unexpected, the verdict on the hate-crime charge, on top of the first-degree murder conviction, would ensure that Sam would spend the rest of his life in prison with no chance of parole.

"We are thrilled with the verdict," Jeanne told reporters gathered at the courthouse afterward.

"No verdict can bring back Blaze," she said, but it "brings a measure of closure." It was that elusive "closure" that they had craved through the long six and a half years of delay and anguish.

Gideon found an old photo of a smiling Blaze taken exactly ten years to the day before the verdict; it showed his son standing in front of the columns at the historic Pantheon in Rome as a teenager on a family trip to Italy. Now Gideon was walking out of the Orange County courthouse, a guilty verdict finally in hand, but "exhausted from a long, dark vacuum of time where Blaze no longer could pose for a picture with our family," he wrote to the family's supporters afterward. Like the Pantheon itself, a monument preserved through the centuries, the guilty verdict seemed to him as if it preserved his son's memory, Gideon said, "with dignity and truth."

For Todd Spitzer, the Orange County district attorney who had made prosecuting hate crimes a cornerstone of his election campaign six years earlier, the verdict meant justice not just for Blaze, but "for every victim of hate," he said. "Hate is here," Spitzer had declared at the start of his term, as Orange County was seeing a groundswell of violent bigotry, and Blaze's murder was a flashpoint. "Every one of the 28 stab wounds... was an act of hate that was carried out over and over again not just to kill Blaze, but to send a message," he said after the verdict; it was a message of hatred aimed at "the most vulnerable members of our society."

To his fellow neo-Nazis, Sam had become a martyr, a figure of twisted reverence, for the killing of a gay Jew. But with the guilty verdict, he had now become a powerful symbol of a different sort, Spitzer said; a symbol that "hate will never be tolerated here in Orange County."

EPILOGUE

# "POISONING THE BLOOD"

A decade of soaring, violent bigotry in America ended much the same way it had started, with a burst of fiery invective from Donald Trump against minorities of all kinds fanning the flames ever higher. In 2015, riding down his golden escalator, Trump had started his first campaign for president with a broadside against Mexican "rapists" and criminals. Ten years later, in 2025, Trump returned to the White House on the strength of a campaign he had built even more heavily on racist and dehumanizing rhetoric against minorities, and the attacks from the White House only intensified in his first year back in office. A country already racked by fraught racial tensions, its historic bugaboo, was growing more hostile than ever for the *others*.

Trump spoke unapologetically in his '24 campaign of immigrants as "animals" who were "poisoning the blood of our country," echoing Hitler's own language. He described his opponents as "vermin," another favorite term of the Nazis. Baselessly, he claimed again and again that "millions" of immigrants were pouring into the country from foreign prisons and insane asylums, and he promised mass deportations that began immediately after the election, with even some American citizens and legal residents swept up in the raids.

He seized on a racist lie started by neo-Nazis to claim at a televised debate with Kamela Harris that legal Haitian immigrants in Springfield, Ohio, were "eating the dogs... they're eating the cats." That led to days of bomb threats and attacks on legal Haitian immigrants in the city; there were eleven reports of hate crimes against Black residents in Springfield that month alone, nearly three times the entire year before. The debunked myth was spread by a neo-Nazi clan called Blood Tribe, started by an ex-Marine, and the group reveled in the newfound influence that Trump had once again given to neo-Nazis. "The president is talking about it now," the group wrote on Gab. "This is what real power looks like."

He sowed enmity and division time and again with a drumroll of other racial, ethnic, and religious attacks, challenging the loyalty and sanity of Jews who voted against him, attacking rival Kamala Harris's Black identity, and posting photos of flag-burning Middle Easterners and knife-wielding immigrants. He warned of a "bloodbath" if he lost and declared in autocratic tones to a gathering of Christian conservatives that if he won, "you won't have to vote anymore, my beautiful Christians."

It was an escalation of the inflammatory and divisive rhetoric Trump had employed in 2016, when he first won the White House, and in 2020, when he lost it, and it had the same effect again, like kerosene on a fire, turning his most virulent supporters violently against minorities and his perceived "enemies." Some of Trump's supporters made their motivation plain in the crimes they were accused of committing. In Iowa, a young white man was arrested on hate-crime charges after he posted racist signs supporting Trump's campaign at eight Hispanic-owned businesses. "Illegal Immigrant Hunting Permit," read the signs he'd made. "No bag limit. No tagging required. Trump 2024." At a polling place in northern Florida, a young white man waving a two-foot-long machete, part of a group of teenagers with Trump flags, was arrested for allegedly harassing and threatening two women supporting Harris. The day after the election, Black and Hispanic students in a slew of states from New York to California reported receiving racist text messages, some referencing Trump, that threatened them with enslavement "at the nearest plantation," or deportation.

The fuse of bigotry had been lit once again.

White supremacists claimed Trump's victory as their own. "Total. Aryan. Victory," declared a neo-Nazi site on Telegram. "Hail Trump!" trumpeted a Proud Boys account. They used his win to lash out online, and sometimes in person, at Hispanics, Blacks, Jews, gays, and other minorities in violent, graphic terms, with talk of rape, kidnapping, and murder against the *others* in the wake of his reelection. White supremacist and "Groyper" leader Nick Fuentes, a guest of Trump's at Mar-a-Lago, went on X the night of Trump's win with a video rant against women, proclaiming: "Hey, bitch, we control your bodies! Guess what, guys win again." It quickly became a viral (and vile) rallying cry for misogynistic men around the country.

Threatening posts like the one from the white-supremacist leader would have once been banned as hate speech on X, but no longer. The site had become a go-to destination for white supremacists after Elon Musk bought Twitter, relaxing many of the restrictions on hateful postings and reinstating Trump's account, which had been suspended for inciting violence during the January 6 rioting at the Capitol. Neo-Nazi material soared, with one Hitler-loving song called "Heil Hitler" by the rapper Ye (formerly Kanye West) attracting some 6.5 million viewers on X in 2025, even as other platforms removed it due to its blatant antisemitism and hateful rhetoric.

One white-supremacist account on X, posting overtly racist and wildly violent material targeting Hispanic immigrants, Blacks, and other minorities, was all too typical on Musk's site. What was striking was the identity of its anonymous creator: a Texas newspaper outed him in 2025 as a senior lawyer in ICE's Dallas office who handled deportations. "America is a White nation," the X account declared. Even the artificial-intelligence chatbot on Musk's site joined in the fusillade, going on an antisemitic rant and praising Hitler as an answer to "anti-white hatred" after it was asked about deaths in the Texas floods in the summer of 2025.

Two months after Trump's reelection, Meta's Mark Zuckerberg did much the same thing as Musk, rolling back restrictions on what could be posted on Facebook and Instagram, lowering the guardrails against hate speech, and getting rid of fact-checkers altogether. Attacking gay people as "freaks" and "abnormal" was now specifically allowed on Facebook and Instagram. So was calling immigrants "grubby, filthy pieces of shit," declaring African-Americans a violent race, or degrading women as "crazy" and pieces of property.

Hateful speech—the gateway to violent bigotry—had been reined in on social media only sporadically before, but now the restraints were practically nonexistent at some of America's most popular platforms. Zuckerberg cast the changes as a win for free speech, but many outsiders saw the new policies as a transparent effort to placate the returning president. Trump had been at loggerheads with Facebook after that platform, too, suspended his account over his January 6 posts. But soon after his reelection, Zuckerberg was dining with Trump at Mar-a-Lago, attending his inauguration after his company donated $1 million for the event, and tearing down the standards that Trump and GOP leaders long complained had "censored" them. It was a sea change at Meta that one outside watch group said was sure to produce "a tidal wave of hate and disinformation," and the leader of Meta's oversight board saw "huge problems" ahead because of it. "We are seeing many instances," said Helle Thorning-Schmidt, co-chair of the panel, "where hate speech can lead to real-life harm."

The day after his inauguration, Trump faced a poignant plea for greater tolerance from the pulpit of the National Cathedral in Washington. Bishop Mariann E. Budde, leader of the Episcopal diocese in Washington, spoke out in her sermon against what she called "the culture of contempt that has become normalized in this country [and] threatens to destroy us." With Trump and his family sitting barely forty feet away from her, she spoke to him directly and said: "Let me make one final plea, Mr. President...I ask you to have mercy upon the people in our country who are scared now." There were gay and transgender children, she said, "who fear for their lives"; children of law-abiding immigrants who "fear that their parents will be taken away"; and refugees fleeing war and persecution who were seeking "compassion and welcome here." For them, she asked the returning president for mercy.

Trump squirmed silently in his seat as he listened to the bishop's words. He was accustomed to being the one with the microphone in front of him. He seemed unmoved by her plea. Hours later, in fact, he demanded an apology for Budde's "nasty" and "ungracious" remarks, as she faced death threats and one Republican congressman's call for her deportation.

Toning down the rhetoric of fear was not part of Trump's playbook. At times, he and those around him seemed to almost invite comparisons to the Third Reich and fascist imagery. When Trump was criticized during the campaign for echoing Hitler's Aryan-inspired rhetoric with his own talk of immigrants "poisoning the blood" of America, Trump doubled down. "They don't like it when I said that," he told rally-goers in Iowa. "They said, 'Oh, Hitler said that,' in a much different way." He then proceeded to repeat the language once more. "They're destroying the blood of our country," he said, drawing another round of comparisons to Hitler and the Nazis.

Musk, who already had a history of making antisemitic remarks, flaunted his support for a far-right German political party with deep ties to neo-Nazis, the Alternative for Germany, appearing by video to boost its election hopes in 2025. At a Trump inauguration event, a celebratory Musk pounded his right hand to his chest and thrust his arm, palm down, straight out to the crowd—twice, in fact—in a gesture that looked to many like a Nazi salute. Musk denied any Nazi connection in the gesture, then compounded the controversy on X with a series of mocking, Nazi-themed puns ("Stop Göring your enemies!"). The Nazi puns fell flat with many, but others lapped it all up—and the "loving Hitler energy" exuded by Musk's salute, as Groyper's Fuentes put it.

One Fox News satirist, Greg Gutfeld, went on the network's show *The Five* and said with a straight face—before breaking into laughter—that criticism from the left calling conservatives Nazis "doesn't matter to us," and that conservatives should adopt the labels themselves. "We need to learn from the Blacks. The way they were able to remove the power from the n-word by *using* it," he said. "So, from now on, it's, 'What up, my Nazi? Hey, what up, my Nazi? Hey, what's hanging, my Nazi?'" Even some of his co-panelists seemed shocked. "Oh, my God," one muttered.

## "Poisoning the Blood"

From his very first days back at the White House, Trump took aim at minority groups with a flurry of executive orders that rolled back decades of civil rights advances. He banned anything even remotely connected to "diversity, equity, and inclusion" programs in the federal government, going so far as to revoke a part of the historic 1964 Civil Rights Act outlawing workplace discrimination against minorities. Trump was going after the *others,* using the levers of power to do it in ways he never had in his first term as president.

Defense Secretary Pete Hegseth—who had been flagged as a possible "insider threat" at the National Guard because of tattoos adopted by white supremacists—declared that "DEI is dead," and the Pentagon ordered the removal of tens of thousands of photos and online records seen as promoting "diversity," including milestone achievements of Black, Hispanic, and female service members and even a photo of the *Enola Gay,* the World War II bomber that had dropped the atomic bomb on Hiroshima. They were simply erased. Events like Black History Month, Holocaust Remembrance Day, and LGBTQ Pride Month were suspended in some offices, too. Hundreds of pages of data on the soaring number of hate crimes were purged from online federal records, and the Justice Department eliminated altogether local grants to deter hate crimes and aid the victims.

For Trump, "diversity" became a catchall for almost any problem. The morning after a midair collision between a commercial airline and a military helicopter killed sixty-seven people at Reagan National Airport in February of 2025, Trump quickly turned a time of national mourning into a time of baseless blame. Even as rescue teams were still pulling bodies from the Potomac River, Trump blamed "diversity" for the disaster. He claimed, without any evidence, that lax hiring standards at the Federal Aviation Administration may have caused the crash because the workforce had been considered "too white." He was seizing on the racist belief that non-whites were less capable. There was nothing to support the racially incendiary charge, but Trump stood by it, he said, "because I have common sense and unfortunately a lot of people don't." Civil rights leaders were aghast. "People are suffering," said congressman Hakeem Jeffries, the top-ranking House Democrat, "and the leader of this country decides to go out and pedal lies, conspiracy theories, and attack people of color and women without any basis whatsoever. Have you no decency?"

Trump's demonization of immigrants in particular reached a boil in June of 2025, when thousands of protesters, many of them Hispanic, took to the streets of Los Angeles to condemn the widespread immigration raids in Trump's first seven months in office, which ensnared many legal residents with little due process. The protests were largely peaceful, with isolated episodes of vandalism, looting, or arson, but Trump sent in nearly five thousand National Guard and Marine personnel to quell protesters whom he depicted in dystopian terms as violent "insurrectionists," invaders, criminals, and "paid troublemakers," among other outsize accusations. "If they spit, we will hit," Trump declared in one post. California's governor, Gavin Newsom, condemned Trump's dire description of the protests as fiction and his military response as a "brazen abuse of power" that only served to sow division and chaos, especially for minorities. "They're traumatizing our communities," Newsom said.

The raids didn't let up, nor did the violent demonization of Hispanic immigrants—legal and otherwise. After Trump opened a new Florida detention center dubbed "Alligator Alcatraz," his confidante, the controversial far-right activist Laura Loomer, wrote—on X, once again—that "the good news is, alligators are guaranteed at least 65 million meals," a clear reference to the number of all Hispanics in America.

Trump made plain his desire to see more white people coming to America. He indicated as much during the campaign when he complained to a roomful of wealthy donors at a Palm Beach mansion that more people weren't arriving from "nice countries, you know, like Denmark, Switzerland?... How about Norway?"—in contrast with people from countries in Latin America, Africa, or the Middle East, whom he regularly derided as criminals, gang members, terrorists, or mentally ill. Back at the White House, he ended the resettlement of Afghan refugees while inviting potentially tens of thousands of white Afrikaners from South Africa to resettle in America because he claimed, using false and manufactured evidence, that they had been victims of violence and

## "Poisoning the Blood"

discrimination. The idea of a "white genocide" in South Africa was a debunked myth that had originally been spread, like Trump's claim about dog-eating Haitians, by neo-Nazi and white-supremacist groups—and fueled by Musk, a native of South Africa, in his time in Trump's White House prior to his bitter falling out with Trump in the spring of 2025.

Trump targeted transgender people almost as ferociously as non-white immigrants. During the campaign, he spent many millions airing commercials that attacked and mocked them, and he made the shocking—and also debunked—claim that schools were performing same-day gender surgery on children without their parents even knowing. As president, he declared that the federal government would recognize only two "immutable" sexes, an assertion at odds with the findings of scientists. He effectively purged transgender Americans of their gender identities in federal records and sought to ban them from the military and deny gender-affirming medical care for those under nineteen, as well. The military ban was "soaked in animus," a judge said in blocking it, and it was "unabashedly demeaning" and stigmatizing to transgender people.

A climate of fear took hold for many in the LGBTQ+ community, with yet another escalation in hate crimes nationwide. Outside a gay bar in Seattle, on a night popular with transgender people, three young white men in a Lexus sedan circled the bar again and again, revving the engine menacingly as they passed. They shouted "Faggots!" and other homophobic slurs at about a dozen club-goers milling about outside the front door, and they told them to die. Finally, the young man in the passenger seat fired a burst of rounds from a pellet gun at them, hitting one woman and scattering the terrified crowd in what police called a hate crime.

The attack came as no surprise to bar manager Anouk Rawkson after a series of other recent confrontations targeting gays. People had become more emboldened than ever by the mood in America, he said. "All this hate is coming out," he said, "because you have the man in the White House, the president, who says it's OK to hate. It brings the haters out."

Violent hatred was "a societal ill that is currently raging throughout this country," Orange County Judge Kimberly Menninger observed from the bench ten days after Trump's election win.

The judge was speaking to a jam-packed courtroom as she delivered the maximum possible sentence against Sam Woodward—life in prison without the possibility of parole—following the guilty verdicts handed down by a jury four months earlier. His brutal killing of Blaze Bernstein, his old high school classmate, was driven by "hate and rage," and it reflected the unsettling climate in America as a whole, Menninger said as she levied the sentence.

"This was a hate crime," Menninger said. Sam's involvement with a neo-Nazi group; his many homophobic, antisemitic memes and writings; his "adoration" of Adolf Hitler, of Charles Manson, of James Mason, and of Trump himself—it all pointed to the hatred that fueled the killing, the judge said. "He idolized all of these men because... he believed they were promoting hate-filled rhetoric about people who were of the LGBTQ and Jewish communities," she said.

Sam wasn't in court to learn his sentence. He was too ill to attend, his lawyer said, and he was allowed to watch the proceedings by video from jail instead. Blaze's father, Gideon, wished he'd been there in person because he wanted the chance to tell his son's killer—to his face—how much his hatred had taken away, in promise and potential, from him and his family. "Life without my son will never be the same," Gideon told the judge.

With the sentence, Sam Woodward joined an infamous and growing fraternity of white supremacists sent away to prison for killing their victims out of pure hatred in a decade of rage and violence, starting in 2015. Dylann Roof at the historic Black church in South Carolina. Robert Bowers at the Tree of Life synagogue in Pittsburgh. Patrick Crusius at the Hispanic-friendly Walmart in El Paso. Payton Gendron at the Tops grocery in Buffalo's majority-Black neighborhood. Anderson Aldrich at the gay nightclub in Colorado Springs. John Earnest at the Jewish synagogue in San Diego. And many more. Angry white supremacists lashing out violently against whichever minority group they loathed the most.

## "Poisoning the Blood"

More than a dozen of Sam Woodward's fellow neo-Nazis at Atomwaffen have also been prosecuted and imprisoned for hate crimes, illegal explosives and firearms, cyber-swatting of minorities and other targets, and a myriad of other charges. Brandon Russell, the founder of Atomwaffen Division, was headed back to prison for a second time after his conviction in early 2025 for plotting with his neo-Nazi girlfriend to bring down the power grid in Baltimore in hopes of starting a race war. Russell had been out of prison only a few months after his first stint—for stockpiling illegal explosives at his Tampa condo—when authorities said he began working with his girlfriend on the new plot. The former nuclear physics student had devised a plan for creating a "cascading failure" in the electrical system by unleashing sniper attacks and Mylar balloons on five of the city's substations. Working with an informant, the FBI moved in to arrest Russell and his girlfriend before they could launch what Maryland governor Wes Moore said would have been "a potentially catastrophic attack" on the city of Baltimore.

Atomwaffen Division itself officially "disbanded," but in reality, many of its members simply went off to a renamed group, the National Socialist Order, or joined up with other neo-Nazi groups. Atomwaffen's inspiration and guru, James Mason, remained free in Denver, still spewing hatred through a new website that a follower created for him, and still daring the FBI to find enough evidence to lock him up.

Rob Rundo, the street-brawling leader of Orange County's "Rise Above Movement," was sentenced in December of 2024 for political violence and rioting that Southern California's top federal prosecutor said "sought to further his white supremacist ideology." Five other RAM members under Rundo were convicted as well, while hundreds of white supremacists from other extremist groups around the country were prosecuted for violent crimes.

But some of the most prominent of the country's violent white supremacists were back on the streets after drawing an unprecedented reprieve from Trump himself. On his first day back in the White House, Trump pardoned virtually all of the more than 1,500 people charged in the rioting at the US Capitol on January 6, 2021, including many who had assaulted and injured some 140 police officers. An infamous day of violence and mayhem became, in Trump's whitewashed retelling, "a day of love." The rioters released from prison were "hostages" and "patriots," he insisted.

With a stroke of the pen, Trump had overturned four years' worth of federal prosecutions in the biggest FBI investigation in its history. The extremists celebrated their good fortune. "They thought we would break, they thought we would fail, but look at us now!" declared Enrique Tarrio, the newly freed Proud Boys leader, outside the US Capitol weeks later, as he stood alongside other members of his group who had likewise been pardoned by Trump. (Tarrio faced new legal problems by the end of the Capitol event, though, after his arrest for allegedly assaulting a counter-protester who was videotaping him.)

"You can't get rid of us," crowed a California chapter of the Proud Boys after the pardons came out.

Indeed, white supremacists' numbers were surging, and new hate groups were sprouting up like weeds in an overgrown garden, with a record 165 white supremacist groups catalogued by the Southern Poverty Law Center in its annual report in 2024, a 50 percent spike in a single year. Hate crimes rose with them, hitting a record high in the annual data released by the FBI and climbing for the ninth time in ten years. A reported attack was now coming every forty-five minutes somewhere in the country. Violent hatred had become the sad state of normalcy in modern-day America.

Hate crimes and civil-rights offenses "are, unfortunately, not likely to go away," then-FBI director Christopher Wray acknowledged in a speech he gave in the spring of 2024 on the hallowed ground of one of America's most notorious hate crimes—the Ku Klux Klan's bombing in 1963 of the 16th Street Baptist Church in Birmingham, Alabama, which killed four Black girls. Wray spoke with an air of resignation in his voice. He and the FBI had elevated such civil rights cases to national "priority" status, devoting more funding, more agents, more training, and more collaboration with local authorities. And still, hate crimes and violent bigotry continued to soar.

## "Poisoning the Blood"

What Wray called "a particularly heinous example" had come to a close just weeks earlier, in fact, with the sentencing of six Mississippi police officers in a police brutality case reminiscent of the darkest days of the Jim Crow South in the 1960s.

The episode hadn't generated nearly the outrage or attention of George Floyd's killing or of police brutality cases against other Black victims, notably Breonna Taylor in Kentucky and Sonya Massey in Illinois. There was no video of this one to shock the conscience. But the pure racial savagery was perhaps even more unsettling.

Six white officers from a self-described "Goon Squad" at the rural Rankin County Sheriff's Office in Mississippi kicked in the door of a home where two Black men were staying in 2023 after a white neighbor complained they were living with a white woman. (One of the men was a friend helping to care for the paralyzed woman.) The officers didn't have a warrant, or any reason to think the men had done anything wrong, an FBI investigation determined. Bombarding the pair with racist slurs as "monkeys" and "n****rs," the officers held them captive for ninety minutes, forced them to strip naked, tortured them, sexually assaulted them, beat them, and tased them more than a dozen times. Then they warned them to leave town and go back to "their side" of the local Pearl River, where many Blacks lived.

As a final *coup de grâce*, one officer staged a "mock" execution, taking a bullet from his gun and shoving the barrel in the mouth of one of his terrified victims, Michael Jenkins. The officer fired once, his gun clicking. Then he fired a second time, a live bullet crushing Jenkins' jaw. Remarkably, he survived.

"No human being," Wray said, "should ever be subjected to the torture, the trauma, the horrific acts of violence carried out by these individuals." Convicted on civil rights charges, the six officers received prison sentences ranging from ten to forty years. But Wray himself was gone from the FBI nine months later, announcing his resignation after Trump won reelection and vowed to fire him. He wouldn't be around to see whether the FBI could stem the tide of racially fueled crimes racking America.

The latest wave of mass hate crimes to hit American streets started overseas, with the war in Gaza setting off a rash of attacks against both Jews and Muslims in America after Hamas's terror attack on Israel in October 2023 killed more than 1,200 people. Like the rampant attacks on Asian Americans after the coronavirus outbreak three years before, another international crisis unleashed a flood of bigotry at home as people looked for someone convenient to blame. Jewish and Muslim advocacy groups reported a doubling or tripling of attacks, threats, and harassment against them, with white supremacist groups often feeding the fury to advance their own agendas and to target Jews in particular.

In Orange County, what started as an argument about Gaza between two groups of strangers at a Laguna Beach bar spiraled into violence in the parking lot, with one angry patron ramming his car into a Jewish man in December 2024, police said. The victim was hospitalized with a broken leg and other injuries, and the attacker was arrested in what police said they were investigating as a hate crime.

In upstate New York, a Cornell University student was arrested and convicted after posting threats online saying that he was "gonna bomb [a] Jewish house" and "shoot up" a dining hall serving kosher food over the strife in Gaza. The episode was "a disturbing reminder of the terrifying hatred our Jewish communities encounter simply because of their beliefs," the FBI agent on the case said.

High-profile Jewish-Americans came under attack as well. In Pennsylvania, Governor Josh Shapiro and his wife and four children were asleep in the governor's official residence in April 2025 after a night spent celebrating the Passover holiday, when a state trooper started banging on their bedroom doors and yelling for them to evacuate. A fierce fire was ravaging the mansion after a man with a history of mental illness allegedly smashed two windows and tossed homemade Molotov cocktails inside. The suspect admitted, police said, that he "harbored hatred" for Shapiro, a strong Jewish supporter of Israel, and was angry about the governor's stance on Palestine.

Less than two weeks later came another Jewish gathering, another rallying cry for violence, and another horrific attack. A group of Jewish

## "Poisoning the Blood"

demonstrators, most of them elderly, were rallying at a popular park in Boulder, Colorado, for the release of Israelis still held hostage by Hamas. "End Zionist!... Free Palestine!" shouted a man nearby as he launched two Molotov cocktails at the group and lit several rally-goers aflame, killing one elderly woman and leaving nearly a dozen other people with burns and other injuries. One of them was a Holocaust survivor.

The annual hate-crime data released by the FBI in August 2025 confirmed what a perilous time it had become for Jewish Americans, in particular, as the war in Gaza ground on. Hate crimes against Jewish victims rose to their highest number ever on record, with more than five reports a day of antisemitic attacks in 2024, while hate crimes overall were the second highest ever recorded.

As attacks mounted one after the other, Jews across America lived in fear of when the next one might hit. It was a fraught time for Palestinians in America, too. In Chicago, a white landlord brutally stabbed a six-year-old Palestinian boy in his building twenty-six times, killing him and badly injuring his mother in another grisly hate crime. Prosecutors, searching for a motive for such a senseless attack, said the landlord had become agitated about the threat from Hamas after listening to conservative talk radio, lashing out violently against his own Palestinian tenants—mother and son—because of it. An Illinois jury found him guilty of murder and hate-crime charges.

And in Burlington, Vermont, three Palestinian students attending college in America were walking along a street near the University of Vermont after a night of bowling when a man on his front porch wordlessly fired his pistol and shot all three of them, paralyzing one, police said. Two of the young men were wearing traditional Palestinian scarves, or *keffiyehs*, speaking a mix of Arabic and English, when the white shooter, a former Boy Scout leader, allegedly opened fire.

Growing up in the West Bank, the three Palestinian students had come to expect the threat of violence there, but not in America, not walking down the street on a holiday break from college. The shooting, an apparent hate crime, was "a symptom of something larger" going on in America, one of the victims, Kinnan Abdalhamid, said stoically as he recovered from his injuries. The root cause, he said, was a "systemic dehumanization" that bred hatred against people, like him, who were seen as outsiders: the *others*.

It was a common, battle-tested belief among both Jews and Muslims on opposite sides of the Israel–Hamas war—especially on college campuses, which became the focal point for rancor over the Gaza conflict. Protests, encampments, and walkouts swept through more than a hundred universities around the country as the war in Gaza escalated, with many liberal students on the left flocking to the pro-Palestinian side in criticizing Israel's counteroffensive. While most of the protests were peaceful, some veered into violence, vandalism, and blatant antisemitism, with calls for the destruction of Israel and praise for Hamas's violent actions leading some Jewish students to say that they felt unsafe on their campuses.

Joining the pro-Palestinian protesters was an unwanted ally looking to vent their antisemitism. White supremacist groups showed up in force at many college protests, staged their own demonstrations, and went online to broadcast their antisemitic tropes and attack Jewish people over Gaza. At one white supremacist demonstration outside the White House weeks after the Gaza war started in October 2023, about forty members of the rabidly antisemitic National Justice Party chanted anti-Jewish slogans and waved signs reading "No White Lives for Israel" and "Zionism = Terrorism."

Groyper's Nick Fuentes, again at the forefront, was blunt about the white supremacists' strategic motives: to hurt the Jews. They had no genuine concern for Palestinians, he acknowledged, but siding with them over Gaza served their anti-Semitic aims. "I don't really care about this conflict," he said in one video, but "this becomes a situation where the enemy of our enemy becomes our friend." Laughing, he scoffed at the notion that white supremacists, typically no fans of Middle Easterners, should be opposed to the Palestinians' cause, not supporting them. "Sorry, Shlomo, you forgot one thing: We're antisemitic!" Fuentes said. "We're more antisemitic than we are racist!"

In an age of rampant hatred, it was a rallying cry for more.

# AUTHOR'S NOTE AND ACKNOWLEDGEMENTS

I started writing this book after a spree of haunting hate crimes in America at the hands of violent white supremacists. I wanted to understand how America had returned to a place of such violent hatred and had inspired a generation of young neo-Nazis. As I complete this book, the epidemic of hate has only grown fiercer today in the Trump era, both in frequency and ferocity. Violent bigotry, spurred by emboldened white supremacists, has become the norm.

In my research, I conducted more than three hundred interviews with victims and survivors of hate crimes, including friends and the parents of Blaze Bernstein — Gideon Bernstein and Jeanne Pepper; federal and local law enforcement officials; hate-crime scholars and historians; advocates focused on combatting white supremacy and extremism; and neo-Nazis and white supremacists themselves, including many hours spent interviewing James Mason, a neo-Nazi leader in Denver of particular influence among young right-wing extremists. The sources of my interviews are listed in the endnotes, unless otherwise reflected in the text.

I also reviewed more than 8,000 pages of documents on hate and extremism, including court records, government and academic reports, archival records, and other material as cited in the endnotes, and I conducted research and reporting at the 2024 murder trial of Samuel Woodward in Orange County, California, in the tragic killing of Blaze Bernstein, as well as at other events that were critical to the telling of this story.

My research took me back to the place where I started my career in journalism more than three decades ago — in Orange County, a

## Author's Note and Acknowledgements

hotbed of white supremacy that serves as a dark reflection of the resurgence of violent bigotry across the country in the past decade. As a young reporter with the *Los Angeles Times* in the early 1990s, I remember interviewing the victim of a savage hate crime in Orange County: an Asian American teenager who was beaten unconscious in a park by a group of fifteen skinheads who were shouting racial slurs and giving Nazi salutes. "What freaks me out," the victim told me, "isn't the fact that I got beat up, but that I got jumped by Nazi skinheads so close to where you live." At the time, the violence seemed like an outlier, a throwback to another era in America when white supremacy ran rampant. But today, in an era of record hate crimes fueled by Donald Trump's frequent race-baiting, such violent bigotry has become a sad, everyday reality for minorities—for the "others"—as white supremacists have made a brash resurgence in Orange County and well beyond.

I want to thank Alex Littlefield, my editor at Little, Brown and Company; Michael Fleming, the copyeditor; and Gail Ross, my agent, for making this book possible. I also want to thank my primary researcher, Jonathan Krohn, who wrote a poignant article on the Blaze Bernstein murder for *Mother Jones;* and Michael Wolivar, who also provided research help. For their insight and feedback, I'm also grateful to my early readers of the manuscript, including my wife; Leslie Zirkin; my children, Matthew, Andrew, Elliot, and Harold; and my sister, Anita Lichtblau; as well as Lenny Bernstein, Kevin Johnson, and Martin Kanovsky (still the fastest reader I know). I also want to give particular thanks to Brian Levin, a longtime scholar of hate crimes, for his insight and help on a topic that is more important than ever today.

# NOTES

### Prologue

4    *just to "catch up"*: Online messages between Sam Woodward and Blaze Bernstein on Tinder, January 2, 2017; court exhibits in murder trial of *People v. Samuel Woodward* (2024), Orange County Superior Court, reviewed by author.

4    *they are going to get hate-crimed*: "Diary of Hate" written by Woodward; court exhibits in Woodward murder trial.

4    *chilling sketch*: Testimony at Woodward murder trial and court exhibits reviewed by author.

6    *reached the highest levels ever recorded*: The FBI's annual report on hate crimes for 2023 as part of Uniform Crime Reporting program, released on Sept. 23, 2024; it was the most recent FBI report at the time of this book's publication. FBI tracking began in 1990. The 2024 report was based on voluntary reporting on hate-crime episodes from about 16,000 law enforcement agencies. As discussed on page 285, the FBI hate-crime data provides a picture of the general trend lines on the frequency of hate crimes, but it is an incomplete tally that undercounts the actual number because thousands of police agencies do not submit any data, or reported they had zero hate crimes.

6    *more than doubling in a decade*: The FBI reported 13,829 hate-crime offenses in its 2024 report for 2023, compared to 6,418 offenses in its 2014 report for 2013.

6    *as many as three of every four, by one accounting*: University of New Hampshire report funded by US Justice Department, "U.S. Hate Crime Investigation Rates and Characteristics: Findings from the National Hate Crime Investigations Study," 2022, 18.

6    *Seven Asian and Hispanic shoppers, including three young children, murdered*: In addition to the seven shoppers, all minorities, a white security guard was also killed in the shooting on May 6, 2023 in Allen, Texas, outside Dallas. The shooter, Mauricio Garcia, thirty-three, who identified as a white supremacist and neo-Nazi, was killed at the scene by a police officer.

6    *Five gay club-goers at a Colorado Springs bar shot dead*: November 19, 2022, at Club Q, a gay nightclub in Colorado Springs. The shooter, Anderson Lee Aldrich, twenty-three, who ran a neo-Nazi website, was sentenced to life in prison without the possibility of parole in a Colorado state court and also faced federal hate-crime charges that were still pending as of this writing. The 2015 massacre at a gay club in Orlando killed far more people — forty-nine — than did the Colorado

## Notes

Springs attack, but as discussed on page 81, the FBI concluded that the Orlando shooter, Omar Mateen, was driven by Islamist extremism, not by a hatred of gays, in an act of terror, and the FBI said that he apparently didn't even know the club catered to LGBT clientele.

6 *ten Black shoppers at a Buffalo grocery killed*: The shooter, Payton Gendron, 19, pleaded guilty in state court to murder charges in the Tops massacre on May 14, 2022 and faced a possible death sentence in federal charges that were pending as of this writing.

6 *The worst massacre of Hispanics*: The shooter, white supremacist Patrick Crusius, 21, pleaded guilty in 2023 to federal charges in the Walmart shooting, which took place August 3, 2019, and was sentenced to 90 consecutive life terms in prison. He also pleaded guilty to state charges in March 2025 in a deal to avoid the death penalty.

6 *worst massacre of Jews ever on American soil*: The shooter, white supremacist Robert Bowers, 46, was sentenced to the death penalty in 2023 for the massacre at the synagogue, which took place on October 27, 2018.

6 *worst massacre ever of Sikh Indian Americans*: The shooter, neo-Nazi Wade Michael Page, 40, was killed by police in a shootout after his attack on the Sikh temple, which took place on August 5, 2012.

7 *trumpeted by Trump himself*: Jude Joffe-Block and Odette Yousef, "How Trump is relying on a racist conspiracy theory to question election results," National Public Radio, September 13, 2024.

7 *far-right figures like Elon Musk*: Greg Sargent, "Elon Musk Pushes a Vile, Toxic Hate Video—and Exposes His Own Scam," *New Republic*, March 21, 2024.

7 *far-right figures like… Tucker Carlson*: Erin Jensen, "'That's just insane': Tucker Carlson resents ADL's response to 'Replacement' theory remarks," *USA Today*, September 28, 2021.

8 *a record spike in the number of hate groups*: The Southern Poverty Law Center catalogued a record 1,108 hate groups in 2011 during Obama's presidency.

9 *attacking us in every way*: Kui Mwai, "Haitian Americans in Springfield, Ohio, Fear for Their Lives amid Trump's Viral Claims," *Yahoo News*, September 13, 2024, 4.

9 *the good Republicans go before they die*: "Reagan on Mortality and Orange County," *New York Times*, September 3, 1984.

9 *his unapologetic racism*: In an infamous interview he did with *Playboy* magazine in 1971 at his Newport Beach home, Wayne said, "I believe in white supremacy until the blacks are educated to a point of responsibility." The movie star also spoke dismissively of gays in film as "fags" and "perverted" and said that he saw nothing wrong with American settlers "taking this great country away" from Native Americans, who he said "were selfishly trying to keep it for themselves." His outspoken bigotry has led some critics to call for the removal of his statute at the airport. See Michael Hiltzik, "Take John Wayne's name off O.C. Airport," *Los Angeles Times*, February 21, 2019.

10 *make up about 65 percent*: 2023 US Census Bureau data. See: https://www.census.gov/quickfacts/fact/table/US/PST045222.

# Notes

10   *a "kill list" of prominent local Jews*: The young white supremacist, Nicholas Rose, pleaded guilty in 2019 to charges of plotting attacks against three houses of worship in Orange County and of carrying a loaded, unregistered firearm.

10   *one of Orange County's busiest freeways*: Author interview with Mayor Farrah Khan; and Alicia Robinson, " 'No place in Irvine' for hate, Mayor Khan says after second antisemitic banner incident," *Orange County Register*, November 29, 2021.

11   *to be "a badge of honor"*: Statement from Mark Weber, director of the Institute for Historical Review, on the organization's website in March 2021; https://ihr.org/news/sept08report-html.

11   *Hate is here*: Orange County District Attorney Todd Spitzer, "Hate Has No Place in Orange County," *Orange County Register*, September 29, 2019.

11   *the growing violence of white supremacists*: Brian Levin, Testimony before House Committee on Homeland Security, September 10, 2019. "The Base" video can be seen at: https://tinyurl.com/yc26utdh.

## Chapter 1

16   *a "Renaissance" student*: Author interview with Ralph Opacic, founder and former executive director of the Orange County School of the Arts.

16   *the homosexuals would convert Sam*: Testimony of Blake Woodward, father of Sam Woodward, at Woodward murder trial.

16   *Orange County conservative to the core*: Blake Woodward testimony and opening statement of Kenneth Morrison, defense counsel, at Woodward murder trial.

17   *He taunted Sam*: Testimony at Woodward murder trial.

17   *a long heart-to-heart*: Blake Woodward testimony.

17   *his stash of pornography*: Trial testimony from law enforcement officials.

17   *Could I be gay?*: Sam Woodward, recorded interview with Orange County sheriff's department, when asked if he had experimented with homosexuality; played back at murder trial and in court exhibits.

18   *I'm going to kill you*: Orange County sheriff's interview with Cassandra Branch, cited at pretrial evidentiary hearing in Woodward murder case.

18   *felt like a minority*: Testimony of Michele Woodward, defendant's mother, in Woodward murder trial.

18   *There's this mixed race*: Author interview with Sean Budge, friend of Sam at Orange County School for the Arts.

18   *made them a power*: Budge interview.

19   *a large Confederate flag*: Budge interview

19   *much of his time sketching*: Author interviews with former classmates.

19   *shoot up a school*: Author interview with Raiah Rofsky.

19   *a raw plea for help*: Jonathan Krohn, "How a Gay Teen, an Internet Nazi, and a Late-Night Rendezvous Turned to Tragedy," *Mother Jones*, March/April 2019.

20   *apparently Nazis*: Budge interview.

20   *Make the cry-babies cry*: Budge interview.

20   *the most violent corners*: Budge interview.

20   *he ventured off*: Author interview with Josh Woods, teacher at Orange County School of the Arts.

# Notes

21 *started writing poetry*: Author interview with Jeanne Pepper and Gideon Bernstein, parents of Blaze Bernstein.
21 *I write until I can't*: Quoted in eulogy for Blaze Bernstein given by Jamie-Lee Josselyn, his academic advisor at the University of Pennsylvania.
21 *they called me gay*: Author interview with Jeanne Pepper.
22 *saw the country as a "simmering pot"*: Jeanne Pepper interview.
22 *Gabe had been out as gay*: Author interview with Gabe García Combs Morris, friend and classmate of Blaze Bernstein at Orange County School of the Arts.
23 *a "gay haven," as he called it*: García Combs Morris interview.
23 *go to hell*: "The Year in Hate," *OC Weekly*, December 28, 2017.
23 *lie awake thinking about you*: Messages from Sam Woodward to García Combs Morris, provided to author.
23 *Damn forgot how fun it was*: Testimony at Woodward trial and court exhibits.
24 *"Bullshit," Blaze said*: Author interview with García Combs Morris.
24 *say good-bye*: Messages from Sam Woodward to García Combs Morris.
24 *that could have been me*: García Combs Morris interview.

## Chapter 2

25 *places to avoid*: Author interviews with Orange County School of the Arts students.
26 *the Skinhead capital of the world*: Rich Kane, "Springboard for Hitler," *OC Weekly*, September 6, 2001.
26 *Imagine what we could do*: Geoff Edgers, "White Trash," *GQ* magazine, August 6, 2012.
27 *jeers, fists, or worse*: Author interview with Tim Zaal, former neo-Nazi in Orange County, who now works with the Simon Wiesenthal Center in Los Angeles.
27 *surf Nazis*: Interview with Dave Dictus, leader of punk band MDC, conducted by researcher Jonathan Krohn.
27 *turned to bedlam*: Steve Donofrio, "Neo-Nazis Get Their Asses Kicked During Reagan Youth Show at Garden Amp," *OC Weekly*, January 23, 2019.
27 *a dozen neo-Nazi skinheads*: Mike Boehm, "Punk Show Violence Prompts Call for Change," *Los Angeles Times*, December 24, 1994.
27 *What do you have*: Mike Boehm, "It's time to stop the 'heil' raisers," *Los Angeles Times*, January 19, 1995.
27 *"Heil' raisers"*: Ibid.
28 *positive results in our society*: Jim Farber, "Label 56 signed Wisconsin Sikh temple killer Wade Michael Page to recording contract," *New York Daily News*, August 6, 2012.
29 *It's obvious the fuckin' Jews*: Pete Simi, *American Swastika* (Lanham, MD: Rowman & Littlefield, 2010), 69.
29 *dedicated its signature song*: OC Weekly, "Springboard for Hitler."
30 *music festival dedicated to hate music*: Southern Poverty Law Center profile of Tom Metzger. See: https://www.splcenter.org/fighting-hate/extremist-files/individual/tom-metzger.
30 *the Mecca of white separatism*: Michael Connelly, David Freed, and Sonia Nazario, "Southland is ripe turf for white hate groups," *Los Angeles Times*, July 25, 1993.

## Notes

30   *good, law-abiding people*: Shawn Lay, *The Invisible Empire in the West* (Chicago: University of Illinois Press, 1992), 112.
30   *robed in Klan regalia*: Lay, *The Invisible Empire in the West*, 103.
31   *all hell would be raised*: Ellen Wu, "Diver's Ambassador Life Showed Bigotry Is Never Far from the Surface," National Public Radio, December 7, 2016.
31   *I don't want to sound*: "Olympic Star Sammy Lee Again Threatened by Calif. Racists," *Honolulu Record*, February 14, 1957, 1.
31   *lesbian spear-chuckers*: "Every lesbian spear-chucker in this country is hoping I get defeated," said Orange County congressman Bob Dornan in his successful 1992 campaign. Danielle Herubin, "Dornan slur jars viewers," *Orange County Register*, June 3, 1992.
31   *likening South African icon Nelson Mandela*: Orange County congressman William Dannemeyer made the vicious comparison in boycotting Mandela's historic talk before Congress in 1990. Robert H. Stewart, "O.C. Delegation Shuns Mandela In Congress," *Los Angeles Times*, June 29, 1990.
31   *a large contingent of barefoot Africans*: The baseless claim by Orange County congressman James Utt in 1963 caused a national furor. Larry Peterson, "Image makers: Men who have reinforced OC's reputation," *Orange County Register*, June 29, 1987.
32   *even the far-right John Birch Society dumped him*: Associated Press, "Ex-congressman, senator dies; Schmitz defined Southern California right-wing Republicanism," *Ventura County Star*, January 12, 2001.
32   *uniformed private security guards*: The FBI opened an investigation into possible civil rights violations, and the state Republicans settled numerous lawsuits growing out of the alleged voter intimidation for at least $480,000. Dave Lesher, "O.C. Poll Guard Case Ends in Settlement by State GOP," *Los Angeles Times*, November 17, 1992.
33   *makes Orange County look bad*: Author interview with Rusty Kennedy, former executive director of the Orange County Human Relations Commission, and notes of commission hearing in 2017.
33   *creating a homeland*: Rick Romell, *Milwaukee Journal Sentinel*, August 6, 2012.
34   *he hated them all*: Ibid.
34   *spotted him goose-stepping*: Gina Barton, "Racist groups drawn to military," *Milwaukee Journal Sentinel*, August 7, 2012.
34   *maybe I'll earn my spiderweb*: F. T. Norton, "Fayetteville's infamous crimes," *Fayetteville (North Carolina) Observer*, April 4, 2021.
35   *the kind of stuff that happens*: "Academic Who Knew Sikh Shooter Wade Michael Page Says Neo-Nazi Soldiers, Musicians Shaped His Hatred," *Democracy Now!*, August 9, 2012.
36   *if it turns out you're a cop*: Simi, *American Swastika*, 41.
36   *German-themed club*: Author interview with Pete Simi.
37   *killing six congregants*: Six people were killed at the time of shooting, including five congregants and a police officer; another victim, Baba Punjab Singh, a priest who was shot in the head and paralyzed, died from his injuries eight years later, bringing the total number of fatalities to seven, in addition to Wade Page, who killed himself at the scene.

## Notes

37  *the US Holocaust Museum*: The shooter, James von Brunn, died in 2010 while awaiting trial on a federal murder charge.

37  *a Jewish summer camp*: Buford O'Neal Furrow Jr. received a sentence of life in prison without the possibility of parole.

38  *immersed himself in dozens of online chats*: John Diedrich, "FBI warrant details Sikh Temple shooter's online white power searches," *Milwaukee Journal Sentinel*, May 14, 2013.

38  *He just hated*: Bill Glauber, "Officer wounded in Sikh temple attack still can't speak," *Milwaukee Journal Sentinel*, August 8, 2012.

39  *they see the turban*: Steven Yaccino, Michael Schwirtz, and Marc Santora, "Gunman Kills 6 at a Sikh Temple Near Milwaukee," *New York Times*, August 5, 2012.

39  *go out and shoot*: Anita Snow, "Sikh preaches love 18 years after brother killed over turban," Associated Press, September 14, 2019.

39  *it is very shocking*: "Details Emerge on Alleged Gunman in Sikh Temple Shooting," *PBS News Hour*, August 6, 2012, https://shorturl.at/Fy2Vw.

39  *he would have been at the temple*: Author interview with Pardeep Singh Kaleka, son of shooting victim.

39  *There's been a shooting*: Kaleka interview and *The Gift of Our Wounds: A Sikh and a Former White Supremacist Find Forgiveness After Hate*, by Arno Michaelis and Pardeep Singh Kaleka (New York: St. Martin's, 2018), 143.

41  *formed a nonprofit group*: Serve2Unite; see: https://pluralism.org/serve2unite.

42  *the defunct British band Skrewdriver*: Research findings from author and researcher Jonathan Krohn on white-power music widely available on music platforms.

42  *Hate speech has the potential*: United Nations *Strategy and Plan of Action on Hate Speech*, issued June 18, 2019, https://shorturl.at/rLSOm.

43  *About a third of all of all Internet users*: US Government Accountability Office, "Online Extremism" report, January 2024.

43  *failing grades*: See, for instance, GLAAD's "2024 Social Media Safety Index (SMSI) & Platform Scorecard," https://shorturl.at/sRB4D.

43  *a safe space for hate*: Sacha Roytman Dratwa, chief executive of the Combat Antisemitism Movement, February 2023.

43  *an anti-hate group reported to X*: Center for Countering Digital Hate report, "X Content Moderation Failure," September 2023, https://shorturl.at/A1kLq. X sued the CCDH over its findings, but the case was thrown out.

### Chapter 3

44  *almost mute in school*: Author interviews with classmates at Corona del Mar High School in Newport Beach.

45  *"fags and kikes," as he called them*: Woodward murder trial and exhibits.

45  *force them to carry*: Testimony at Woodward murder trial presented by prosecution. All the quotations from Woodward's social media postings and other writings were presented at the trial, except where otherwise noted.

46  *if you're a race mixer*: Court exhibits in Woodward murder trial. Selfie posted on ifunny.com.

# Notes

47  *prompted the filmmakers to rewrite*: "Edward Norton's primal fear," *Ottawa Citizen*, October 22, 1998.
47  *You are violent*: Hannah Fry, "Suspect in ex-classmate's death boasted of his faith," *Los Angeles Times*, January 20, 2018.
47  *looked like a school shooter*: Testimony of Blake Woodward at Woodward murder trial.
47  *He went long stretches*: Trial testimony from Michele Woodward at Woodward murder trial.
47  *Sam got into a series of fights*: Trial testimony from Michele Woodward and Dr. Martha Rogers, psychologist for the defense.
48  *balancing that with classwork*: Trial testimony and exhibits on messages between Woodward and Tristan Evans.
48  *joining the military*: Ibid.
48  *his "Diary of Hate"*: Trial testimony and exhibits in Woodward murder trial with excerpts from his "Diary of Hate."
48  *Get them hooked*: Trial testimony and exhibits.
49  *That didn't happen*: Author interview with Penn classmate Amy Marcus.
49  *snippets of poetry*: Ibid.
50  *his confidence*: Author interview with Gideon Bernstein.
50  *encouraged him to think*: Ibid.
50  *lavish feasts*: Amy Marcus interview.
51  *You don't need to worry*: Author interview with Jeanne Pepper.
52  *OMG WE ALL KNEW IT*: Author interview with Alex Tomlinson.
52  *mainly because of women*: Messages between Sam Woodward and Blaze Bernstein introduced in court testimony and exhibits in Woodward murder trial.
52  *"Very gay," Blaze answered*: Ibid.
53  *They talked excitedly online*: Messages between Sam Woodward and Tristan Evans introduced in trial testimony and included in court exhibits in Woodward murder trial.
53  *our entire society is polluted*: Sam Woodward–Tristan Evans messages.
54  *angry diatribes*: Blake Woodward testimony at murder trial.
54  *neo-Nazi symbols*: "88" is the neo-Nazi shorthand for "Heil Hitler" because H is the eighth letter of the alphabet, and "14" symbolizes the "14 Words" of the white supremacist creed composed by David Lane to secure the future of the white race.
54  *Revolution is not a spectator sport*: Testimony of Dr. Martha Rogers at Woodward murder trial.
55  *joining up with a band of neo-Nazis*: Testimony at Woodward murder trial from Woodward's parents and opening statement of defense counsel Morrison.
55  *Blake told Sam he was worried*: testimony of Blake Woodward at Woodward murder trial.
55  *wind up in prison*: Ibid.
55  *This movement is for real men*: Sam Woodward–Tristan Evans messages at murder trial.

# Notes

## Chapter 4

56  *a HUGE role in electing Trump*: "White Nationalists of the world congratulate President-elect Trump," *Jerusalem Post*, November 11, 2016.

56  *We won, brothers*: Ibid.

56  *Everything you love*: Vegas Tenold, *Everything You Love Will Burn* (New York: Nation Books, 2018), 13.

57  *promptly got himself arrested*: Liam Stack, "Two Klan Leaders Are Charged in a North Carolina Stabbing," December 7, 2016.

57  *can act like a virus*: US Department of Justice, Bureau of Justice Assistance monograph, "A Policymaker's Guide to Hate Crimes," March 1997, 22.

58  *Grant personally marched*: Ron Chernow, *Grant* (New York: Penguin Books, 2017), 705.

58  *the duty of putting forth*: Ibid., 707.

59  *Peace has come*: Ibid., 706.

59  *ruling it unconstitutional*: United States v. Harris (1883). The Supreme Court concluded that the enforcement law was "overbroad" and unconstitutional because, the court said, the federal government did not have the power to take action against and punish "private persons" who violated the equal rights of Black people.

60  *talking too much*: Equal Justice Initiative, "White Georgia Mob Lynches Man for 'Talking Too Much' About Another Lynching," https://shorturl.at/sBKA7, accessed January 13, 2025. The victim, Mitchell Daniel, was a leader in local Negro activism.

60  *surrender to a ragged rabble of Negroes*: David Zucchino, *Wilmington's Lie* (New York: Grove Atlantic, 2020), 146.

60  *If it is necessary, every Negro*: John Barry, *Rising Tide: The Great Mississippi Flood of 1927 and How It Changed America* (New York: Simon & Schuster, 1998), 124.

61  *Purge that plague hole*: Roxane Kopetman, "Santa Ana City apologizes for Chinatown blaze of 1906," *Orange County Register*, May 25, 2002.

61  *only a lone Chinese resident*: "Chinatown Torched in Ugly '06 Incident," *Los Angeles Times*, May 31, 1993.

61  *the racist and xenophobic actions*: Roxana Kopetman, "Santa Ana Apologizes for 1906 Burning of Its Chinatown," *Orange County Register*, May 24, 2022. What was once a thriving Chinatown in Santa Ana ultimately became a parking lot, the destruction there long forgotten. No marker or memorial commemorates what happened there.

61  *not of white blood*: Michael Traynor, "The Infamous Case of *People v. Hall* (1854): An Odious Symbol of Its Time," California Supreme Court Historical Society newsletter, Spring/Summer 2017.

62  *little Mexican Revolution*: Gustavo Arrelano, "The Citrus War of 1936 Changed Orange County Forever and Cemented Our Mistrust of Mexicans," *OC Weekly*, June 8, 2006.

62  *SHOOT TO KILL*: Ibid.

62  *All law has been suspended*: Ibid.

## Notes

62  *I had no idea*: Richard Gergel, *Unexampled Courage: The Blinding of Sgt. Isaac Woodard and the Awakening of President Harry S. Truman and Judge J. Waties Waring* (New York: Sarah Crighton Books, 2019), 73.

63  *On the eve of the final passage*: The Senate had passed the civil rights measure three weeks earlier, and the House gave it final approval on April 10, 1968, six days after King's assassination.

64  *in retaliation for an African American man*: Justice Department announcement, January 7, 2009.

64  *a pair of white supremacist skinheads*: Eric Lichtblau, "Arrests in Plan to Kill Obama and Black Schoolchildren," *New York Times*, October 27, 2008.

64  *spiked three or four times*: Ezra Klein, "President Obama has faced three times as many threats on his life as past presidents," September 29, 2014. Other sources, including journalist Ron Kessler, said that the threats actually quadrupled, assertions rejected by the Secret Service, which was under criticism for security failures.

65  *Americans were "not ready"*: Jonathan Edwards, "Michelle Obama says Americans weren't ready for her natural Black hair," *Washington Post*, November 17, 2022.

65  *what Johnson was seeing*: Author interview with Darryl Johnson, former DHS domestic security senior analyst.

66  *another plot to kill President Obama*: Johnson interview; and Daryl Johnson, *Right-Wing Resurgence* (Lanham, MD: Rowman & Littlefield, 2012), 213.

66  *strapped on a bulletproof vest*: Paula Reed Ward, "911 Call Set Battle Plan In Motion; Accused Killer Put Bulletproof Vest On and Armed Himself," *Pittsburgh Post-Gazette*, June 25, 2011.

66  *Boy Scout fundraiser*: Johnson interview.

66  *criminalize political dissent*: Johnson, *Right-Wing Resurgence*, 252.

66  *Napolitano withdrew the report*: Author interview with Janet Napolitano. Asked if she had any regrets about withdrawing the report, Napolitano said, "I don't second-guess that way."

67  *nearly nine hundred reports*: Southern Poverty Law Center report, "Ten Days After: Harassment and Intimidation in the Aftermath of the Election," issued November 29, 2016.

68  *Laziness is a trait*: John R. O'Donnell, *Trumped!: The Inside Story of the Real Donald Trump—His Cunning Rise and Spectacular Fall* (New York: Simon & Schuster, 1991).

68  *Trump even had a copy of Hitler's collected speeches*: "Report: Trump keeps Hitler book at bedside," United Press International, August 9, 1990.

69  *more than tripled*: Ayal Feinberg, Regina Branton, and Valerie Martinez-Ebers, "The Trump Effect: How 2016 Campaign Rallies Explain Spikes in Hate," *PS: Political Science and Politics* (April 2022), DOI:10.1017/S1049096521001621. Conservatives attacked the data as unfounded.

69  *America's Hitler*: Gram Slattery and Helen Coster, "JD Vance once compared Trump to Hitler. Now, he is Trump's vice president–elect," November 6, 2024.

70  *I am very surprised*: *60 Minutes* interview with Donald Trump, November 13, 2016.

## Notes

70 *not looking to energize them*: "Donald Trump's New York Times Interview: Full Transcript," *New York Times,* November 23, 2016.

71 *You fucking generals*: Susan B. Glasser and Peter Baker, "Inside the War Between Trump and His Generals," *The New Yorker,* August 8, 2022.

71 *Hitler did some good things*: Michael S. Schmidt, "As Election Nears, Kelly Warns Trump Would Rule Like a Dictator," *New York Times,* October 22, 2024.

71 *Attacks on women*: Meghan Keneally, "'Horseface,' 'crazy,' 'low IQ': Trump's history of insulting women," ABC News, October 17, 2018.

72 *screamed "White power"*: BBC, "Trump retweets video of supporter shouting 'White power,'" June 28, 2020.

72 *confined to a "small group"*: "Trump says white nationalism is a 'small group of people' with 'very serious problems,'" *Washington Post,* March 15, 2019.

72 *invade my country*: Bruce Vielmetti, "Man arrested in Milwaukee acid attack was convicted of false imprisonment of hunters," *Milwaukee Journal Sentinel,* November 14, 2019.

72 *the next Donald Trump rally*: Amelia Dickson, "Man to serve 4 years in downtown Olympia hate crime stabbing," *The Olympian,* October 25, 2017.

72 *Get out of my country*: Joshua Barajas, "Kansas man sentenced to life in prison for 2017 shooting that targeted Indian men," PBS, August 7, 2018.

72 *President Trump will cleanse America*: US Justice Department indictment of William Patrick Syring, February 21, 2018. He was sentenced to five years in prison.

73 *It is hard to differentiate*: "'No Blame?' ABC News finds 54 cases invoking 'Trump' in connection with violence, threats, alleged assaults," ABC News, May 30, 2020.

73 *Rough-and-tumble verbal pummeling*: Sentencing memorandum from the defense in *United States v. Patrick Stein* (February 29, 2018), United States District Court for the District of Kansas. Stein and two other defendants in the bombing plot each received prison sentences ranging from twenty-five to thirty years.

74 *attacks on Muslims increased*: Nazia Parveen, "Boris Johnson's burqa comments led to surge in anti-Muslim attacks," *The Guardian,* September 19, 2019.

74 *No president has ever gone there*: Author interview with Michael Yaki.

76 *Thank you President Trump*: Greg Price, "White Supremacist David Duke Thanks Donald Trump for Slamming Antifa and Leftists," *Newsweek,* August 15, 2017.

76 *hate incidents targeting Jews*: Anti-Defamation League report, "ADL Data Shows Antisemitic Incidents Continue Surge in 2017 Compared to 2016," November 2, 2017.

76 *drafted a letter of resignation*: Kate Kelley and Maggie Haberman, "Gary Cohn, Trump's Adviser, Said to Have Drafted Resignation Letter after Charlottesville," *New York Times,* August 25, 2017.

77 *your words matter*: Tim Alberta, "Nikki Haley's Time for Choosing," *Politico,* February 2021.

### Chapter 5

79 *Gas the Kikes*: Southern Poverty Law Center, Extremist Files: Atomwaffen Division.

## Notes

79  *fucking edgy*: Brandon Russell police interview with Tampa Police Department and FBI; audio obtained by author under Florida Public Records Act in *State of Florida v. Devon Shawn Ryan Arthurs* (2020), Hillsborough County Court.
79  *evil, evil, evil*: Russell police interview.
80  *ultimate goal of uncompromising victory*: Exhibit 19 in *United States v. Brandon C. Russell* (2017), United States District Court, Middle District of Florida.
80  *committed to their beliefs:* US Justice Department's Amended Motion for an Order Revoking Defendant's Release in *US v. Russell*, filed June 12, 2017.
80  *radiation tattoo*: "How to spot neo-Nazis in the military," *Tampa Bay Times*, June 4, 2018.
80  *are you worried*: John M. Donnelly, "Pentagon report reveals inroads white supremacists have made in military," *Roll Call*, February 16, 2021.
81  *vocalized his hatred for homosexuality*: A. C. Thompson, "An Atomwaffen Member Sketched a Map to Take the Neo-Nazis Down. What Path Officials Took Is a Mystery," ProPublica, November 20, 2018.
81  *a recruiting tool*: Justice Department amended motion in Russell case, June 12, 2017.
82  *a chilling statement*: Brian Chasnoff, "Racist at vigil posts hate-filled messages," *San Antonio Express News*, June 8, 2016.
83  *the Holocaust never really happened*: "Breaking Hate: Episode 2," MSNBC, May 12, 2019.
83  *Are you serious*: Ibid.
83  *do you know what this stands for*: Author interview with Emily Oneschuk, sister of Andrew Oneschuk.
83  *a stranger, a sociopath:* Emily Oneschuk interview.
84  *Breivik V. 2*: Southern Poverty Law Center, *Iron March*.
84  *a Heil Hitler salute*: Emily Oneschuk interview.
84  *all the shit we can get dragged into*: "Breaking Hate," MSNBC.
84  *time for fishing*: Associated Press, August 22, 2017.
85  *paintballing and target-shooting*: Brandon Russell police interview.
85  *Ball-busting*: Tampa Police Department report in murder case against Devon Arthurs, April 2017, 121.
85  *Get out of here*: "Breaking Hate," MSNBC.
85  *Get the fuck on the ground*: Tampa Police Department report; also John Martin and Tony Marrero, "'Neo-Nazi' in Florida National Guard arrested after explosives found at Tampa Palms murder scene," *Tampa Bay Times*, May 23, 2017.
86  *He angrily swiped*: Tampa Police Department report, 126.
86  *Pointed his gun*: Ibid.
86  *Put the gun down*: Tampa Police Department report, 133.
87  *they're dead*: David Goodhue, "Admitted neo-Nazi stopped in Keys wanted for making explosives at home, cops say," *Miami Herald*, May 22, 2017.
87  *Dropped to his knees*: Tampa Police Department report.
87  *that's my roommate*: Tampa Police report, 135.
87  *motionless body*: Tampa Police report, 138.

## Notes

88    *magic marker on the cooler*: Tampa Police report, 121.
88    *corrosive elements*: Video of Tampa Police interrogation of Devon Arthurs obtained by author under Florida Public Records Act.
89    *Listening in from another room*: Tampa Police report, 118.
89    *I screwed up*: Max Kutner, "Radicalized," *Audible Original* (podcast, 2020).
90    *targets in mind*: Tampa FOIA report, May 20, 2017, 119.
90    *Power lines, nuclear reactors*: Tampa PD interview video produced by State Attorney under Public Records Act.
90    *kind of stupid*: Devon Arthurs, police interview.
92    *another Atomwaffen member*: Jason Dearen and Michael Kunzelman, "Deadly Shooting Ends Friendships Forged in Neo-Nazi Group," Associated Press, August 22, 2017.
92    *he wasn't sure*: Russell search warrant.
92    *an assault-style weapon*: Ibid.
92    *an ATF bomb expert*: ATF search warrant in Russell case.
93    *shaking and sweating*: Monroe County Police report.
93    *What's wrong?*: Monroe County video FOIA.
93    *My life's over*: Audio from Torres body cam, Monroe County.
93    *What are we going to find in that car?*: "Documenting Hate: New American Nazis," *PBS Frontline*.
93    *decided to go hunting*: Dearen and Kunzelman, "Deadly Shooting Ends Friendships Forged in Neo-Nazi Group."
93    *all the weapons*: "Documenting Hate."
94    *The harder the storm rages*: Iron March logs filed into evidence in US District Court in Tampa in *US v. Russell*, filed June 3, 2017 (exhibit 19).

### Chapter 6

95    *trashing of the "subhuman"*: Testimony of former Atomwaffen member Brenan Duffy at Woodward murder trial and preliminary hearing. Brenan was allowed to testify at the trial by using the alias of Brian Murphy. He had previously been identified publicly by his real name in anti-Nazi social media posts.
96    *I admired these men*: Defense attorney Morrison at Woodward murder trial, citing Woodward interviews with Dr. Rogers.
97    *a darker, more satanic type of vision*: Former Atomwaffen member Tyler Wising, testifying at Woodward murder trial.
97    *I'm a misanthrope*: Jonathan Krohn, "How a Gay Teen, an Internet Nazi, and a Late-Night Rendezvous Turned to Tragedy," *Mother Jones*, March/April 2019.
97    *occult held a strange fascination*: Author interview with Andrew Stewart, criminal lawyer for John Denton.
97    *"RAPE," "DEATH," and "TORMENTOR"*: Justice Department affidavit in criminal case against John Denton, US District Court, Eastern District of February, February 25, 2020.
97    *instructions on bomb-making*: Justice Department affidavit in Denton case.
98    *Bring your uniform*: Thompson, Winston, and Hanrahan, "Inside Atomwaffen."

## Notes

98 *cut me off*: Online messages between Woodward and Evans from Woodward murder trial exhibits.
98 *sleep in the back of Evans's truck*: Testimony from Woodward and Duffy at Woodward murder trial.
99 *senior member named Brenan Duffy*: As noted above, Duffy was allowed to testify at trial under the alias "Brian Murphy."
99 *just three Nazis getting together to go hiking*: Duffy testimony at pretrial hearing in Woodward murder trial, January 29, 2024.
99 *an IQ of 121*: Messages between Woodward and Evans.
100 *wasn't sure they were "serious" enough*: Duffy testimony at pretrial hearing in Woodward trial.
100 *greatest man that ever lived*: Author interview with James Mason.
101 *I'm a Nazi*: Mason interview.
101 *FBI has had James Mason in its sights*: Author interviews.
101 *The closer they watch me*: Mason interview.
101 *just as good*: Ibid.
102 *worried at all the neo-Nazi literature*: Author interview with Mason; also James Mason appearance at University of Phoenix in Denver, 2003, https://shorturl.at/VkH5O.
102 *swiping a .44 magnum*: Mason interview; and James Mason, *Siege* (Atlanta, GA: Black Sun Production, 2003), 15. This edition includes an introduction by Mason follower Ryan Schuster.
103 *take my chances*: Mason interview.
103 *slept on the floor*: Mason, *Siege*, 17.
103 *A healthy state*: Mason, *Siege*, 55.
103 *Amerikan apple pie*: Mason, *Siege*, 14.
103 *slothful group*: Mason interview; and Mason, *Siege*, 18.
104 *child porn charges*: News brief, *Cincinnati Enquirer*, August 19, 1991.
104 *ordained in the Bible*: Mason interview.
104 *being a "race traitor"*: Alan Prendergast, "Double Exposure, Underage Girls, a Nazi with a Camera, and Partying Cops—What's Wrong with This Picture?," *Westword*, September 20, 1995.
104 *a prophet*: Mason interview.
105 *clarion call*: Mason, *Siege*, 28.
106 *Glad I got to see that*: James Mason, video on Bitchute that has been removed by the site.
106 *"Graveyard" channel*: Justice Department affidavit in John Denton case.
106 *illicit relations*: Anna Schecter and Rich Schapiro, "Influential neo-Nazi eats at soup kitchens, lives in government housing," NBC News, November 26, 2019.
107 *My life*: Mason interview.
107 *soup kitchen*: NBC News, November 26, 2019.
107 *an elderly African American woman*: Author interview with Lady Clark. She said she didn't believe the things she heard about him and liked him because he was always friendly to her and he fed the squirrels.

# Notes

108 *He was nervous*: Messages between Woodward and Evans; exhibits in Woodward murder trial.
108 *the important passages*: Exhibits in Woodward murder trial.
109 *He told them a story*: Mason interview.
110 *should've been more*: Mason interview.
110 *a fine, upstanding young man*: Mason interview.
110 *came to terrorize*: Author interviews; court records in *Commonwealth of Virginia v. Nicholas Giampa* (2023), Circuit Court of Fairfax County, reviewed by author.
111 *trying to get transgender people*: Jessica Schulberg and Luke O'Brien, "We Found the Neo-Nazi Twitter Account Tied to a Virginia Double Homicide," *Huffington Post*, January 4, 2018.
111 *Show them how to use a gun*: Ibid.
111 *discovered a giant swastika*: Justin Jouvenal, "A swastika was mowed into a field. Was it part of a chain of events that led to murder?" *Washington Post*, December 26, 2017.
111 *He called himself a "freak"*: Justin Jouvenal, "Her son, facing murder charges, is being called an alt-right killer," *Washington Post*, March 27, 2018.
111 *connected to child pornography*: Court records in *Virginia v. Giampa*.
112 *sounds like heaven*: Jessica Shulberg and Luke O'Brien, "We Found the Neo-Nazi Twitter Account Tied to a Virginia Double Homicide," *Huffington Post*, January 4, 2018.
112 *signs of hope*: Justin Jouvenal, "Her son, facing murder charges, is being called an 'alt-right killer.' This mother blames herself," *Washington Post*, March 17, 2018.
112 *found somebody that loves me*: "Was an Ivy League student slain in the name of hate?" *48 Hours* (CBS), May 30, 2021.
112 *Did you know that the Jews*: *Washington Post*, March 17, 2018.
112 *We can't allow*: Justin Jouvenal, "A teen is charged with killing his girlfriend's parents. They had worried he was a neo-Nazi," Washington Post, December 23, 2017.
113 *He is a monster*: Ibid.
113 *put him in an in-patient psychiatric hospital*: Order of Fairfax County Chief Judge Penney Azcarate, April 13, 2023, *Reed Calvert Kuhn v. Michael Troy Giampa et al.*, Nineteenth Judicial District of Virginia.
113 *She dozed off*: Judge Azcarate court order; and *Washington Post*, March 17, 2018.
113 *"He is here"*: *Washington Post*, March 17, 2018.
113 *heard something down the hall*: Court records, Fairfax County Police probable-cause report in *Virginia v. Giampa*; reviewed by author.
113 *They banged on the door*: Ibid.
114 *a skilled shooter*: Order of Judge Azcarate.
114 *First, he shot*: Fairfax police probable-cause report and autopsy notes in *Virginia v. Giampa*.
114 *He raced out*: Interview notes from police interview with victims' son in court records in *Virginia v. Giampa*.
114 *She had given Giampa*: Fairfax County Police probable-cause report.
115 *put the gun to her head*: Ibid.

## Notes

115 *Giampa shooting himself*: While awaiting trial on murder charges more than six years after the killings, Giampa was found dead in his Fairfax County jail cell in August 2024 in an apparent suicide.

115 *deranged adolescent*: Schulberg and O'Brien, "We Found the Neo-Nazi Twitter Account."

### Chapter 7

117 *Combat-ready, militant brand*: Appellate decision in *United States v. Robert Rundo, Robert Boman, et al.* (2024), Ninth Circuit Court of Appeals, July 18, 2024.

117 *Training is a go*: FBI affidavit in *US v. Rundo, Boman, et al.*, filed by FBI special agent Scott Bierwirth, October 20, 2018.

117 *many of them shirtless*: RAM videos accessed by author.

117 *#RightWingDeathSquad*: Statement of Facts filing in plea agreement in *United States v. Michael Paul Miselis* (2020), US District Court for the Western District of Virginia (Charlottesville), May 3, 2019.

118 *FATHERLAND*: RAM video.

118 *a hooligan type*: Rob Rundo video interview with Nordic Resistance Movement/Bellum, a Sweden-based neo-Nazi group, May 2021.

118 *juvenile custody*: Ibid.

118 *Original Flushing Crew*: "Documenting Hate: New American Nazis," *Frontline* (PBS), 2018.

118 *a lot of like-minded people*: Rundo video interview.

118 *right on the beach*: Rise Above Media video formerly on YouTube; accessed by author.

119 *consuming videos*: Ibid.

119 *grossly exaggerated*: Most violent crimes are committed by people of the same race as the victim, according to a 2017 study by the Justice Department's Bureau of Justice Statistics, and white people were four times more likely to be victimized by other whites than by Black people. See: David Neiwert, "White supremacists' favorite myths about black crime rates take another hit from BJS study," October 23, 2017.

119 *mess with your psyche*: Ibid.

119 *a big supporter*: Ibid.

119 *we haven't been replaced yet*: Emails between Rundo and author.

119 *mass homeless*: Ibid.

119 *suit-and-tie politics*: Rundo video interview with Nordic Resistance.

120 *I care about my race*: Ibid.

120 *even an aerospace engineer*: A. C. Thompson and Ali Winston, "He Is a Member of a Violent White Supremacist Group. So Why Is He Working for a Defense Contractor with a Security Clearance?" *ProPublica*, July 5, 2018. The engineer, Michael Miselis, was fired by Northop Grumman the day after ProPublica's report, and he later was charged and pled guilty to federal rioting charges.

120 *notorious Hammerskin Nation*: Ibid.

120 *near the Jewish victim's blood*: Salvador Hernandez and Erika I. Ritchie, "FBI Probing Hate-Crime Assault in Coto," *Orange County Register*, April 8, 2011.

120 *personally handled*: FBI complaint in *US v. Rundo*.

# Notes

121 *warms the heart*: RAM video.
121 *giving a white supremacist salute*: FBI affidavit in *US v. Rundo*.
122 *confront the counter-protesters*: Ibid.
123 *a flurry of kicks and punches*: Ibid.
123 *we're not racist*: Angel Jennings and Anh Do, "Reporter and photographers say they were assaulted by Trump supporters at Huntington Beach rally," *Los Angeles Times*, March 26, 2017.
123 *Celebrity status*: Michelis statement of facts.
123 *only alt right crew*: FBI affidavit in *US v. Rundo*.
124 *punching and kicking them*: Ibid.
124 *kicked one counter-protester*: Plea agreement in *United States v. Benjamin Drake Daley* (2019), Western District of Virginia (Charlottesville), May 3, 2019.
124 *not even room*: Miselis statement of facts.
124 *had led anti-fascist protests*: Felarca herself faced criminal charges over an earlier protest against neo-Nazis in Sacramento, but the case was dismissed after she agreed to plead "no contest" to the charges and was sentenced to community service.
124 *she needs the rope*: FBI affidavit in *US v. Rundo*.
125 *breaking it on a guy's head*: Ibid.
125 *"palm strikes" and elbows*: Daley plea agreement.
126 *Fuck those Jews*: FBI affidavit in *US v. Rundo*.
126 *had to work*: Rundo video interview with Nordic Resistance.
126 *so he could buy torches*: Miselis affidavit.
127 *disastrous results*: "Independent Review of the 2017 Protest Events in Charlottesville Virginia," conducted by law firm of Hunton & Williams; published December 2017.
127 *essentially serial rioters*: Thomas Cullen, US attorney for the Western District of Virginia, in announcing the charges agains the RAM members, October 2, 2018.
127 *small little fistfights*: Rundo video interview with Nordic Resistance.
128 *liked beer, action movies*: Rich Lord, "How Robert Bowers Went from Conservative to White Nationalist," *Pittsburgh Post-Gazette*, November 11, 2018.
128 *post three or four memes*: Southern Poverty Law Center, "Analyzing a terrorist's social media manifesto: The Pittsburgh synagogue shooter's posts on Gab," October 28, 2018.
129 *hello there HIAS*: Justice Department superseding indictment in *United States v. Robert Bowers* (January 29, 2019).
129 *prank gone bad*: Author interview with Brad Orsini. Three young men were ultimately charged and convicted in the cross-burning case in 2011.
130 *if a shooter attacked*: Orsini interview.
130 *arrested a Florida man*: Cesar Soyoc was sentenced to twenty years in prison in the pipe-bomb mailings.
130 *I won't shoot you*: Justice Department, June 24, 2021. Bush was sentenced to life in prison.
131 *Dylann Roof!*: Billy Kobin, "Prosecutors: Gregory Bush shouted 'Dylann Roof' after killing two Black shoppers at Kroger," *Louisville Courier Journal*, June 8, 2021.

# Notes

131 *a volley of pop-pop-pops*: This account of the rampage at the Tree of Life synagogue is drawn from author interviews, Justice Department filings, trial testimony in *US v. Bowers*, and Shelly Bradbury, "Timeline of terror: A moment-by-moment account of Squirrel Hill mass shooting," *Pittsburgh Post-Gazette*, October 28, 2012.
131 *unthinkable*: Jonathan Greenblatt, Anti-Defamation League, statement of October 27, 2018.
132 *happy family*: Earnest manifesto. See: https://bcsh.bard.edu/files/2019/06/Earnest-Manifesto-042719.pdf.
132 *vengeful manifesto*: Ibid.
132 *receptive audience*: Drew Harwell, "Three mass shootings this year began with a hateful screed on 8chan. Its founder calls it a terrorist refuge in plain sight," *Washington Post*, August 4, 2019.
132 *go-to forum*: After the run of hate crimes, 8chan changed its name to 8kun. It remained popular with far-right extremists, including January 6 rioters who used it to organize the raid on the Capitol.
134 *picked up at a local gun shop*: Lindsay Winkley, "Accused Poway synagogue shooter didn't have valid hunting license when gun was purchased," *San Diego Union-Tribune*, August 14, 2019.
134 *Earnest raced*: Ken Stone, "Court Shown Video of Chabad of Poway's Lori Kaye Being Slain by Gunman," *Times of San Diego*, September 19, 2019.

## Chapter 8

136 *a Goodwill store*: Author interview with Liam Williams.
137 *went to her GPS tracking app*: Testimony of Jeanne Pepper at Woodward murder trial.
137 *the name was inspired*: Author interview with Jeanne Pepper and Gideon Bernstein; and family blog posting, https://blazebernstein.org.
137 *getting along well*: Jeanne Pepper and Gideon Bernstein interview.
138 *Text is boring*: Prosecution testimony in Woodward murder trial, and court exhibit.
139 *this is awkward*: Prosecution testimony in Woodward trial.
140 *out of the blue*: Author interview with Liam Williams; testimony at Woodward murder trial.
140 *baffled by the cryptic message*: Liam Williams interview.

## Chapter 9

143 *spigot is on full blast*: Author interview with Christian Picciolini.
144 *an affinity for these alt-right groups*: Zolan Kanno-Youngs, "White House Unveils Strategy to Combat Domestic Extremism," *New York Times*, June 15, 2021.
144 *slowed to a trickle*: "Few Federal Hate Crime Referrals Result in Prosecution," Report of the Transactional Records Access Clearinghouse (TRAC) at Syracuse University, August 19, 2021.
145 *a buried report*: Eric Lichtblau, "In Buried Report, U.S. Government Admits Major Failures in Confronting Domestic Terrorism," *The Intercept*, June 29, 2020.
145 *abruptly quit*: Author interview with Jeff Schoep.

## Notes

145 *died in a shootout*: Neo-Nazi Timothy Wilson, a member of the National Socialist Movement, died March 24, 2020, in Belmont, Missouri.
146 *signed over legal control*: Katie Mettler, "The Race Whisperer," *Washington Post*, October 30, 2019.
146 *first turned him*: Author interview with Burt Colucci.
146 *sounds ridiculous*: Schoep interview.
147 *alienated a lot of good members*: Colucci interview.
147 *embrace the swastika*: Ibid.
147 *America is for whites*: See: https://youtu.be/KI4AMgnGZX8.
148 *both sides were wrong*: Tom Perkins, "Detroit police chief faces backlash over neo-Nazi protest at Pride event," *The Guardian*, June 14, 2019.
149 *calling them "apes"*: Police records, audio, and video obtained by author from Chandler (Arizona) Police Department on the two Colluci episodes in the hotel parking lot on April 19, 2021.
149 *Grabbed a pistol*: Chandler Police Department arrest report.
149 *You fucking monkeys*: Ibid., 26.
150 *Nazi salute*: Ibid.
150 *Ground Zero*: Ibid.
150 *railing anew*: Author interview with Colucci.
151 *wasn't willing to give it to him*: Author interview with Brian Levin.
151 *landmark verdict*: Supreme Court decision in *Wisconsin v. Todd Mitchell* (1993).
151 *$1.1-million verdict*: Eric Lichtblau, "Neo-Nazi Must Pay $1.1 million to Fair Housing Activist," *Los Angeles Times*, July 21, 2000.
152 *poster boy for Nazism*: Author interview with Brian Levin.
153 *I don't care*: Ibid.

### Chapter 10

156 *a surreal episode*: Author interview with Gideon Bernstein.
156 *I'm really worried*: Text provided to author by Liam Willams.
157 *who's Sam Woodward*: Author interview with Liam Williams.
157 *He's been missing*: The audio was played in its entirety during the Woodward murder trial and included in exhibits.
158 *I think he did it*: Testimony of Gideon Bernstein.
159 *Six computer stations*: Gideon Bernstein, *Giving* (Orange County, CA: Modern Philanthropy Publishing, 2021), 187.
159 *any way you can come home*: Alene Tchekmedyian and Maria Alejandra Cardona, "Drones used in hunt for missing O.C. student," *Los Angeles Times*, January 8, 2018.
160 *turned into something worse*: Testimony of Dylan Jantzen at preliminary hearing in Woodward murder case.
160 *seemed nervous*: Testimony from Jantzen at Woodward preliminary hearing and murder trial and sheriff's report.
161 *"Who am I to judge?"*: Ibid.
161 *cuts and scrapes*: Ibid.
162 *sensed instantly*: Ibid.

# Notes

163   *eyes were still open*: Pretrial evidentiary hearing, Woodward murder trial, February 2024.

163   *"Stay away from the park"*: Gideon Bernstein interview.

163   *a big piece of who we were*: Bernstein, *Giving*, 46.

163   *Our family is devastated*: Kelly Puente, Scott Schwebke, and Alma Fausto, "Missing teen found dead," *Orange County Register*, January 11, 2018.

163   *We thank God*: Ari Feldman, "Loved Ones Mourn Blaze Bernstein's 'Sweet Smile' as Death Is Ruled Homicide," *The Forward*, January 11, 2018.

164   *the passing of life*: Thompson, Winston, and Hanrahan, "Inside Atomwaffen."

165   *more rare than one in one trillion*: Testimony of forensic examiner Corrie Maggay at Woodward preliminary hearing.

167   *Gay Jew Wrecking Crew*: Thompson, Winston, and Hanrahan, "Inside Atomwaffen."

## Chapter 11

168   *I'm sorry*: Howard Altman, "5 Years For Explosives," *Tampa Bay Times*, January 10, 2018.

169   *hinder our efforts*: The Brandon Russell video was originally posted to Bitchute, a favorite spot for neo-Nazi video postings, but it has since been removed.

169   *dropping another project*: Author interview with A. C. Thompson.

170   *not enough rope*: Threats and postings provided to author by Thompson.

170   *siphon thousands of dollars*: Thompson interview.

171   *come to sleep*: Ibid.

172   *killed a twenty-eight-year-old father*: Tyler Barriss was sentenced to twenty years in prison in the "swatting" death of Andrew Finch of Wichita, Kansas, on December 28, 2017.

172   *left shaken*: FBI affidavit in *United States v. John Cameron Denton* (2020), Eastern District of Virginia (February 25, 2020).

172   *having nightmares*: Thompson interview and victim-impact statement.

173   *bombings and mayhem*: FBI affidavit and court documents in *US v. Denton*.

173   *entertainment and bragging*: Ibid.

173   *Who did you swat*: Ibid.

173   *in New Hope, Pennsylvania*: It's unclear why the Atomwaffen members decided to target that town.

173   *This was hilarious*: FBI affidavit in *US v. Denton*.

173   *find themselves terrorized*: Justice Department criminal complaint in *United States v. Cameron Shea et al.* (2020), Western District of Washington (Seattle), filed February 25, 2020.

174   *VISITED BY YOUR LOCAL NAZIS*: Ibid.

175   *Kelley called Old Dominion*: FBI affidavit in *US v. Denton*.

175   *ITS GONNA GET REAL*: Ibid.

176   *DON'T BOMB THREAT*: Ibid.

177   *In one news story*: Thompson, Winston, and Hanrahan, "Inside Atomwaffen."

177   *I'm A. C. Thompson*: "Documenting Hate: New American Nazis, *Frontline* (PBS), November 20, 2018.

# Notes

177 *He was "furious" with Thompson*: FBI affidavit in *US v. Denton*.
178 *a voice changer*: Ibid.
178 *a top-tier crime*: Ibid.
178 *vouched for him*: Author interview with Andrew Stewart, defense attorney for John Denton.
179 *loosened the standards*: Eric Lichtblau, *Bush's Law: The Remaking of American Justice* (New York: Pantheon, 2008), 84.
179 *paid him more than $80,000*: Filing in defense motion in *United States v. Kaleb Cole* (2023), Western District of Washington. The filing did not name the undercover operative paid by the FBI, but journalist Ali Winston identified him as neo-Nazi publisher Joshua Caleb Sutter.
179 *irreversible trauma*: Raj Parekh, acting US attorney for the Eastern District of Virginia, May 4, 2021, following Denton's sentence of three and a half years in prison.
180 *It's simply just evil*: KING 5 Staff, "Former neo-Nazi to KING 5 reporter he targeted: 'I just want to apologize,'" King-TV (Seattle, WA), January 7, 2021.

## Chapter 12

181 *an avowed neo-Nazi*: A. C. Thompson, Ali Winston, and Jake Hanrahan, "California Murder Suspect Said to Have Trained with Extremist Hate Group," *ProPublica*, January 26, 2018.
182 *wasn't a damn bit sorry*: Author interview with James Mason.
182 *deep inside the neo-Nazi group*: Duffy testimony at Woodward murder trial.
183 *deployed to Kuwait*: Duffy testimony at Woodward pretrial evidentiary hearing, 2024.
183 *destroying my marriage*: Duffy Testimony at Woodward murder trial.
183 *paper tiger*: Heidi L. Beirich, cofounder of the Global Project Against Hate and Extremism, testifying before subcommittee of the US House Armed Services Committee, February 12, 2020.
184 *didn't help at all*: Ibid.
185 *a trove of evidence*: Testimony from Jantzen at Woodward preliminary hearing and murder trial.
185 *weren't certain they could prove*: District attorney Jennifer Walker, closing arguments at Woodward murder trial.
186 *jailhouse "snitches"*: The Orange County District Attorney's office reached a settlement with the Justice Department in January of 2025 over its use of jailhouse informants, agreeing to put in place added safeguards and training to prevent their misuse. The Justice Department concluded that the DA's prolonged use of jailhouse informants over nearly a decade violated defendants' right to counsel and due process under the Constitution.
186 *spews hate*: Orange County district attorney's press conference, August 2, 2018.
186 *Today, we suffer*: Ibid.
187 *Tanber kicked out*: Author interview with Paul Tanber, uncle of Craig Tanber.
187 *killing was payback*: Tanber's earlier prison stint came in the 2004 killing of Cory Lamon in Orange County.

## Notes

187  *white boys*: Pete Simi, Lowell Smith, and Ann Reeser, "From Punk Kids to Public Enemy Number One," *Deviant Behavior*, October 13, 2008.
187  *his family learned*: Paul Tanber interview.
188  *proudly showed off*: Ibid.
188  *"Proud as a peacock"*: Ibid.
188  *never held a steady job:* Ibid.
188  *they scheduled*: Ibid.
189  *began picking on him*: Author interview with Shazhad Mazroei, mother of Shayan Mazroei.
189  *design turbocharged engines*: Ibid.
190  *felt disrespected*: Court of Appeals of California decision in *People v. Craig Matthew Tanber* (2021); and news accounts of Tanber trial.
190  *telling him to "go home"*: "The Life and Death of Shayan Mazroei," *Now This*, March 23, 2018.
190  *He called Mazroei*: *People v. Tanber* appellate decision.
190  *disrespects me like that*: Ibid.
190  *Tanber and Thornburg*: Thornburg pleaded guilty in December of 2024 to a charge of being an accessory after the fact in the killing and was sentenced to 200 hours of community service and two years' probation.
192  *powerful message*: Shazhad Mazroei interview.
192  *never imagined*: Ibid.
192  *We lost everything*: Alma Fausto and Sean Emery, "Supremacist who killed man gets 56 years to life," *Orange County Register*, February 29, 2020.
192  *ethnic slurs*: *People v. Tanber* appellate decision.
193  *make no mistake*: Todd Spitzer, "The OCDA should pursue justice, not just high conviction rates," *Orange County Register*, September 15, 2018.
193  *He kept warning*: Author interview with Lowell Smith, former Orange County probation officer.
194  *felt the sting of persecution*: Author interview with Todd Spitzer.
194  *threatened with a knife*: Ibid.
194  *protect the independence*: Ibid.
194  *whenever Trump would go after*: Ibid.
194  *okay to hate*: Ibid.
194  *two hundred cases*: Orange County district attorney's office, May 2021.
195  *beating a young man to death*: Author interview with Julie Mayfield, stepmother of Tyson Chandler.
195  *Her name was Jasmine*: The victim was identified in court papers as Jasmine C.
195  *got his "kicks"*: Court opinion, *People v. Tyson Theodore Mayfield* (2020), Court of Appeal of the State of California, Fourth Appellate District, Division Three, filed June 23, 2020.
196  *No one got hurt*: Author interview with Tyson Mayfield from Orange County jail.
196  *Hate is here*: Todd Spitzer, "Hate has no place in Orange County," *Orange County Register*, September 29, 2019.
197  *walked into Judge Robbins's chambers*: Spitzer interview.

# Notes

197 *Are you aware*: Ibid. Robbins did not respond to a request for comment on the case.
197 *a dangerous person*: Sean Emery, "5-year Sentence for Fullerton hate crime draws criticism from OC district attorney," *Orange County Register*, May 20, 2019.
198 *someone so evil*: Orange County district attorney's office, May 20, 2019.
198 *ultimately received a whopping new sentence*: After seven years of litigation in the hate-crime case, Mayfield received the new twenty-seven-year sentence in Orange County Superior Court on August 29, 2025.
198 *just think it's wrong*: Author interview with background source.

## Chapter 13

200 *they have people here*: Author interview with Farrah Khan.
200 *record heights*: The Orange County Human Relations Commission report for 2023 showed a 195 percent increase over the last five years in hate crimes and hate incidents.
200 *a "kill list" he'd compiled*: Nicholas Rose pleaded guilty in 2019 to criminal charges and was sentenced to twenty-seven months in the Orange County jail plus a year in a mental health institution.
202 *found drawings*: Evidentiary hearing and testimony in Woodward murder trial.
202 *"extorting" him*: Ken Morrison, public defender for Sam Woodward, at hearing.
202 *Delay, delay, delay*: Jeanne Pepper interview.
203 *actively supported*: Motion from the Bernsteins in civil lawsuit, *Jeanne Pepper Bernstein and Gideon Bernstein v. Samuel Woodward, Blake Woodward, Michelle Woodward* (2019), Orange County Superior Court, filed December 12, 2019.
203 *a significant sum*: Author interviews.
203 *as little as they could*: Author interview with Gideon Bernstein.
204 *a Vietnamese café*: Bernstein, *Giving*, 48.
204 *the worst days*: Ibid., 187.
204 *crashed the server*: Bernstein, *Giving*, 188.
205 *"divisive" and even "sinful"*: Brandon Pho and Hosam Elattar, "OC Supervisors Ban Pride Flag at County Properties under New Policy," *Voice of OC*, June 6, 2023.
205 *rising at least 22 percent*: The FBI's 2024 hate-crime report, an incomplete snapshot, showed a total of 2,949 episodes in 2023 targeting victims based on either their sexual orientation or gender identity, up from 2,416 the year before. About one in five of all hate crimes targeted LGBTQ+ victims.
205 *LGBTQ+ students were at particular risk*: Laura Meckler, Hannah Natanson, and John D. Harden, "In states with laws targeting LGBTQ issues, school hate crimes quadrupled," *Washington Post*, March 12, 2024.
205 *first-ever guilty verdict at a trial for transgender-related violence*: Daqua Lameek Ritter was sentenced to life in prison for the August 2019 murder of Dime Doe, a Black transgender woman from Allendale, South Carolina.
206 *act on their worst instincts*: *Pepp Talks with Jeanne Pepper* podcast, YouTube, June 29, 2023; and author interview with Dave Min.
206 *STOP COMPROMISING*: Noah Goldberg, "Killer in Pride flag dispute appears to have posted anti-LGBTQ+ rants and conspiracies online," *Los Angeles Times*, August 21, 2023.

# Notes

207 *Why do you need*: Paul Feig, Hollywood director and friend of Carleton, on X, August 21, 2023.
207 *seemed to flinch*: Noah Goldberg, "Final moments before pride flag killing emerge, along with disturbing portrait of gunman," *Los Angeles Times*, August 22, 2023.
207 *senseless killing*: Beau Yarbrough, "Shooting death of Cedar Glen shop owner over pride flag still under investigation," *San Bernardino Sun*, August 23, 2023.
207 *hard to believe*: Ibid.
208 *assault rifle with a handwritten*: FBI affidavit in *United States v. Chance Brannon and Tibet Ergul* (2023), US District Court, Central District of California, filed June 12, 2023.
208 *the two men drove*: FBI affidavit in *US v. Brannon, Ergul*; and Brannon plea agreement, November 20, 2023.
209 *they planned another one*: Brannon plea agreement.
209 *rifle is in a box*: Tibet Ergul plea agreement in *US v. Brannon, Ergul*, February 15, 2024.
210 *attack a Gay Pride night*: Brannon plea agreement.
210 *it's going to be so bad*: Jesse Bedayn and Matthew Brown, "Judge warned in 2021 of gay bar attacker's shootout plans," Associated Press, December 16, 2022.

## Chapter 14

212 *what first lured*: Author interview with Haijun Si.
214 *figured her English*: Author interviews with Si and his daughter.
214 *children wondered*: Si interview.
215 *beat him up so badly*: "Teen Student in LA Assaulted as Coronavirus Fears Stoke 'Racial Backlash,'" KCAL, February 13, 2020.
215 *slashing one of the boys in the face*: "Local heroes meet victims recovering after Sam's Club stabbing," NewsWest9 (Midland, Texas), February 16, 2020.
215 *get out of America*: Justice Department statement, February 23, 2022.
215 *infecting people*: Josh Margolin, "FBI warns of potential surge in hate crimes against Asian Americans amid coronavirus," ABC News, March 27, 2020.
216 *hours-long string of assaults*: The attacker, Steven Zajonc, received a sentence of fifteen months to four years in prison on assault and hate-crime charges in New York Supreme Court in Manhattan in 2023.
216 *1,800 percent increase*: Orange County Human Relations Commission annual report for 2020.
216 *Olympic athlete*: Sakura Kokumai competed for the United States in karate in the 2020 Summer Olympics.
216 *mocked with chants*: Orange County Human Relations Commission annual report for 2020.
216 *Get out of our country!!*: Ibid.
216 *there's a feeling now*: Author interview with Patty Yoo.
216 *you see a new attack*: Bryan Pietsch, "Recent killings of Asian American women force Asians abroad to rethink their relationship with the U.S.," *Washington Post*, February 17, 2022.
217 *a 73 percent rise*: FBI updated hate-crime report issued October 25, 2021.

## Notes

217 *an alarming level*: Report of the UN's Special Rapporteur, issued August 12, 2020.
217 *tsunami of hate and xenophobia*: Secretary-General António Guterres, speech to UN General Assembly, May 8, 2020.
217 *not racist at all*: White House press briefing on Covid, March 18, 2020.
218 *go to synagogues*: Alert issued by FBI's New York field office, March 2020.
218 *carried out by whites*: Melissa Borja and Jacob Gibson, "Anti-Asian Racism in 2020," *Virulent Hate Reports*, University of Michigan.
218 *pitting them against Asians*: Author interviews.
218 *firebombed the refugees' fishing boats*: "A Look Back," Southern Poverty Law Center, July 15, 2011; and Kathleen Belew, *Bring the War Home: The White Power Movement and Paramilitary America* (Cambridge, MA: Harvard University Press, 2018), 43.
218 *a hell of a lot more violent*: "A Look Back," Southern Poverty Law Center.
218 *rape and kidnapping*: Belew, *Bring the War Home*, 43.
219 *weren't the kind of men*: Frances Kai-Hwa Wang, "Who is Vincent Chin? The History and Relevance of a 1982 Killing," NBC News, June 15, 2017.
220 *I killed a jap*: Geoff Boucher and Lee Romney, "Grisly Account of Ly Killing Believed Penned by Suspect," *Los Angeles Times*, March 7, 1996.
220 *if you're not white*: R. Scott Moxley, "When Gunner Jay Lindberg Killed Thien Minh Ly, Was It Actually a Hate Crime?" *OC Weekly*, July 17, 2018.
221 *like a high*: People v. Gunner Jay Lindberg (2008), Supreme Court of California decision, August 28, 2008.
221 *defendant was a racist*: Ibid.
221 *sexual addiction*: Richard Fausset, Nicholas Bogel-Burroughs, and Marie Fazio, "8 Dead in Atlanta Spa Shootings, with Fears of Anti-Asian Bias," *New York Times*, March 17, 2021.
222 *the first to test Georgia's new hate-crime law*: The Fulton County trial of Long on murder and hate-crime charges was still pending at the time of publication.
223 *the only response*: Author interview with Haijun Si.
223 *Kung Flu virus*: Video of Ladera Ranch rally held September 19, 2020; provided to the author.
223 *game of "ding-dong-ditch"*: Author interview with Layla Parks.
224 *so disgusted*: Parks interview.
224 *an Orange County ritual*: Gustavo Arrelano, "Racism in O.C. schools is nothing new—but it's surprisingly diverse," *Los Angeles Times*, January 27, 2022.
225 *give this family some peace*: Parks interview.
225 *have a good dinner*: Author interview with Dave Uemura.
226 *sexual obscenities*: Video footage from Haijun Si.
226 *take down the video*: Parks interview.
226 *hundreds of residents gathered*: Hannah Fry, "An Asian American family in O.C. was being harassed. Now their neighbors stand guard," *Los Angeles Times*, March 2, 2021.
226 *if these kids were Black*: Author interview with Dave Min.
226 *very grateful*: Si interview.
227 *electronic version of a cross-burning*: Petula Dvorak: "America's ugly front-lawn racism is on display," *Washington Post*, October 9, 2021.

# Notes

227   *did not rise to a level*: Statement from Virginia Beach Police Department on Twitter, October 7, 2021.

227   *It's quieter*: Lisa Vernon Sparks, "Activists march in solidarity against taunts of 'racist stuff' from next door," *Daily Press* (Newport News, VA), October 10, 2021.

## Chapter 15

228   *white picket fence*: Author interview with Shereen and Marc Rahming.

229   *they didn't want us there*: Jerry Bembry, "Chargers' Brandon Mebane: 'You could just tell they didn't want us there,'" *Andscape*, July 31, 2017.

231   *radical left, bad people*: Eric Lichtblau, "In Buried Report, U.S. Government Admits Major Failures in Confronting Domestic Terrorism," *The Intercept*, June 29, 2020.

231   *another Boogaloo Boy*: Lichtblau, *The Intercept*, June 29, 2020.

231   *Can't you just shoot them*: Michel Martin and Tinbete Ermyas, "Former Pentagon chief Esper says Trump asked about shooting protesters," *All Things Considered*, National Public Radio, May 9, 2022. Esper said he talked Trump out of the idea of shooting the protesters. Trump insisted he had never made such a remark.

231   *was no racist*: Author interview with Dyke Huish, attorney for Russell Taylor.

232   *why you would publicly call me*: Messages between Rahming and Taylor, September 7, 2020.

233   *followers of "Q"*: Paige St. John, Anita Chabria, Hannah Fry, and Michael Finnegan, "Suburban radicals: Inside the resurgence of right-wing extremism in Orange County," *Los Angeles Times*, March 21, 2021.

233   *prohibit such tax-exempt nonprofits*: In the indictment of Hostetter and Taylor over the January 6 rioting, federal prosecutors said that the American Phoenix project, registered as a 501(c)(3) nonprofit organization, was used to "advocate violence" and support Trump, but they did not bring any tax-related charges in the case. *United States v. Alan Hostetter, Russell Taylor, et al.* (2021), United States District Court for the District of Columbia, June 9, 2021.

233   *President Trump must be inaugurated*: Federal indictment in *US v. Hostetter, Taylor, et al.*, US District Court for the District of Columbia, filed June 9, 2021.

234   *My name is Russell Taylor*: Orange County Board of Supervisors archives, December 15, 2020.

234   *at least eleven aides*: Rosalind S. Helderman, Jacqueline Alemany, Josh Dawsey, and Tom Hamburger, "New evidence shows Trump was told many times there was no voter fraud—but he kept saying it anyway," *Washington Post*, March 3, 2022.

234   *claims of fraud were "bullshit"*: Bill Barr testimony before the US House Select Committee on the January 6th Attack on the United States Capitol, June 9, 2022.

234   *Who is going?*: Federal indictment, *US v. Hostetter, Taylor, et al.*

234   *California Patriots*: Ibid.

234   *able-bodied individuals*: Ibid.

234   *we were meant to come together*: Justice Department motion for revocation of release of Taylor, June 15, 2021.

235   *a hatchet, a fixed-blade knife*: *US v. Hostetter, Taylor, et al.*

# Notes

235 *Get violent*: Report of General Accountability Office, "Capitol Attack: Federal Agencies' Use of Open Source Data and Related Threat Products Prior to January 6, 2021," May 2, 2022, 35.

235 *the officers' riot gear*: "Examining the US Capitol Attack," report of the US Senate Committee on Homeland Security and Governmental Affairs, 2021, 2.

236 *a troubling text*: Author interview with Harry Dunn and testimony at House Select Committee, July 27, 2001.

236 *medieval battlefield*: US Capitol Police Sgt. Aquilino Gonell at July 27, 2021, hearing of House Select Committee.

236 *knocked down one rioter*: Dunn interview with author.

237 *throng of racist rioters*: Ibid.

237 *Is this America?*: Dunn testimony, July 27, 2021, hearing; and Dunn interview.

237 *93 percent*: Robert Pape, "American Face of Insurrection: Analysis of Individuals Charged for Storming the US Capitol on January 6, 2001," Chicago Project on Security and Threats, January 5, 2022.

237 *to understand white rage*: Alex Horton, "Top U.S. military leader: 'I want to understand white rage. And I'm white,'" *Washington Post*, June 23, 2021.

237 *huge Confederate flag*: Kevin Seefried, the man with the Confederate flag, was sentenced to three years in prison. His son was also convicted in the rioting.

238 *open Nazi sympathizer*: Timothy Hale-Cusinelli was sentenced to four years in prison.

238 *"Camp Auschwitz" sweatshirt*: Robert Packer pleaded guilty and received a sentence of seventy-five days in jail.

238 *the Nazi salute*: "Examining the US Capitol Attack," Senate homeland security report.

238 *notorious white-nationalist symbols*: "Identifying far-right symbols that appeared at the U.S. Capitol riot," *Washington Post*, January 15, 2021; and "Day of Rage: How Trump Supporters Took the U.S. Capitol," *New York Times* video.

238 *So proud*: Aaron C. Davis, "Red Flags," *Washington Post*, January 31, 2021.

239 *No Trump—no peace:* Indictment of Enrique Tarrio in *United States v. Ethan Nordean et al.* (2022), United States District Court for the District of Columbia, February 14, 2022.

239 *Ministry of Self-Defense*: Ibid.

239 *force multiplier*: Messages from Kelly Meggs cited in Justice Department motion in *United States v. Kelly Meggs* (2021), United States District Court for the District of Columbia, March 23, 2021.

239 *turn out in record numbers*: Indictment in *United States v. Dominic Pezzola and William Pepe* (2021), United States District Court for the District of Columbia, January 29, 2021.

239 *Let's take the fucking Capitol*: Justice Department complaint in *United States v. Daniel L. Scott* (2021), United States District Court for the District of Columbia, April 29, 2021. Lyons was sentenced to five years in prison.

239 *Dude, we're right in front of the Capitol*: US v. Nordean et al.

240 *banned him*: Peter Hermann and Keith Alexander, "Proud Boys leader barred from District by judge following his arrest," *Washington Post*, January 5, 2021.

## Notes

240 *Don't fucking leave*: Tarrio indictment in *US v. Nordean et al.* Tarrio was sentenced to twenty-two years in prison in 2023 for seditious conspiracy and other charges in the January 6 rioting.

240 *in serious danger*: Rich Schapiro, Anna Schecter, and Chelsea Damberg, "Officer who shot Ashli Babbitt during Capitol riot breaks silence: 'I saved countless lives,'" NBC News, August 26, 2021.

240 *hatred in the eyes*: "'Hatred in the eyes': How racist rage animated Jan. 6 riots," Associated Press, January 6, 2022.

241 *no way I'm taking off my pin*: Ibid.

241 *galvanizing effect*: Pape, "American Face of Insurrection."

242 *voted for Biden over Trump*: Biden won 53.5 percent of the county to 44 percent for Trump. For California state results, see: https://tinyurl.com/2umtz4xn.

242 *at least sixteen people*: Author review of criminal case files by hometowns.

242 *political science at UCLA*: Grace Johnston-Glick, James Nee, Lacy Green, Gavin Quan, Brandon Broukhim, and Talla Khelghati, "From Student Politics to Capitol Insurrection: The Intensification of Extremism at UCLA and Beyond," UCLA Luskin Center for History and Policy, March 2021.

242 *extremist ideology*: *United States v. Christian Secor* (2021), United States District Court for the District of Columbia, February 13, 2021.

243 *half Mexican*: Author interviews.

243 *No immigration*: Interview that Secor did after the insurrection for *New American Patriots*, a conservative podcast on YouTube on May 10, 2021. The video was later taken down.

243 *You know what'd be funny*: Ibid.

244 *killed eleven people*: Alek Minassian was sentenced to life in prison in Canada. Ten people died at the time of the attack, and an eleventh victim passed away from his injuries later.

244 *another "incel" admirer*: Tres Genco, twenty-four, of Hillsboro, Ohio, was sentenced to four years in prison on hate-crime charges.

244 *radical, reckless*: Rebecca Bihn-Wallace, "UCLA student and founder of America First Bruins arrested by FBI for participation in insurrection at Capitol," *California Aggie* (University of California, Davis), February 19, 2021.

244 *America First Bruins*: Secor criminal complaint.

244 *Fascism was "epic"*: Ibid.

244 *America is a white country*: Twitter archives of Secor's deleted postings, https://tinyurl.com/vkvwez42.

244 *Orange County has fallen*: Ibid.

244 *I want holy war*: Ibid.

244 *online bravado of a college kid*: Author interviews.

245 *called out Secor by name*: Grayson Peter, "Disloyal: Fascists Come to UCLA," *Ha'am*, April 1, 2020.

245 *showing up with other "Groypers"*: "Inside the resurgence of right-wing extremism in Orange County," *Los Angeles Times*, May 21, 2021.

245 *thirteen men*: Nine of the Michigan men were ultimately convicted in state or federal court.

## Notes

245 *their fierce resistance*: John Agar, "'Covid started everything': Jury set in trial of 4 men accused of plotting Gov. Whitmer's kidnapping over coronavirus orders," *Michigan Live*, March 8, 2022.

245 *shouting "America First!"*: "Inside the resurgence of right-wing extremism in Orange County."

246 *just "to make us look bad"*: Ibid.

246 *a communist coup*: Cited in *US v. Hostetter, Taylor, et al.*

246 *getting ready for tomorrow*: Ibid.

246 *couldn't risk*: Ibid.

247 *be glad it's 2020*: Hearing of the US House Select Committee on the January 6th Attack on the United States Capitol, June 21, 2022.

247 *should be locked up*: Jason Szep and Linda So, "Trump Campaign Demonized Two Georgia Election Workers—And Death Threats Followed," Reuters, December 1, 2021.

247 *called 911 for help*: Moss testimony at Select Committee hearing.

248 *nowhere I feel safe*: Freeman video deposition aired at Select Committee hearing.

249 *had to apologize*: Editor's Note appended to: John Eastman, "Some Questions for Kamala Harris about Eligibility—Opinion," *Newsweek*, August 14, 2020.

249 *serpent in the ear of the president*: Email exchanges between Eastman and Jacob introduced at hearings of the Select Committee, March 12, 2022, and June 16, 2022; and included in "Final Report: Select Committee to Investigate the January 6th Attack on the United States Capitol," December 22, 2022.

249 *BOLD, Certainly*: Decision of Judge David O. Carter, US District Court, Central District of California, Southern Division, in the case of John C. Eastman, Plaintiff, v. Bennie G. Thompson, Select Committee to Investigate the January 6th Attack on the United States Capitol, and Chapman University (March 28, 2022).

249 *a coup in search of a legal theory*: Ibid.

250 *made no sense*: Jacob testimony before the House Select Committee.

250 *knew it was illegal*: Testimony of Jacob before the Senate Select Committee to Investigate the January 6 Attack on the United States Capitol; cited in committee hearing on June 16, 2022.

250 *asking you to reject*: Cited in Judge Carter's decision.

250 *we would lose*: Jacob testimony before the House Select Committee.

251 *you weren't jumping up*: Ibid.

251 *You're asking*: House Select Committee hearing, June 21, 2022.

252 *go down in history*: Peter Baker, Maggie Haberman, and Annie Karni, "Pence Reached His Limit with Trump. It Wasn't Pretty," *New York Times*, January 12, 2021.

253 *had a hatchet*: Court testimony in *US v. Hostetter, Taylor, et al.*

253 *who these guys end up working for*: Indictment in *US v. Hostetter, Taylor, et al.*

253 *flipping off the police officers*: Getty Images; and "Suburban radicals."

253 *blocking back*: Hostetter sentencing, December 7, 2023. He received eleven years in federal prison.

253 *saying that Pence "deserves" to be hanged*: Rep. Liz Cheney at Select Committee hearing on June 9, 2022.

# Notes

253 *nothing but a traitor*: Video played at Select Committee hearing, June 16, 2022.
254 *thanks to your bullshit*: Judge Carter decision; and Jacob testimony at disbarment hearing for Eastman before the California Bar, June 16, 2023.
254 *WE STORMED THE CAPITOL*: Indictment in *US v. Hostetter, Taylor, et al.*
254 *shoved their way past*: Justice Department motion to detain in *US v. Secor*; and Luke Mogelson, "A Reporter's Video from Inside the Capitol Siege," *The New Yorker*, January 16, 2021.
255 *Where the fuck are they?*: "A Reporter's Video from Inside the Capitol Siege."
255 *It was Trump supporters*: Justice Department's "Statement of Offense" in *US v. Secor*; May 19, 2022.
257 *completely crazy*: Herschman testimony before Select Committee, June 16, 2022.
257 *alt-right firebrand*: Bannon was facing possible fraud charges for allegedly diverting money from donors to a private group to build a wall along the Mexican border. After the federal pardon, prosecutors in Manhattan brought state charges against Bannon over the same scheme.
258 *he retired under pressure*: Michael T. Nietzel, "John Eastman Retires from Chapman University," *Forbes Magazine*, January 13, 2021.
258 *jeopardized our democracy*: Statement of Chapman University President Daniele Struppa, January 8, 2021. Eastman retired under pressure the next week amid calls for his ouster.
258 *What happened*: "What happened to John Eastman?" *Orange County Register*, June 16, 2022.

## Chapter 16

260 *the future of the White race*: Justice Department complaint in *United States v. Payton Gendron* (2022), US District Court for the Western District of New York, June 15, 2022.
260 *sought refuge in a freezer*: Ibid.
260 *"Sorry," Gendron told him*: Ibid.
261 *Pure evil*: Charlie Specht, "'Pure evil': Racial motives cited in mass shooting that killed 10 at Buffalo supermarket," *Buffalo News*, May 15, 2022.
261 *filled with rage*: John Persons, president of Tops Friendly Markets, quoted in Bill Hutchinson, Alysha Webb, and Jade Lawson, "Buffalo grocery store president speaks out after massacre as tensions rise with some workers," *ABC News*, November 1, 2022.
261 *really started to turn racist*: Office of the New York State attorney general Letitia James, "Investigative Report on the role of online platforms in the tragic mass shooting in Buffalo on May 14, 2022," released October 18, 2022.
261 *a video she posted*: Tracey Maciulewicz, *TikTok*, July 27, 2022.

## Chapter 17

263 *saw you with injuries*: Cross-examination of Sam Woodward by Assistant District Attorney Jennifer Walker, June 20, 2024. All material in this section is drawn from the murder trial or court exhibits reviewed by the author, except as noted.
264 *threw a Dixie cup*: Author interviews.

# Notes

265 *I got upset*: Pretrial hearing in Woodward murder case, January 29, 2024.
265 *whether he was faking*: Direct examination of Sam Woodward by Ken Morrison at murder trial.
266 *horribly disgusting*: Pretrial hearing, January 29, 2024.
266 *Oh my Lord*: Pretrial hearing, January 12, 2024.
267 *under an alias*: Duffy was allowed to testify under the alias "Brian Murphy."
270 *how he had come out*: Former Atomwaffen member Tyler Wising.
272 *listen to lie after lie*: Jeanne Pepper on *Pepp Talks with Jeanne Pepper* podcast, YouTube, November 20, 2024.
274 *Thank God*: Louis Keene, "Jury convicts Blaze Bernstein's killer of premeditated murder and a hate crime," *The Forward*, July 3, 2024.
274 *Blaze's rock-garden memorial*: Jeanne Pepper, *Pepp Talks* podcast, November 20, 2024.
275 *exhausted from a long, dark vacuum*: Gideon Bernstein on Facebook "Blaze It Forward" page, July 4, 2024.
275 *for every victim of hate*: Todd Spitzer, district attorney, video on X, July 3, 2024.

## Epilogue

277 *eating the dogs*: Eric Lichtblau, "Opinion: Trump amplifies racist lies, giving neo-Nazis 'real power,'" *USA Today*, September 23, 2024.
277 *eleven reports of hate crimes:* Data from Brian Levin, chairman of the California Commission on the State of Hate.
277 *what real power looks like*: *USA Today*, September 23, 2024.
277 *he posted racist signs*: Brianne Pfannenstiel and Stephen Gruber-Miller, "Police arrest man for racist anti-immigrant signs invoking Donald Trump," *Des Moines Register*, August 14, 2024. The defendant, Daniel Embree, pleaded guilty and was sentenced to probation.
277 *waving a two-foot-long machete*: Neptune police arrested Caleb J. Williams on a charge of aggravated assault against an elderly person, displaying a deadly weapon, and voter intimidation, but prosecutors in the state attorney's office for the 4th District in Florida later dropped the charges, saying that although the young man "was ill advised and perhaps zealous," they did not believe that his actions "rise to the level of voter intimidation." Voting rights groups objected to what they believed was undue leniency in the decision.
278 *racist text messages*: The White House denied any involvement in the text messages. No one had been charged in connection with the texts at the time of publication.
278 *Total. Aryan. Victory.*: "Following Election, American Extremists Celebrate and Call For Violence Against the Communities Trump Has Targeted," Global Project Against Hate and Extremism, November 6, 2024.
278 *Hey, bitch, we control your bodies*: Nicholas J. Fuentes on X, @NickJFuentes, November 5, 2024.
278 *for inciting violence*: Twitter statement on January 8, 2021 announcing Trump's "permanent suspension." Musk lifted the suspension the next year after buying Twitter.

## Notes

278 *Texas newspaper outed him*: Steven Monacelli, "ICE Prosecutor In Dallas Runs White Supremacist X Account," *Texas Observer*, February 19, 2025. The lawyer was a former Marine named James Rodden. His racist writings were under investigation at ICE as of this writing.

278 *going on an antisemitic rant*: Kate Conger, "Elon Musk's Grok Chatbot Shares Antisemitic Posts on X," *New York Times*, July 8, 2025. Musk downplayed the episode and blamed the Nazi propaganda on a chatbot that was "too eager to please and be manipulated." His artificial-intelligence company promised changes in its programming.

279 *at loggerheads with Facebook*: Meta agreed in January 2025, nine days after Trump's inauguration, to pay him $25 million to settle a lawsuit he brought over his suspension from Facebook after the January 6 rioting.

279 *tidal wave of hate:* Report of the Center for Countering Digital Hate, "More Transparency and Less Spin: Analyzing Meta's Sweeping Policy Changes and Their Impact on Users," February 24, 2025.

279 *hate speech can lead*: Graham Fraser, "'Huge problems' with Instagram and Facebook changes, says oversight board," BBC, January 8, 2025.

280 *poisoning the blood*: Trump rally in Waterloo, Iowa, on December 19, 2023.

280 *deep ties to neo-Nazis*: Maik Baumgärtner and Ann-Katrin Müller, "The True Proximity of Germany's AfD to Neo-Nazis," *Der Spiegel*, July 27, 2023.

280 *"What up, my Nazi"*: Fox News, *The Five*, July 15, 2025.

281 *possible "insider threat"*: The National Guard barred Hegseth from duty in protecting the 2021 inauguration of President Biden as a result of the concerns about extremist ties over his tattoos, one of the Latin phrase "Deus Vult"("God Wills It") and another of the Jerusalem Cross. Hegseth said they were symbols of his Christian faith with no extremist meaning.

281 *removal of tens of thousands of photos*: Tara Copp, Lolita C. Baldor, and Kevin Vineys, "War heroes and military firsts are among 26,000 images flagged for removal in Pentagon's DEI purge," Associated Press, March 7, 2025.

281 *alligators are guaranteed at least 65 million meals*: Isabel Keane, "Alligator lives matter": Trump pal Laura Loomer slammed for saying Florida "Alcatraz" beasts will get "65 million meals," *The Independent*, July 3, 2025.

282 *nice countries*: Maggie Haberman and Michael Gold, "Trump, at Fund-Raiser, Says He Wants Immigrants From 'Nice' Countries," *New York Times*, April 7, 2024.

283 *at odds with the findings*: Megan Molteni, "Trump executive order declaring only 'two sexes' gets the biology wrong, scientists say," *STAT*, January 23, 2025.

283 *soaked in animus*: Memorandum Opinion from Judge Ana C. Reyes, United States District Court for the District of Columbia, March 18, 2025. The ban on medical care for transgender youth was also blocked in federal court. Challenges by the Trump administration to those rulings were still pending as of this writing.

283 *circled the bar again and again*: Author interview with Anouk Rawkson, manager at Pony bar in Seattle; and Seattle Police Department blotter, February 21, 2025.

283 *all this hate*: Rawkson interview.

284 *societal ill that is currently raging*: Sentencing of Samuel Woodward, November 15, 2024, Orange County Superior Court.

# Notes

285 *cascading failure*: Criminal complaint in US v. Sarah Beth Clendaniel and Brandon Clinton Russell, United States District Court for the District of Maryland, February 2, 2023. Clendaniel pleaded guilty and was sentenced to eighteen years in prison.

285 *sought to further his white supremacist ideology*: United States attorney Martin Estrada at federal sentencing of Rundo, United States District Court, Central District of California, December 13, 2024.

286 *"hostages"*: Trump's signing of the pardons at the Oval Office, January 20, 2025. The pardons covered more than 1,500 people out of about 1,600 who had been charged in the January 6 rioting; about 1,270 of them had already been convicted.

286 *They thought we would break*: "Ernique Tarrio and the Proud Boys" video, Fox5 News (Washington, DC), February 21, 2025. His latest case was still pending in court as of this writing.

286 *a record 165 white supremacist groups*: "The Year in Hate and Extremism 2023: Decoding the Plan to Undo Democracy," Southern Poverty Law Center, report released June 2024.

286 *not likely to go away*: Speech by FBI director Christopher Wray at the Birmingham Civil Rights Conference in Birmingham, Alabama, April 15, 2024.

287 *go back to "their side"*: Plea documents from US Justice Department in *United States v. Brett McCalpin et al.* (filed July 31, 2023).

288 *ramming his car*: The incident took place on December 7, 2024. The victim was Roy Gross.

288 *gonna bomb a Jewish house*: The student, Patrick Dai, was ultimately sentenced to twenty-one months in federal prison on charges of posting threats of death or injury.

288 *fire was ravaging the mansion*: Criminal complaint in Commonwealth of Pennsylvania v. Cody Balmer, April 13, 2025; and Marc Scolforo and John Sewer, "Arson attack probe at Pennsylvania governor's mansion looking into suspect's hatred of Josh Shapiro," Associated Press, April 13, 2025. The case against the man accused in the arson, Cody Balmer, was still pending as of this writing.

289 *agitated about the threat from Hamas*: David Struett, "Plainfield man fatally stabbed 6-year-old Muslim boy after listening to conservative talk radio, prosecutors say," *Chicago Sun-Times*, October 16, 2023. An Illinois jury found the landlord, Joseph Czuba, guilty on murder and hate-crime charges in February of 2025.

289 *fired his pistol*: The trial of the man arrested in the shooting, Jason Eaton, was still pending as of this writing.

290 *leading some Jewish students*: A poll conducted by Hillel International, among others, found that 63 percent of Jewish students felt less safe because of the protests.

290 *chanted anti-Jewish slogans*: @DLamontJenkins, X, October 23, 2023.

290 *enemy of our enemy*: Nick Fuentes, X, October 13, 2024.

# ILLUSTRATIONS

Page 5 – Napkin with doodle. Exhibits in *People vs. Samuel Woodward*, Orange County Superior Court.

Page 28 – Wade Michael Page. Anti-Defamation League website (original photographer unknown).

Page 46 – Sam Woodward. Exhibits in *People vs. Samuel Woodward*, Orange County Superior Court.

Page 50 – Blaze Bernstein. Exhibits in *People vs. Samuel Woodward*, Orange County Superior Court.

Page 96 – Sam Woodward. Exhibits in *People vs. Samuel Woodward*, Orange County Superior Court.

Page 108 – James Mason, et al. Exhibits in *People vs. Samuel Woodward*, Orange County Superior Court.

Page 122 – Rob Rundo/Rise Above Movement. Mindy Schauer, *Orange County Register/SCNG* via Getty Images.

Page 162 – Borrego Park site. Exhibits in *People vs. Samuel Woodward*, Orange County Superior Court.

Page 165 – Knife. Exhibits in *People vs. Samuel Woodward*, Orange County Superior Court.

Page 166 – Woodward mug shot. Exhibits in *People vs. Samuel Woodward*, Orange County Superior Court.

Page 176 – John Denton. Exhibits in *People vs. Samuel Woodward*, Orange County Superior Court.

Page 203 – Rock garden. Eric Lichtblau (author).

Page 211 – Club Q, Colorado Springs. Isaiah Downing for Reuters.

Page 265 – Sam Woodward on the witness stand. *Orange County Register* via Getty Images.

# INDEX

Abdalhamid, Kinnan, 289
accelerationism, 174, 209
African Americans. *See* Blacks; neo-Nazis; racism; white supremacy
Aldrich, Anderson, 210–211, 284
"Alligator Alcatraz," 282
Alternative for Germany, 280
alt-right movement, 70, 119. *See also* neo-Nazis; white supremacy
America First Bruins, 244
*American History X* film, 47
American Nazi Party, 101–103, 109
American Phoenix Project, 233, 245, 246
American Vanguard, 54, 75
Anaheim, California, 25
Anglin, Andrew, 56
anti-Klan law, 58–59
anti-Muslim event, RAM attendance at, 125
antisemitism
    attacks set off by war in Gaza, 288–290
    Chabad of Poway synagogue attack, 132, 133–135
    of Mason, 103
    in Orange County, 10–11
    Tree of Life synagogue attack, 127–131
Apple, conflict between law enforcement and, 184
Arberry, Ahmed, 7
Arbery, Ahmaud, 222
Arellano, Gustavo, 224
Arthurs, Devon, 84, 85–91, 94, 96–97
Asian Americans, hate crimes targeting
    Atlanta spa shootings, 221–223

    history of, 218–221
    neighborhood pushback against, 223–226
    Si family experience, 211–214
    surge in during Covid pandemic, 212–213, 214–218
Atlanta spa shootings, Georgia, 221–223
Atomwaffen Division, 53, 64, 120, 144, 271
    accelerationism, 174
    Arthurs' shooting of members, 85–91
    background of, 78–82
    Denton as de facto chief of, 96–97
    doxxing operations by, 170
    early members of, 82–85
    escalation after Bernstein's murder, 168
    hailing of Bernstein's murder by, 167
    hate camps by, 95–96, 97–98
    influence on Giampa, 110–115
    Mason's protégés at, 105, 106
    prosecution and imprisonment of members, 285
    public call to arms by Russell, 168–169
    publication of details about by ProPublica, 181–184
    Russell's arrest, 91–94
    swatting operations by, 170–173, 174–178
    threatening posters sent or delivered by, 173–174
    Woodward's role in
        discovery of connection, 181–182, 184–185
        hate camp attendance, 95–96

# Index

Atomwaffen Division (*cont.*)
  initiation, 98–100
  introduction to group, 53, 54–55
  messages sent after Bernstein's death, 164
  Orange County branch, 138
  support for Woodward, 201–202
  testimony about, 268, 273
Azov Brigade, 83, 84, 90, 121

Babbitt, Ashli, 240
Baker, Jay, 222
Bannon, Steve, 257–258
Barr, William, 234
"The Base" neo-Nazi group, 11
Beam, Louis, 218
Bernstein, Beaue, 137, 156–157
Bernstein, Blaze, *50*
  disappearance of, 155–162
  discovery of body of, 162–163
  discussion with García about Woodward's interest in, 24
  effect of murder on Duffy, 183
  funeral for, 166
  leak about murder of, 166–167
  matching of DNA from Woodward's belongings to, 165
  meetup with Woodward
    events leading up to, 136–140
    messaging with Woodward before, 51–53
    overview, 3–4
  memorial garden in memory of, *203*, 204
  motive for murder of
    discovery of, 184–186
    focus on in trial of Woodward, 264–267
    initial lack of evidence about, 181
  sexual orientation of, 22, 51, 205
  teenage years, 15–16, 20–21, 22
  trial of Woodward for murder of
    defense in, 262–263, 270–273
    delays of, 263–264
    focus on motive for murder in, 264–267
    prosecution in, 267–270
    verdict, 274–275
  at University of Pennsylvania, 49–51
Bernstein, Gideon, 50, 137
  attempts to talk with Blaze about sexuality, 51
  Blaze It Forward project, 203–204
  call to Woodward about Blaze's disappearance, 157–158
  focus on charity work, 204
  and leak about Blaze's death, 167
  notification of Blaze's death, 163
  reaction to delays in case against Woodward, 202
  reaction to hate-crime enhancement in case, 186
  reaction to verdict, 274, 275
  and search for Blaze, 155–156, 159
  and sentencing of Woodward, 284
  tensions with Woodward family, 202–203
  testimony at Woodward trial, 269
Bernstein, Jeanne Pepper
  attempts to talk with Blaze about sexuality, 51
  background of, 21–22
  Blaze It Forward project, 203–204
  call to Woodward about Blaze's disappearance, 157, 158
  events leading up to Blaze's disappearance, 137
  exit from courtroom during Woodward's testimony, 272
  and leak about Blaze's death, 167
  notification of Blaze's death, 163
  reaction to banning of gay pride flag, 204–205
  reaction to delays in case against Woodward, 202
  reaction to hate-crime enhancement in case, 186
  reaction to verdict, 274, 275
  and search for Blaze, 155–156, 159
  tensions with Woodward family, 202–203
  testimony at Woodward trial, 269

# Index

Bernstein, Richard, 137, 163
Biden, Joe, 144, 229, 233, 261
bigotry. *See also* hate crimes; Nazi Party; neo-Nazis; racism; white supremacy; Woodward, Sam
   history of in US, 57–63
   nationwide surge in, 5–9, 64, 143–145, 151–152, 286–287
   Orange County as epicenter of, 9–11, 25, 30–33
   pushback to Obama's election, 64–67
   by Rise Above Movement, 121–125
   role of Trump's first win in spreading, 56–57, 67–74
   and Trump's rhetoric during second term, 276–283
Billingsley, Steve, 81, 82, 88
birtherism, 64, 68, 248–249
Black Lives Matter protests, 230–232
Blacks. *See also* hate crimes; neo-Nazis; racism; white supremacy
   Colucci's arrest for threats to, 148–150
   fixation on violence of by white supremacists, 119
   hate crimes against during Obama presidency, 64
   history of violent bigotry against, 58–60, 62–63
   Mason's hatred of, 101, 107
   racial climate in Orange County in 2020, 228–232
   Tops grocery store attack targeting, 259–261
   Trump's racism against, 68
Blake, Jacob, 232
Blaze It Forward project, 203–204
Blood Tribe, 277
Blue-Eyed Devils band, 28
Bolsonaro, Jair, 73
Boogaloo Boyz, 231
Borrego Park, 158, 159, 160, 162–163
Bowers, Robert, 127–131, 133–134, 260, 284
Bowers, Rusty, 251
Branch, Cassandra, 18

Brannon, Chance, 207–210
Breivik, Anders, 84
Bruin Republicans club, 244
brute force attacks, 184
Bryant, Kobe, 159
Budde, Mariann E., 279–280
Budge, Sean, 18–19, 20
Buffalo, New York grocery store attack, 259–261
Burmeister, James, 34
Bush, George W., 74, 251
Bush, Gregory, 130
Byrd, Michael, 240

California. *See* Orange County, California
California State University Channel Islands, 48
Camp Pendleton, California, 207–208
Capitol attack, 8
   demographics of rioters in, 241
   lack of warning to officers about, 235
   racist nature of, 237–242
   Secor's actions during, 254–256
   Taylor's involvement in, 234–235, 252–253, 254
   Trump's pardons for participants, 285–286
   violence and mayhem during, 236–237, 252–255
Carleton, Lauri, 206–207
Carlson, Tucker, 7
Carter, David O., 249
Cellebrite, 184
"Central Park Five" case, 68
Chabad of Poway synagogue attack (San Diego), 132, 133–135
Chansley, Jacob, 255
Chapman University, 258
Charlottesville, Virginia. *See* "Unite the Right" rally
Chauvin, Derek, 230
Cherokee County, Georgia, 221–222
Chin, Vincent, 219
China, blame placed on during Covid pandemic, 217–218

## Index

Chinese immigrants, bigotry against, 61, 211–214, 223–226
Christchurch, New Zealand mosque massacre, 72
*Citizen Kane* film, 49
"Citrus War" of 1936, 62
Civil Rights Act, 63, 281
Club Q attack (Colorado Springs), 210–211
Cohn, Gary, 76
Cole, Kaleb, 167
Colucci, Burt, 145–150
Confederate flag, 19, 46, 237–238
conservative self-identity of Orange County, 9–10, 30–32
copycat hate crimes, 132–135
Corona del Mar High School (Newport Beach, CA), 44–45, 208
counter-protesters, attacks on, 122–127, 147–148
Covid pandemic
 "Curfew Breaker" protests, 245–246
 and hate crimes against Asian Americans, 212–213, 214–218
Craig, James, 148
Crow, Jason, 240
Crusius, Patrick, 7, 133, 284
Cruz, Ted, 69
Crystal Cathedral, 21
Cung, Bawi, 215
"Curfew Breaker" protests, 245–246

*Daily Stormer* website, 56, 123, 152
Daley, Ben, 119, 120, 123, 124, 125, 126
*The Dark Knight Rises* premiere shooting, 38
Democrats, in Orange County, 199–200
Denton, John Cameron, 106, 143, *176*
 as de facto chief of Atomwaffen, 96–97
 and swatting operations, 176–178, 179
Department of Homeland Security (DHS), 65, 66–67
DeSantis, Ron, 205
diversity, equity, and inclusion (DEI) programs, 281

domestic extremism, 65–67. *See also* hate crimes; neo-Nazis; violent bigotry; white supremacy
Douglass, Frederick, 59
doxxing operations, by Atomwaffen, 170
Duffy, Brenan, 265
 initiation of Woodward into Atomwaffen, 99, 100
 leaks of Atomwaffen internal communications by, 182–184
 testimony at Woodward trial, 267, 268
Duke, David, 56, 69, 76
Dunn, Harry, 235–237
Duterte, Rodrigo, 73
Dvorak, Petula, 227

Earnest, John, 132, 133–135, 284
Eastman, John, 248–252, 254, 256–258
Edwards, John, 38
8chan online forum, 132–133
El Paso Walmart attack, Texas, 6, 7
Ergul, Tibet, 207, 208–210
Estrada, Martin, 210
Evans, Tristan, 96, *108*, 183, 271
 Atomwaffen branch started by, 138
 friendship with Woodward, 53–54, 98–99
 out given to Woodward by, 55
 visit to Mason, 100, 107–110
Evers, Medgar, 63
Evola, Julius, 99
extremists. *See* Atomwaffen Division; hate crimes; neo-Nazis; Rise Above Movement; white supremacy

Facebook, 279
far-right politics, in Orange County, 30–32. *See also* alt-right movement; neo-Nazis; white supremacy
fascists. *See* Nazi Party; neo-Nazis
Federal Aviation Administration, 281
Federal Bureau of Investigation (FBI)
 focus on racially fueled crimes, 286, 287

# Index

investigation after Capitol attack, 255–256
investigation after murder of Atomwaffen members, 91, 92–93
investigation of Planned Parenthood clinic arson, 209, 210
investigation of swatting by Atomwaffen, 176–177, 178–180
Mason as being in sights of, 101
Felarca, Yvette, 124
Fields, James, 75, 109–110
First Amendment, 148
Florida National Guard, 80–81
Flournoy, Vernon, 32–33
Floyd, George, 230, 287
4chan, 261
Francis (Pope), 17, 161
Freeman, Ruby, 247–248
Fricker, Amelia, 112, 113, 114–115
Fricker, Scott, 112–113, 114
Fuentes, Nick, 243, 244, 278, 280, 290
Fulton County, Georgia, 222–223

Gab website, 128, 132, 170
Garcia, John, 261
García Combs Morris, Gabe, 22–24, 49, 51, 52, 268
Garden Grove, California, 31
Garland, Merrick, 211
Garza, Johnny Roman, 180
gays. *See also* Bernstein, Blaze
  banning of gay pride flag, 204–205, 206
  hate crimes against, 81–82, 88, 205–211, *211*
  National Socialist crashing of Gay Pride festival, 147–148
  planned attack on Los Angeles Gay Pride Night, 210
  presentation of Woodward as in trial, 270–271
  and Trump's rhetoric during second term, 283
  Woodward's hatred for, 16–18, 160–161
  Woodward's pranking of, 22–24, 48–49, 138, 139
Gaza, war in, 288–290
Gendron, Payton, 259–261, 284
Georgia, hate crimes in, 221–223
Giampa, Marilyn, 112, 113
Giampa, Nicholas, 110–115, 143
Gilbert-Kaye, Lori, 134
Giuliani, Rudy, 246, 247, 248, 257
Goebbels, Joseph, 109
Goldsmith, Craig, 184, 268–269
Goldwater, Barry, 102
"Goon Squad" (Rankin County, Mississippi), 287
Gore, Al, 251
Graham, Lindsey, 69
Grant, Ulysses S., 58
"Great Replacement Theory," 7, 10–11, 174, 242
Green Planet Smoke Shop hostage situation (Tampa), 85–86
Groyper Army, 243–244, 245–246, 290
Guterres, António, 217–218

Hagen, William, 57
"Hail Trump!" convention, 70
Haitian immigrants, Trump's rhetoric about, 277
Haley, Nikki, 76–77
Hammerskin Nation, 38, 120
Harris, Kamala, 59, 229, 248–249, 251, 277
Hasson, Christopher, 73
hate camps, Atomwaffen Division, 95–96, 97–98
"Hate Crime Streetwear" shop (Orange County), 11
hate crimes. *See also* Bernstein, Blaze; neo-Nazis; white supremacy; Woodward, Sam
  by Burmeister, 34
  Chabad of Poway synagogue attack, 132, 133–135
  Colucci's arrest for, 148–150
  decision not to charge Tanber with, 192–193
  focus on in Orange County under Spitzer, 193–198

## Index

hate crimes (*cont.*)
  history of in US, 57–63
  lack of focus on in Trump administration, 144
  against LGBTQ+ community, 81–82, 88, 205–211
  by Mason, 103, 110
  Mason's endorsement of, 109–110
  against Muslims, 72, 73–74, 288–290
  nationwide surge in, 5–9, 151–152, 286–287
  neighborhood pushback against, 223–227
  Orange County as epicenter of, 9–11, 32–33, 200
  role of Trump's first term in spreading, 67, 69, 70, 72–74
  set off by war in Gaza, 288–290
  Sikh Temple of Wisconsin attack, 36–42
  targeting Asian Americans
    Atlanta spa shootings, 221–223
    history of, 218–221
    Si family experience, 211–214
    surge in during Covid pandemic, 212–213, 214–218
  Tops grocery store attack, 259–261
  Tree of Life synagogue attack, 127–131
  and Trump's rhetoric during second term, 277–278, 283
  and "Unite the Right" rally, 75
hate music. *See* "white power" music
hate speech
  First Amendment as protecting, 148
  online, 42–43, 45–47, 111, 117, 278–279
Hegseth, Pete, 281
Heimbach, Matthew, 56
"Helter Skelter" murders, 98, 104–105
Herschmann, Eric, 257
Heyer, Heather, 75
HIAS (originally Hebrew Immigrant Aid Society), 128–129, 130
Himmelman, Jeremy, 82, 84, 87
Hispanics
  immigration raid protests, 282
  Walmart attack on in El Paso, 6, 7

Hitler, Adolf, 82, 119, 169. *See also* Nazi Party
  as inspiration for Earnest, 133–134
  Mason's idolization of, 100
  *My New Order*, 68
  National Socialist Movement love of, 147
  Trump as inviting comparisons to, 280
  Trump's admiration of, 68, 71
  Woodward's fixation on, 18
Holocaust, 11, 22
homosexuals. *See* gays
Horton, Willie, 31
Hostetter, Alan
  and American Phoenix Project, 233, 245–246
  involvement in Capitol attack, 234, 252–253, 254, 256
  views of Groyper Army, 245–246
House, control by Democrats, 199
Huntington Beach, California, 25, 121–123, 204–205, 206
Hutchinson, Cassidy, 252

Ikeguchi, Travis, 206–207
immigrants
  Bowers' focus on in attack, 128–129
  Secor's opposition to, 243
  Trump's rhetoric about during second term, 276–277, 281–283
  violent bigotry against, 60–61
incels (involuntarily celibate men), 244
Ingalls, Chris, 180
Instagram, 117, 279
Institute for Historical Review, 11
*Iron March* neo-Nazi forum, 78–79, 80–81, 87, 94
Islam. *See* Muslims
Israel–Hamas war, 288–290
Italian immigrants, lynching of in New Orleans, 60

Jacob, Greg, 249, 250–251, 254, 257
James, LeBron, 71
Jantzen, Dylan, 160–162, 183–184, 185, 269

# Index

Jayapal, Pramila, 241
Jeffries, Hakeem, 281
Jenkins, Michael, 287
Jews
   attacks on set off by war in Gaza, 288–290
   Chabad of Poway synagogue attack, 132, 133–135
   Holocaust, 11, 22
   Mason's hatred of, 103
   in Orange County, 10–11, 21–22
   Tree of Life synagogue attack, 127–131
Jiang, Weijia, 217
jihadism, 85, 86–87, 88
John Birch Society, 30, 32
Johnson, Boris, 73–74
Johnson, Daryl, 65, 66–67
Johnson, Lyndon B., 63
Jones, Alex, 83

Kaleka, Pardeep Singh, 39–42
Kaleka, Satwant, 40–41
Kelley, John, 174–176, 179
Kelly, John, 71
Khan, Farrah, 200, 201
King, Martin Luther, Jr., 63, 109
Ku Klux Klan Act, 58–59
Ku Klux Klan (KKK), 37, 144
   at Camp Pendleton, 208
   history of violent bigotry by, 63
   Levin's avoidance of violence toward, 152
   in Orange County, 30
   PBS documentary on, 35
   support for Trump, 56, 57, 69
   and "Unite the Right" rally, 74–77
   violence against Asian Americans by, 218
Kuhn-Fricker, Buckley, 112–113, 114
Kushner, Jared, 128

Ladera Ranch, California, 211–214, 223–226, 228–232, 256
Laube, Tyler, 122
Lee, Robert E., 76
Lee, Sammy, 31
Lemon, Don, 71
Levin, Brian, 11, 151–153
LGBTQ+ community. *See* gays
Limbaugh, Rush, 66
Lindberg, Gunner, 220–221
Lindbergh, Charles, 244
Lloyd, Hardy, 129
"lone wolf" attacks, 65, 100, 108. *See also* Mason, James Nolan; Woodward, Sam
Long, Robert Aaron, 221–223
Loomer, Laura, 282
Ly, Thien Minh, 220, 221
lynching, 59–60, 124

Maciulewicz, Tracey, 261
Mackneil, Andre, 259, 261
"Make America Great" rally (Orange County), 121–123
Mandela, Nelson, 31
manifestos by violent extremists, 132–134
Manson, Charles, 109, 139, 169
   and accelerationism, 174
   as Atomwaffen hate camp inspiration, 98
   Mason's friendship with, 104–105
   Woodward's resemblance to, 262
Marblehead Park (San Clemente), 116–117
Marcus, Amy, 49
Martin, Trayvon, 230
Martinez, Jannique, 226–227
Martinez, Joel, 226–227
Mason, James Nolan, *108*, 178, 202, 285
   and accelerationism, 174, 209
   background of, 100–104
   disappointment with Woodward's murder of Bernstein, 182
   friendship with Manson, 104–105
   hatred of government, 104, 107
   influence on Giampa, 110–115
   interest in underage girls, 104
   mention of at Woodward's trial, 267
   new wave of followers of, 105–107

# Index

Mason, James Nolan (*cont.*)
  *Siege*, 54, 97, 99, 104, 105, 267
  Woodward and Evans' visit to, 100, 107–110
Massey, Sonya, 287
mass-scale hate crimes. *See* hate crimes
Mateen, Omar, 81
Mayfield, Tyson, 195–198
Mazroei, Shahzad, 192
Mazroei, Shayan, 189–190, 192–193
McInnes, Gavin, 239
McVeigh, Timothy, 82, 88, 90, 91, 104, 174
Mebane, Brandon, 229
Menninger, Kimberly, 263–264, 265, 266, 274, 284
Meta, 278–279
Metzger, Tom, 29–30
Mexicans, bigotry against, 62, 68–69
Michaelis, Arno, 41–42
military, white supremacy and neo-Nazis in, 33–35, 80–81, 183
Milley, Mark A., 237
Min, Dave, 205, 206, 226
minorities. *See also* hate crimes; neo-Nazis; racism; white supremacy
  anti-minority rhetoric in Orange County, 31–32
  diversifying Orange County, 10
  history of violent bigotry against, 57–63
  notion of threat of, 7
  Trump's rhetoric about during second term, 276–283
  Woodward's growing hatred for, 18–19
Miselis, Michael, 124–125, 126, 127, 170
Modi, Narendra, 73
Mondragon, George, 32
Moore, Wes, 284–285
Morrison, Kenneth, 264–265, 266, 270–271
Moss, Shaye, 247–248
"Murder Squad" song, 43
Murphy, Brian, 37, 41
Musk, Elon, 7, 43, 278, 280, 283

Muslims
  Arthurs' conversion to Islam, 85, 86–87, 88
  Bush's appeal regarding, 74
  FBI undercover investigations of, 179
  hate crimes against, 72, 73–74, 288–290
  murder of Mazroei, 189–190, 192–193
  RAM attendance at anti-Muslim event, 125
  Sikhs mistaken for, 38–39
  Trump's racism against, 69
*My New Order* (Hitler), 68
Myers, Jeffrey, 130, 131

Napolitano, Janet, 66
National Guard, 80–81
National Justice Party, 290
National Policy Institute, 70
National Socialist Liberation Front, 105
National Socialist Movement
  under Colucci, 145–150
  Schoep's distancing from, 150–154
National Socialist Order, 285
National Socialists of America, 148
nationalism, white. *See* Atomwaffen Division; neo-Nazis; Rise Above Movement; white supremacy
Nazi Low Riders gang, 187, 191
Nazi Party. *See also* neo-Nazis; white supremacy
  Atomwaffen Division as based on love of, 78–80, 82
  Mason's collection of artifacts of, 108–109
  Mason's consideration of himself as belonging to, 100–103
  Trump as inviting comparisons to, 280
  Woodward's fixation on, 18, 19–20
neighborhood pushback against hate crimes, 223–227
neo-Nazis, 7. *See also* Atomwaffen Division; Mason, James Nolan; Rise Above Movement; white supremacy
  at Capitol attack, 238

## Index

and Covid pandemic, 218
focus on in trial of Woodward, 264–267, 273
growing group of imprisoned members, 285
influence on Giampa, 110–115
Metzger's movement, 29–30
in military, 33–35
National Socialist Movement, 145–154
nationwide surge in, 143–145
online hate speech by, 42–43
in Orange County, 10, 11, 30, 33, 195–198
recruitment of young people by, 153–154
Schoep's distancing from, 150–154
Sikh Temple of Wisconsin attack, 36–42
Simi's research on, 35–36
support for Trump by, 56
support for Woodward by, 201–202
surge in during Obama presidency, 64
Tanber's ties to, 186–193
Trump's pardons for Capitol riot participants, 285–286
and Trump's rhetoric during second term, 277, 278
at "Unite the Right" rally, 74–77
"white power" music and, 25–29
Woodward's desire to join group, 44, 53–55
Woodward's online persona, 45–47
Neumann, Elizabeth, 144
Nevada hate camp, Atomwaffen Division, 98
New Hope, Pennsylvania swatting incident, 173
Newsom, Gavin, 282
Nielsen, Kirstjen, 176
Nightlinger, Kenny, 89, 91
9/11 attacks, 39, 178–179
Nixon, Richard, 9

Oath Keepers, 65, 124, 144, 239
Obama, Barack, 8, 45, 64–67, 68, 192
Obama, Michelle, 65

Old Dominion University swatting incident, 174–175
Oneschuk, Andrew, 82–84, 85, 87, 90, 121
Oneschuk, Emily, 83
online hate speech, 42–43, 45–47, 111, 117, 278–279
Orange County, California. *See also* Bernstein, Blaze; Woodward, Sam
attacks in set off by war in Gaza, 288
backlash of white supremacists to political changes in, 200–201
Black Lives Matter protests in, 230–231
"Citrus War" of 1936, 62
Covid protests in, 245
decision to ban gay pride flag in, 204–205, 206
as epicenter of white supremacy, 9–11, 25, 30–33
focus on hate crimes in under Spitzer, 193–198
hate crimes against Asian Americans in neighborhood pushback against, 223–226
Si family experience, 211–214
surge in during Covid pandemic, 216, 219–221
overrepresentation at Capitol attack, 242
racial climate in 2020, 228–232
rapid changes in political makeup of, 199–200
Rise Above Movement in, 116–121
violence against Chinese immigrants in, 61
"white power" music scene in, 25–30
*Orange County Register*, 166–167, 258
Orange County School of the Arts (Santa Ana), 15–16, 18–21, 22
Orbán, Viktor, 73, 74
"Original Flushing Crew" gang, 118
Orsini, Brad, 129–130
*others*, hate for, 8–9. *See also* bigotry; neo-Nazis; racism; white supremacy

# Index

Page, Wade Michael, 28, 81
    indoctrination into white supremacy in military, 33–35
    Sikh Temple of Wisconsin attack by, 36–42
    Simi's research on, 35–36
    "white power" music of, 27–28
Palestinians, 289, 290
Pape, Robert, 241–242
Parks, Layla, 223–226
Pascal, Blaise, 137
Pelosi, Nancy, 255
PEN1 (Public Enemy Number One) street gang, 187, 188
Pence, Mike, 242
    target of attempts by Eastman to delay vote, 257
    pressure on to stop certification of election, 249–250, 252
    threats of violence against during Capitol attack, 238, 253–254
Peterson, George, 191
Picciolini, Christian, 143
Pierce, William, 26–27, 102, 104
Planned Parenthood clinic arson (Costa Mesa, CA), 208–209
police brutality, 287
political rallies, RAM at, 121–125
politics. *See also* Trump, Donald
    Orange County's extreme brand of, 30–32
    resistance to DHS report on domestic extremism, 66–67
    support for violent bigotry in, 60
Poplawski, Richard, 66
ProPublica, 169, 170, 177–178, 181–184
Proud Boys, 124, 144, 238–240, 278, 286
Public Enemy Number One (PEN1) street gang, 187, 188
Pulse nightclub massacre (Orlando), 81–82, 88
punk bands, 27

QAnon, 233

Rachlis, Arnie, 166
racial accelerationism, 174, 209
racism. *See also* bigotry; Nazi Party; neo-Nazis; white supremacy
    and attempts to overturn 2020 election, 247–248
    and Capitol attack, 237–242
    in Orange County, 228–232
    role of Trump's first win in spreading, 56–57, 67–74
    Trump's history of speech showing, 68
    in Trump's rhetoric during second term, 276–283
    "white power" music and, 25–29
    of Woodward during teenage years, 18–19
Rackauckas, Tony, 185, 186, 192, 193
Rahming, Marc, 228, 229–230
Rahming, Shereen, 228, 229–230, 231, 232
RAM. *See* Rise Above Movement
Rankin County, Mississippi, 287
Rawkson, Anouk, 283
Ray, James Earl, 63
Reagan, Ronald, 9, 69
Reagan National Airport collision, 281
Reagan Youth band, 27
*The Real Housewives of Orange County* TV show, 191
Reconstruction era, 58–59
Republicans
    attacks on Trump by, 69
    in Orange County, 31–32
Resistance Records, 26–27
Rhodesian flag, 243
"right-wing death squad." *See* Rise Above Movement
right-wing extremism, 7–8, 65–67. *See also* Capitol attack; hate crimes; neo-Nazis; white supremacy
right-wing political oasis, Orange County as, 9–11
Rise Above Movement (RAM), 144
    background of, 116–121
    and Bowers, 127–131
    conviction of members of, 285

# Index

differences from Atomwaffen Division, 138
at "Unite the Right" rally, 125–127
violence and rioting at political rallies by, 121–125
Rittenhouse, Kyle, 232
Robbins, Roger, 196, 197, 198
Rockwell, George Lincoln, 101–103
Rodger, Elliot, 243–244
Rodman, Dennis, 191
Rofsky, Raiah, 19, 22
Rohrabacher, Dana, 233
Roof, Dylann, 130–131, 260, 284
 manifesto of, 133
 murder of Black churchgoers by, 77, 119
 Rhodesian flag use by, 243
Rubio, Marco, 69
Rundo, Rob, 126, 138
 background of, 118–119
 casting of RAM as political prisoners by, 127
 conviction of, 285
 at "Make America Great" rally, 122–124, *122*
 start of Rise Above Movement by, 119–121
Russell, Brandon, 96, 97, 183
 apartment shared with other Atomwaffen members, 82–83, 84, 85
 arrest of, 91–94
 Arthurs' description of to police, 90
 Denton's taking over for, 176
 founding of Atomwaffen Division, 79–82
 insincere apology by, 168, 180
 public call to arms made from prison by, 168–169
 reaction to murders at apartment of, 87
 search of home and garage of, 88
 second imprisonment of, 285

Santa Ana Chinatown, California, 61
Schmitz, John G., 32
Schoep, Jeff, 145, 146, 150–154
Schuller, Robert H., 21
Secor, Christian, 242–246, 254–256
September 11 attacks, 39, 178–179
Shapiro, Josh, 288
Shea, Cameron, 174
Short, Marc, 250
Si, Haijun, 211–214, 223–226, 228
*Siege* (Mason), 54, 97, 99, 104, 105, 267
Sikh Temple of Wisconsin attack, 36–42
Simi, Pete, 35–36
Singhania, Aruna, 269–270
16th Street Baptist Church bombing (Birmingham), 63
"Skinhead City" (Huntington Beach), 25
skinheads. *See* neo-Nazis; white supremacy
Skokie, Illinois, 148, 151
Skrewdriver band, 42
Smith, Lowell, 193–194
Smith, Morton Irvine, 233, 246
social media, hate speech on, 43, 45–47, 111, 117
South Africa, white genocide myth about, 282–283
Spencer, Richard, 70, 74, 75, 119
spiderweb tattoos, 34
Spitzer, Todd, 193, 194, 196–198, 275
Stahl, Leslie, 70
"State of Hate" hearing (California State Assembly), 151–153
Stern, James, 146
"Stop the Steal" rallies, 233, 246–247, 251–252
surf Nazis, 27
swastikas, 146, 147
swatting operations, by Atomwaffen, 170–173, 174–178
Sweeney, Charlotte, 211
synagogues, attacks on, 127–131, 132, 133–135
Syring, Patrick, 72

Tanber, Craig, 186–193, 195
Tanber, Paul, 188
Tarrant, Brenton, 132–134

# Index

Tarrio, Henry "Enrique," 239–240, 286
Taylor, Breonna, 287
Taylor, Russell, 245
   and Black Lives Matter protests, 230–231, 232
   in events leading up to Capitol attack, 246
   involvement in Capitol attack, 234–235, 252–253, 254
   political involvement of, 232–233
   raid on home of, 256
   warning about coming revolution by, 233–234
terrorism investigations by FBI, 178–179
Texas hate camp, Atomwaffen Division, 95–96, 98
Thanasas, Katie, 86
"Thank God I'm a White Boy" (Youngland), 29, 42
Third Reich. *See* Hitler, Adolf; Nazi Party
Thompson, A. C., 169–172, 173, 177–178, 182
Thompson, Bennie, 240
Thornburg, Elizabeth, 189–190
Thorning-Schmidt, Helle, 279
Three Percenters, 234, 239
Three Strikes law (California), 196, 198
Till, Emmett, 63
Tomlinson, Alex, 52–53
Tops grocery store attack (Buffalo), 259–261
Torres, Deanna, 93
transgender people, 205, 283
Tree of Life synagogue attack, 127–131
Truman, Harry S., 62
Trump, Donald, 4, 43, 192, 194. *See also* Capitol attack
   American Phoenix Project support for, 232–233
   attempts to overturn 2020 election, 228, 233, 234, 246–252, 256–257
   and Black Lives Matter protests, 230–231
   Bowers' distrust of, 128
   and Covid pandemic, 215, 217, 223
   decision not to testify in his own defense, 271
   frontal attack on Pence, 253–254
   "Great Replacement Theory," 7
   history of racist speech, 68
   inflammatory rhetoric during second term, 276–283
   and nationwide surge in violent bigotry, 5, 6, 8–9, 64, 143, 144–145, 151–152
   Oneschuk's opinion of, 83–84
   pardon for Capitol attack participants, 285–286
   pardons in final week in office, 257–258
   and Proud Boys, 238–239
   RAM members' view of, 120
   RAM's actions at protests against, 122–125
   role of first term in spreading bigotry, 67–74
   and "Unite the Right" rally, 76, 144
   white supremacist support for, 56–57
   Woodward's fervent support of, 45–46
Trump, Donald, Jr., 246
Trump, Ivanka, 83
Tschantre, William, 92, 93
*The Turner Diaries* (Pierce), 104
Twitter (now X), 43, 111, 120, 278

Uemura, Dave, 225
ultraconservative self-identity of Orange County, 9–10, 30–32
undercover FBI agents, 178–179
"Unite the Right" rally, 8, 98
   general discussion, 74–77
   Mason's opinion on violence at, 109–110
   National Socialist Movement at, 145
   and nationwide surge in white supremacy, 144
   Rise Above Movement at, 125–127
United States Capitol attack. *See* Capitol attack
University of California, Los Angeles (UCLA), 244–245

## Index

University of Chicago, 241–242
University of Pennsylvania, 49–51, 68
US House, control by Democrats, 199

Vance, J. D., 69
Vardaman, James K., 60
Vietnamese Americans, bigotry against, 218, 219–220
Villa, Anthony, 274
violent bigotry. *See also* hate crimes; Nazi Party; neo-Nazis; racism; white supremacy; Woodward, Sam
   history of in US, 57–63
   nationwide surge in, 5–9, 64, 143–145, 151–152, 286–287
   Orange County as epicenter of, 9–11, 32–33
   pushback to Obama's election, 64–67
   by Rise Above Movement, 121–125
   role of Trump's first win in spreading, 56–57, 67–74
   and Trump's rhetoric during second term, 276–283
Volz, Adriean, 191, 192

Waddell, Alfred Moore, 60
Walker, Jennifer, 262–263, 266, 267–268, 270, 272–274
Wallace, Chris, 238
Wallace, George, 102
Walmart attack (El Paso), 6, 7
Warren, Elizabeth, 71
Wayne, John, 9
weaponry, Woodward's fixation on, 19, 20, 46
West, Kanye (now Ye), 278
White, Patrick, 158–159
White Aryan Resistance (WAR) movement, 29–30
white genocide myth about South Africa, 282–283
"White Lives Matter" movement, 200
"White Man on the Move" (Youngland), 29
"white power" music, 11, 25–30, 42

White Radio, 26
white supremacy. *See also* Atomwaffen Division; Capitol attack; neo-Nazis; Rise Above Movement; "Unite the Right" rally; Woodward, Sam
   alt-right movement, 70, 119
   American Vanguard group, 54, 75
   and Covid pandemic, 218
   and hate crimes against LGBTQ+ community, 205–210
   history of in US, 57–63
   imprisonment of members of groups, 285
   and Israel–Hamas war protests, 290
   Metzger's movement, 29–30
   in military, 33–35, 80–81, 183
   nationwide surge in, 5–9, 64, 143–145, 151–152, 286–287
   online hate speech related to, 42–43
   Orange County as epicenter of, 9–11, 25, 30–33
   pushback to Obama's election, 64–67
   Sikh Temple of Wisconsin attack, 36–42
   Simi's research on, 35–36
   support for Trump, 56–57
   Tanber's ties to, 186–193
   Tops grocery store attack in Buffalo, 259–261
   and Trump's first term, 67–74
   and Trump's second term, 276–283
   and violence at Black Lives Matter protests, 231
Whitmer, Gretchen, 245
Williams, Liam, 22, 50, 52, 136, 139, 156–157
Woodard, Isaac, Jr., 62
Woodward, Blake, 20, 164
   alarm at Sam's growing extremism, 54–55
   and Sam's high school years, 44–45, 47
   seeds of hatred planted by, 16–17
   tensions with Bernstein family, 202–203
Woodward, Clay, 17

# Index

Woodward, Michele, 165
  alarm at Sam's growing extremism, 54–55
  choice of arts school for Sam, 16
  and Sam's high school years, 44–45
  tensions with Bernstein family, 202–203
  worry about Sam's violent behavior, 48
Woodward, Sam, 46, 96, 101, 108, 116, 143, 166
  arrest of, 165–166, 175
  in Atomwaffen Division
    discovery of connection, 181–182, 184–185
    hate camp attendance, 95–96
    initiation, 98–100
    introduction to group, 53, 54–55
    messages sent after Bernstein's death, 164
    Orange County branch, 138
    support for Woodward, 201–202
    testimony about, 268, 273
  and Bernstein's disappearance
    deputy sheriff's call to, 158–159
    Gideon Bernstein's call to, 157–158
    interview of by investigators, 160–162
    investigator's sighting of at Borrego Park, 160
  college experience of, 48
  delays in murder case against, 201–202
  desire to join neo-Nazi group, 11, 44, 53–55
  "Diary of Hate," 4, 23, 48–49, 185, 268
  fixation on weaponry, 19, 20, 46
  hate-crime enhancement in case against, 185–186
  investigation into
    hacking of phone by law enforcement, 184–185
    initial lack of evidence about motive, 181
    search of home and vehicle, 164–165
    trailing by sheriff's investigators, 163–164
  meetup with Bernstein, 3–4, 137–140
  messaging between Bernstein and, 51–53
  pranking of gays by, 4, 22–24, 48–49, 268
  publication of details about by ProPublica, 181–182
  seeds of hatred in, 16–18
  sentencing of, 284
  teenage years
    arts school years, 15–16
    growing belief in white supremacy, 18–20
    online persona during, 45–47
    pranking of García during, 22–24
    transfer to second high school, 44–45
    violent outbursts during, 47–48
  "Text is boring but murder isn't" drawing, 4, 5, 138, 269
  trial of
    defense in, 262–263, 270–273
    delays of, 263–264
    focus on motive for murder in, 264–267
    prosecution in, 267–270
    verdict, 274–275
  visit to Mason, 100, 107–110
Wray, Christopher, 179, 286, 287
Wu, Eric, 216

X (formerly Twitter), 43, 111, 120, 278
xenophobism. *See* bigotry; immigrants; white supremacy

Yaki, Michael, 74
Ye (formerly Kanye West), 278
Yoo, Patty, 216
Youngland band, 29, 42
YouTube, 42, 43

Zimmerman, George, 230
ZOG ("Zionist Occupation Government"), 36, 48
Zuckerberg, Mark, 278–279

# ABOUT THE AUTHOR

**Eric Lichtblau** is a Washington journalist and a two-time Pulitzer Prize winner. He was a reporter in the Washington bureau of the *New York Times* for nearly fifteen years until 2017, and a reporter for the *Los Angeles Times* for fifteen years before that. He has also written for *The New Yorker, TIME, USA Today*, and other publications. He is the author of three nonfiction books, including *The Nazis Next Door: How America Became a Safe Haven for Hitler's Men*, a *New York Times* bestseller; *Bush's Law: The Remaking of American Justice*; and *Return to the Reich: A Holocaust Refugee's Secret Mission to Defeat the Nazis*. He lives outside Washington, DC.

# RAISING READERS
## Books Build Bright Futures

Thank you for reading this book and for being a reader of books in general. We are so grateful to share being part of a community of readers with you, and we hope you will join us in passing our love of books on to the next generation of readers.

**Did you know that reading for enjoyment is the single biggest predictor of a child's future happiness and success?**

More than family circumstances, parents' educational background, or income, reading impacts a child's future academic performance, emotional well-being, communication skills, economic security, ambition, and happiness.

Studies show that kids reading for enjoyment in the US is in rapid decline:

- In 2012, 53% of 9-year-olds read almost every day. Just 10 years later, in 2022, the number had fallen to 39%.
- In 2012, 27% of 13-year-olds read for fun daily. By 2023, that number was just 14%.

Together, we can commit to **Raising Readers** and change this trend. How?

- Read to children in your life daily.
- Model reading as a fun activity.
- Reduce screen time.
- Start a family, school, or community book club.
- Visit bookstores and libraries regularly.
- Listen to audiobooks.
- Read the book before you see the movie.
- Encourage your child to read aloud to a pet or stuffed animal.
- Give books as gifts.
- Donate books to families and communities in need.

**Books build bright futures**, and **Raising Readers** is our shared responsibility.

For more information, visit **JoinRaisingReaders.com**

Sources: National Endowment for the Arts, National Assessment of Educational Progress, WorldBookDay.com, Nielsen BookData's 2023 "Understanding the Children's Book Consumer"